All that glitters...

Even the stars

All things precious...

Even your life

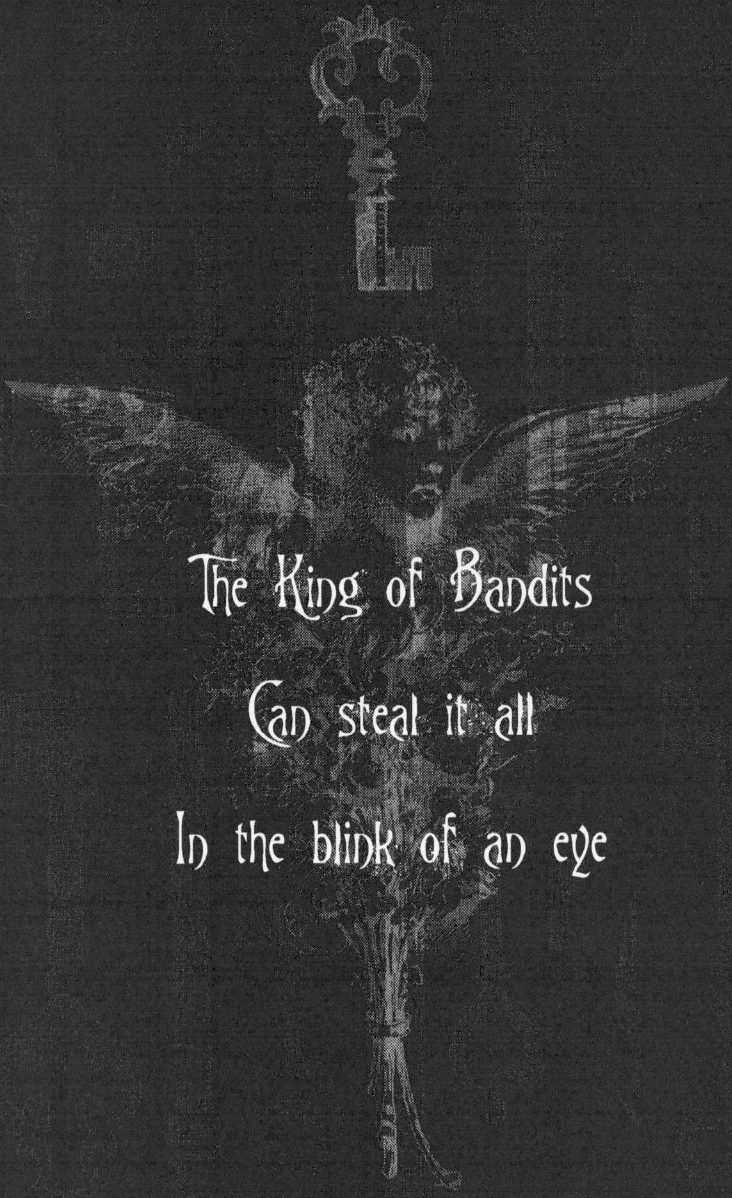
The King of Bandits
Can steal it all
In the blink of an eye

王ドロボウ
JING
新装版
FOUR

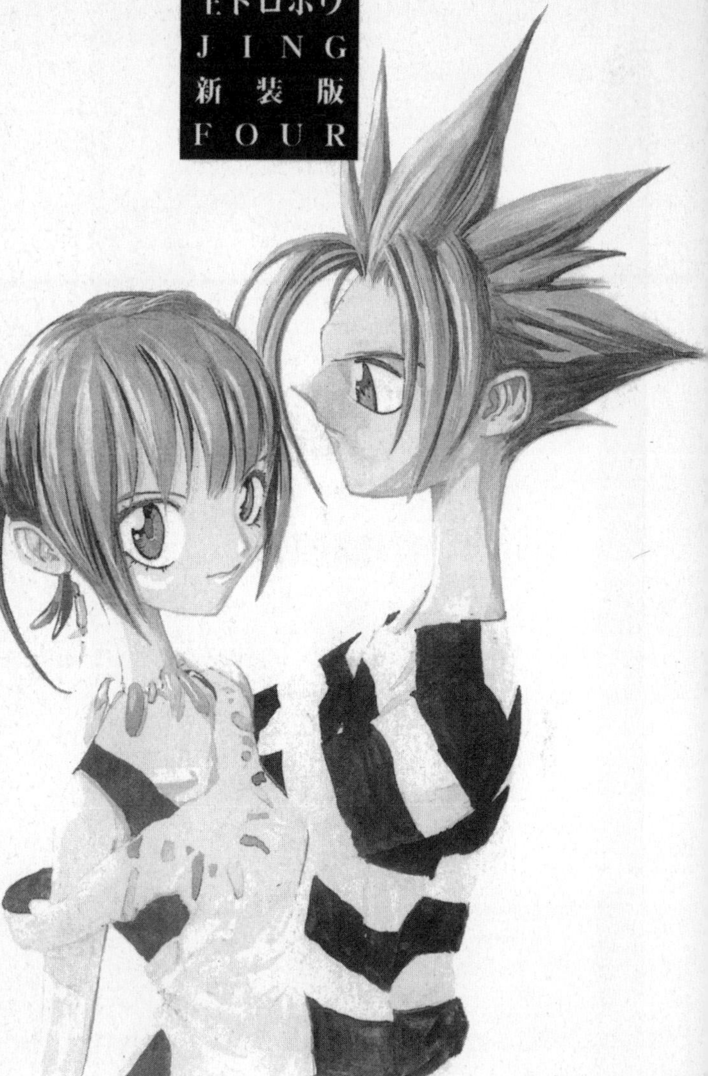

jing&benedictine

Translator - Kong Chang
English Adaptation - Carol Fox
Editors - Jake Forbes & Paul Morrissey
Copy Editor - Tim Beedle
Retouch and Lettering - Jesse Fernley, John Lo & Jose Macasocol, Jr.
Cover Layout - Gary Shum

Managing Editor - Jill Freshney
Production Coordinator - Antonio DePietro
Production Managers - Jennifer Miller & Mutsumi Miyazaki
Art Director - Matthew Alford
Director of Editorial - Jeremy Ross
VP of Production & Manufacturing - Ron Klamert
President & C.O.O. - John Parker
Publisher & C.E.O. - Stuart Levy

Email: editor@TOKYOPOP.com
Come visit us online at www.TOKYOPOP.com

A  **TOKYOPOP**® Manga

TOKYOPOP Inc.
5900 Wilshire Blvd. Suite 2000
Los Angeles, CA 90036

Jing: King of Bandits vol. 4
©2000 Yuichi Kumakura. All rights reserved. First published in Japan
in 2000 as Odorobo Jing - New Edition by Kodansha, Ltd., Tokyo.
English publication rights arranged through Kodansha, Ltd.

English text copyright ©2004 TOKYOPOP Inc.

ISBN: 1-59182-179-7

First TOKYOPOP® printing: January 2004

10 9 8 7 6 5 4 3 2 1
Printed in USA

KING OF BANDITS

王ドロボウ JING

VOLUME 4 OF 7

STORY AND ART BY
YUICHI KUMAKURA

Los Angeles • Tokyo • London

Once upon a midnight dreary, a thief named Jing was weak and weary,
Many strange and forgotten lands he did traverse and explore.
His companion was a bird named Kir, his black wings a flapping,
While Jing nodded, nearly napping, Kir saw booty galore.
"Wake up, Jing," Kir muttered, "all around us is loot galore."
Treasure from ceiling to floor!

Thus, this ebony bird's wiling, sent Jing's sad face into smiling,
For Jing could steal the stars from the sky, thievery he truly did adore.
The albatross sat proudly on Jing's placid bust, his beady eyes did implore,
One more thing Kir did utter, his feathers all a greedy flutter, his voice a roar,
Quoth the albatross, "Let's steal some more!"

JING: King of Bandits

FOUR

CONTENTS

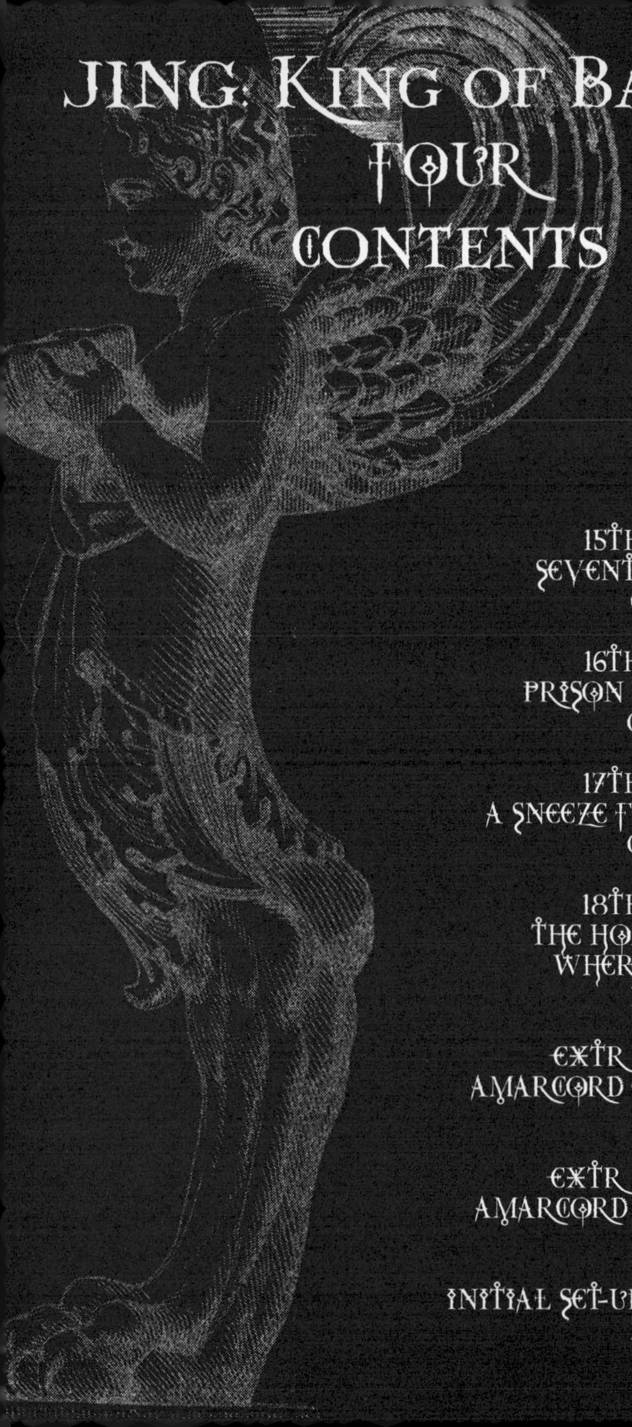

all hope is gone!!!

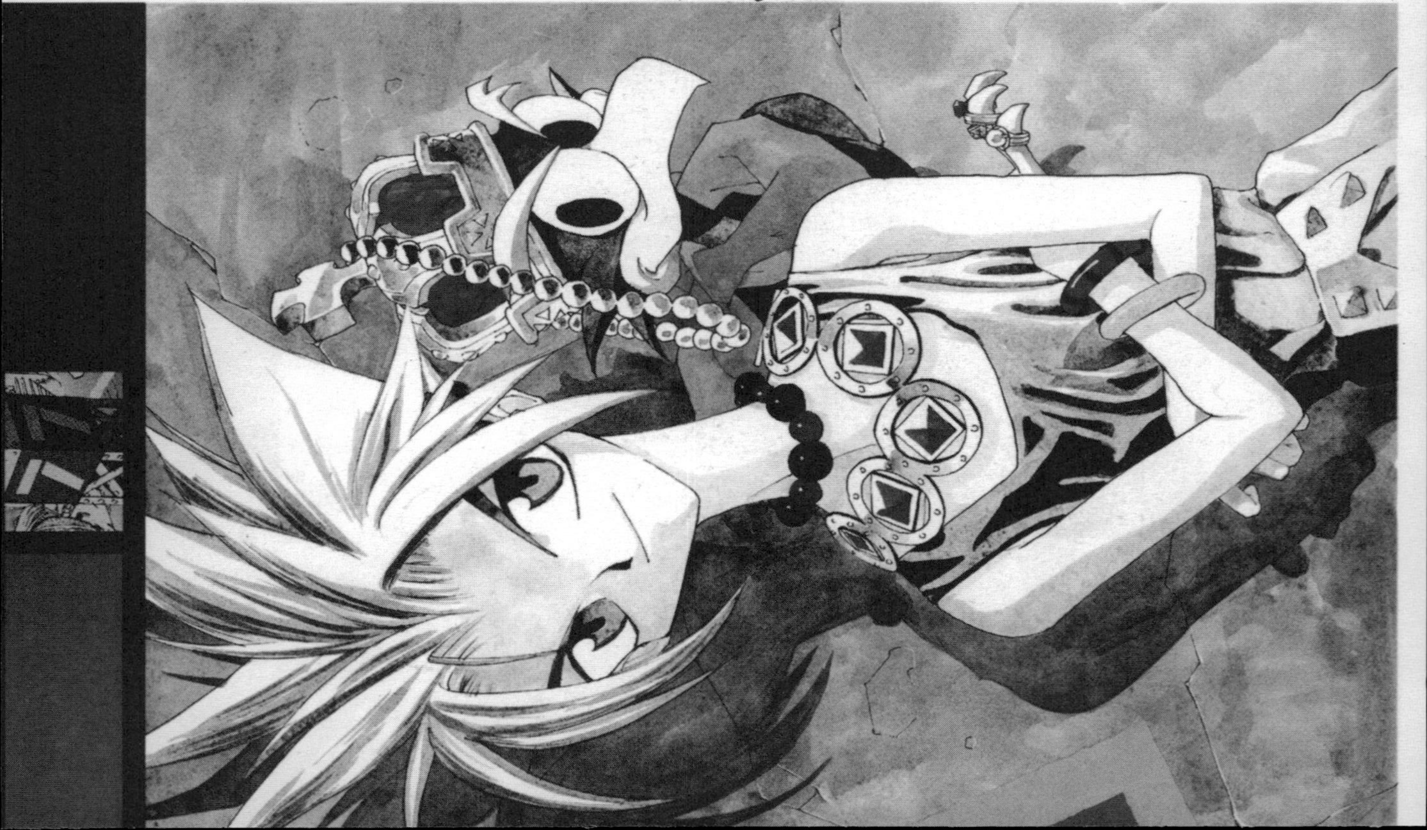

where are we now!!?

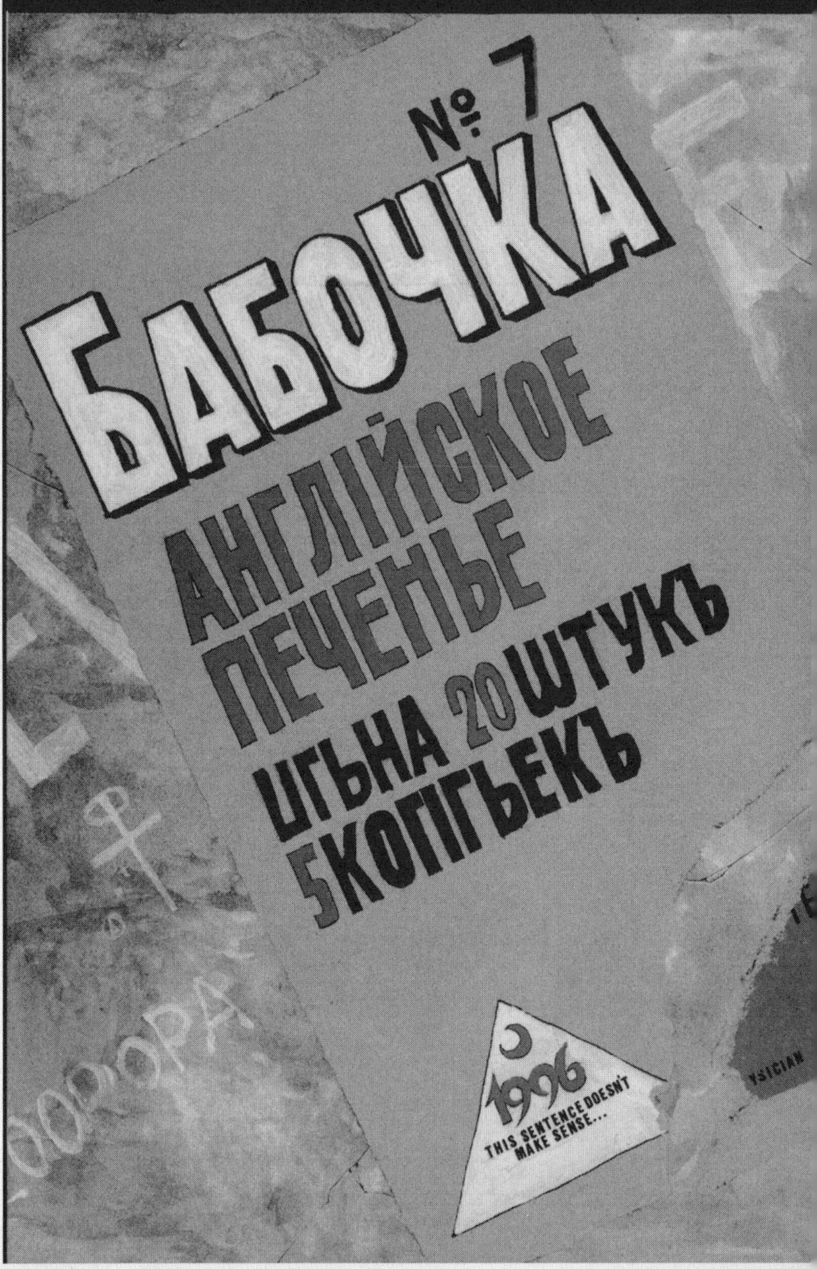

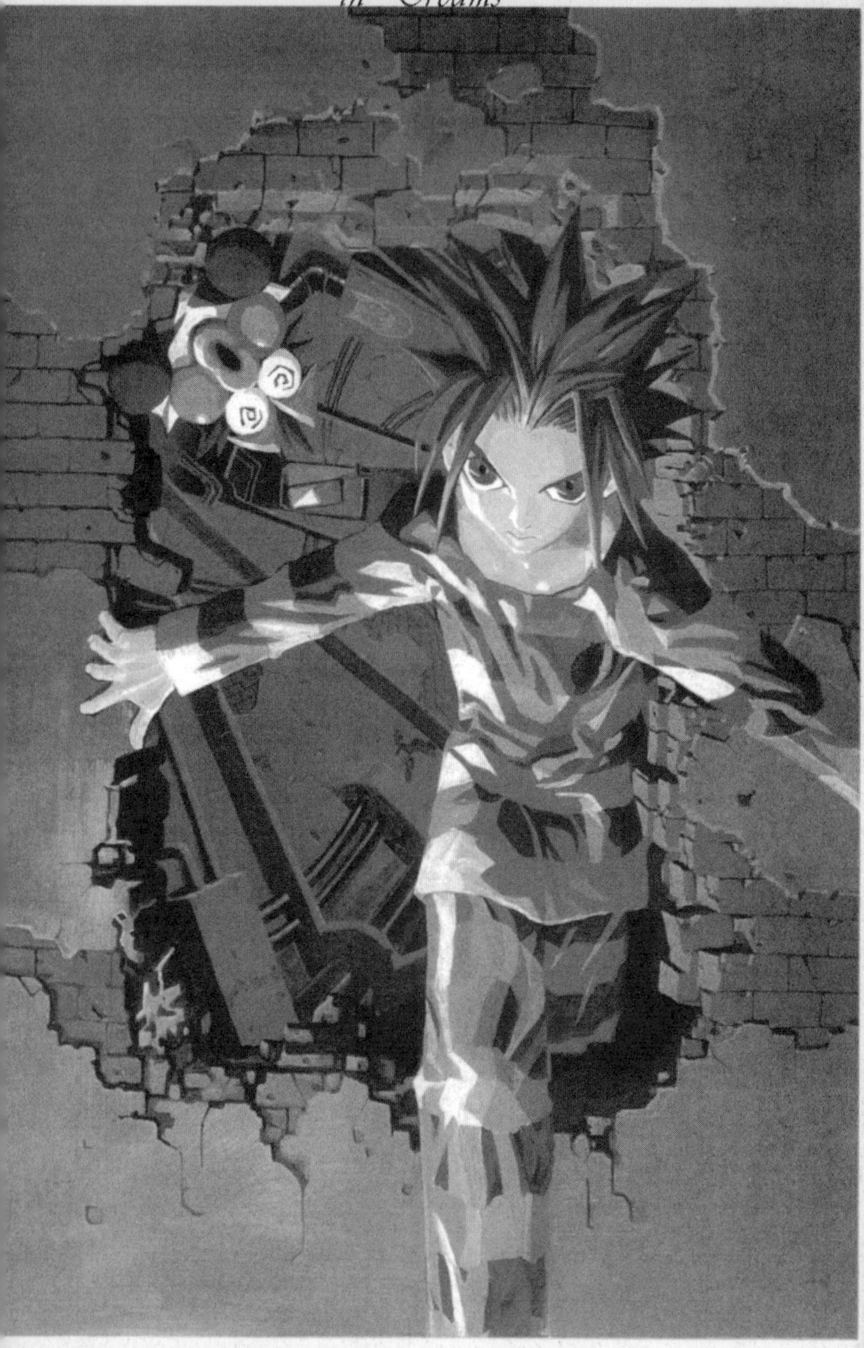

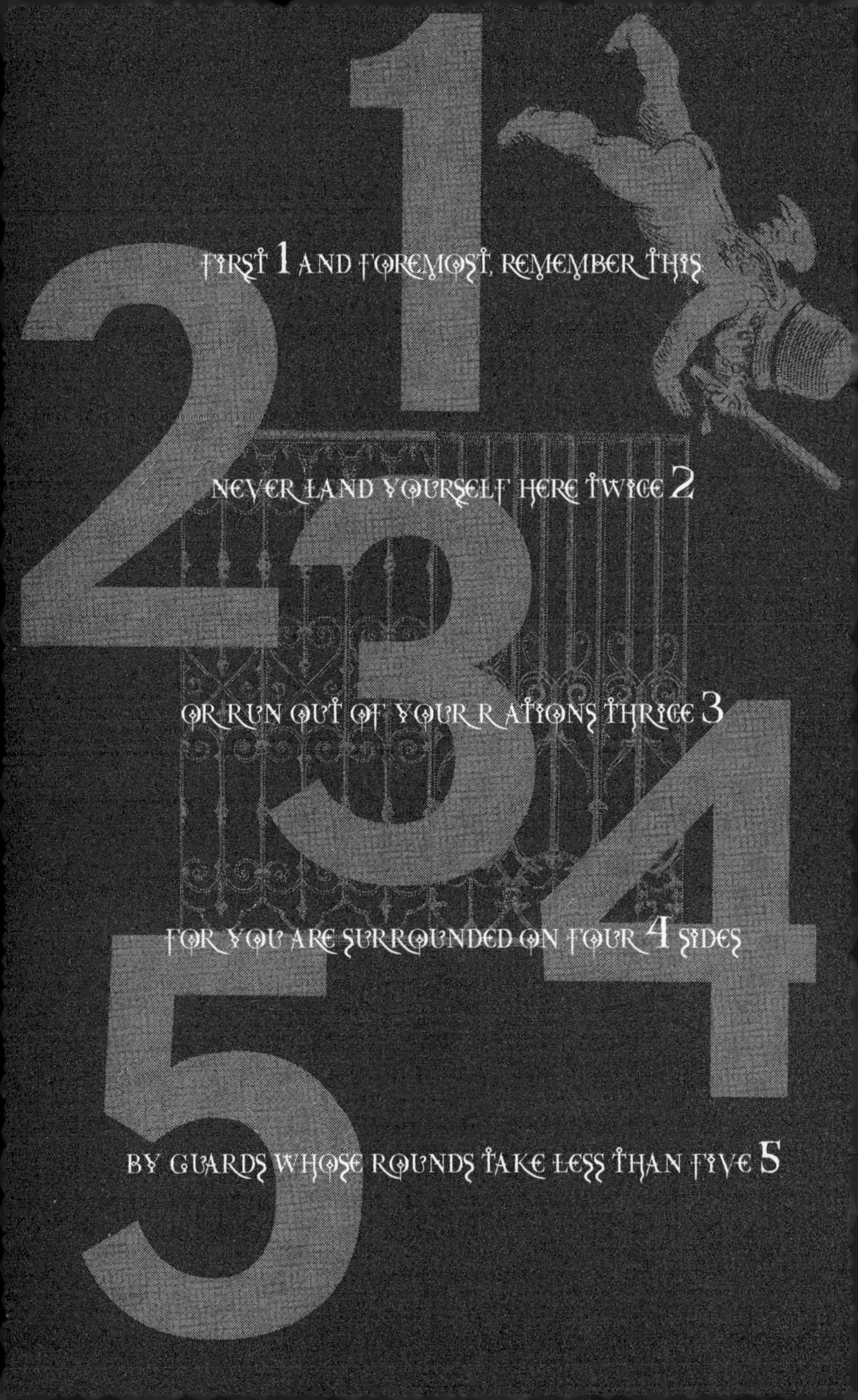
FIRST 1 AND FOREMOST, REMEMBER THIS
NEVER LAND YOURSELF HERE TWICE 2
OR RUN OUT OF YOUR RATIONS THRICE 3
FOR YOU ARE SURROUNDED ON FOUR 4 SIDES
BY GUARDS WHOSE ROUNDS TAKE LESS THAN FIVE 5

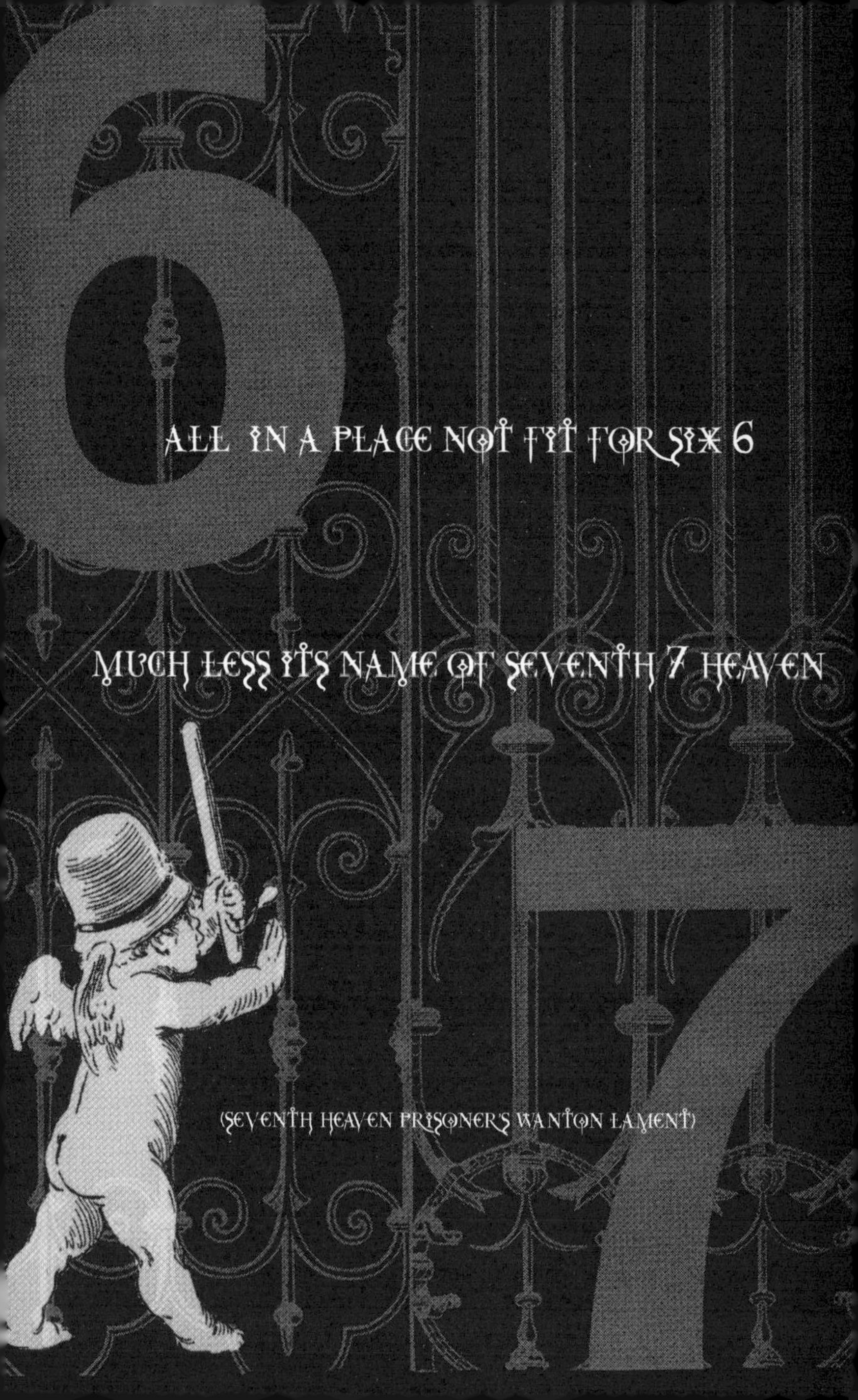
ALL IN A PLACE NOT FIT FOR SIX 6
MUCH LESS ITS NAME OF SEVENTH 7 HEAVEN
(SEVENTH HEAVEN PRISONER'S WANTON LAMENT)

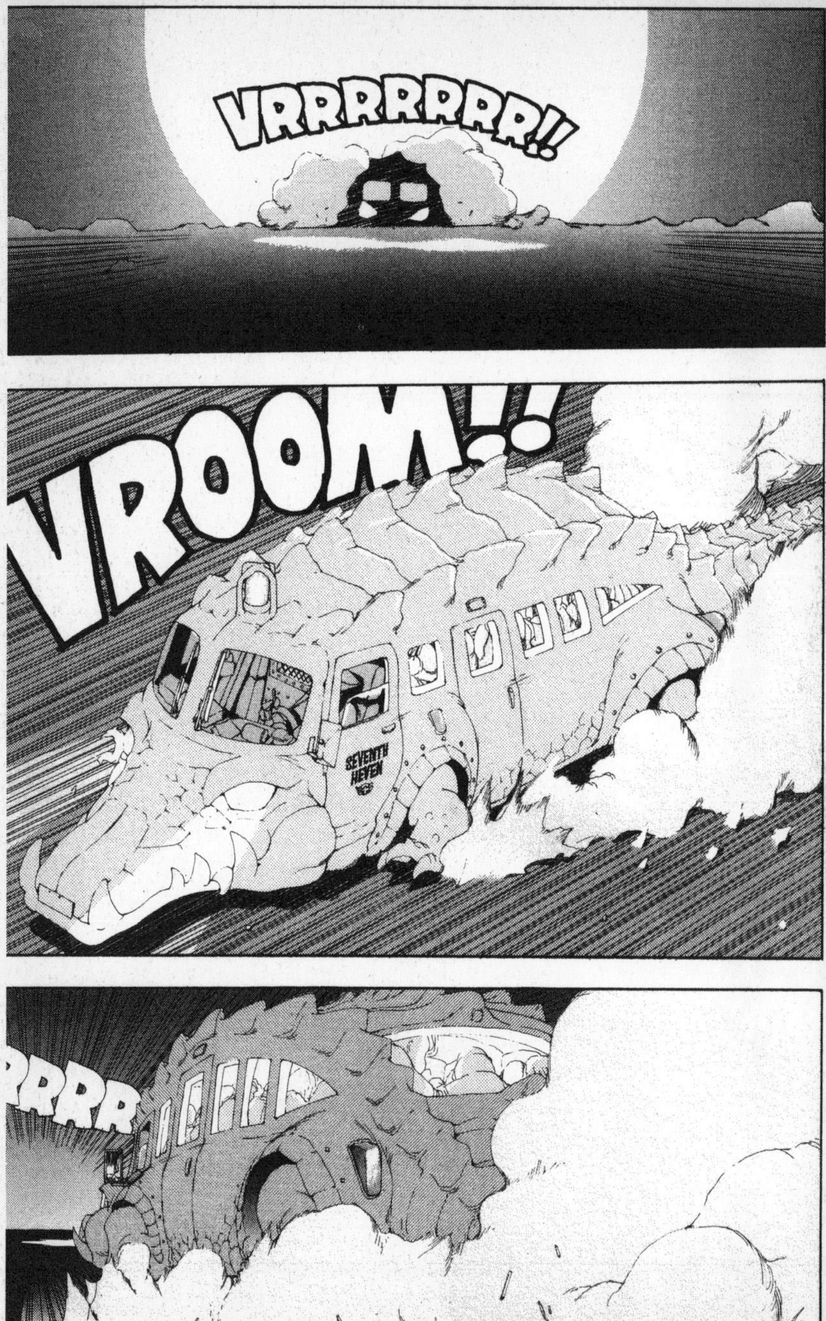
VRRRRRRR!!
VROOM!!
SEVENTH HEVEN
RRRR

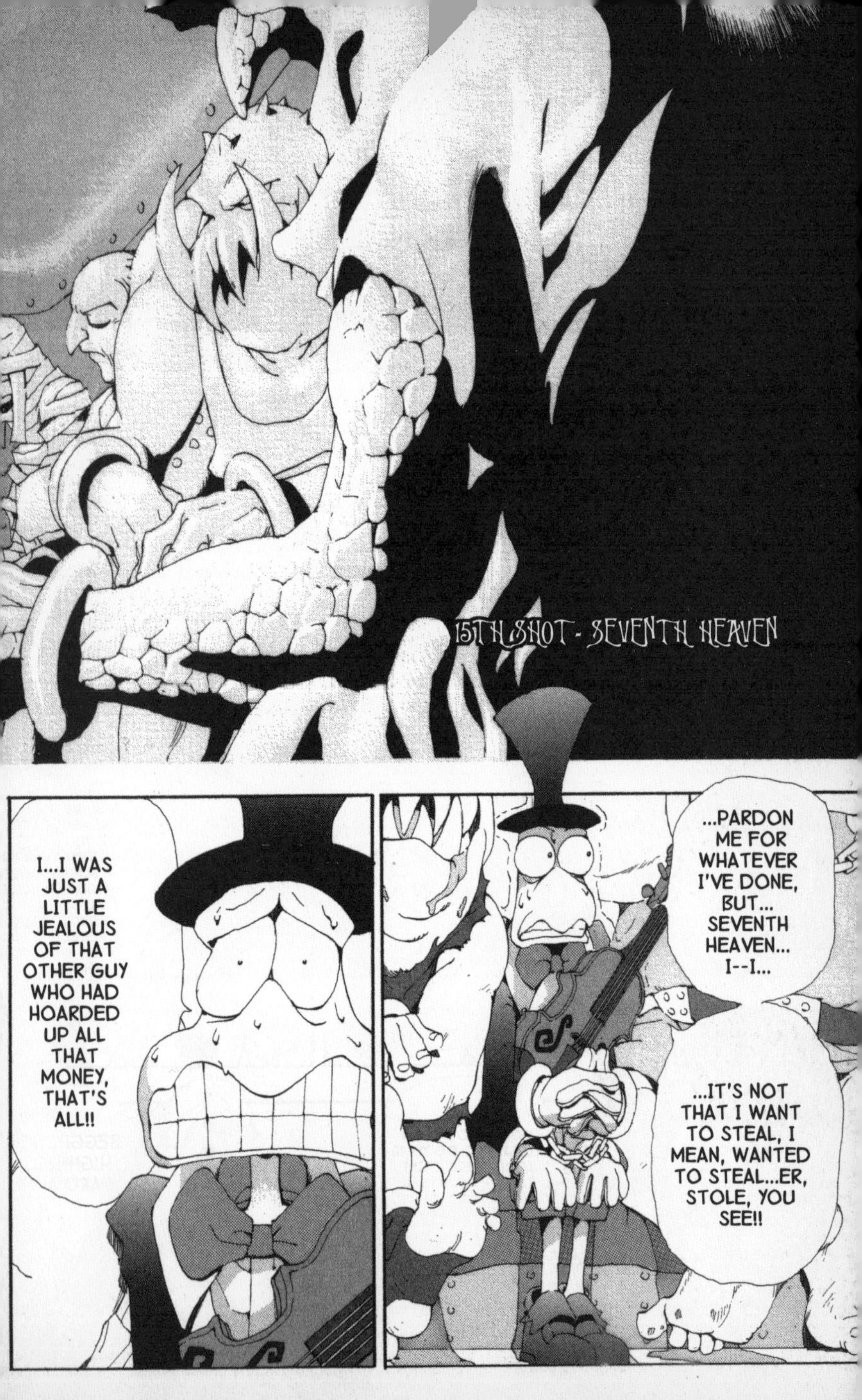
15TH SHOT - SEVENTH HEAVEN
...PARDON ME FOR WHATEVER I'VE DONE, BUT... SEVENTH HEAVEN... I--I...
...IT'S NOT THAT I WANT TO STEAL, I MEAN, WANTED TO STEAL...ER, STOLE, YOU SEE!!
I...I WAS JUST A LITTLE JEALOUS OF THAT OTHER GUY WHO HAD HOARDED UP ALL THAT MONEY, THAT'S ALL!!

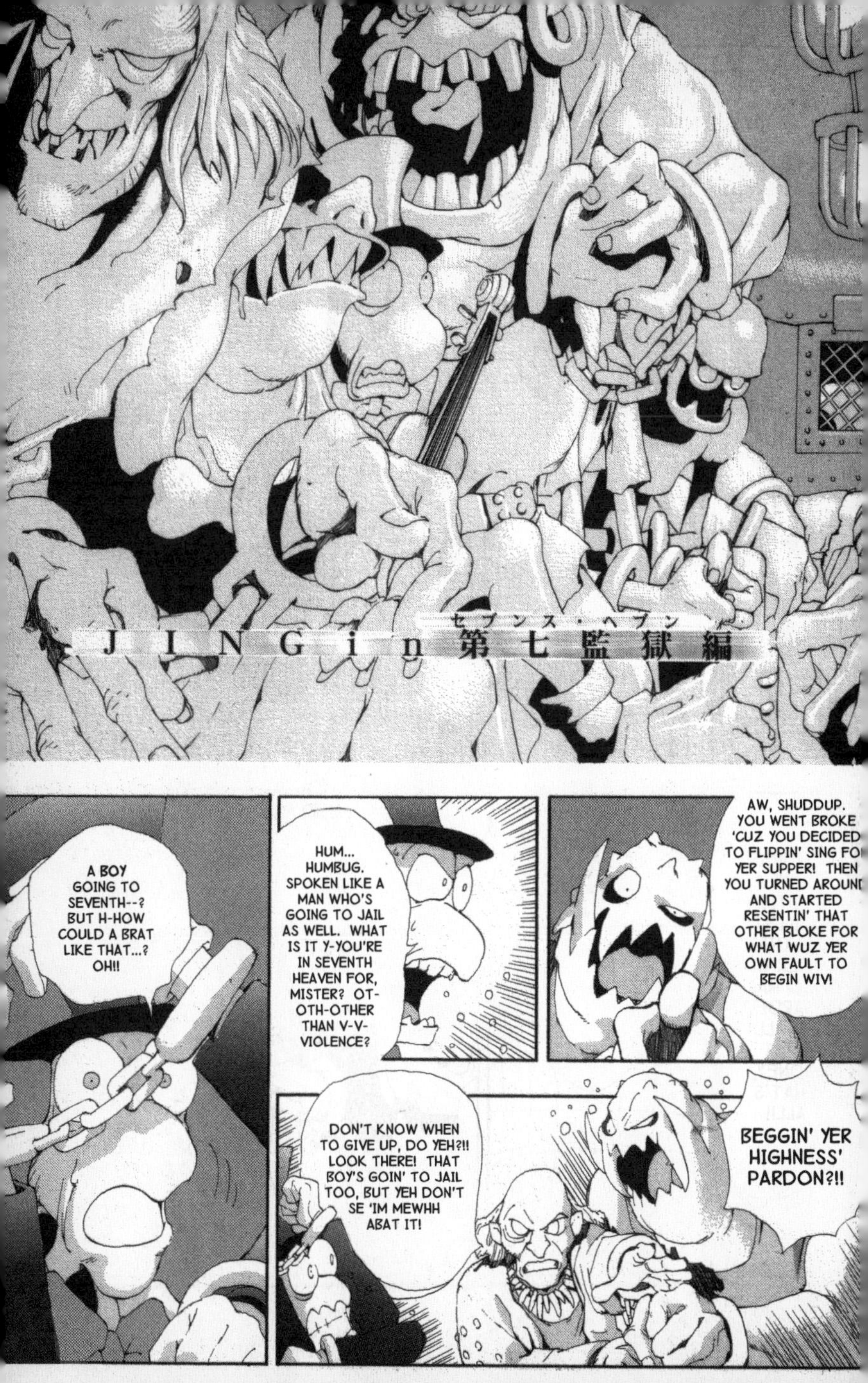
セブンス・ヘブン
JINGin 第七監獄編
AW, SHUDDUP. YOU WENT BROKE 'CUZ YOU DECIDED TO FLIPPIN' SING FOR YER SUPPER! THEN YOU TURNED AROUND AND STARTED RESENTIN' THAT OTHER BLOKE FOR WHAT WUZ YER OWN FAULT TO BEGIN WIV!
HUM... HUMBUG. SPOKEN LIKE A MAN WHO'S GOING TO JAIL AS WELL. WHAT IS IT Y-YOU'RE IN SEVENTH HEAVEN FOR, MISTER? OT-OTH-OTHER THAN V-V-VIOLENCE?
BEGGIN' YER HIGHNESS' PARDON?!!
DON'T KNOW WHEN TO GIVE UP, DO YEH?!! LOOK THERE! THAT BOY'S GOIN' TO JAIL TOO, BUT YEH DON'T SE 'IM MEWHH ABAT IT!
A BOY GOING TO SEVENTH--? BUT H-HOW COULD A BRAT LIKE THAT...? OH!!

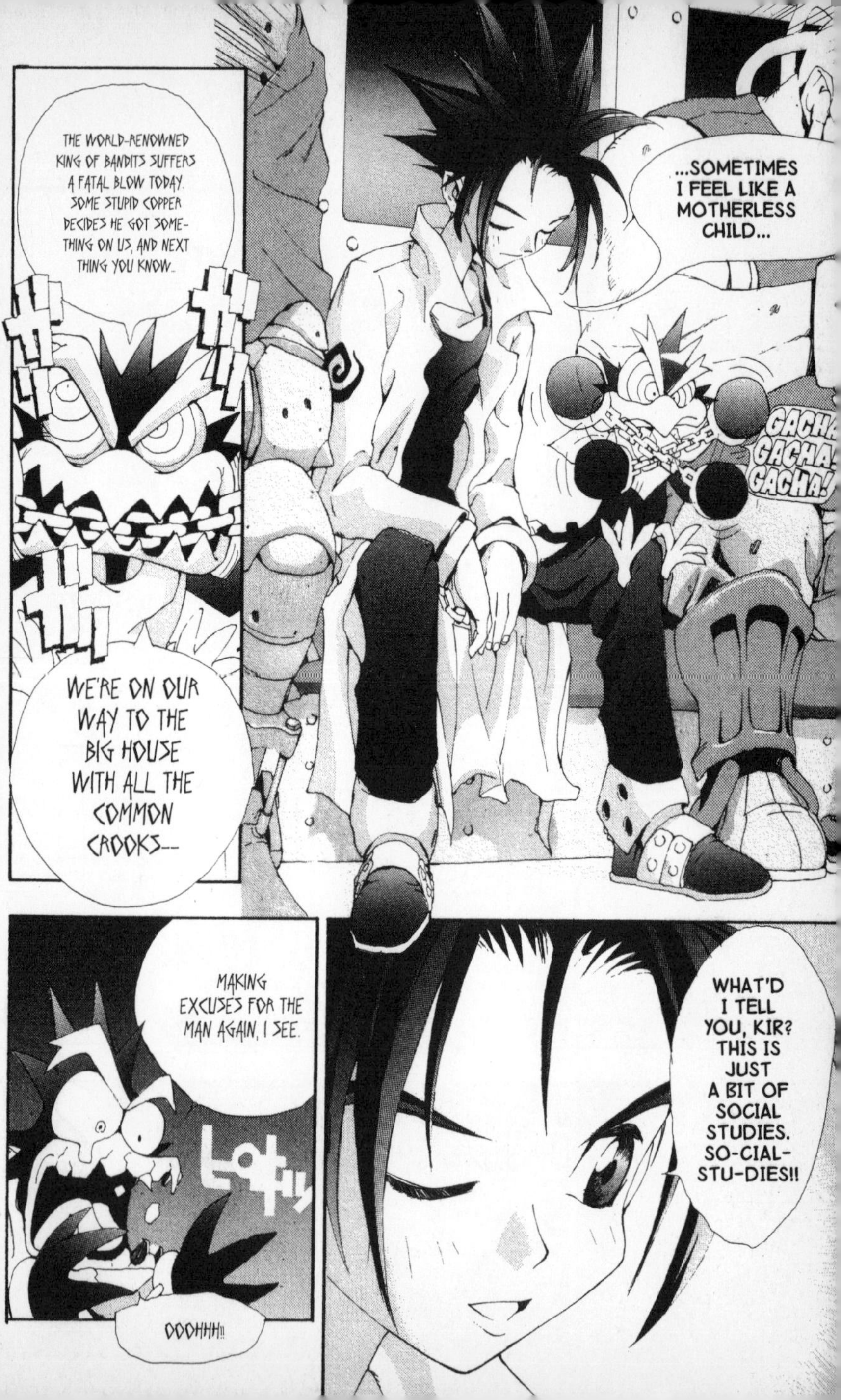
...SOMETIMES I FEEL LIKE A MOTHERLESS CHILD...
GACHA! GACHA! GACHA!
THE WORLD-RENOWNED KING OF BANDITS SUFFERS A FATAL BLOW TODAY. SOME STUPID COPPER DECIDES HE GOT SOMETHING ON US, AND NEXT THING YOU KNOW...
WE'RE ON OUR WAY TO THE BIG HOUSE WITH ALL THE COMMON CROOKS--
WHAT'D I TELL YOU, KIR? THIS IS JUST A BIT OF SOCIAL STUDIES. SO-CIAL-STU-DIES!!
MAKING EXCUSES FOR THE MAN AGAIN, I SEE.
OOOHHH!!

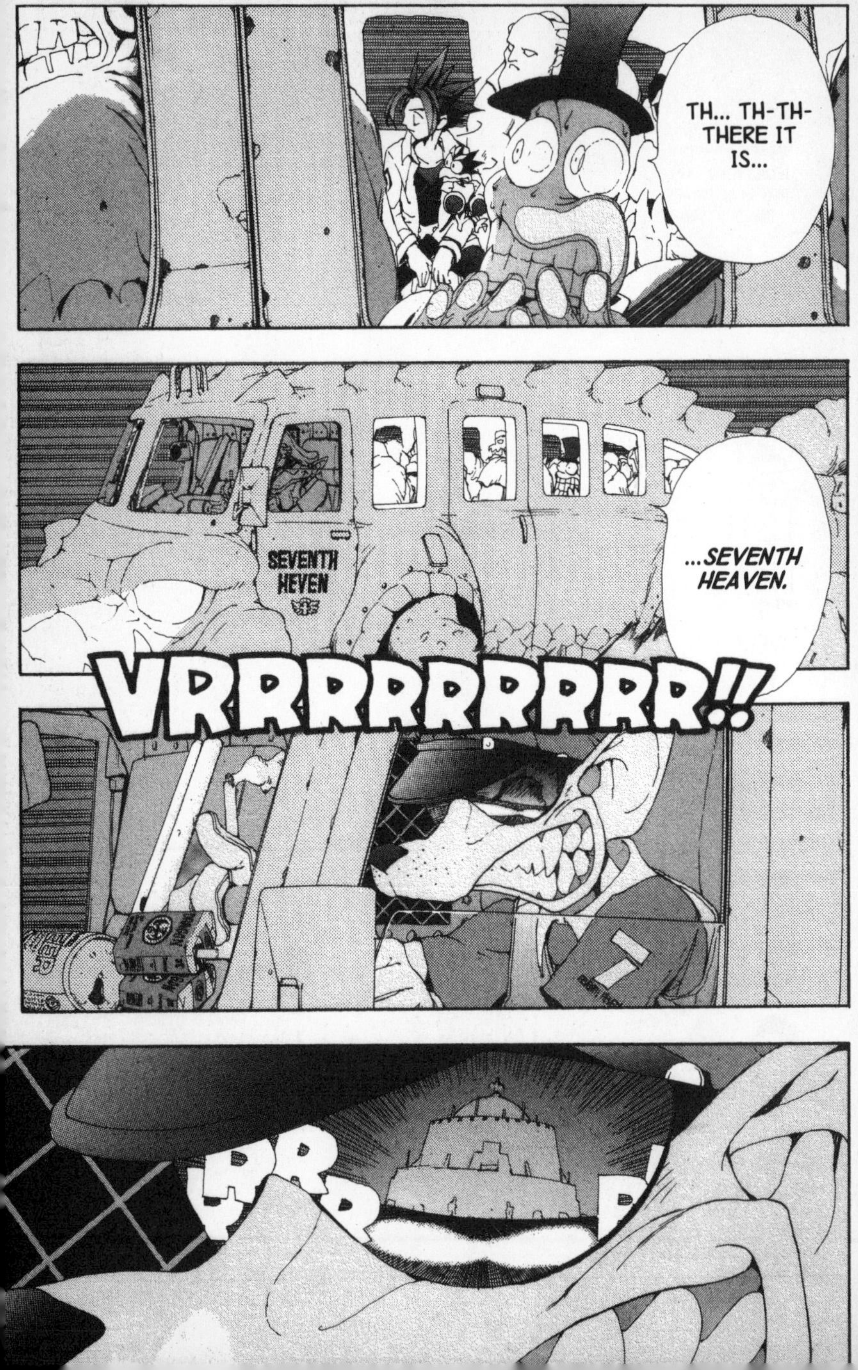
TH... TH-TH- THERE IT IS...
...SEVENTH HEAVEN.
SEVENTH HEVEN
VRRRRRRRRRR!!

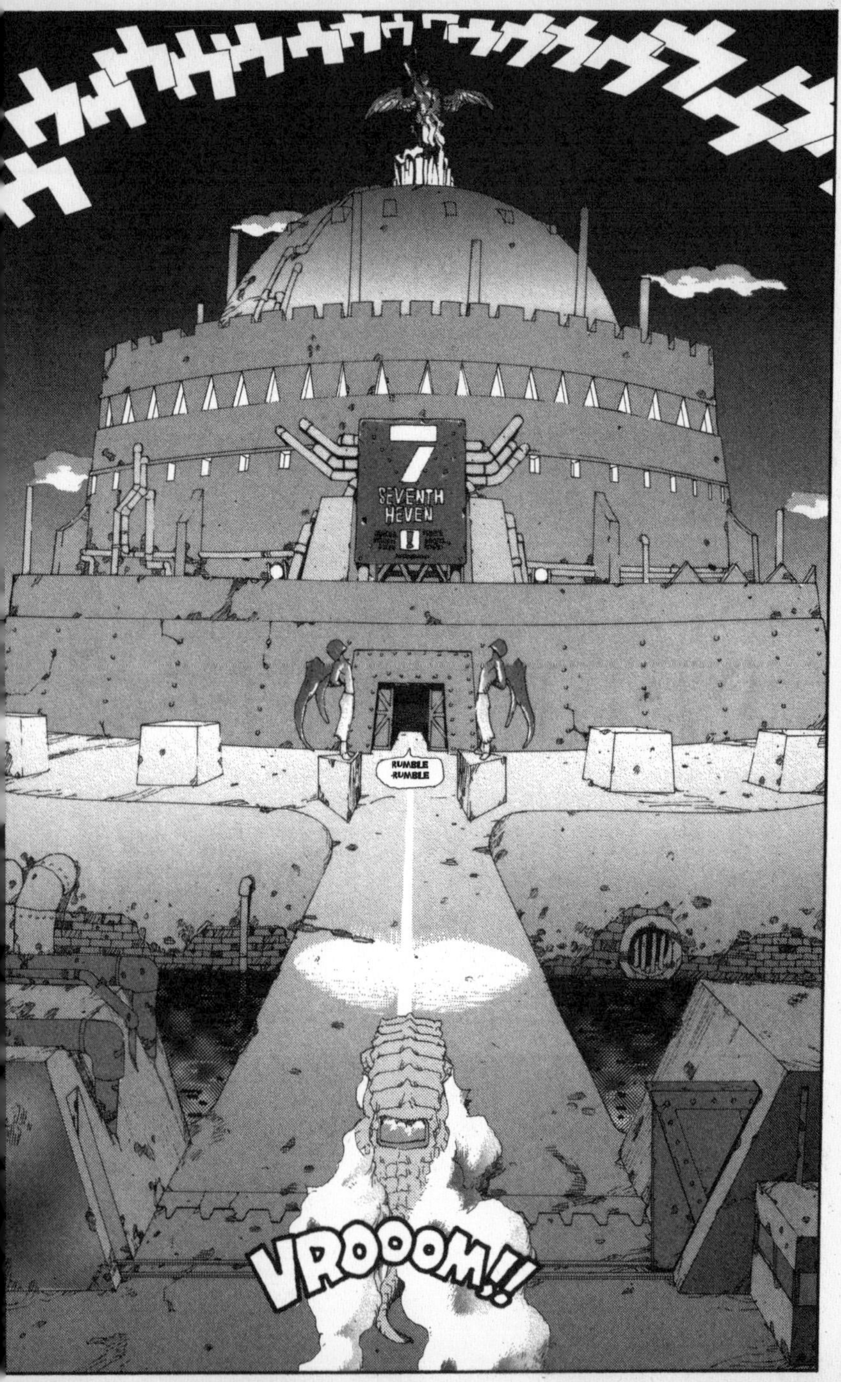
7
SEVENTH
HEVEN
RUMBLE
-RUMBLE
VROOOM!!

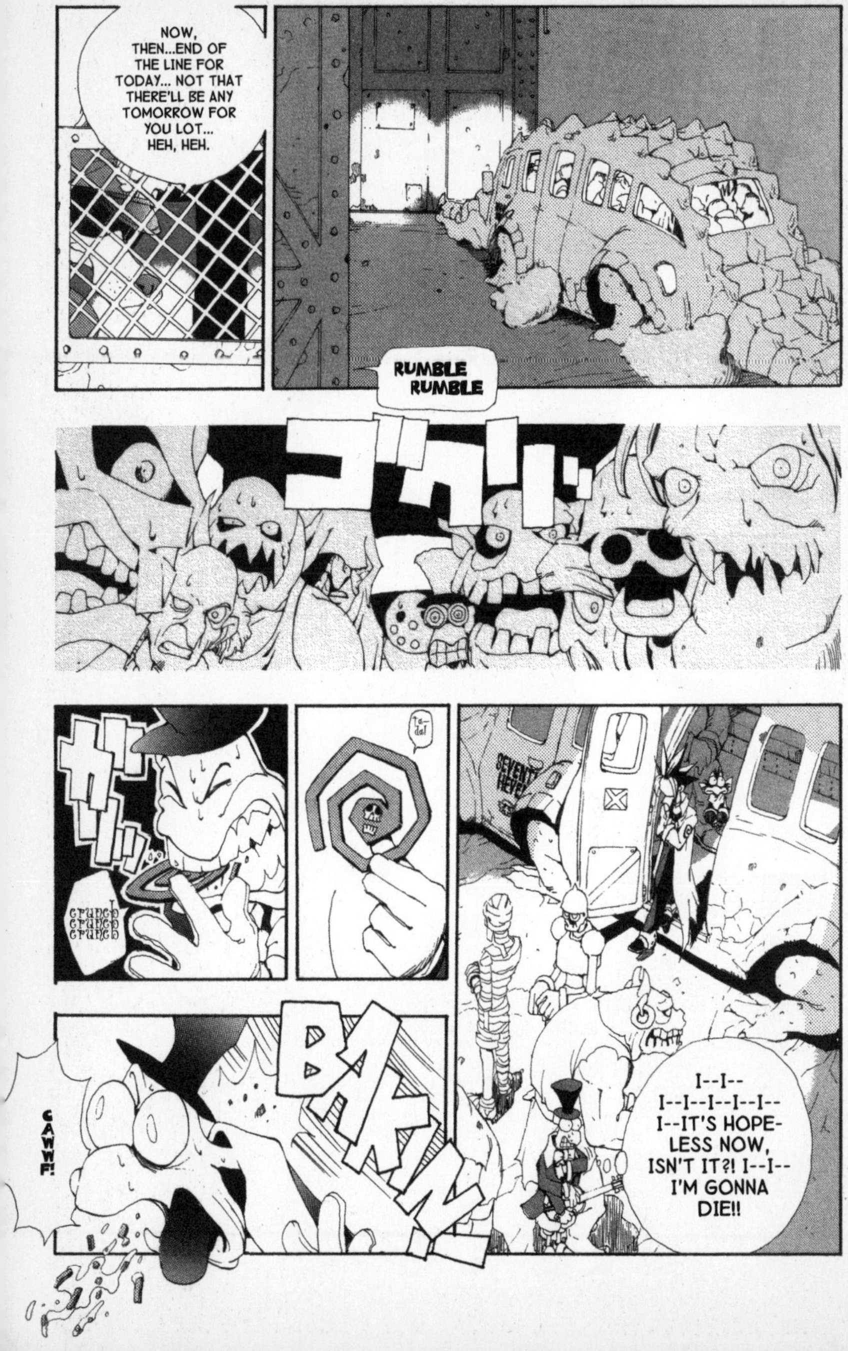
RUMBLE RUMBLE
NOW, THEN...END OF THE LINE FOR TODAY... NOT THAT THERE'LL BE ANY TOMORROW FOR YOU LOT... HEH, HEH.
I--I-- I--I--I--I--I-- I--IT'S HOPE-LESS NOW, ISN'T IT?! I--I-- I'M GONNA DIE!!
Ta-da!
CRUNCH CRUNCH CRUNCH
BAKIN
GAWWF!

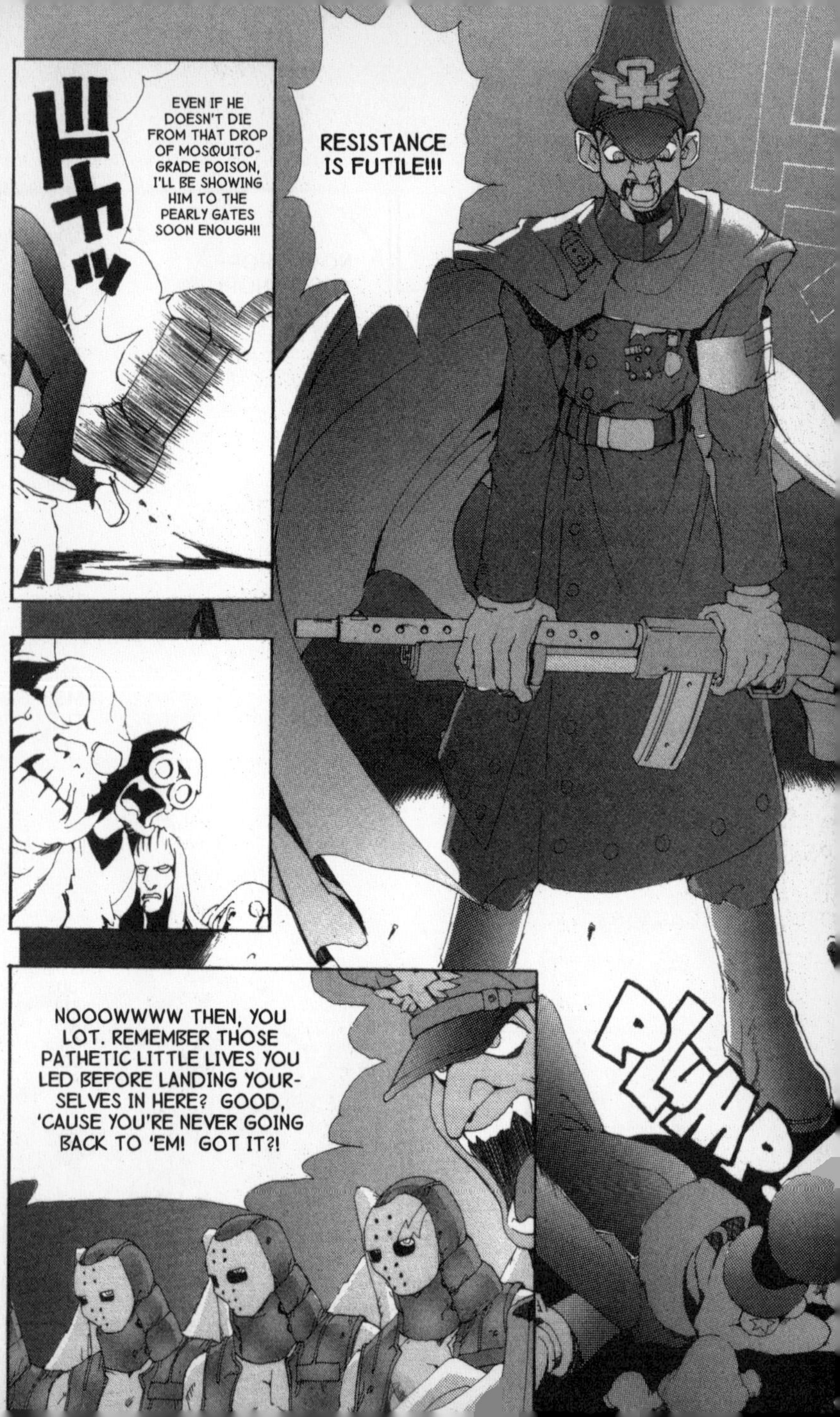
RESISTANCE IS FUTILE!!!
ドカッ
EVEN IF HE DOESN'T DIE FROM THAT DROP OF MOSQUITO-GRADE POISON, I'LL BE SHOWING HIM TO THE PEARLY GATES SOON ENOUGH!!
PLUMP
NOOOWWWW THEN, YOU LOT. REMEMBER THOSE PATHETIC LITTLE LIVES YOU LED BEFORE LANDING YOURSELVES IN HERE? GOOD, 'CAUSE YOU'RE NEVER GOING BACK TO 'EM! GOT IT?!

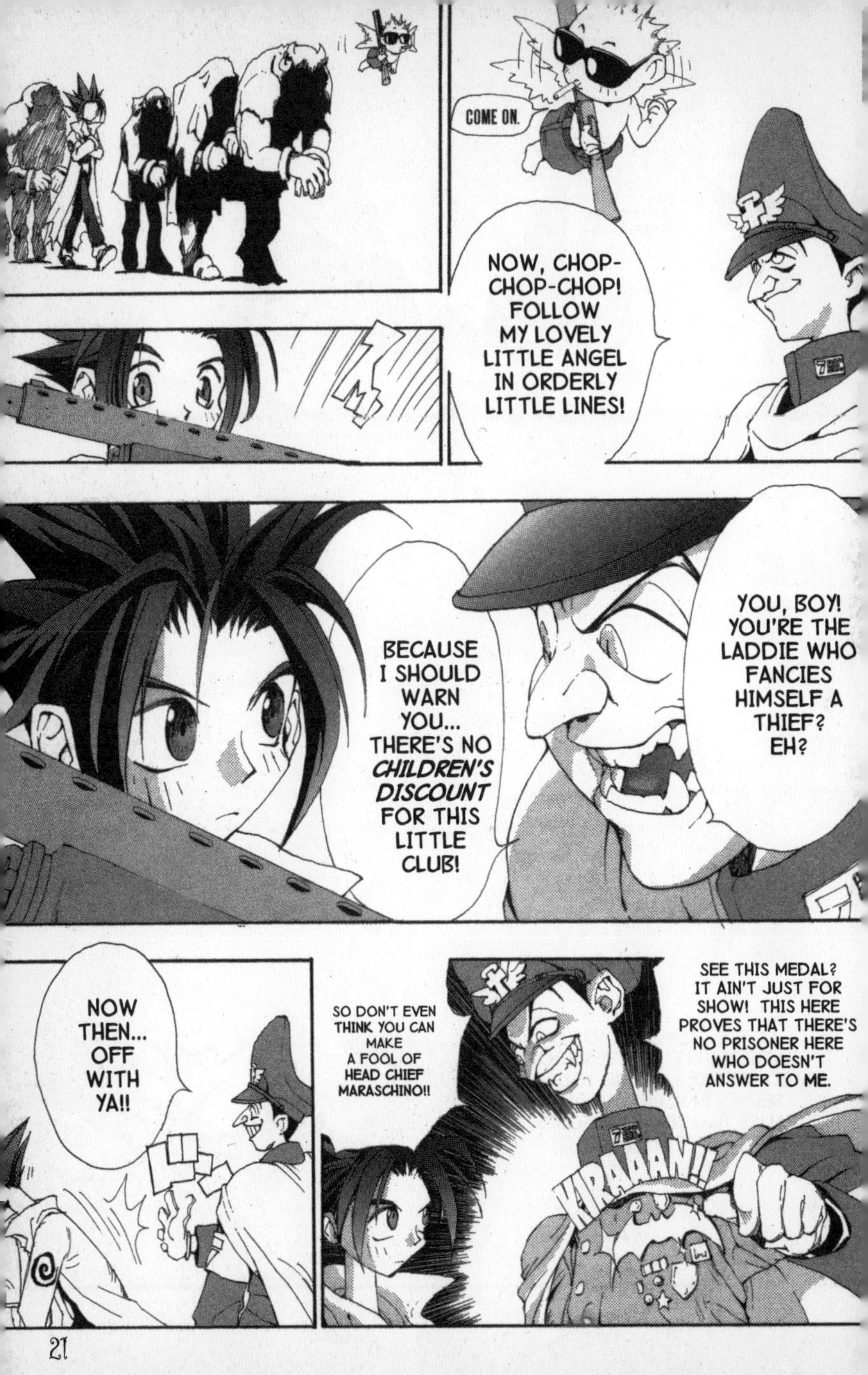
COME ON.
NOW, CHOP-CHOP-CHOP! FOLLOW MY LOVELY LITTLE ANGEL IN ORDERLY LITTLE LINES!
YOU, BOY! YOU'RE THE LADDIE WHO FANCIES HIMSELF A THIEF? EH?
BECAUSE I SHOULD WARN YOU... THERE'S NO *CHILDREN'S DISCOUNT* FOR THIS LITTLE CLUB!
SEE THIS MEDAL? IT AIN'T JUST FOR SHOW! THIS HERE PROVES THAT THERE'S NO PRISONER HERE WHO DOESN'T ANSWER TO ME.
KIRAAAN!!
SO DON'T EVEN THINK YOU CAN MAKE A FOOL OF HEAD CHIEF MARASCHINO!!
NOW THEN... OFF WITH YA!!

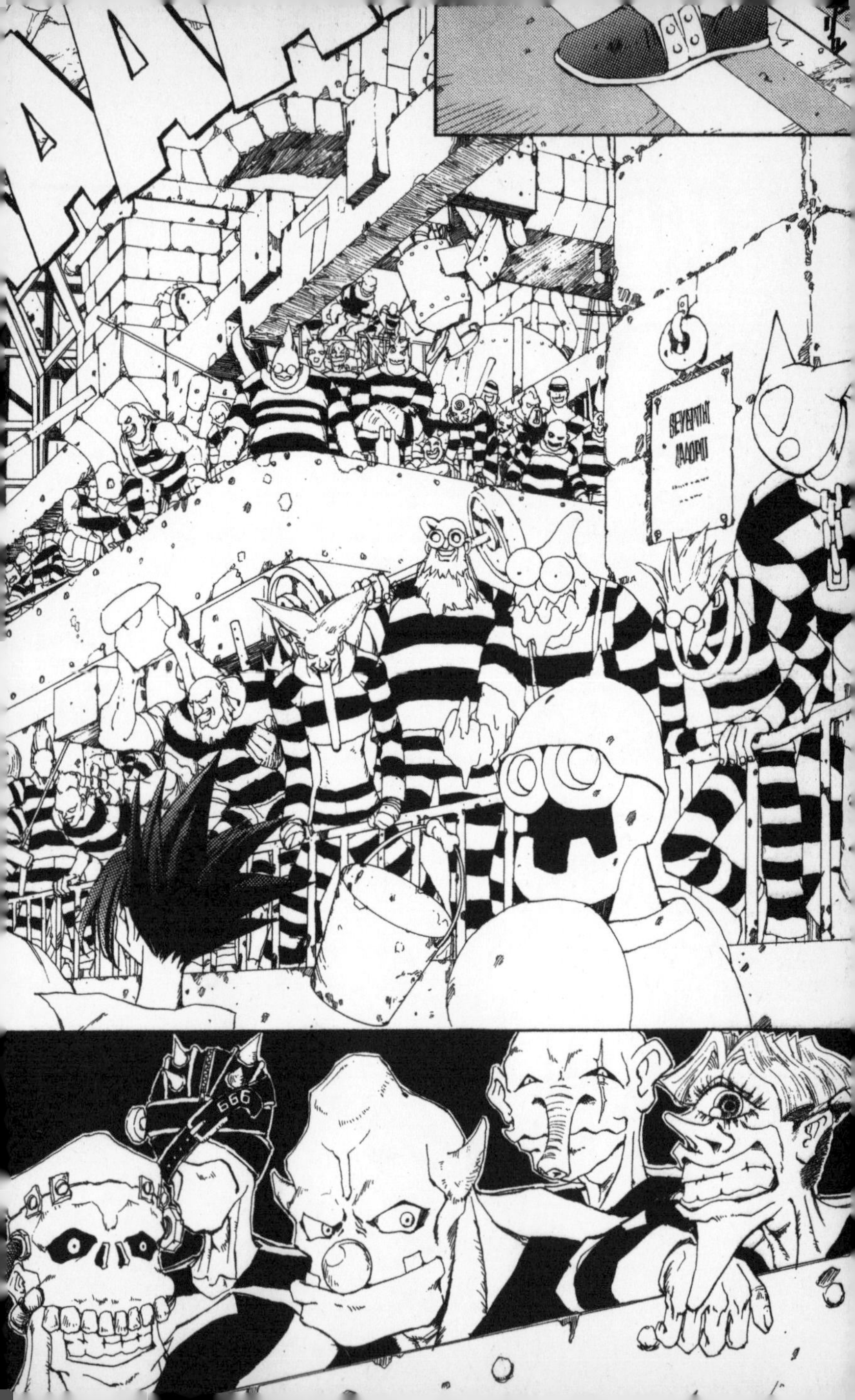
SEVENTH
666

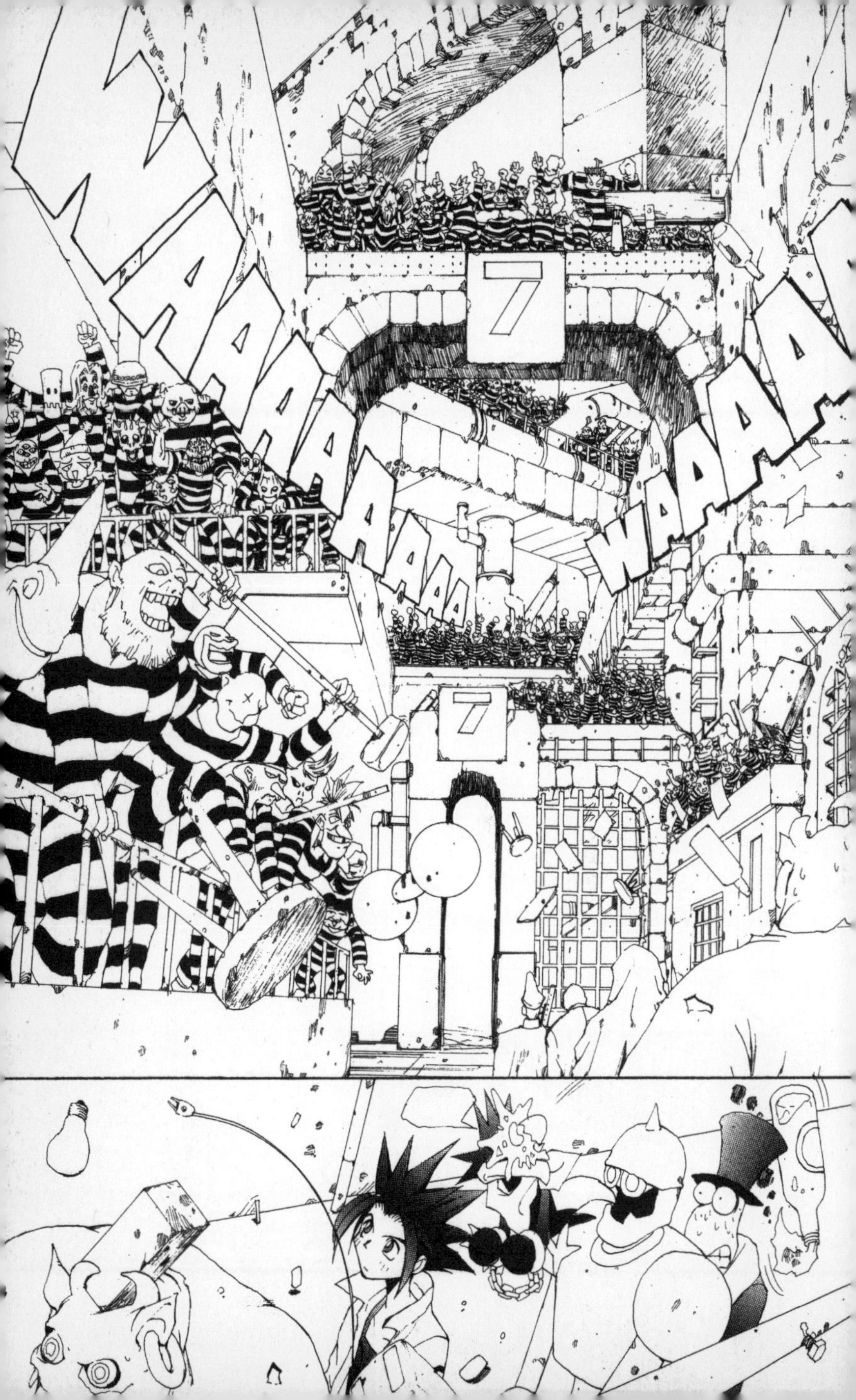
WAAAAA
WAAAAAAAAA
7
7

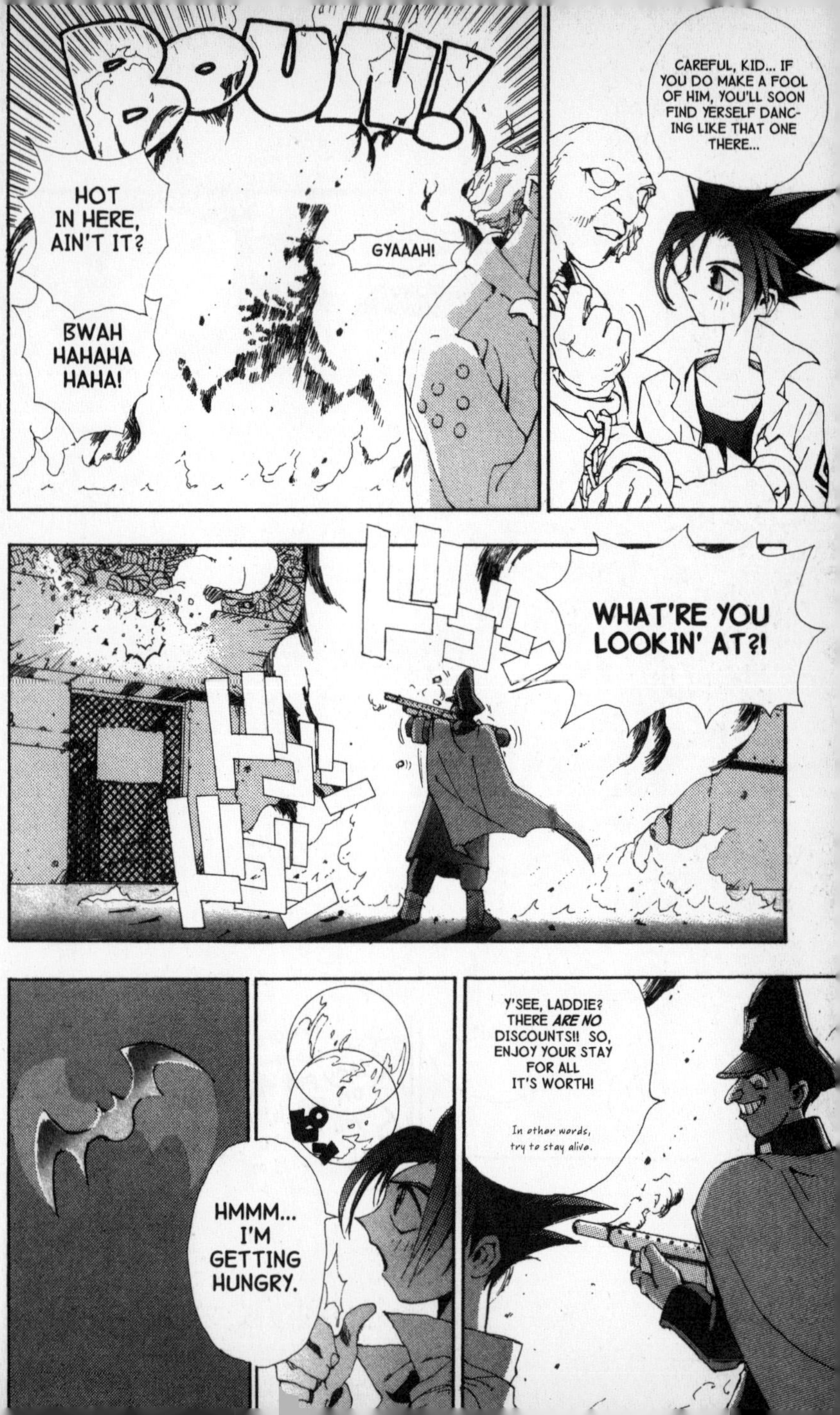
CAREFUL, KID... IF YOU DO MAKE A FOOL OF HIM, YOU'LL SOON FIND YERSELF DANCING LIKE THAT ONE THERE...
BOUN!
GYAAAH!
HOT IN HERE, AIN'T IT?
BWAH HAHAHA HAHA!
WHAT'RE YOU LOOKIN' AT?!
Y'SEE, LADDIE? THERE *ARE NO* DISCOUNTS!! SO, ENJOY YOUR STAY FOR ALL IT'S WORTH!
In other words, try to stay alive.
HMMM... I'M GETTING HUNGRY.

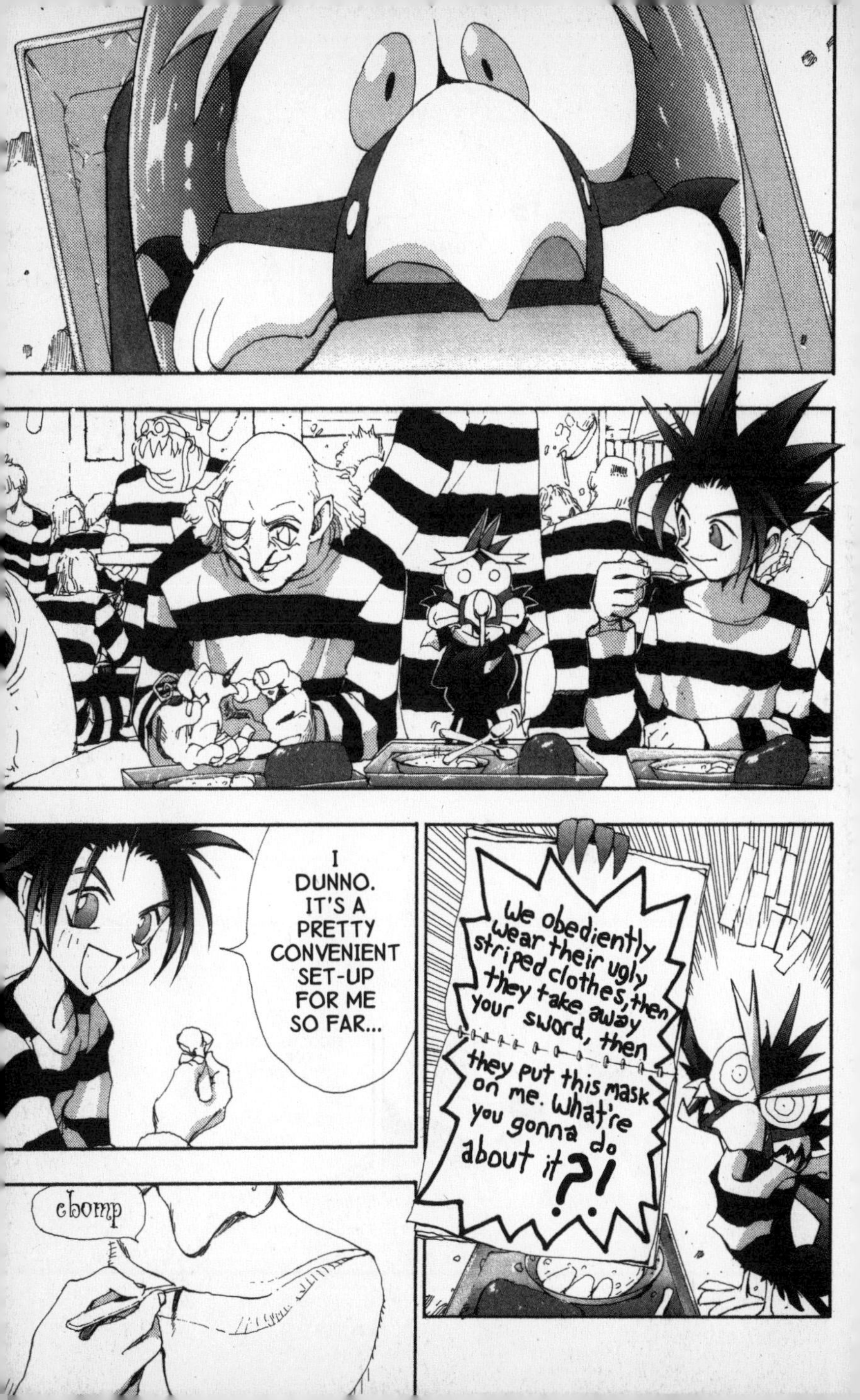
We obediently wear their ugly striped clothes, then they take away your sword, then they put this mask on me. What're you gonna do about it?!
I DUNNO. IT'S A PRETTY CONVENIENT SET-UP FOR ME SO FAR...
chomp

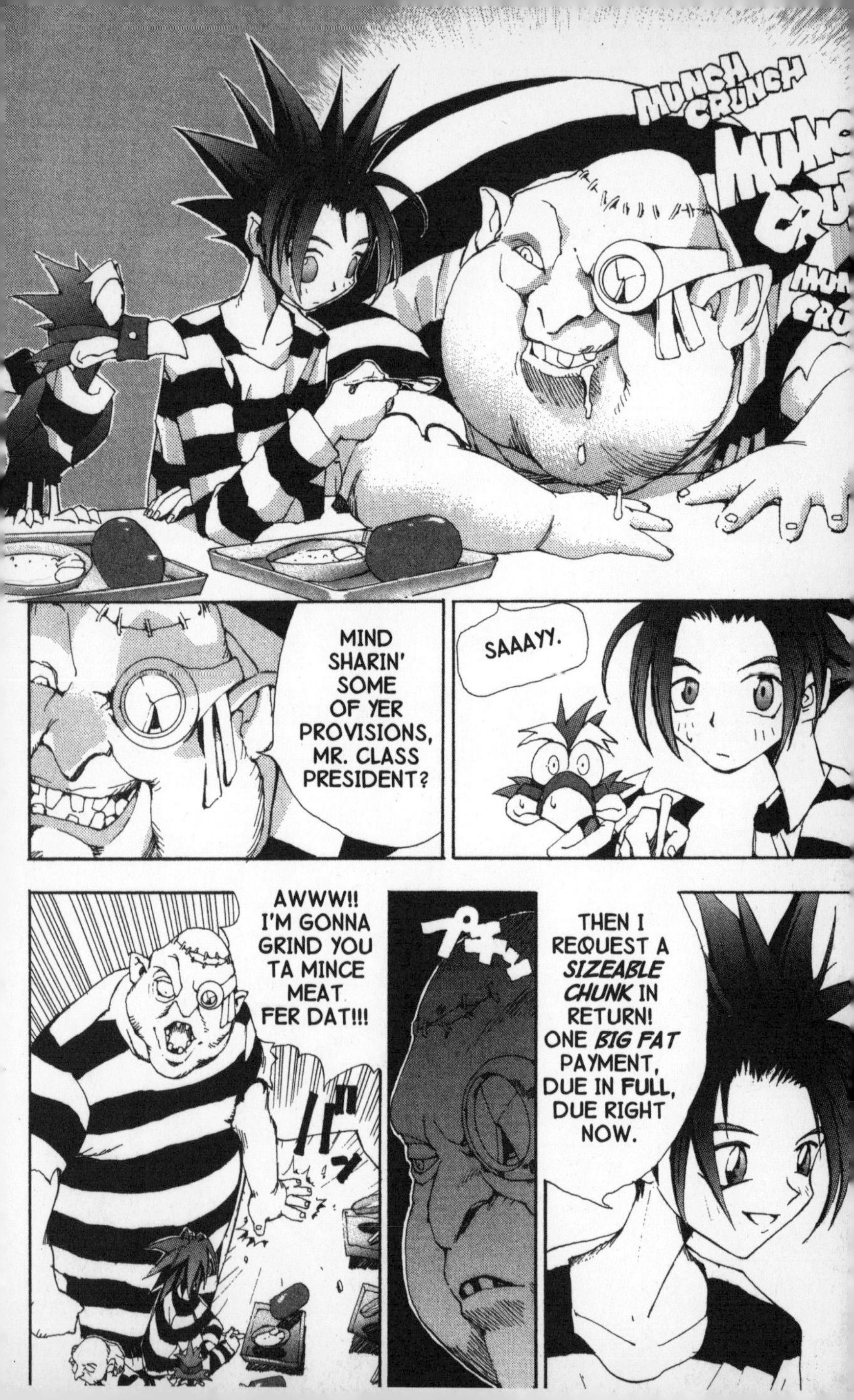
MUNCH CRUNCH
SAAAYY.
MIND SHARIN' SOME OF YER PROVISIONS, MR. CLASS PRESIDENT?
THEN I REQUEST A *SIZEABLE CHUNK* IN RETURN! ONE *BIG FAT* PAYMENT, DUE IN FULL, DUE RIGHT NOW.
プチッ
AWWW!! I'M GONNA GRIND YOU TA MINCE MEAT FER DAT!!!

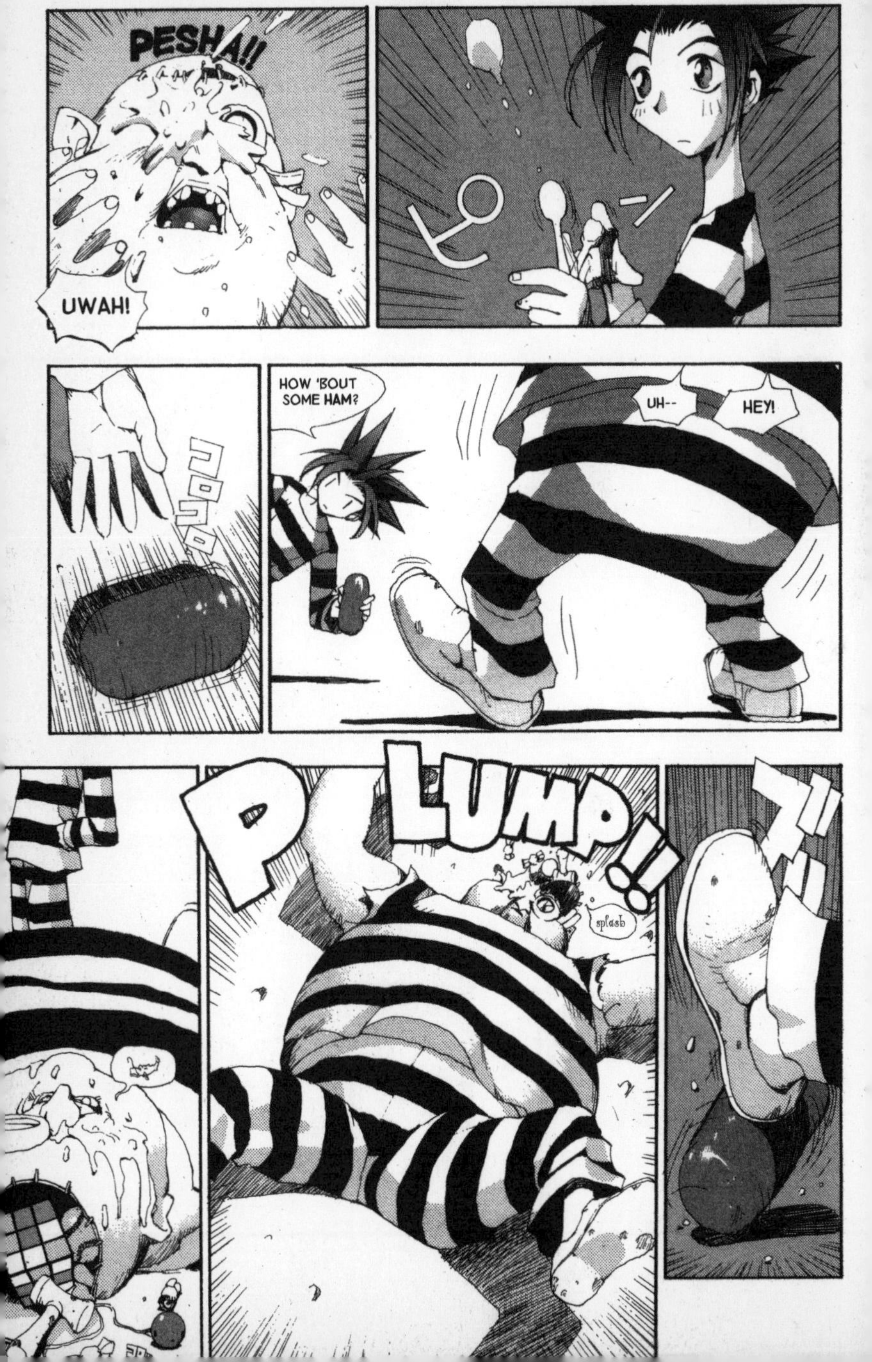
PESHA!!
UWAH!
HEY!
UH--
HOW 'BOUT SOME HAM?
PLUMP!!
splash

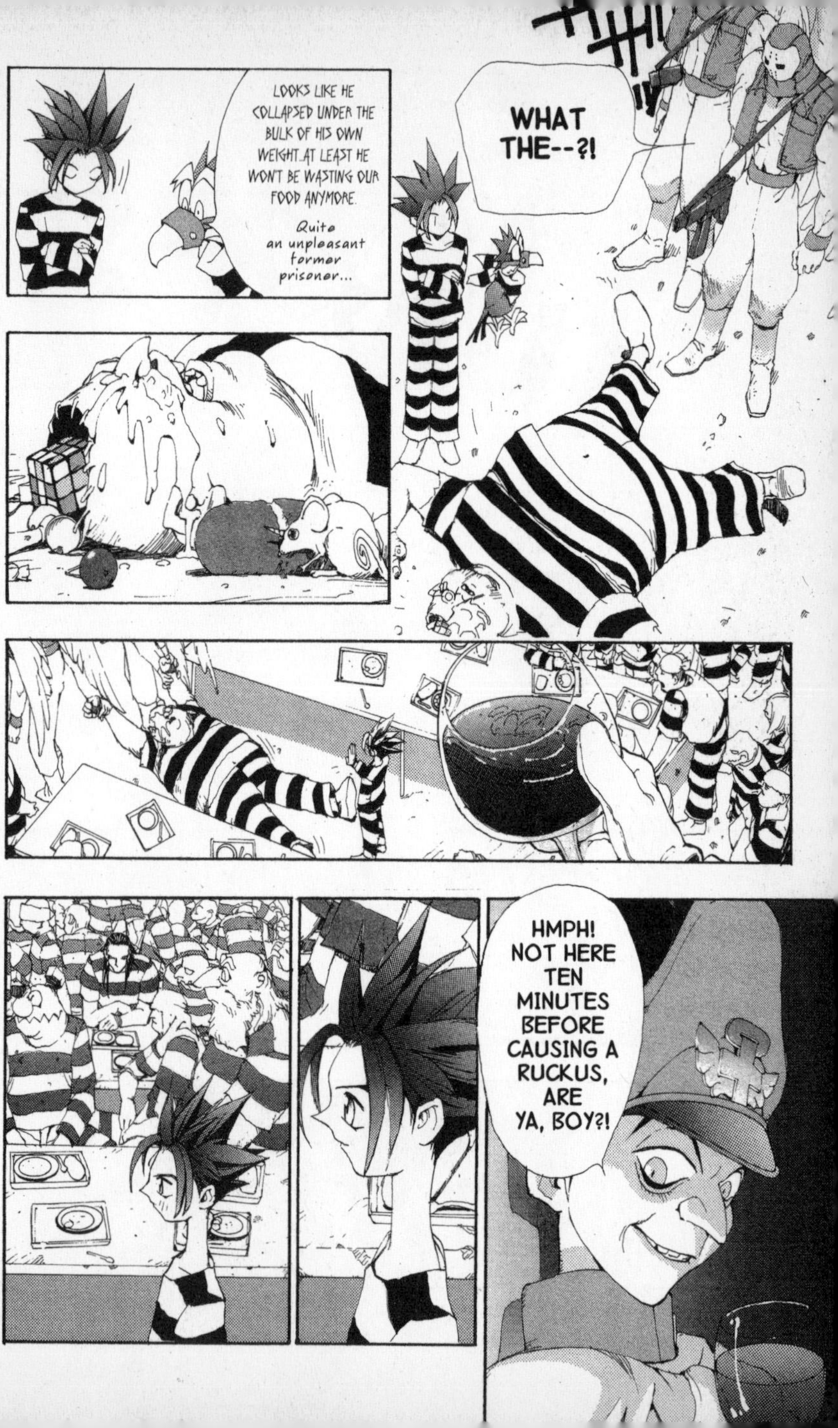
WHAT THE--?!
LOOKS LIKE HE COLLAPSED UNDER THE BULK OF HIS OWN WEIGHT...AT LEAST HE WON'T BE WASTING OUR FOOD ANYMORE.
Quite an unpleasant former prisoner...
HMPH! NOT HERE TEN MINUTES BEFORE CAUSING A RUCKUS, ARE YA, BOY?!

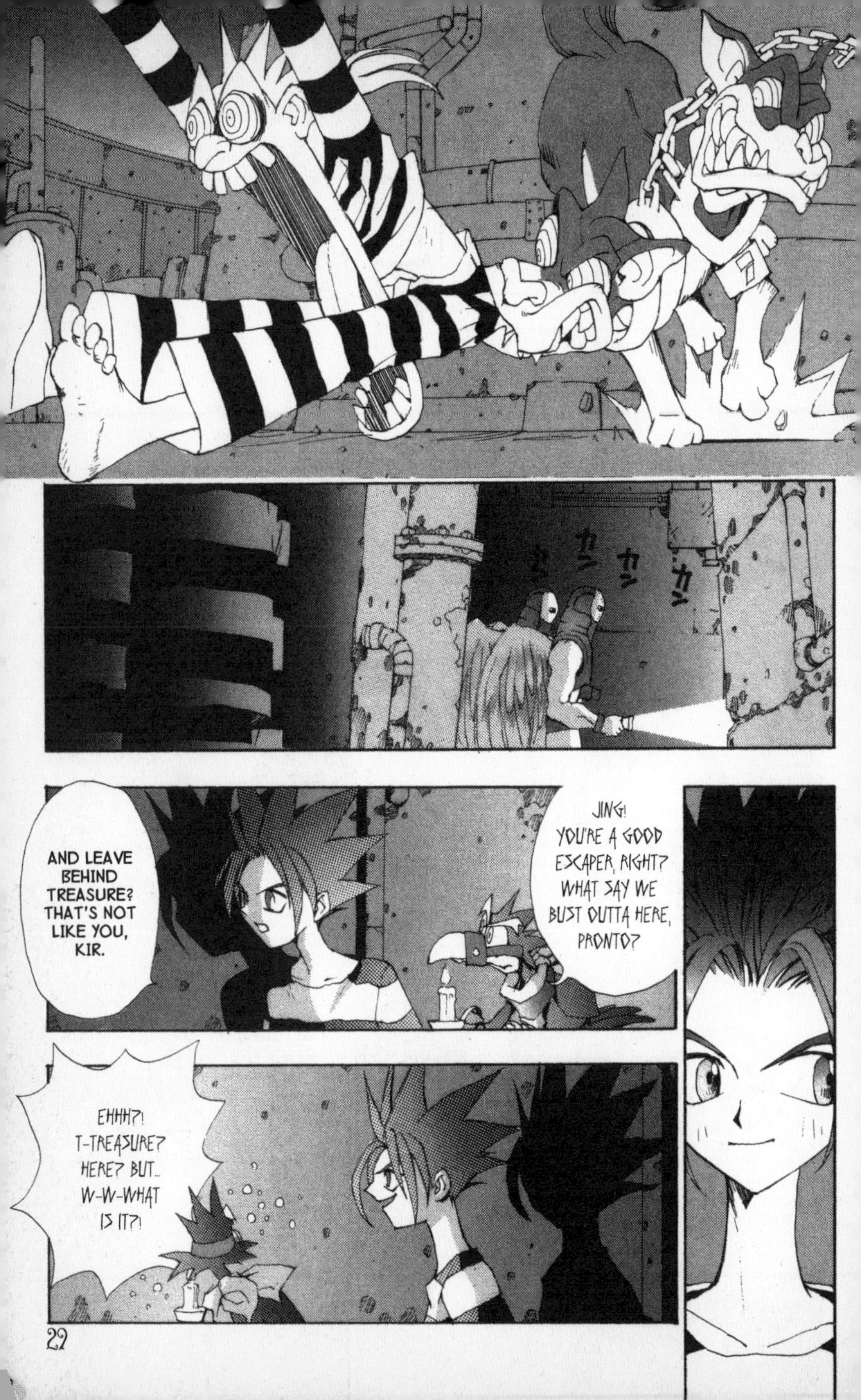
カン
カン
カン
JING! YOU'RE A GOOD ESCAPER, RIGHT? WHAT SAY WE BUST OUTTA HERE, PRONTO?
AND LEAVE BEHIND TREASURE? THAT'S NOT LIKE YOU, KIR.
EHHH?! T-TREASURE? HERE? BUT... W-W-WHAT IS IT?!

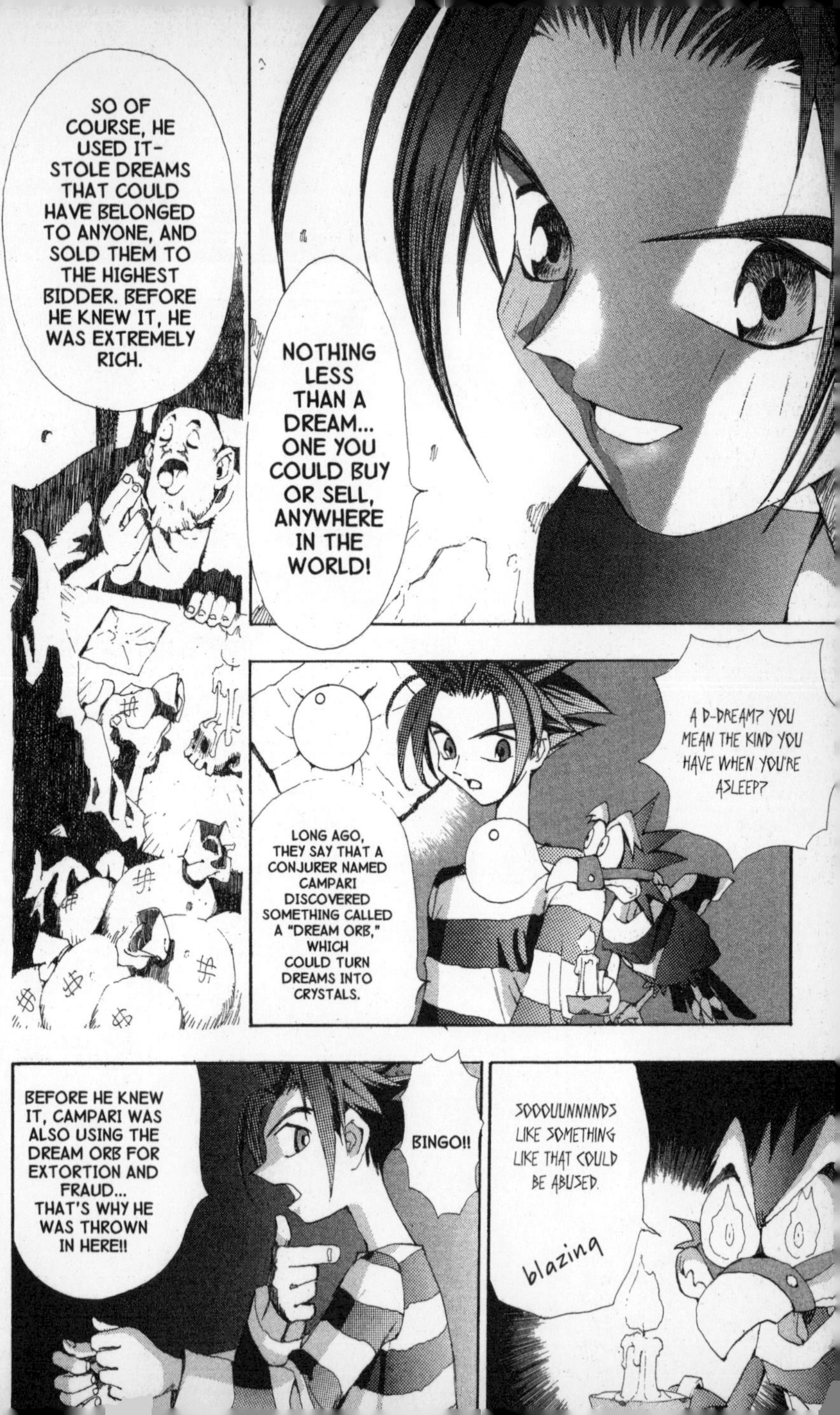
NOTHING LESS THAN A DREAM... ONE YOU COULD BUY OR SELL, ANYWHERE IN THE WORLD!
A D-DREAM? YOU MEAN THE KIND YOU HAVE WHEN YOU'RE ASLEEP?
LONG AGO, THEY SAY THAT A CONJURER NAMED CAMPARI DISCOVERED SOMETHING CALLED A "DREAM ORB," WHICH COULD TURN DREAMS INTO CRYSTALS.
SO OF COURSE, HE USED IT- STOLE DREAMS THAT COULD HAVE BELONGED TO ANYONE, AND SOLD THEM TO THE HIGHEST BIDDER. BEFORE HE KNEW IT, HE WAS EXTREMELY RICH.
SOOOUUNNNDS LIKE SOMETHING LIKE THAT COULD BE ABUSED.
blazing
BINGO!!
BEFORE HE KNEW IT, CAMPARI WAS ALSO USING THE DREAM ORB FOR EXTORTION AND FRAUD... THAT'S WHY HE WAS THROWN IN HERE!!

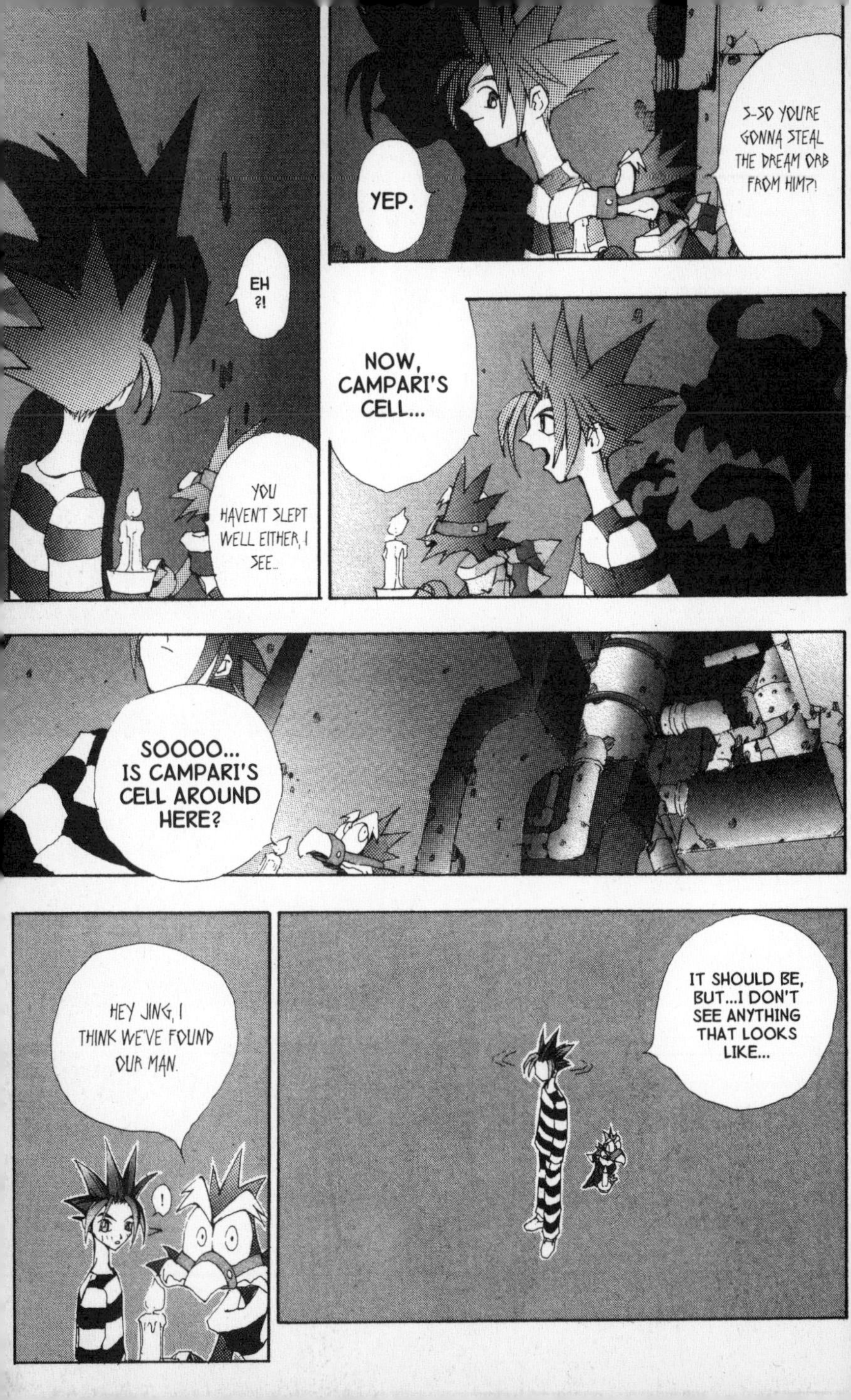
S-SO YOU'RE GONNA STEAL THE DREAM ORB FROM HIM?!
YEP.
NOW, CAMPARI'S CELL...
EH ?!
YOU HAVEN'T SLEPT WELL EITHER, I SEE...
SOOOO... IS CAMPARI'S CELL AROUND HERE?
IT SHOULD BE, BUT...I DON'T SEE ANYTHING THAT LOOKS LIKE...
HEY JING, I THINK WE'VE FOUND OUR MAN.
!

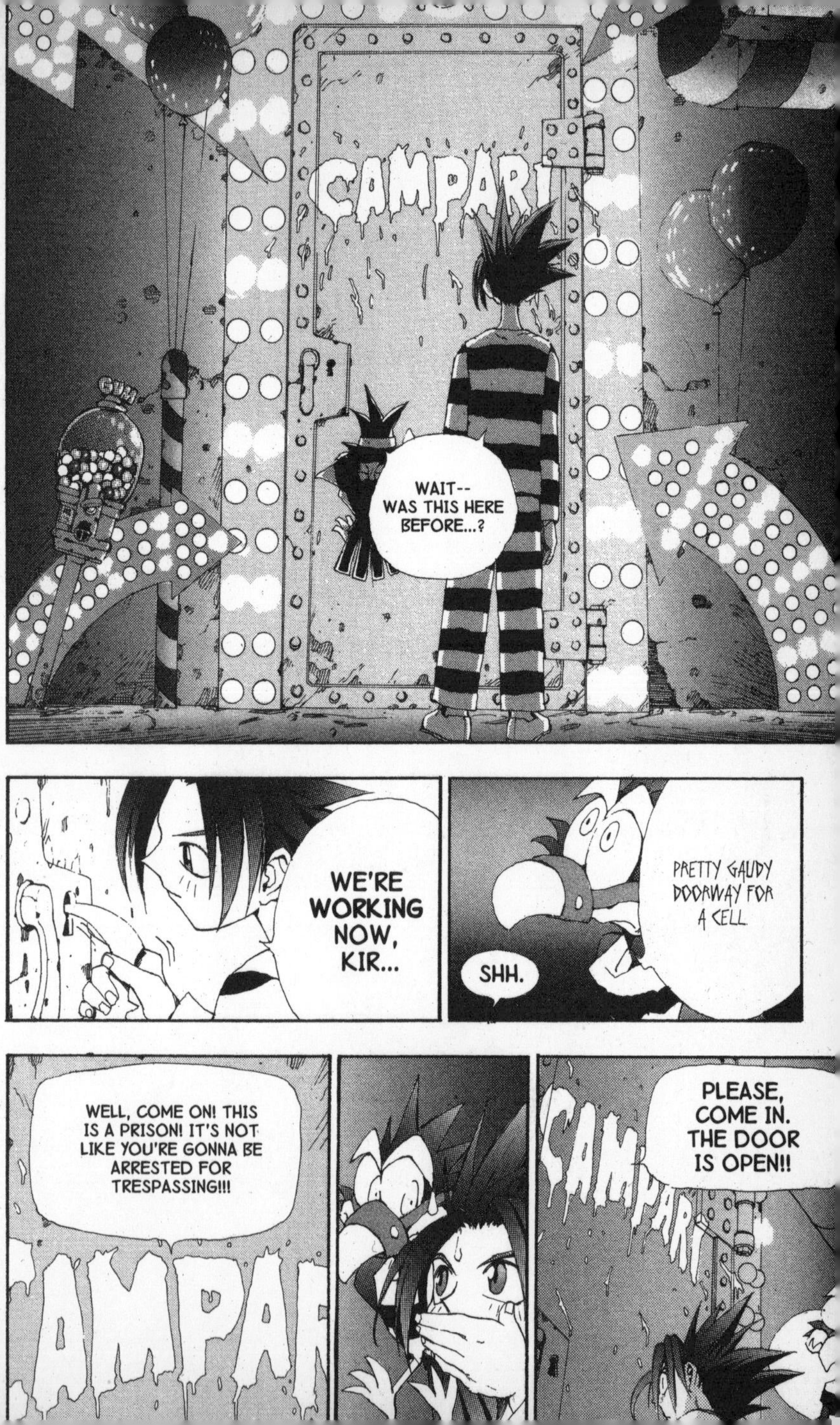
CAMPARI
GUM
WAIT-- WAS THIS HERE BEFORE...?
PRETTY GAUDY DOORWAY FOR A CELL.
SHH.
WE'RE WORKING NOW, KIR...
PLEASE, COME IN. THE DOOR IS OPEN!!
CAMPARI
WELL, COME ON! THIS IS A PRISON! IT'S NOT LIKE YOU'RE GONNA BE ARRESTED FOR TRESPASSING!!!

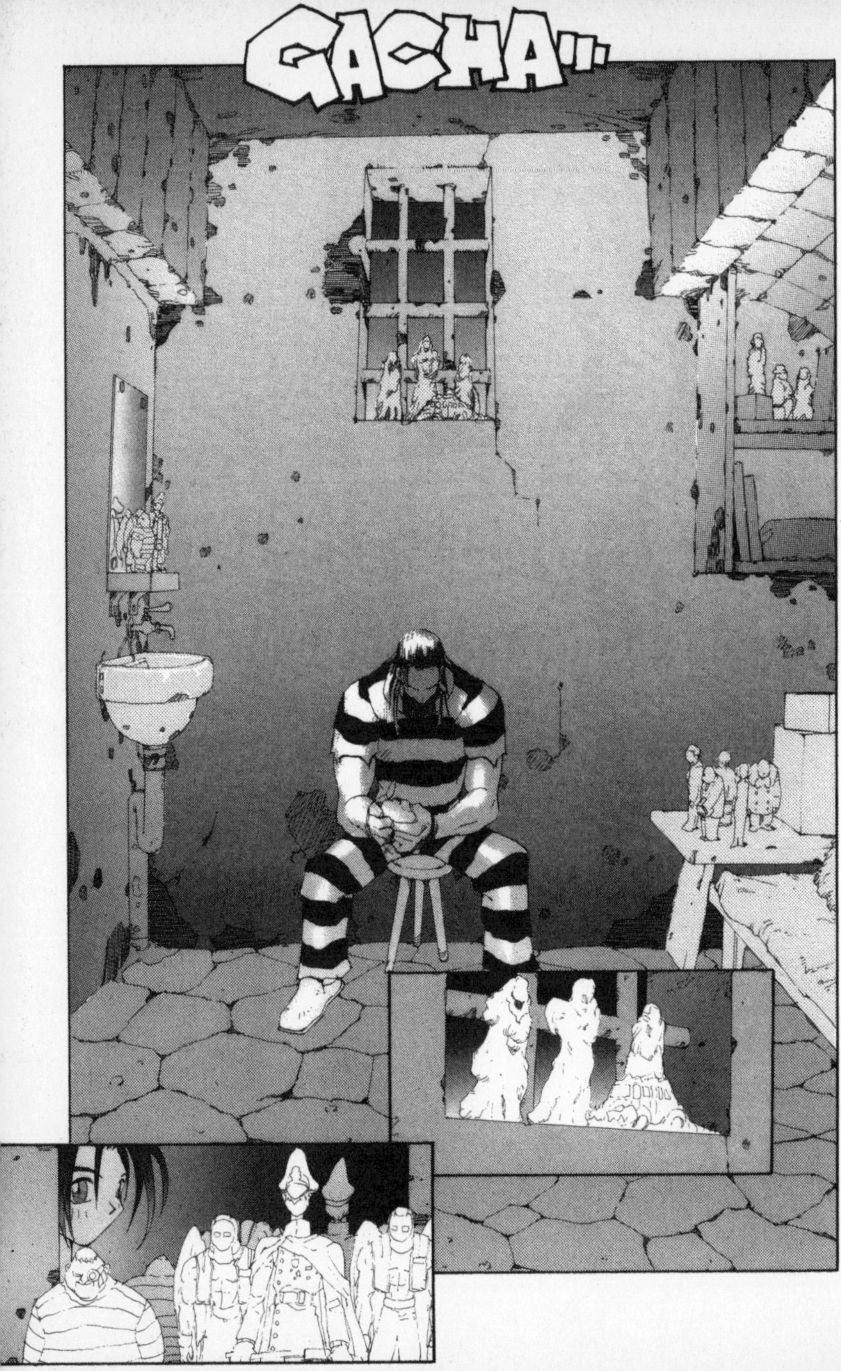
GACHA!!

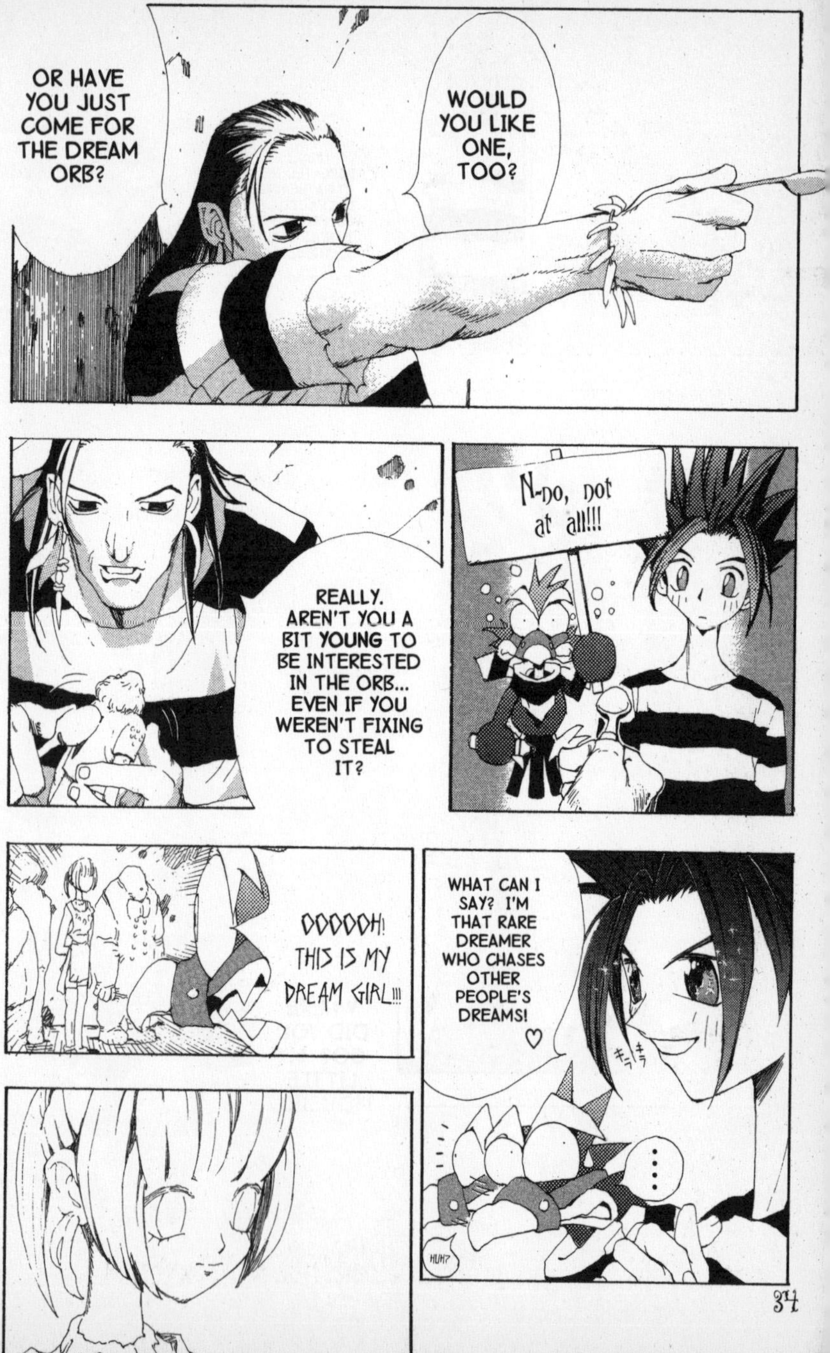
WOULD YOU LIKE ONE, TOO?
OR HAVE YOU JUST COME FOR THE DREAM ORB?
N-no, not at all!!!
REALLY. AREN'T YOU A BIT YOUNG TO BE INTERESTED IN THE ORB... EVEN IF YOU WEREN'T FIXING TO STEAL IT?
WHAT CAN I SAY? I'M THAT RARE DREAMER WHO CHASES OTHER PEOPLE'S DREAMS! ♡
....
HUH?
OOOOOH! THIS IS MY DREAM GIRL!!!

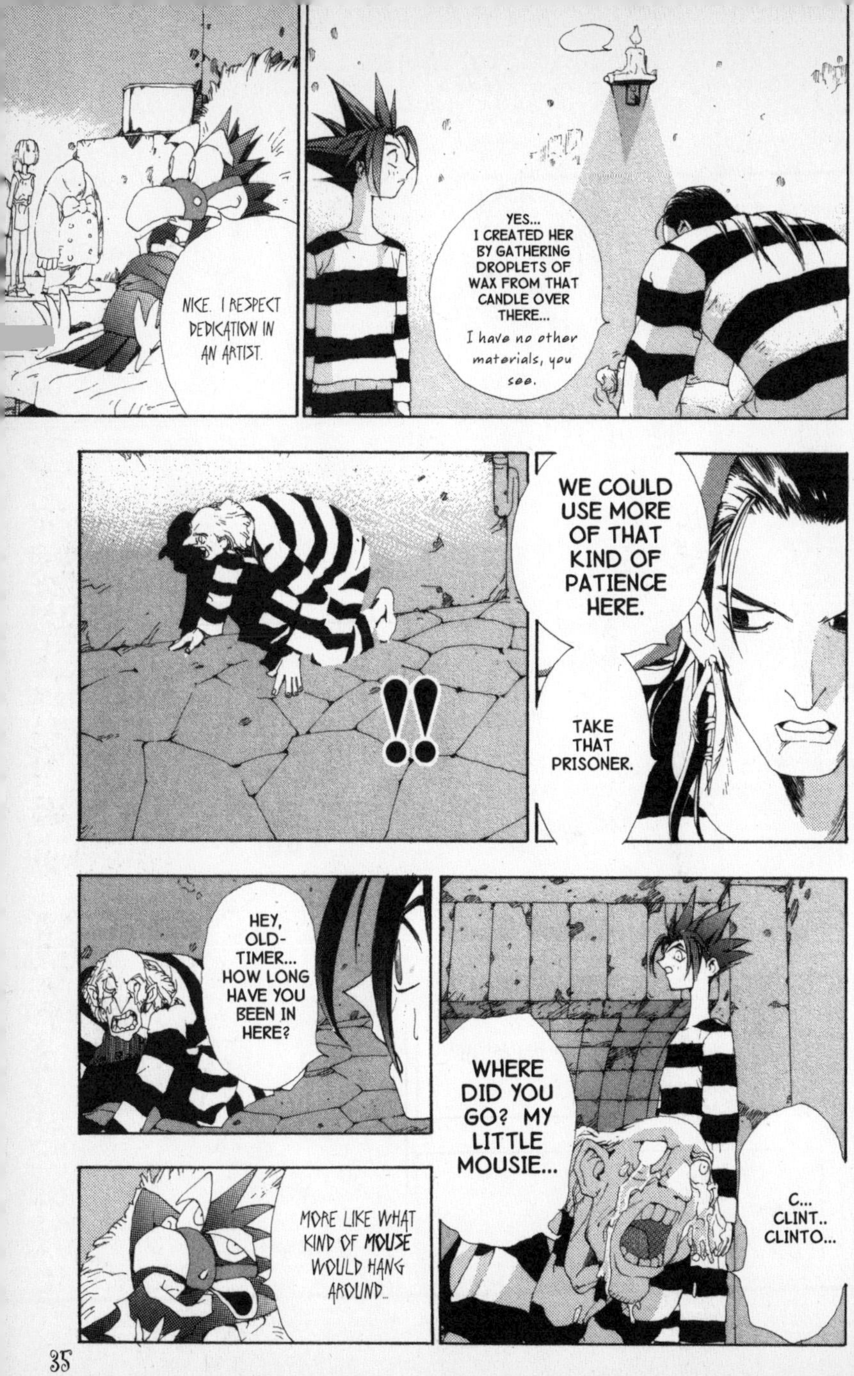
YES... I CREATED HER BY GATHERING DROPLETS OF WAX FROM THAT CANDLE OVER THERE... I have no other materials, you see.
NICE. I RESPECT DEDICATION IN AN ARTIST.
WE COULD USE MORE OF THAT KIND OF PATIENCE HERE.
TAKE THAT PRISONER.
!!
WHERE DID YOU GO? MY LITTLE MOUSIE...
C... CLINT.. CLINTO...
HEY, OLD-TIMER... HOW LONG HAVE YOU BEEN IN HERE?
MORE LIKE WHAT KIND OF MOUSE WOULD HANG AROUND...

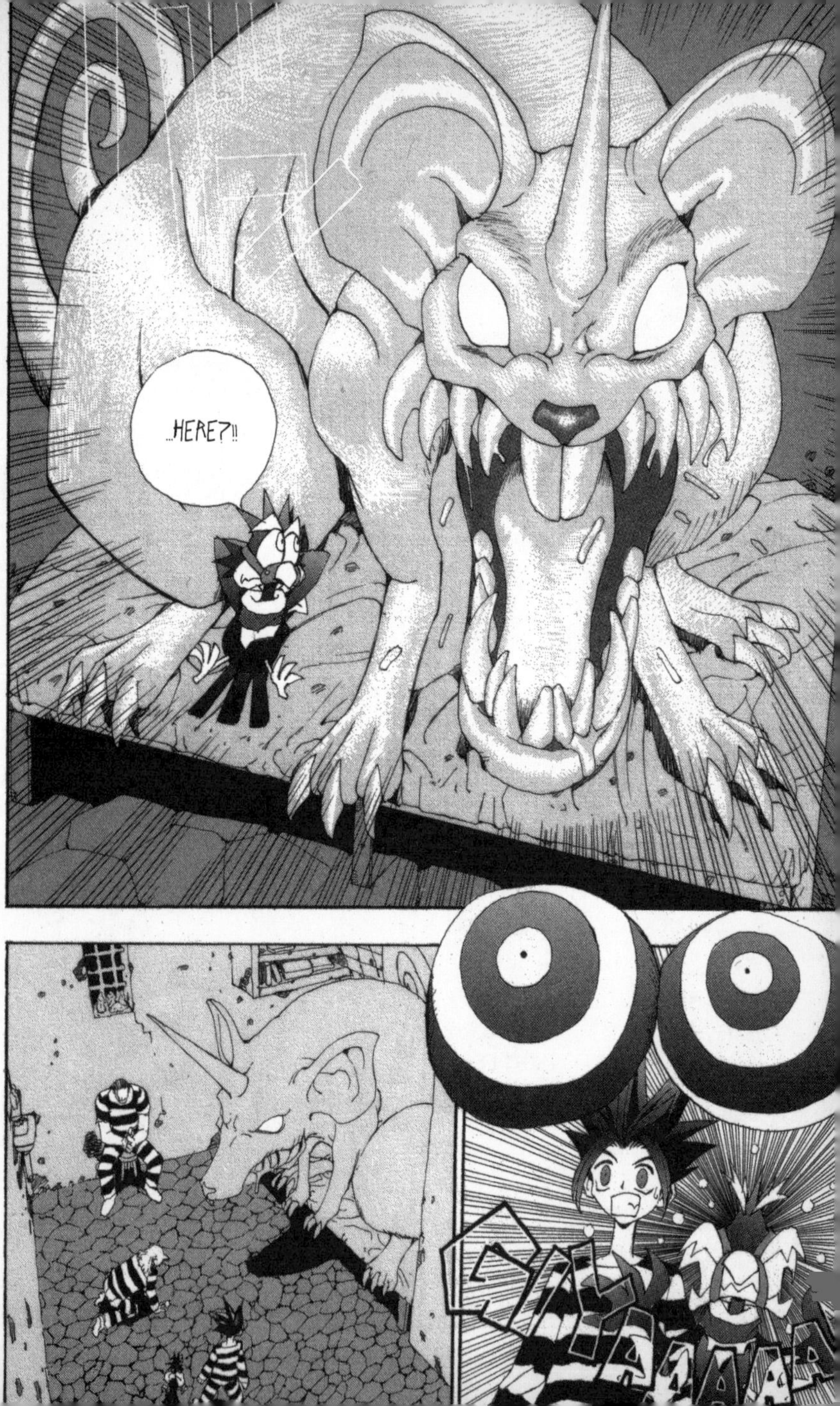
...HERE?!!
GYAAAAA

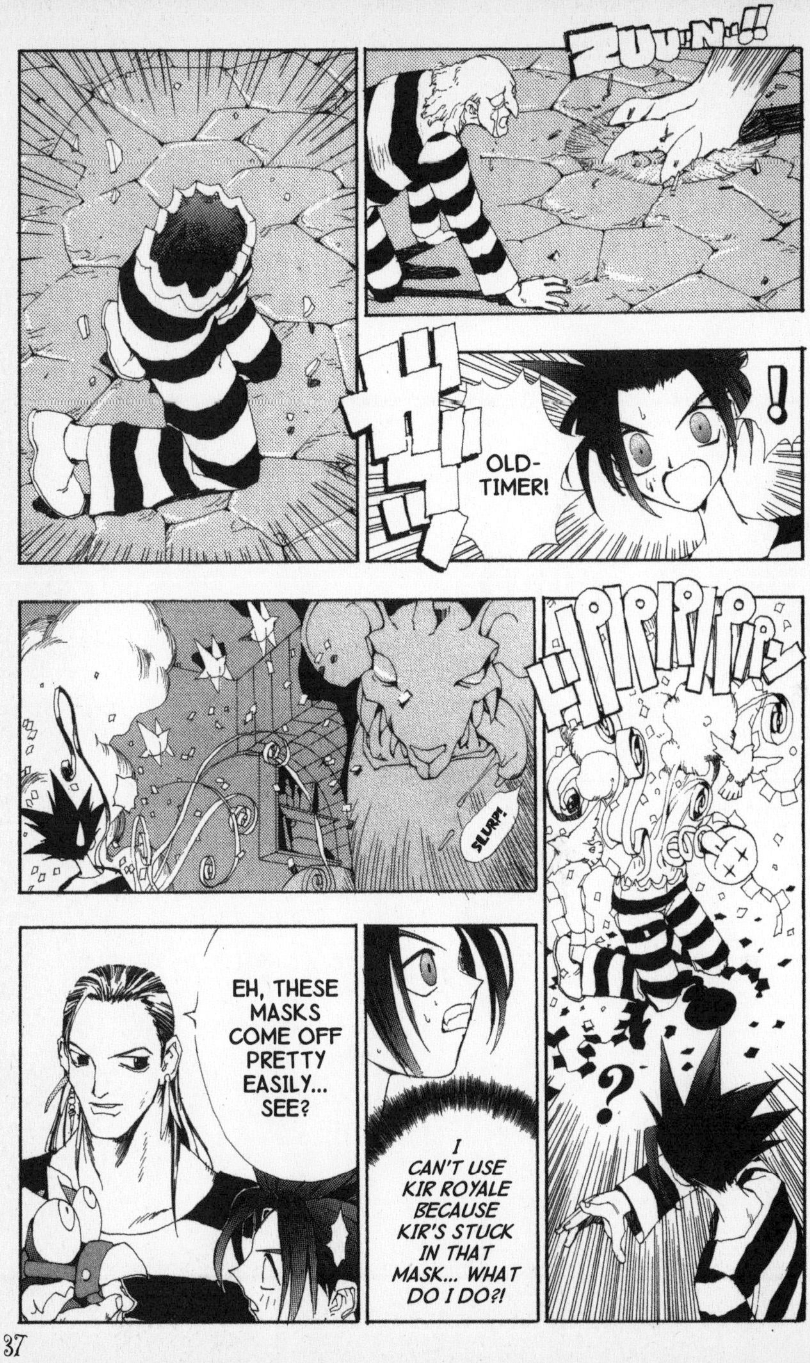

ZUU..N..!!
OLD-TIMER!
!
?
SLURP!
I CAN'T USE KIR ROYALE BECAUSE KIR'S STUCK IN THAT MASK... WHAT DO I DO?!
EH, THESE MASKS COME OFF PRETTY EASILY... SEE?

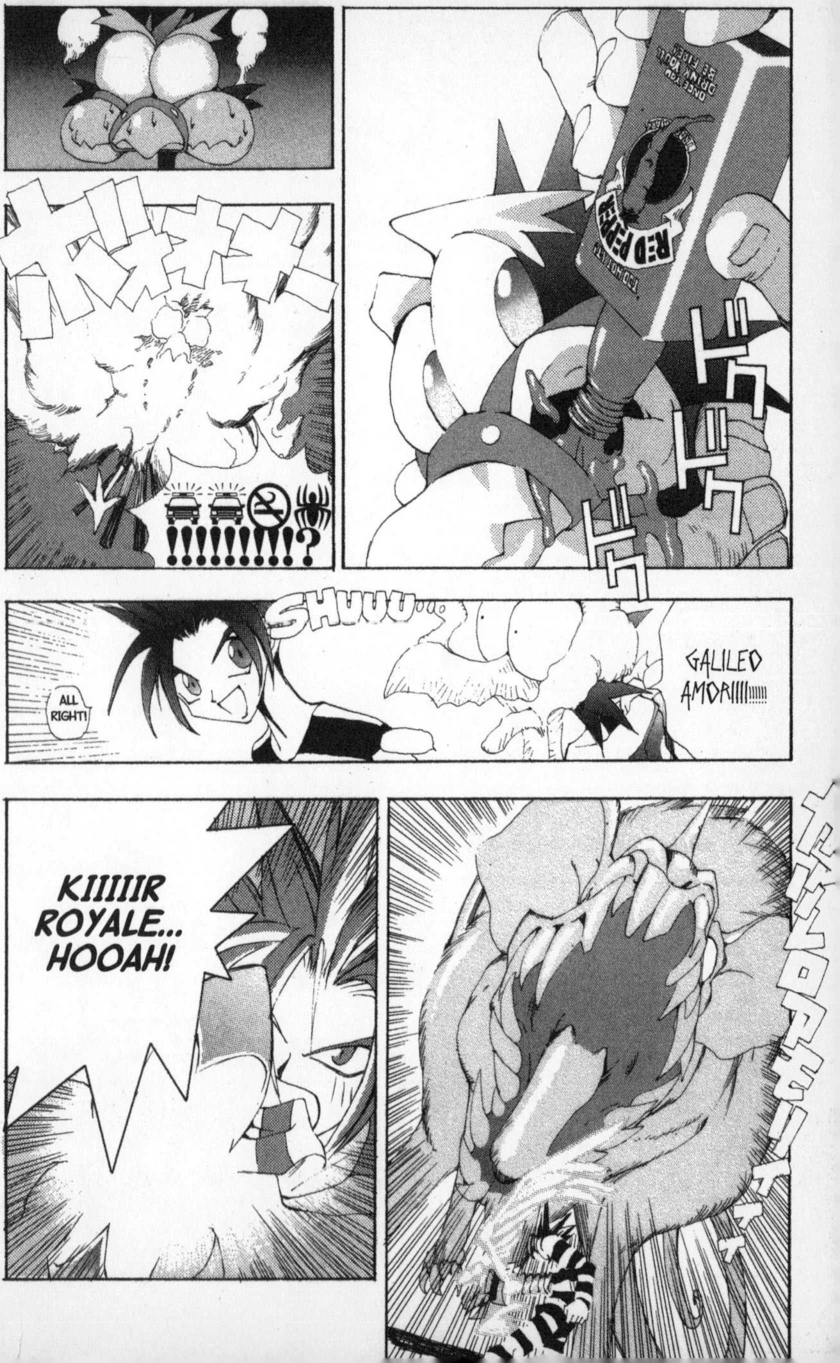
RED PEPPER
!!!!!!!!!?
GALILEO AMOR!!!!!!!!!
SHUUU...
ALL RIGHT!
KIIIIIR ROYALE... HOOAH!

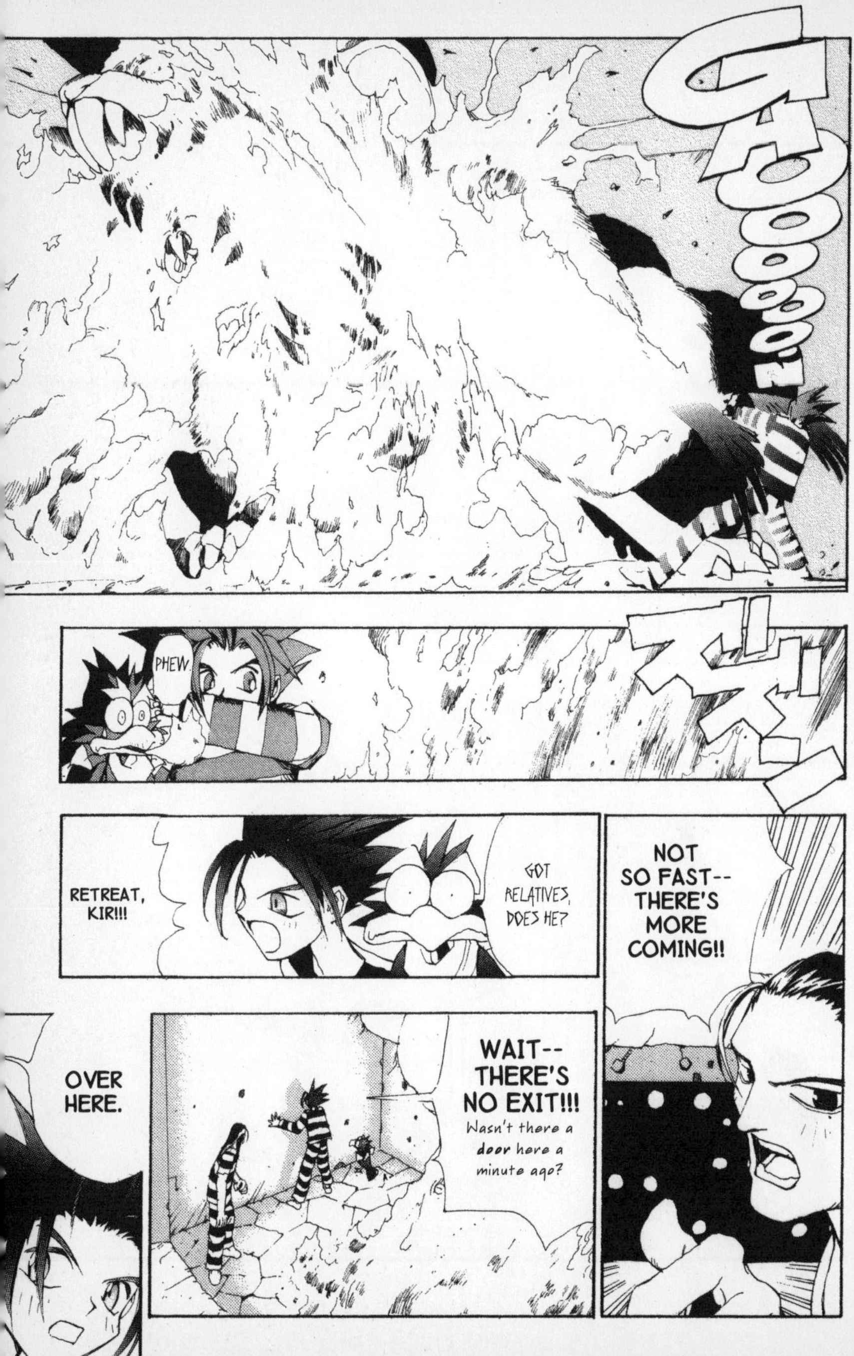
GAOOOOOO!
PHEW.
NOT SO FAST--THERE'S MORE COMING!!
GOT RELATIVES, DOES HE?
RETREAT, KIR!!!
WAIT--THERE'S NO EXIT!!!
Wasn't there a door here a minute ago?
OVER HERE.

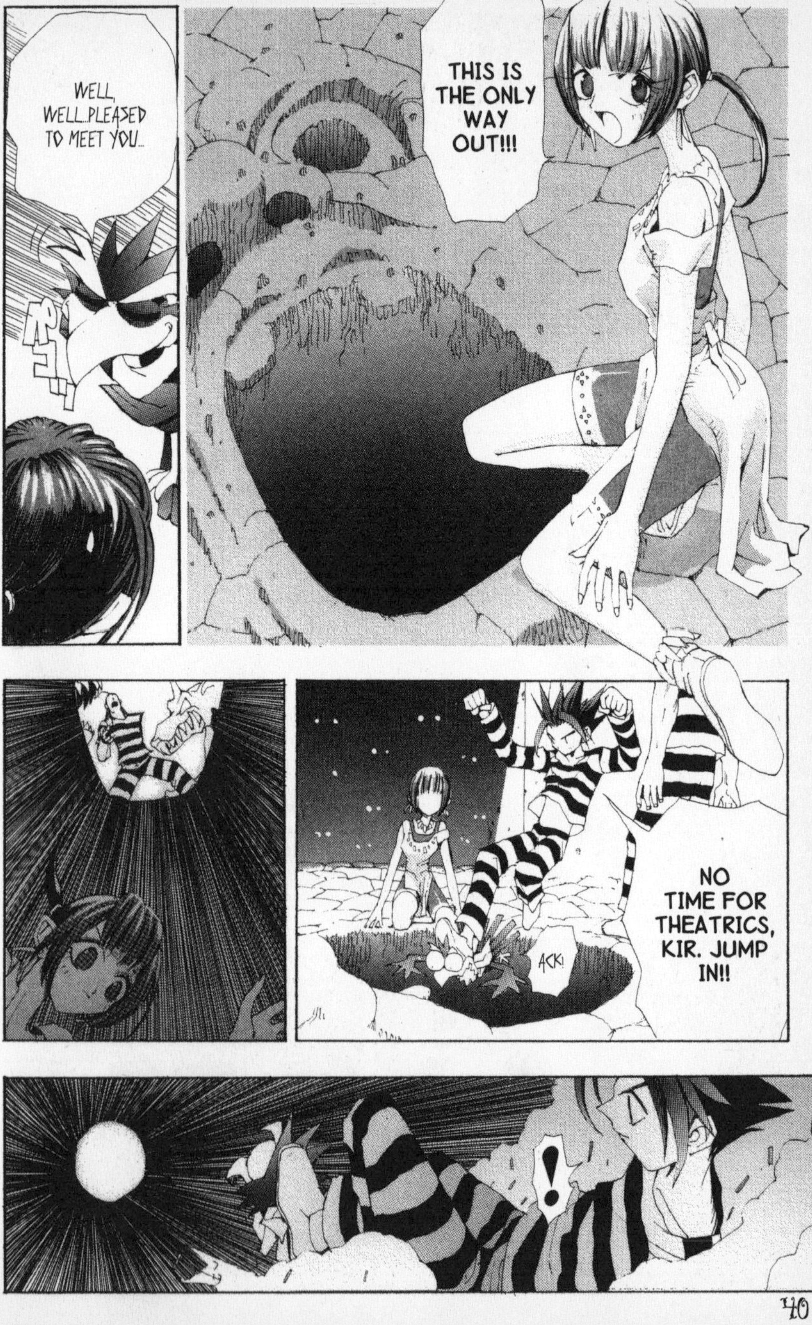
THIS IS THE ONLY WAY OUT!!!
WELL, WELL...PLEASED TO MEET YOU...
NO TIME FOR THEATRICS, KIR. JUMP IN!!
ACK!
!

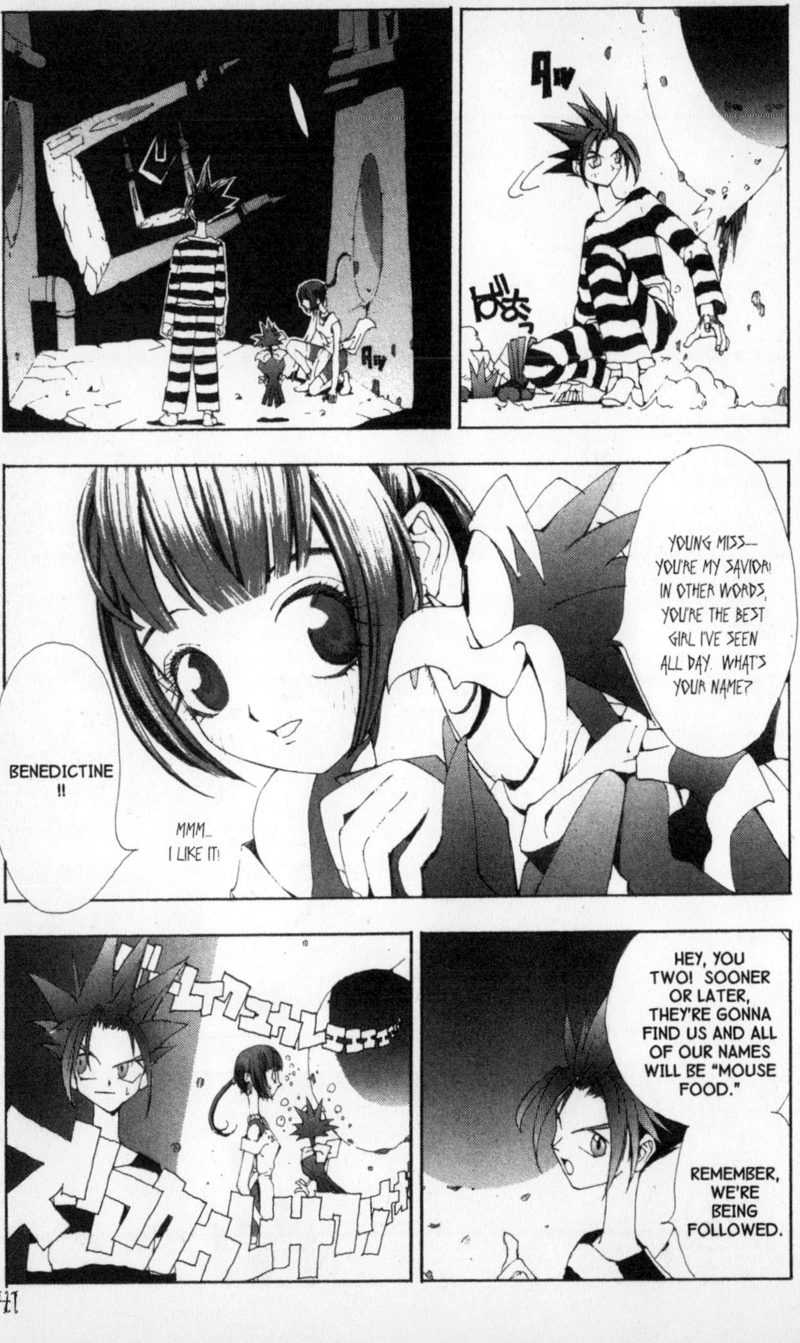
ばおっ
YOUNG MISS--- YOU'RE MY SAVIOR! IN OTHER WORDS, YOU'RE THE BEST GIRL I'VE SEEN ALL DAY. WHAT'S YOUR NAME?
MMM... I LIKE IT!
BENEDICTINE !!
HEY, YOU TWO! SOONER OR LATER, THEY'RE GONNA FIND US AND ALL OF OUR NAMES WILL BE "MOUSE FOOD."
REMEMBER, WE'RE BEING FOLLOWED.

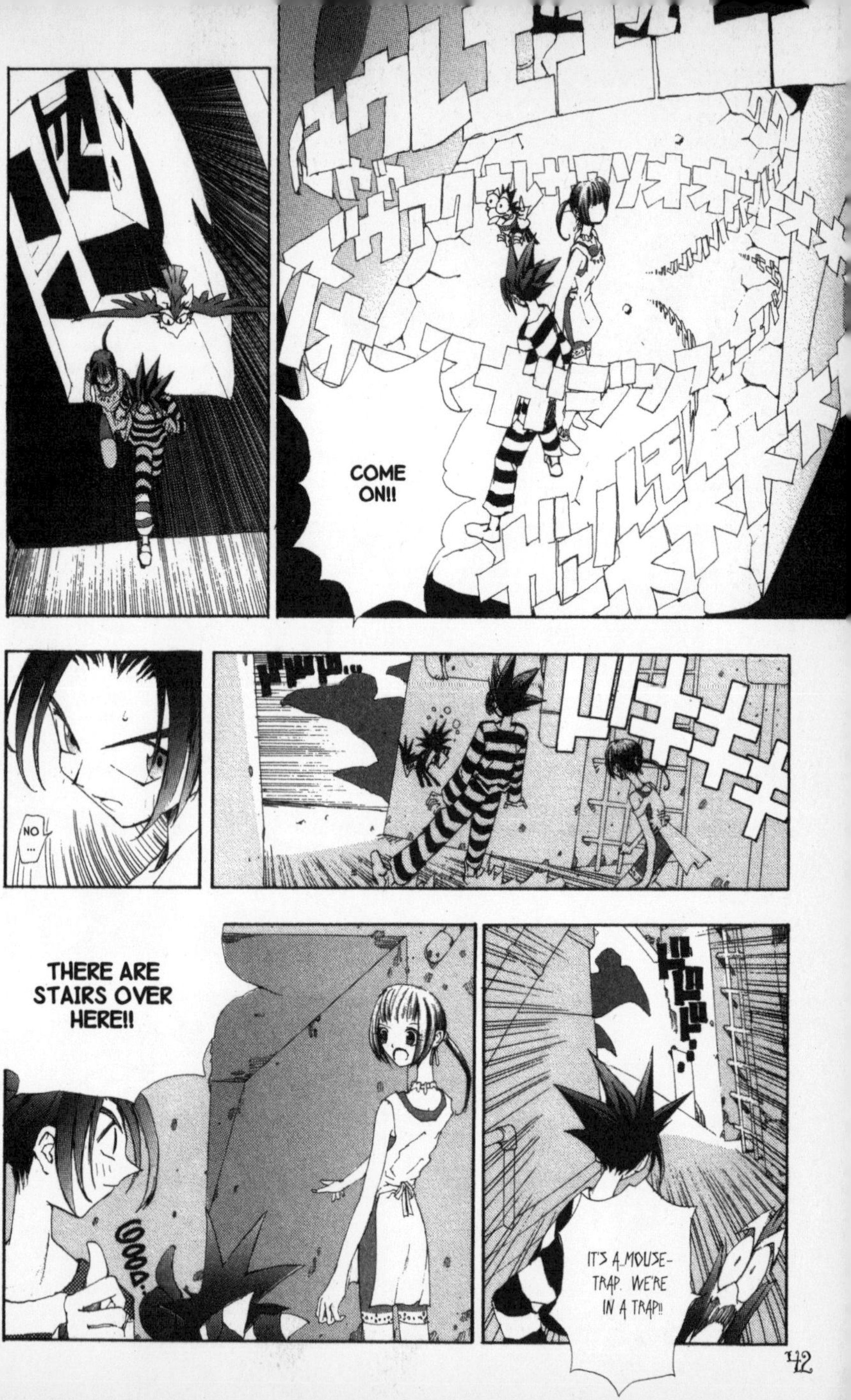
COME ON!!
NO ...
IT'S A MOUSE-TRAP. WE'RE IN A TRAP!!
THERE ARE STAIRS OVER HERE!!
GOOD...

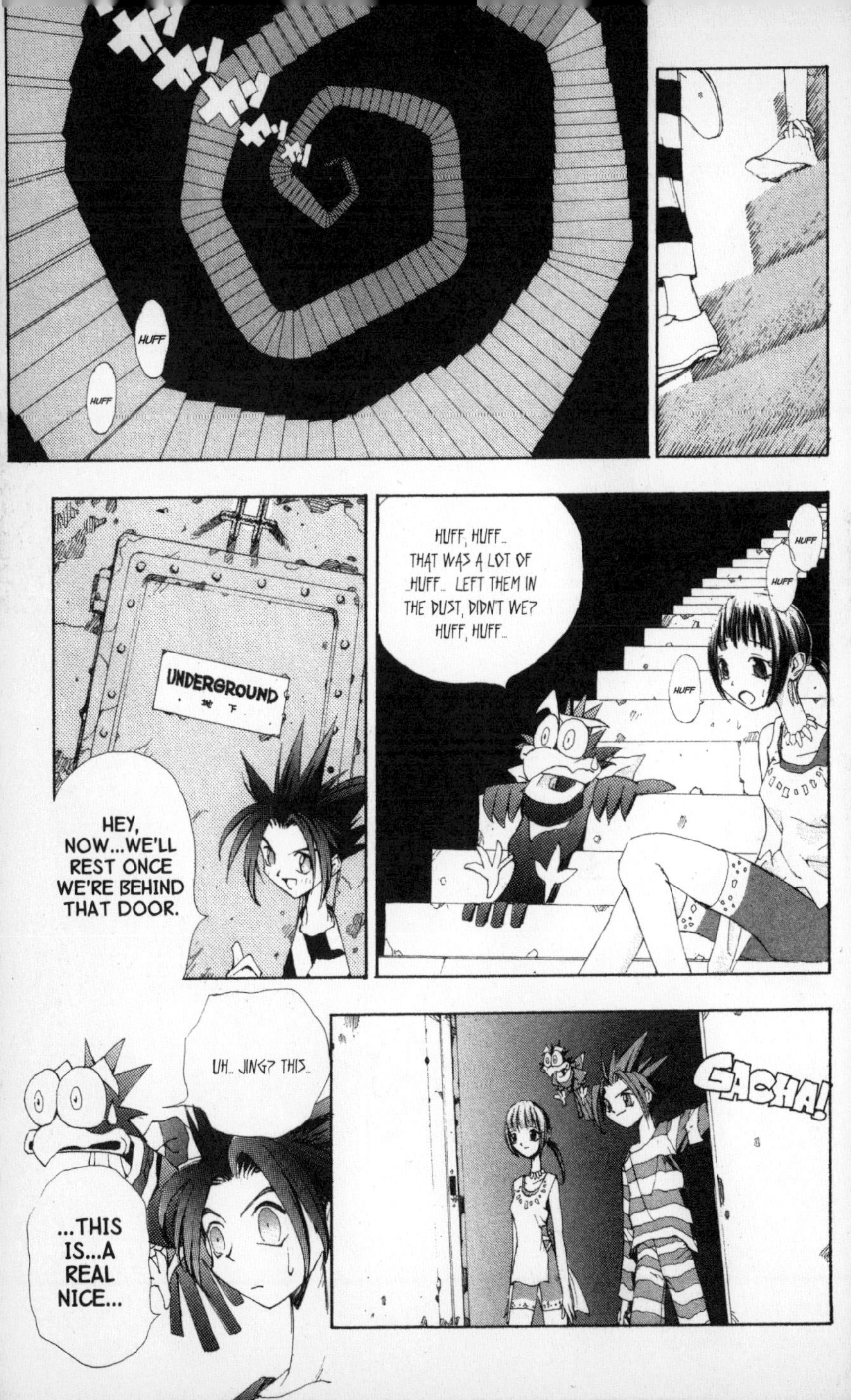
HUFF
HUFF
HUFF, HUFF... THAT WAS A LOT OF ...HUFF... LEFT THEM IN THE DUST, DIDN'T WE? HUFF, HUFF...
HUFF
HUFF
HUFF
UNDERGROUND
HEY, NOW...WE'LL REST ONCE WE'RE BEHIND THAT DOOR.
GACHA!
UH... JING? THIS...
...THIS IS...A REAL NICE...

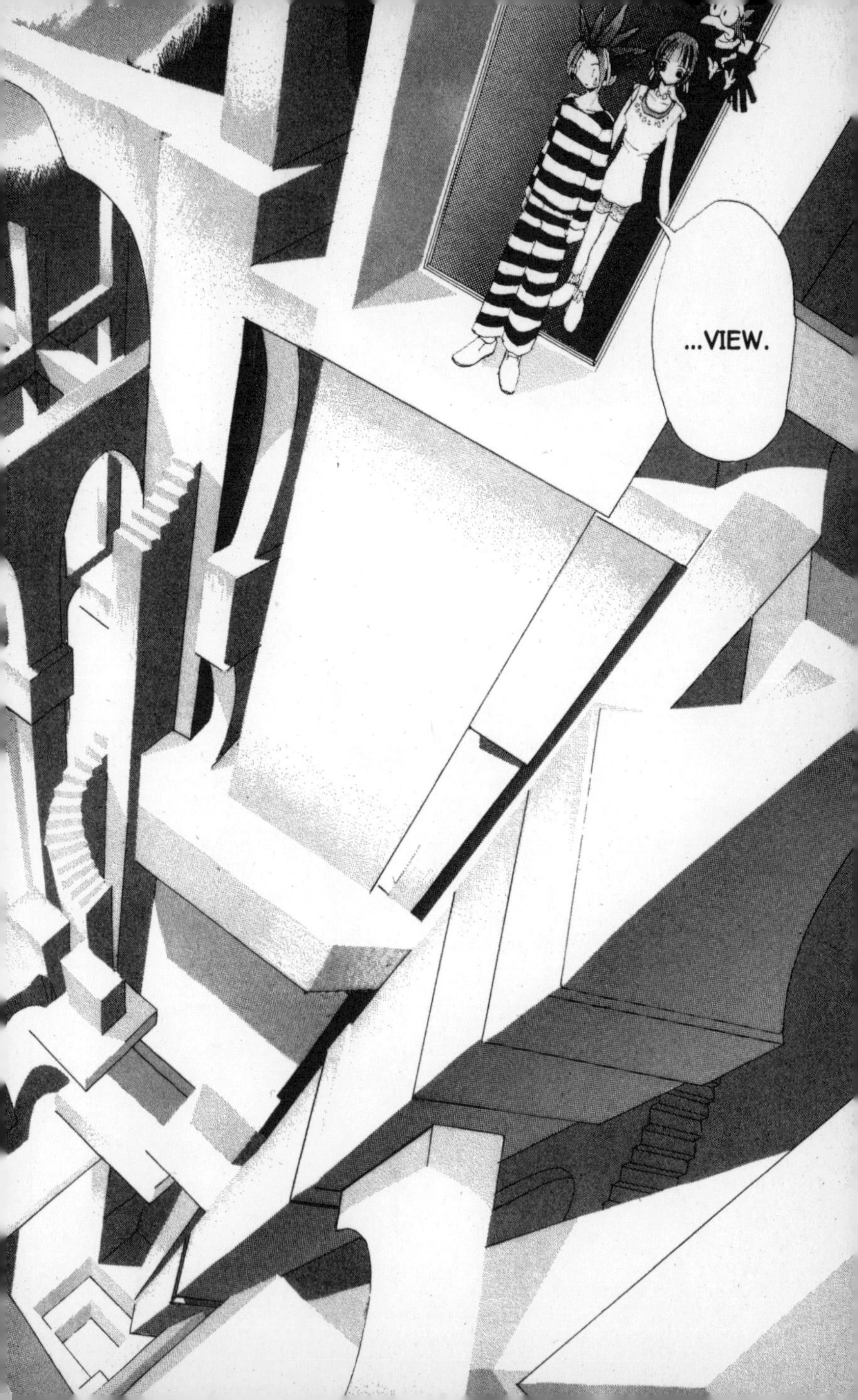
...VIEW.

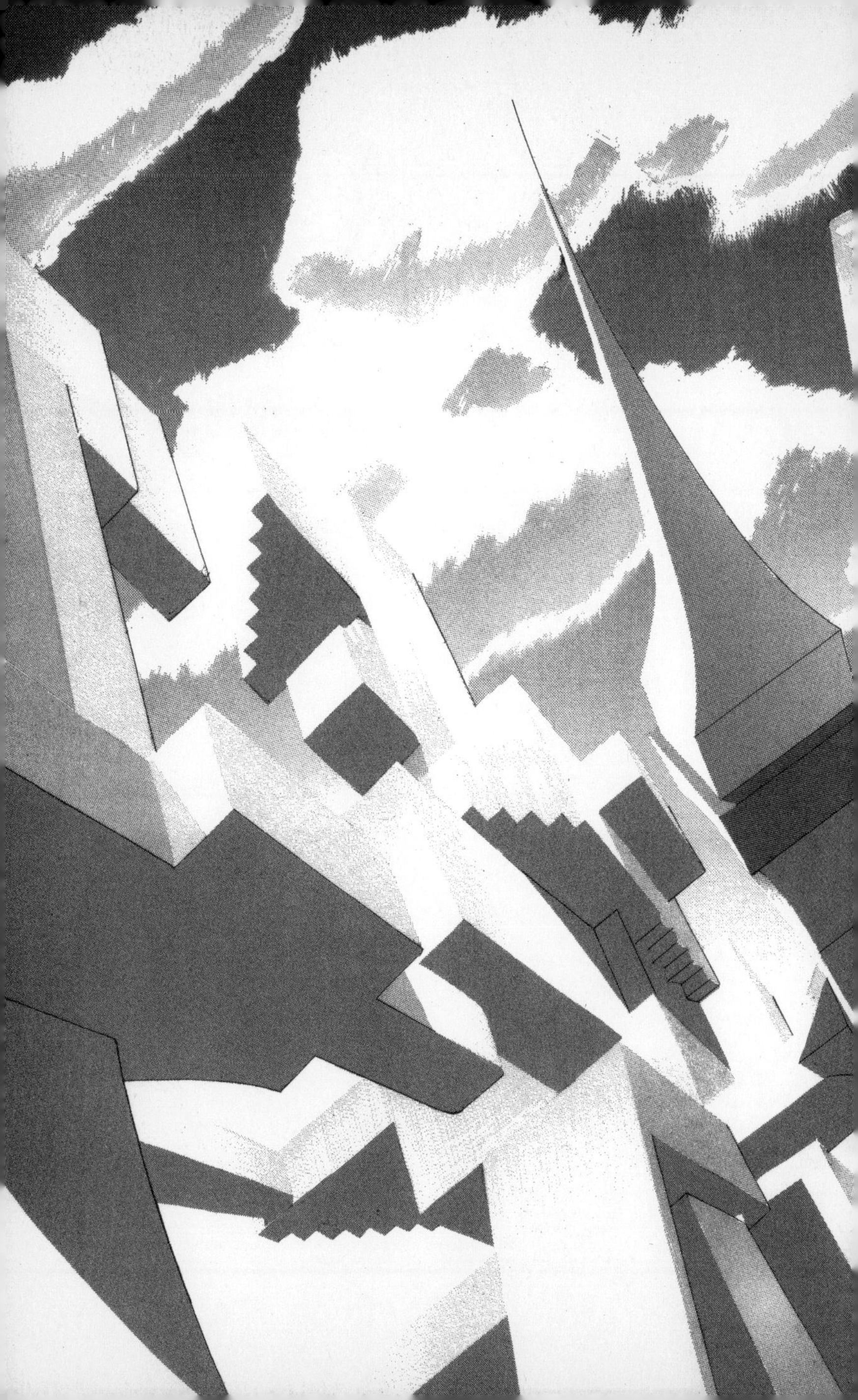

I KNEW THIS PRISON WAS SUPPOSED TO BE HUGE...BUT...

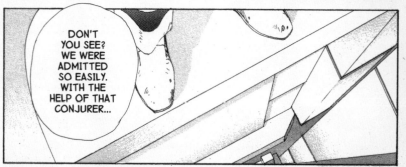

DON'T YOU SEE? WE WERE ADMITTED SO EASILY. WITH THE HELP OF THAT CONJURER...

...WE WERE BOOKED INTO THE PRISON OF DREAMS... A THOUSAND TIMES HARDER TO ESCAPE THAN SEVENTH HEAVEN!!

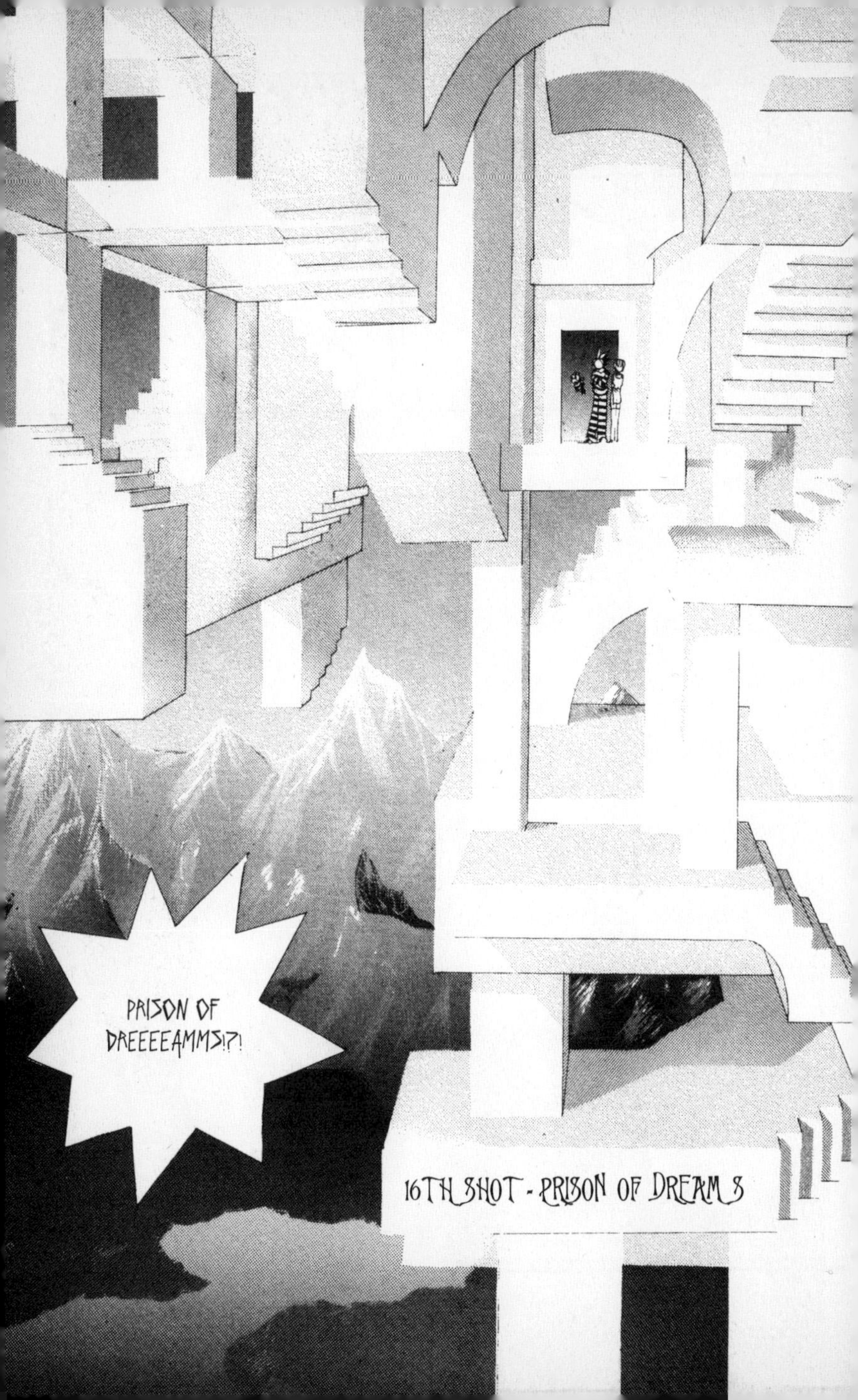
16TH SHOT - PRISON OF DREAMS
PRISON OF DREEEEAMMS!?!

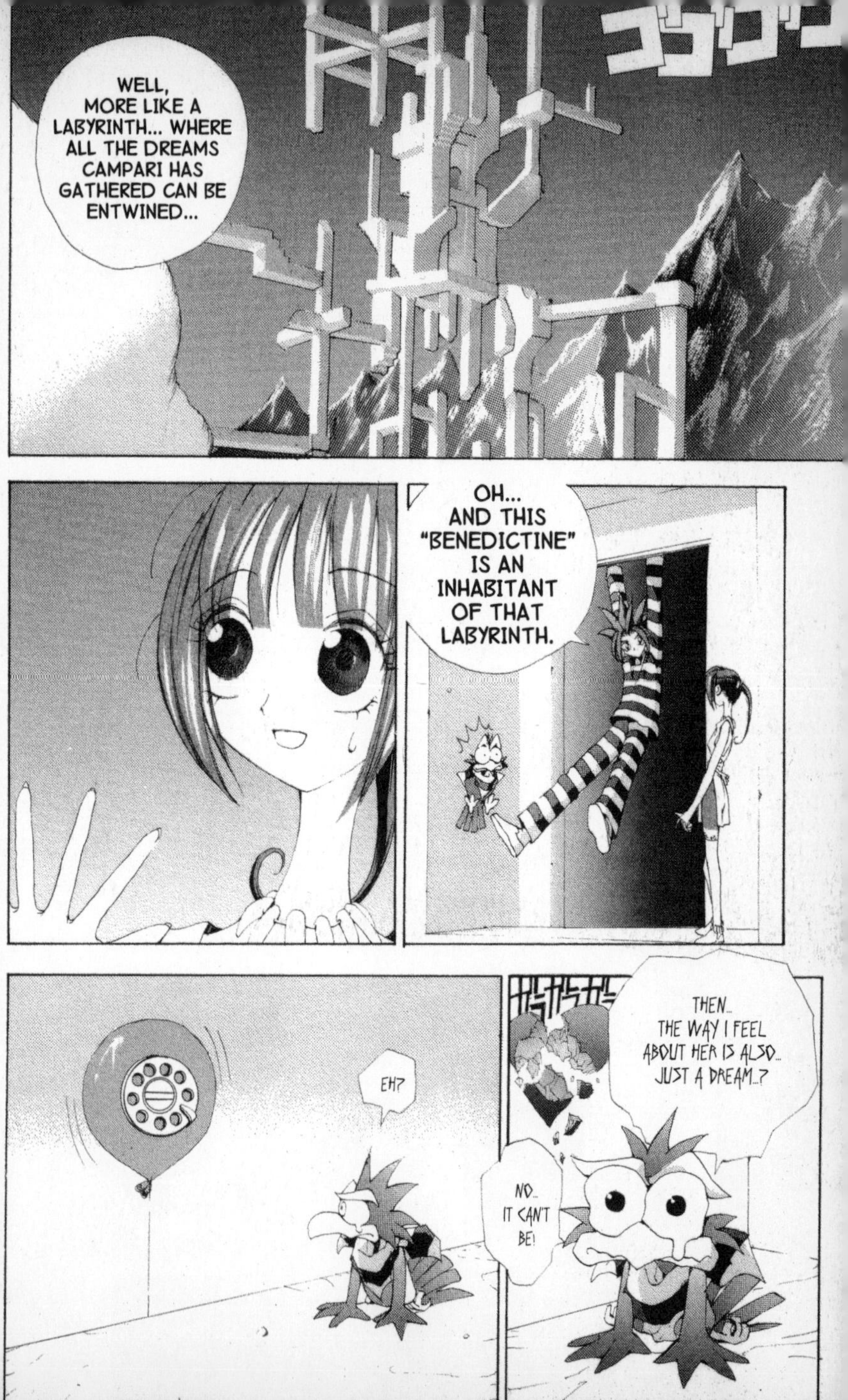
WELL, MORE LIKE A LABYRINTH... WHERE ALL THE DREAMS CAMPARI HAS GATHERED CAN BE ENTWINED...
OH... AND THIS "BENEDICTINE" IS AN INHABITANT OF THAT LABYRINTH.
THEN... THE WAY I FEEL ABOUT HER IS ALSO... JUST A DREAM...?
NO... IT CAN'T BE!
EH?

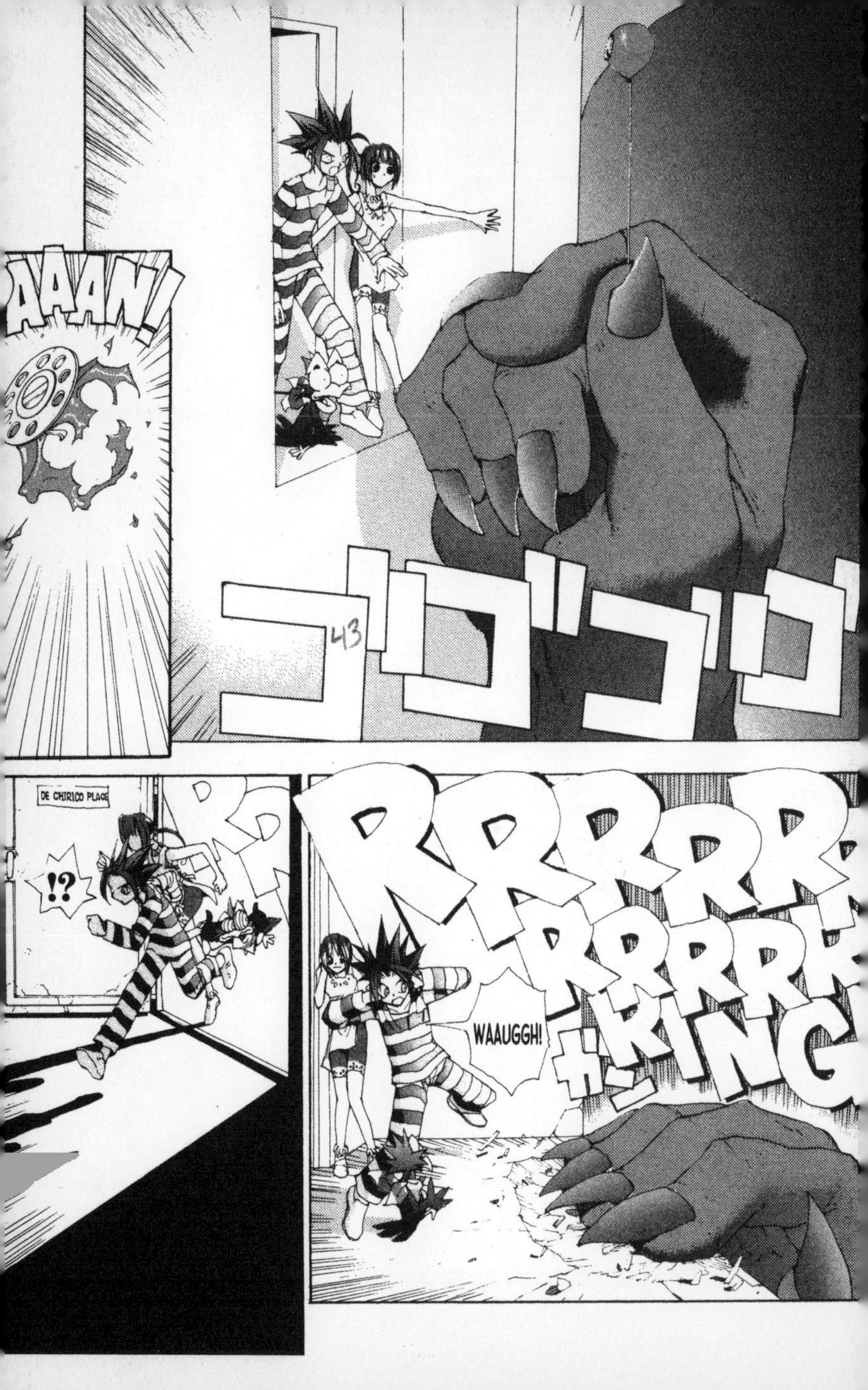
43
AAAN!
RRRRR
RRRRR
RING
WAAUGGH!
DE CHIRICO PLACE
!?

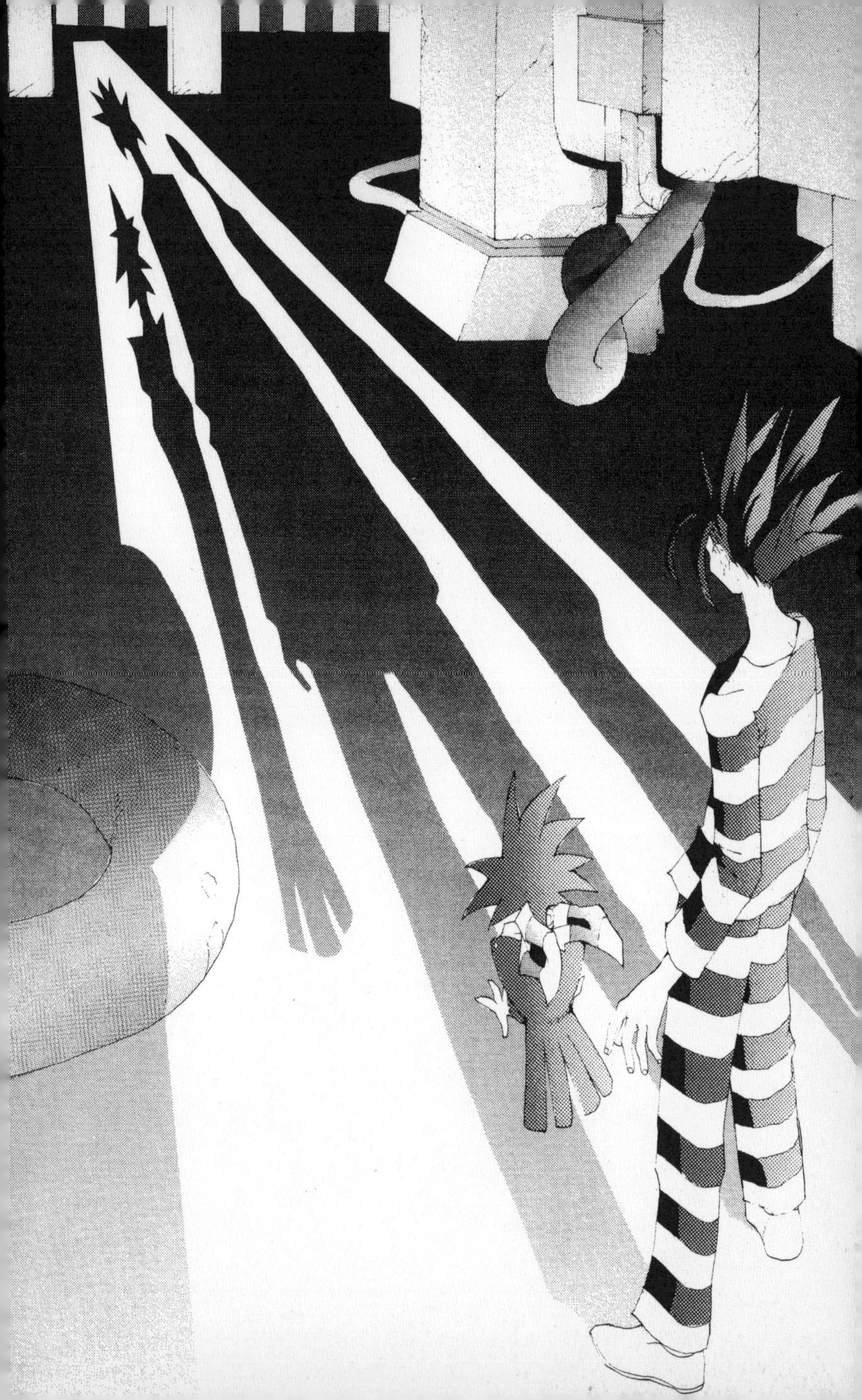

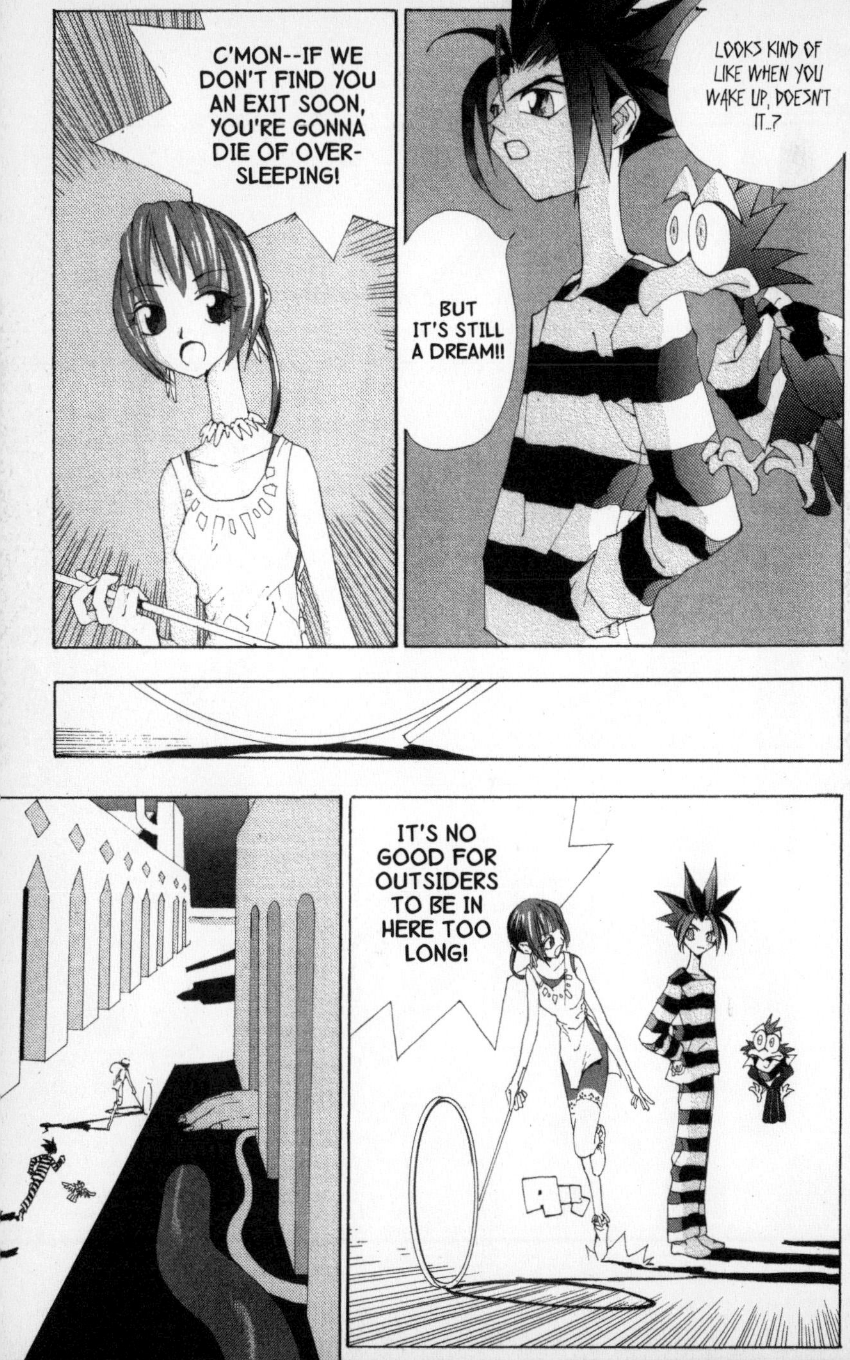
LOOKS KIND OF LIKE WHEN YOU WAKE UP, DOESN'T IT..?
BUT IT'S STILL A DREAM!!
C'MON--IF WE DON'T FIND YOU AN EXIT SOON, YOU'RE GONNA DIE OF OVER-SLEEPING!
IT'S NO GOOD FOR OUTSIDERS TO BE IN HERE TOO LONG!

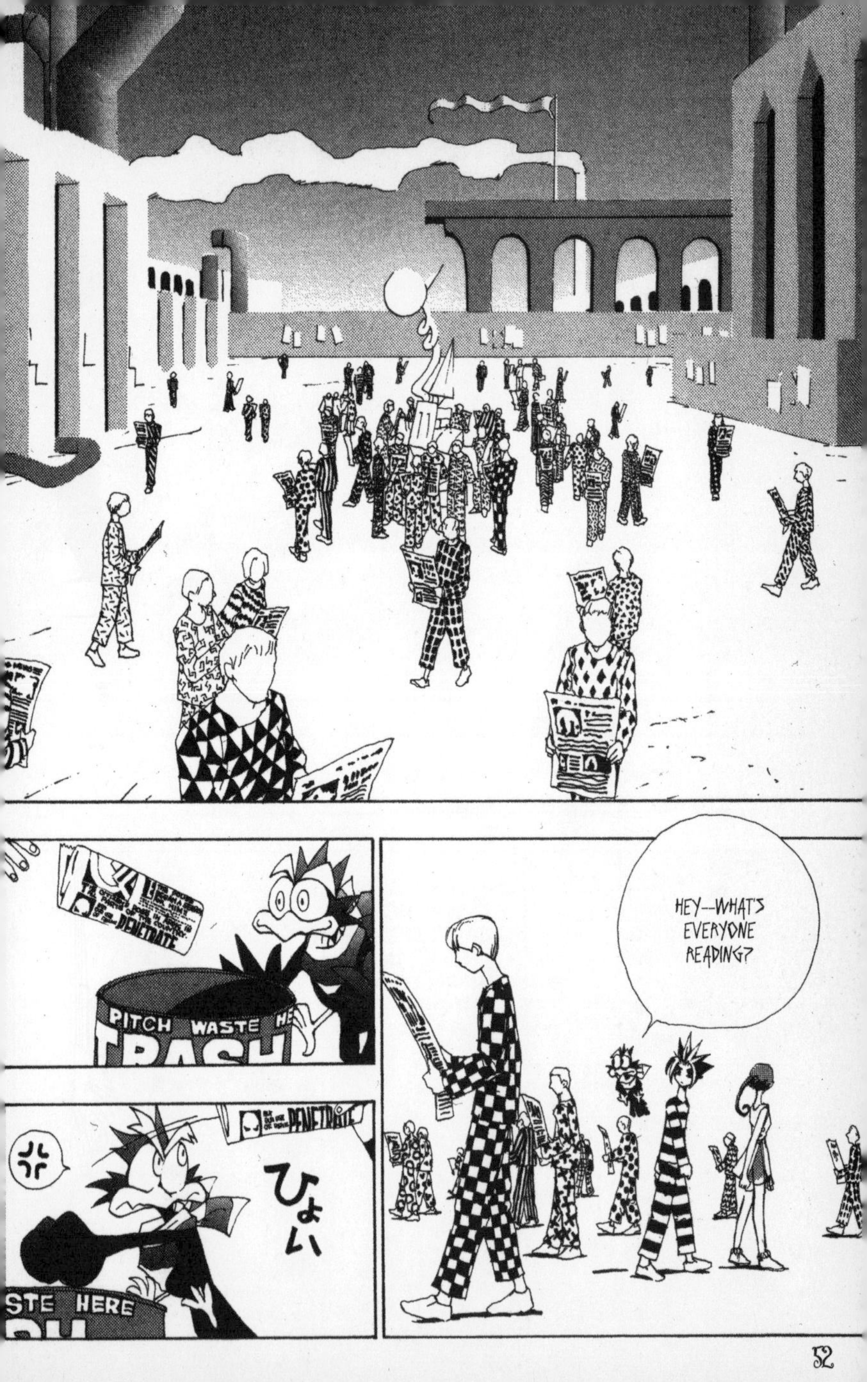
HEY--WHAT'S EVERYONE READING?
PENETRATE
PITCH WASTE HE
PENETRATE
ひょい
STE HERE

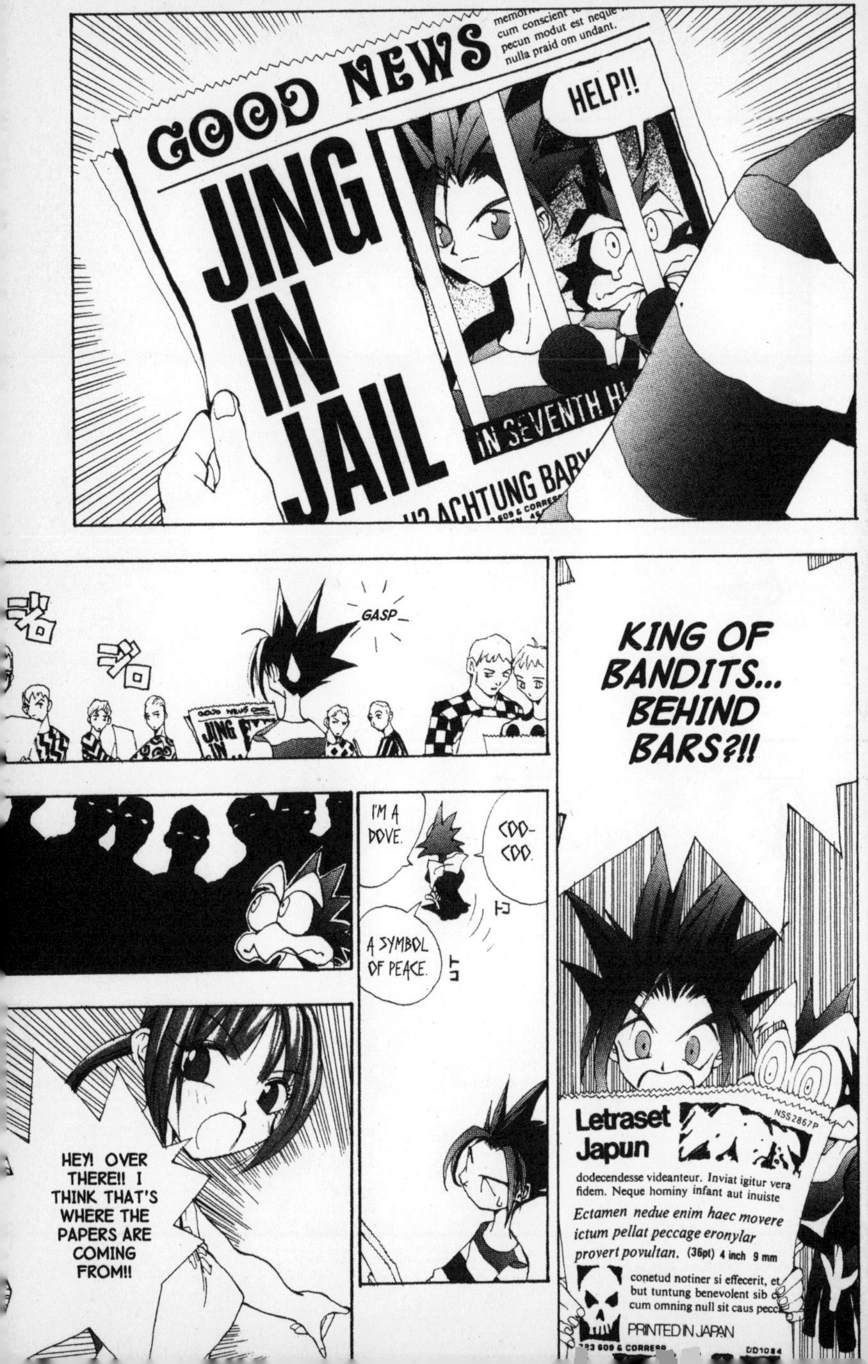
memori...
cum conscient ... pecun modut est neque ...
nulla praid om undant.
GOOD NEWS
JING IN JAIL
HELP!!
IN SEVENTH H
U2 ACHTUNG BABY
KING OF BANDITS... BEHIND BARS?!!
Letraset Japun
NSS2867P
dodecendesse videanteur. Inviat igitur vera fidem. Neque hominy infant aut inuiste
Ectamen nedue enim haec movere ictum pellat peccage eronylar provert povultan. (36pt) 4 inch 9 mm
conetud notiner si effecerit, et but tuntung benevolent sib c cum omning null sit caus pecc
PRINTED IN JAPAN
DD1084
GASP
GOOD NEWS
JING IN...
I'M A DOVE.
COO-COO.
A SYMBOL OF PEACE.
HEY! OVER THERE!! I THINK THAT'S WHERE THE PAPERS ARE COMING FROM!!

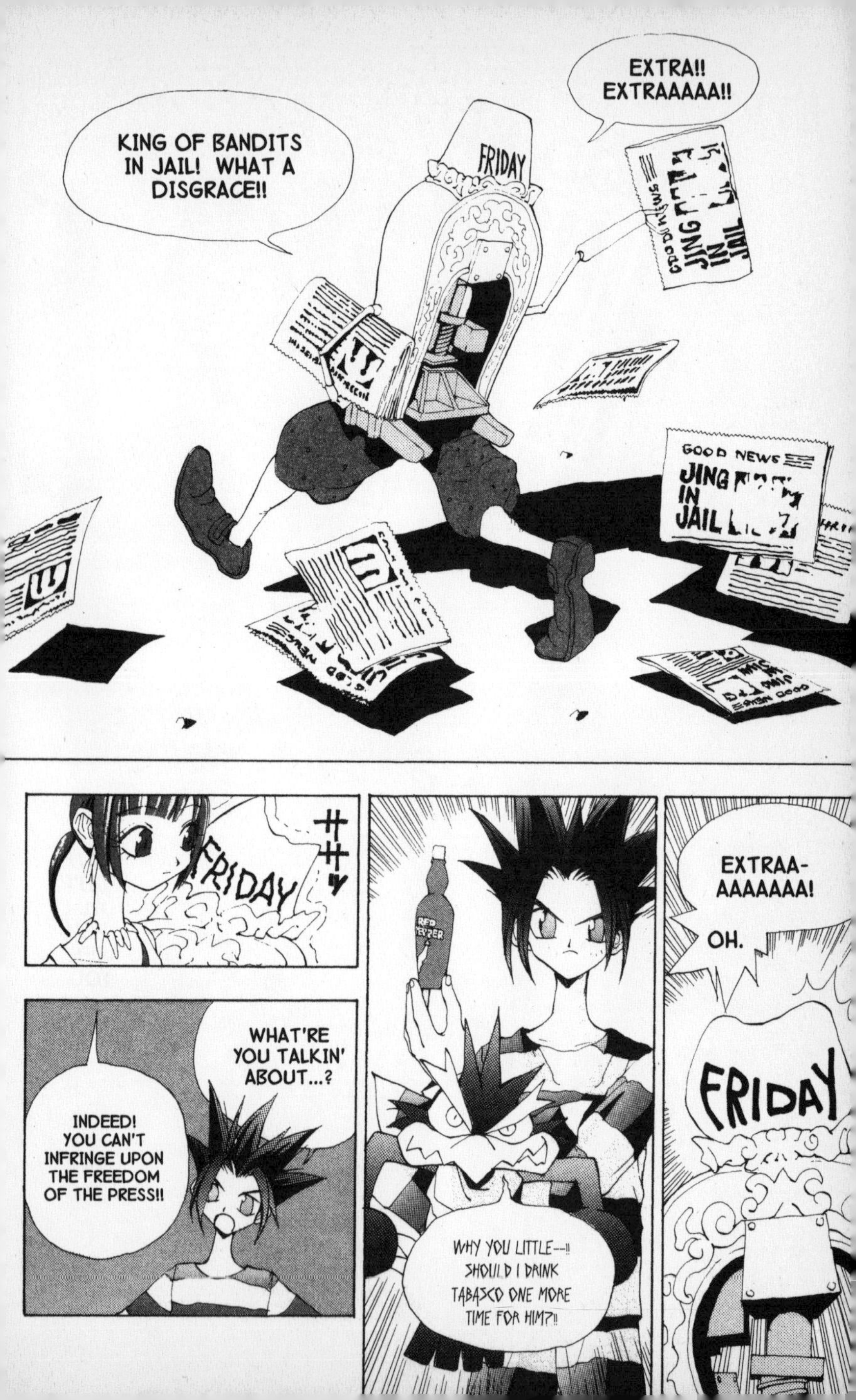
EXTRA!! EXTRAAAAA!!
FRIDAY
KING OF BANDITS IN JAIL! WHAT A DISGRACE!!
GOOD NEWS
JING
IN
JAIL
EXTRAA-AAAAAAA!
OH.
FRIDAY
WHY YOU LITTLE--!! SHOULD I DRINK TABASCO ONE MORE TIME FOR HIM?!!
FRIDAY
WHAT'RE YOU TALKIN' ABOUT...?
INDEED! YOU CAN'T INFRINGE UPON THE FREEDOM OF THE PRESS!!

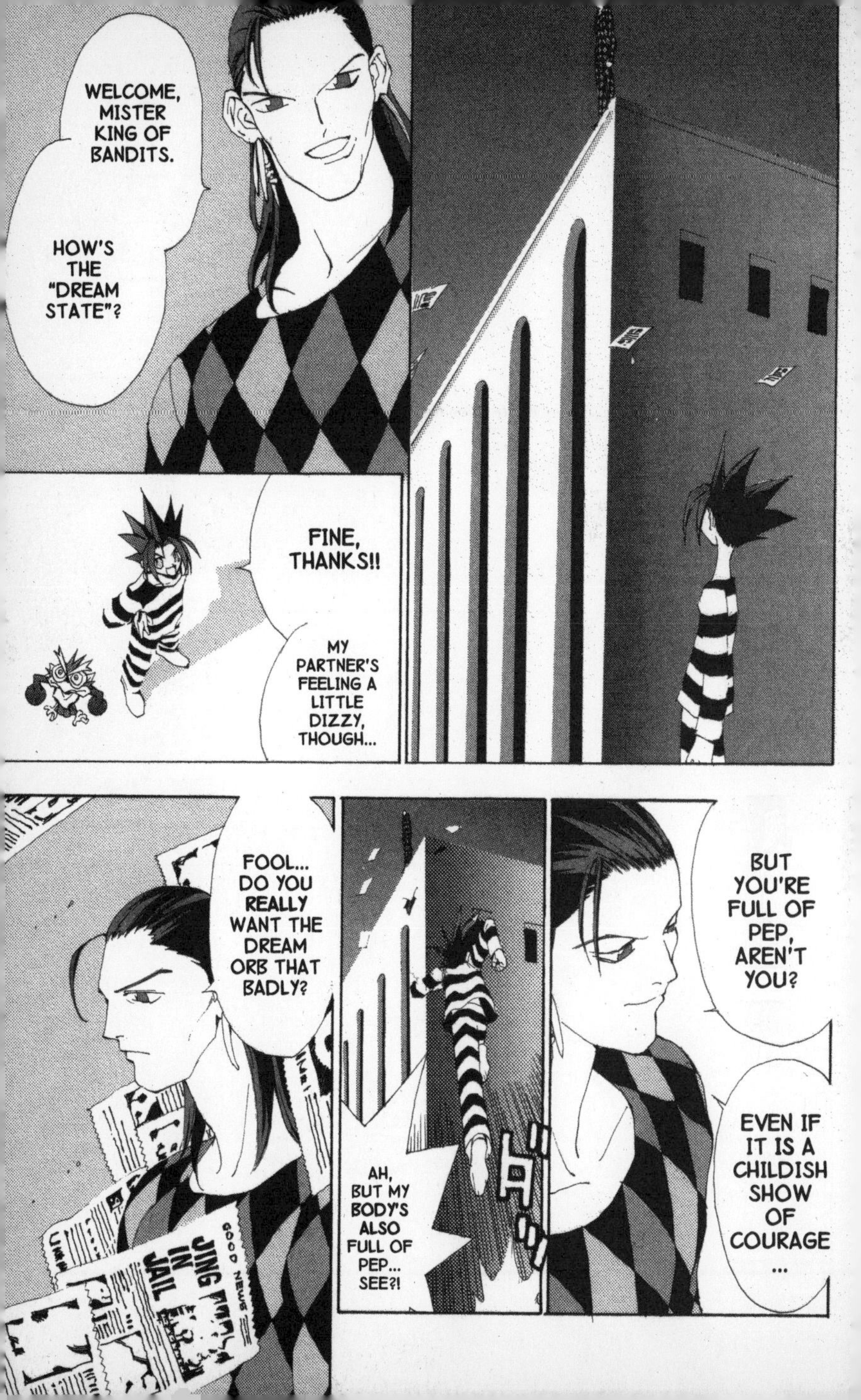
WELCOME, MISTER KING OF BANDITS.
HOW'S THE "DREAM STATE"?
FINE, THANKS!!
MY PARTNER'S FEELING A LITTLE DIZZY, THOUGH...
BUT YOU'RE FULL OF PEP, AREN'T YOU?
EVEN IF IT IS A CHILDISH SHOW OF COURAGE ...
AH, BUT MY BODY'S ALSO FULL OF PEP... SEE?!
FOOL... DO YOU REALLY WANT THE DREAM ORB THAT BADLY?
GOOD NEWS
JING IN JAIL

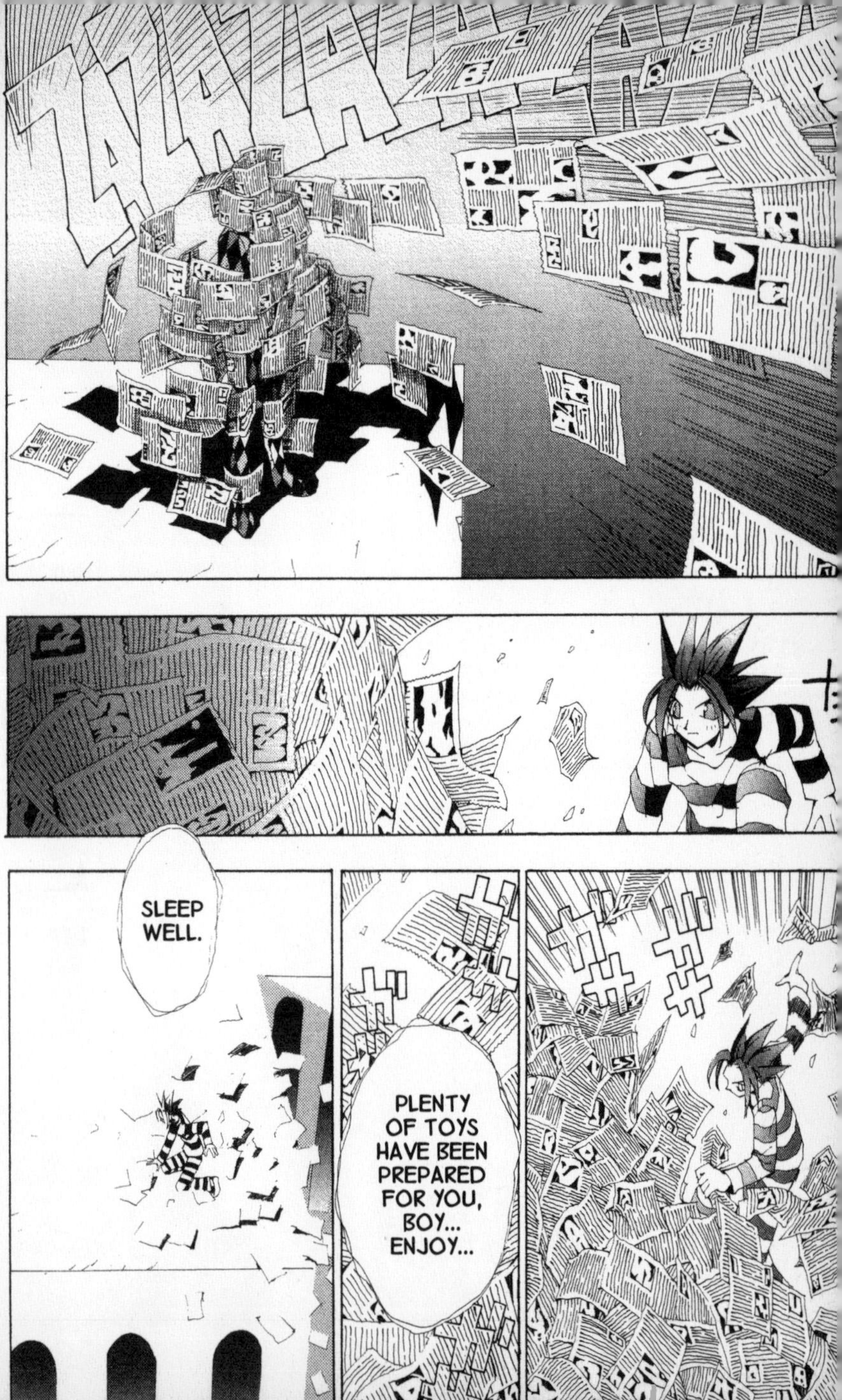

ZAZAZA
PLENTY OF TOYS HAVE BEEN PREPARED FOR YOU, BOY... ENJOY...
SLEEP WELL.

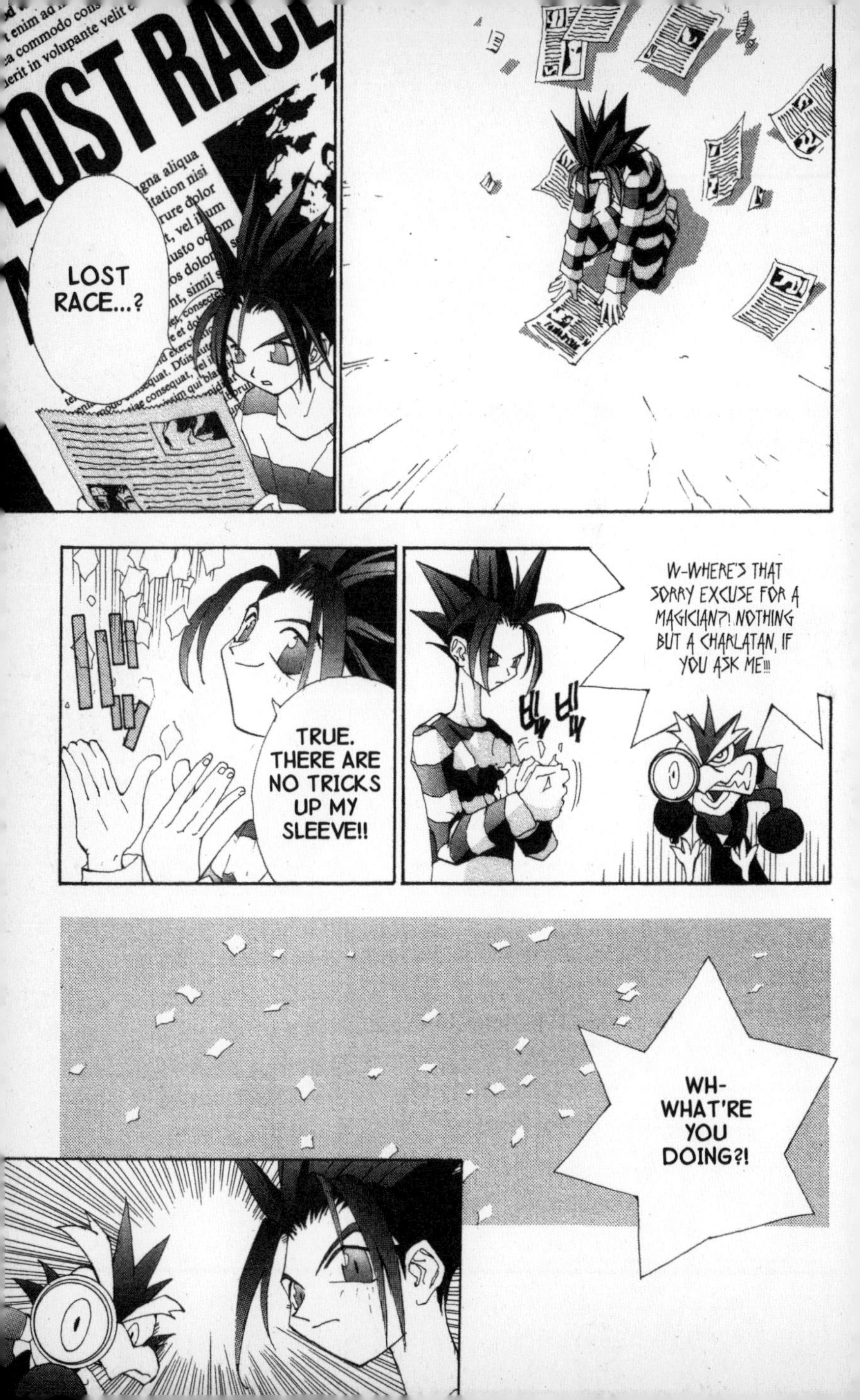
LOST RACE
LOST RACE...?
W-WHERE'S THAT SORRY EXCUSE FOR A MAGICIAN?! NOTHING BUT A CHARLATAN, IF YOU ASK ME!!!
TRUE. THERE ARE NO TRICKS UP MY SLEEVE!!
WH- WHAT'RE YOU DOING?!

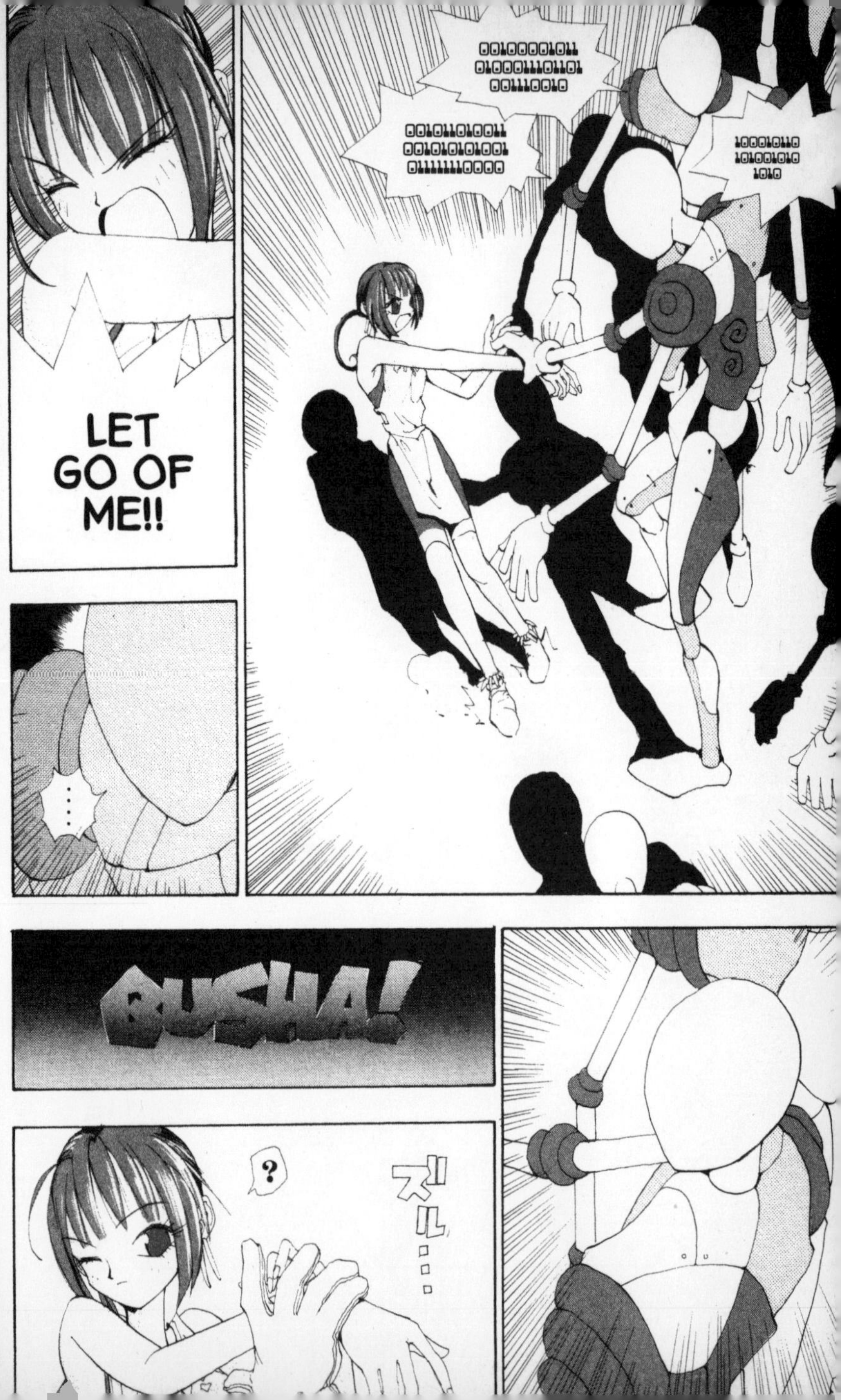
100010110
101001010
1010
001000001011
0100011101101
001110010
001011010011
001010101001
01111110000
LET GO OF ME!!
....
BUSHA!
ズル...
?

YOU SEE?
IT'S JUST A
FRIENDLY
NIGHTMARE...

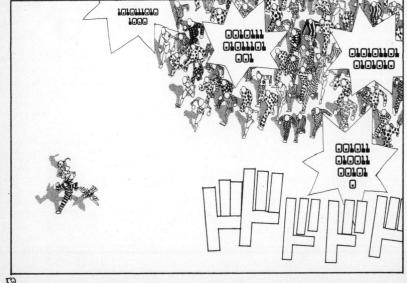

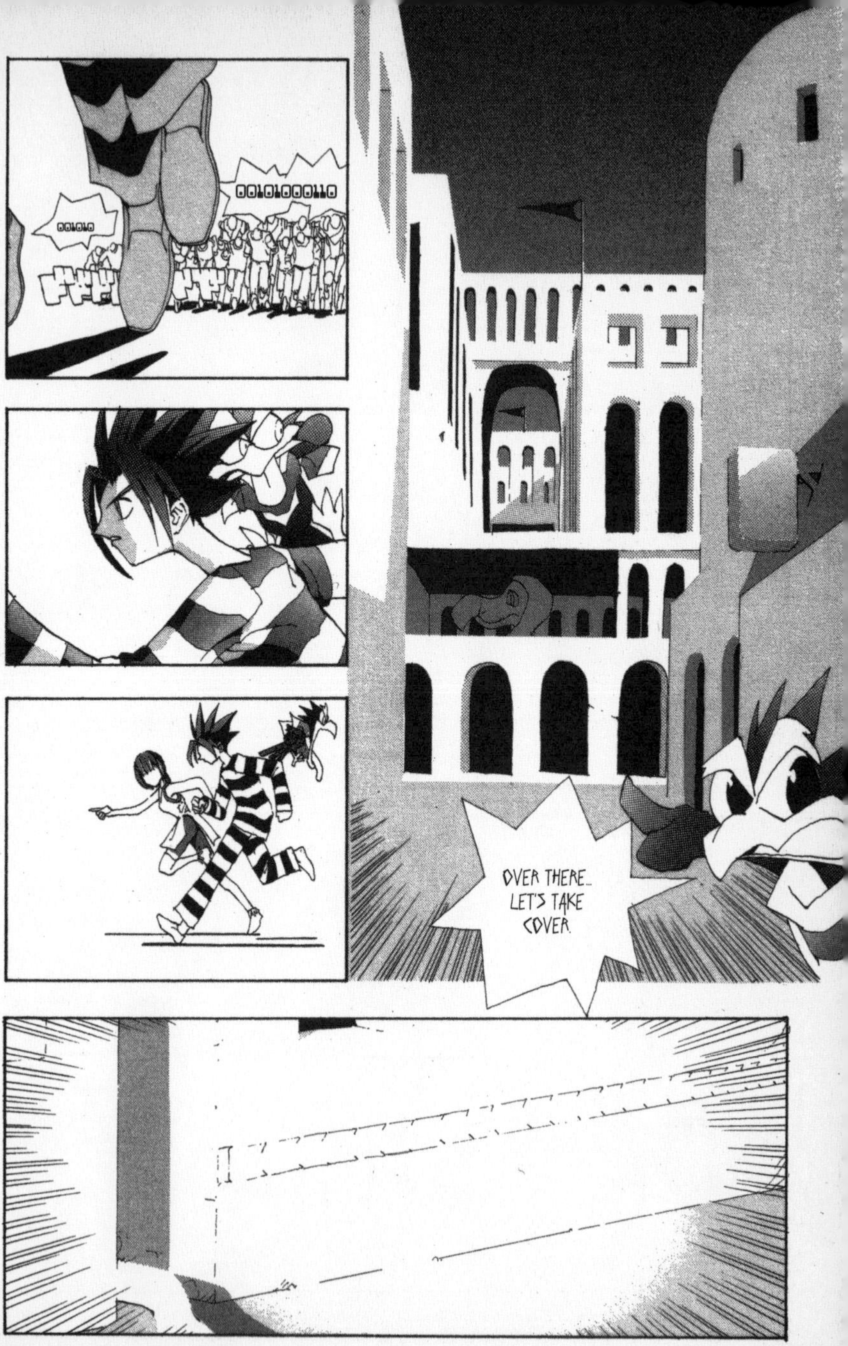

OVER THERE... LET'S TAKE COVER.
00101000110
001010

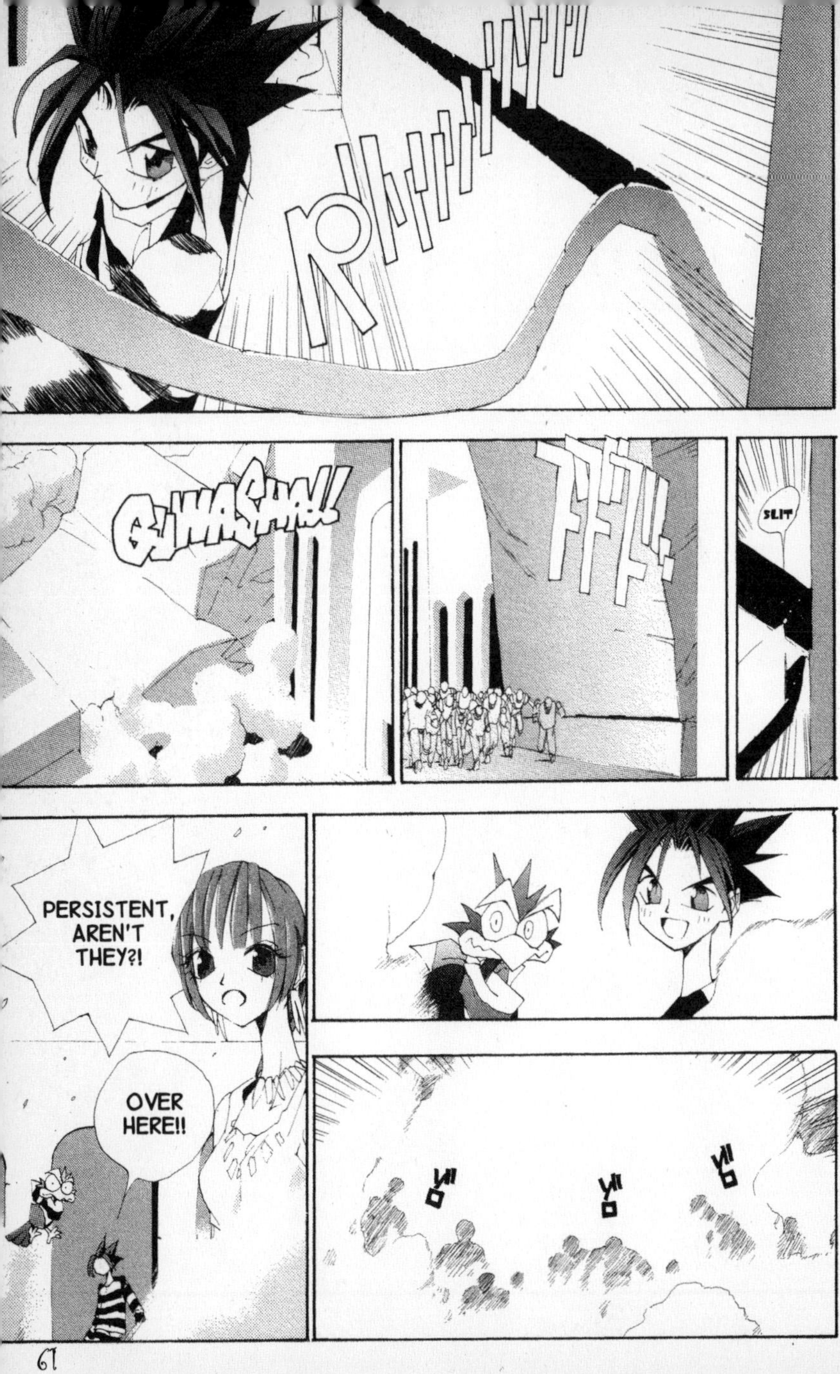
SLIT
GUWASHA!!
PERSISTENT, AREN'T THEY?!
OVER HERE!!

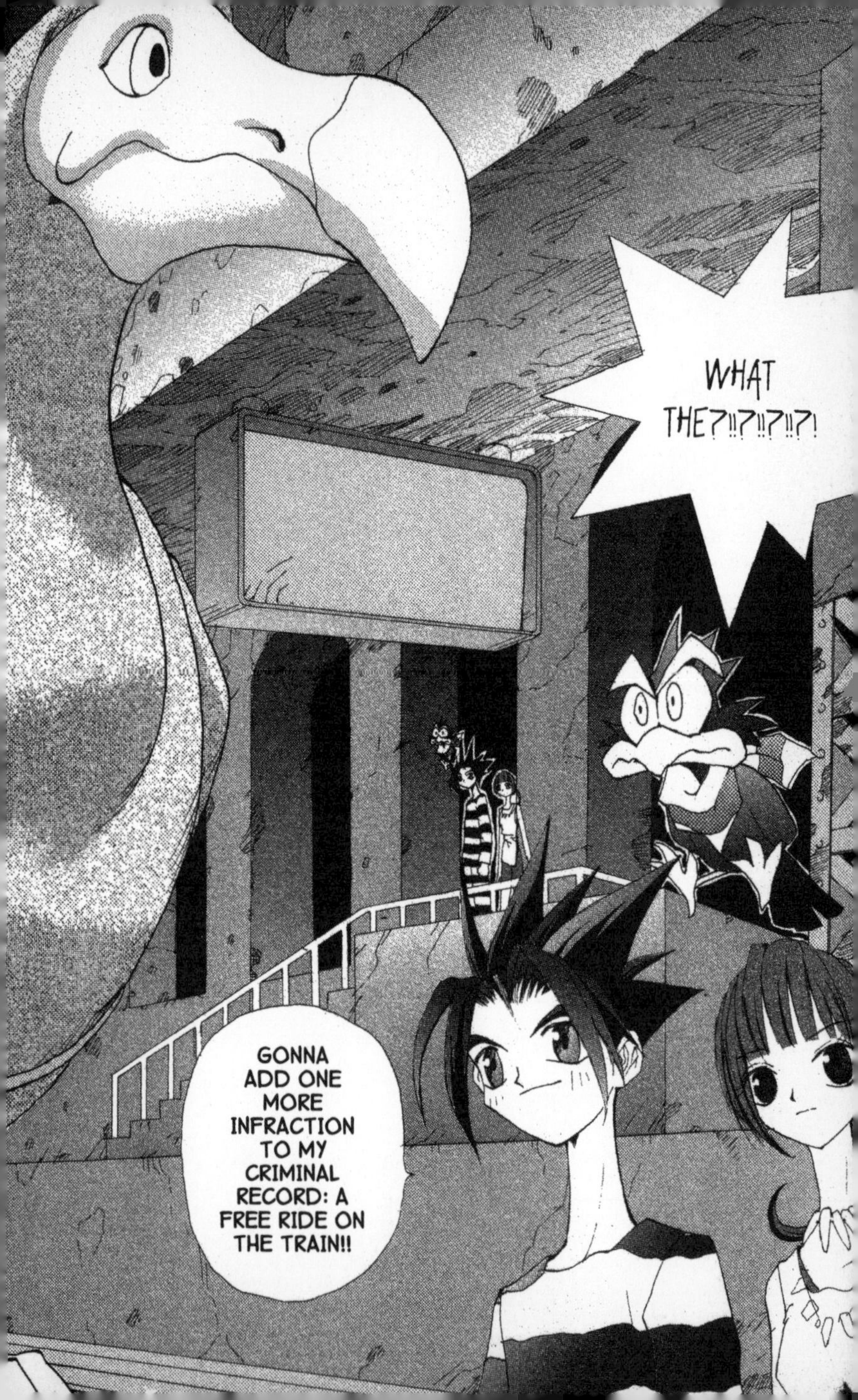
WHAT THE?!!?!!?!!?!
GONNA ADD ONE MORE INFRACTION TO MY CRIMINAL RECORD: A FREE RIDE ON THE TRAIN!!

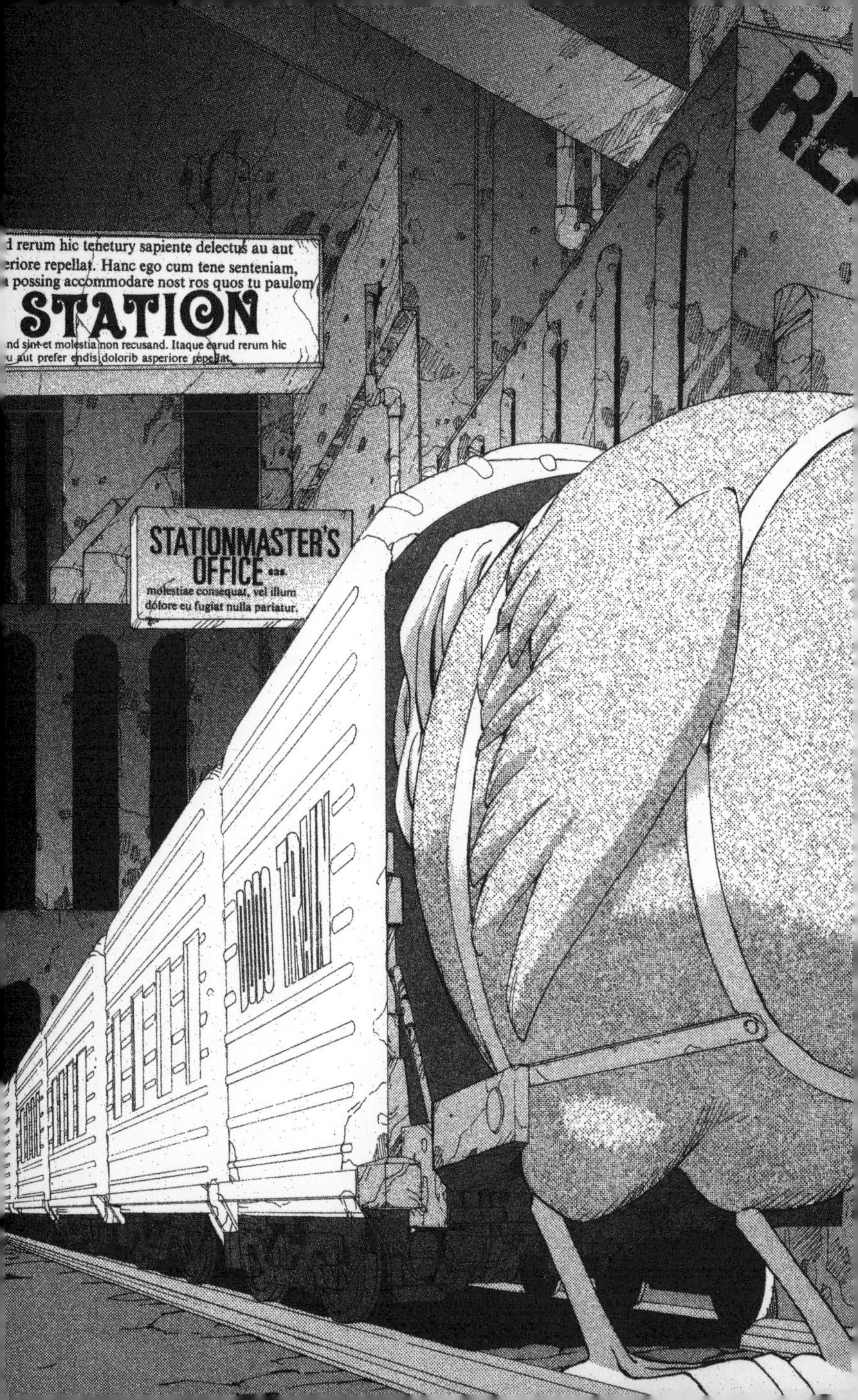
d rerum hic tenetury sapiente delectus au aut
eriore repellat. Hanc ego cum tene senteniam,
possing accommodare nost ros quos tu paulom
STATION
nd sint et molestia non recusand. Itaque earud rerum hic
u aut prefer endis dolorib asperiore repellat.
STATIONMASTER'S OFFICE
molestiae consequat, vel illum
dolore eu fugiat nulla pariatur.

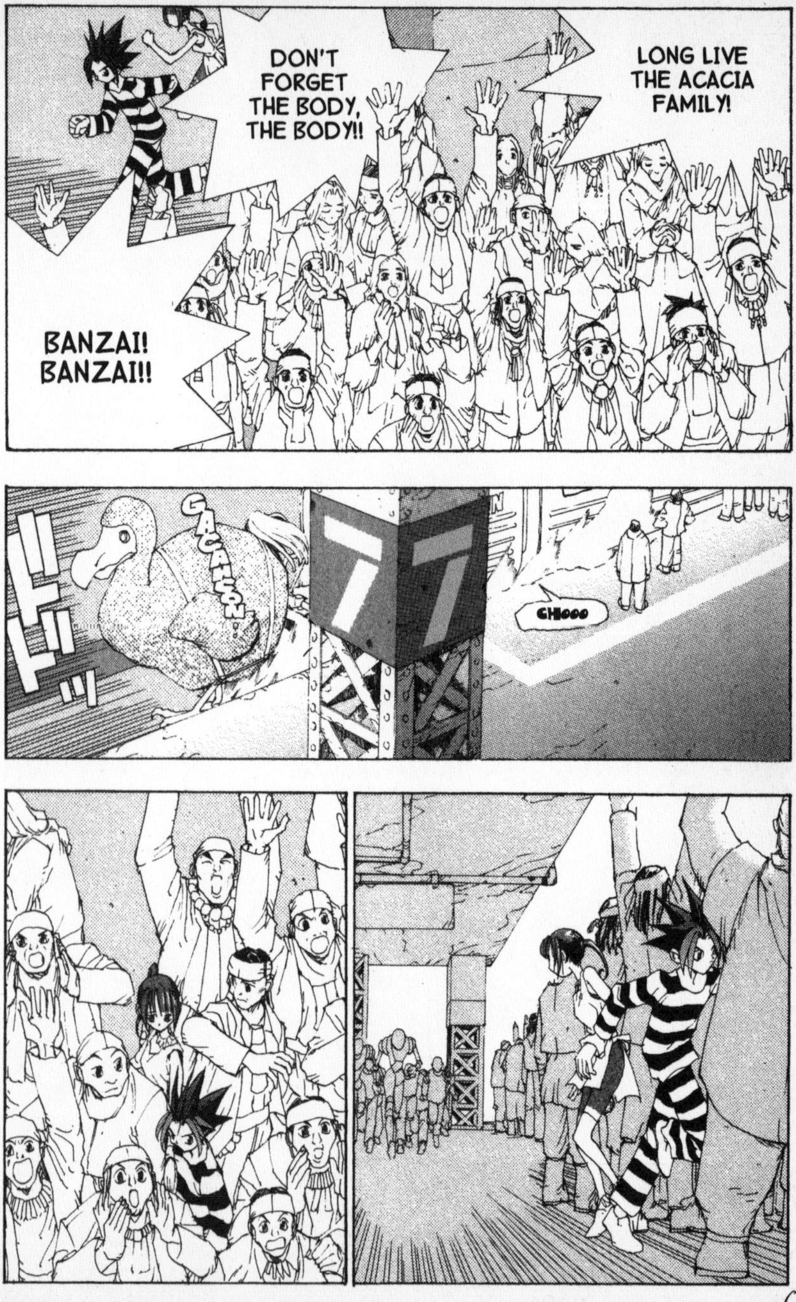
LONG LIVE THE ACACIA FAMILY!
DON'T FORGET THE BODY, THE BODY!!
BANZAI! BANZAI!!
CHOOO
GAGAHSON

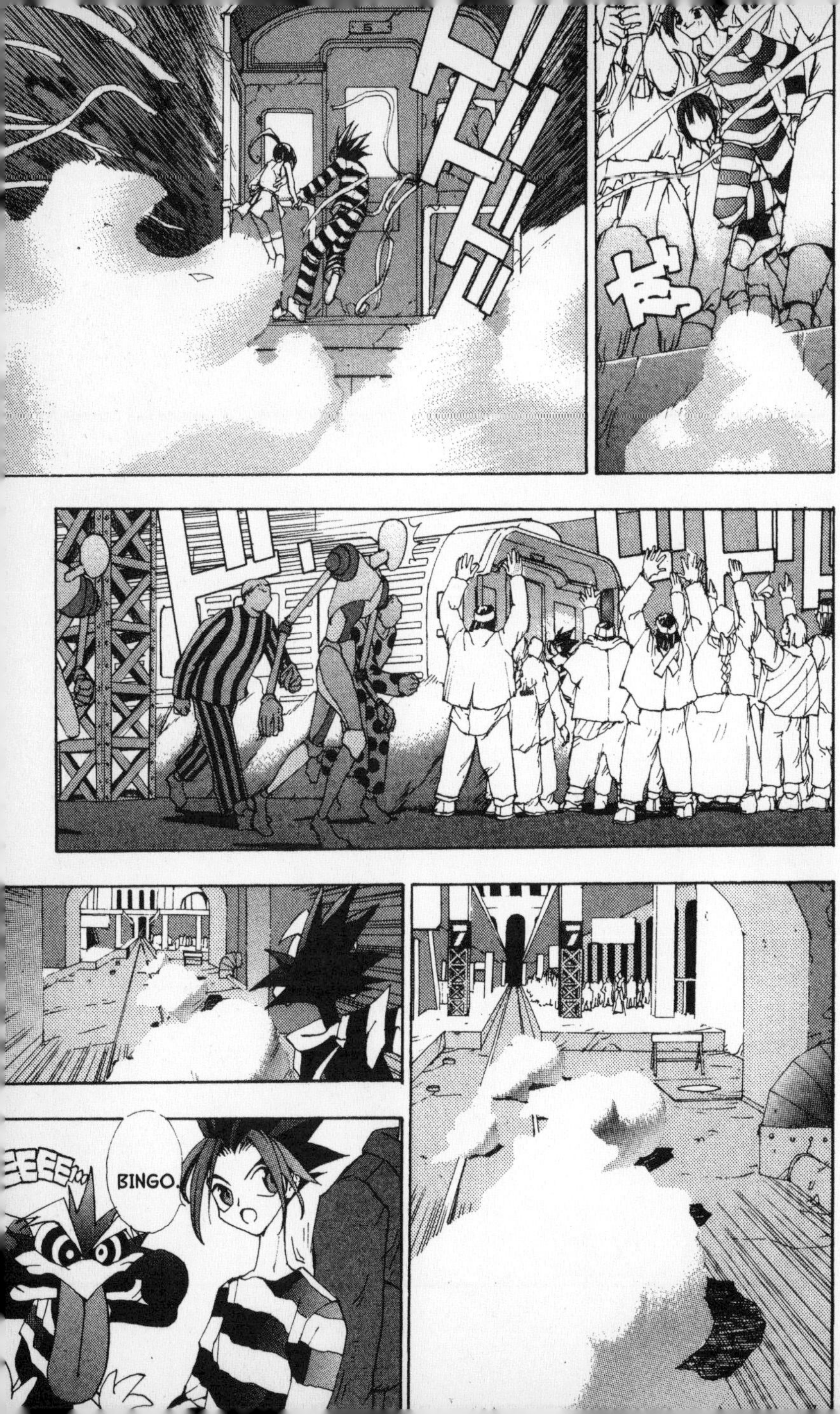
だっ
ドドドドドド
ドドドド
BINGO.
EEEE!!

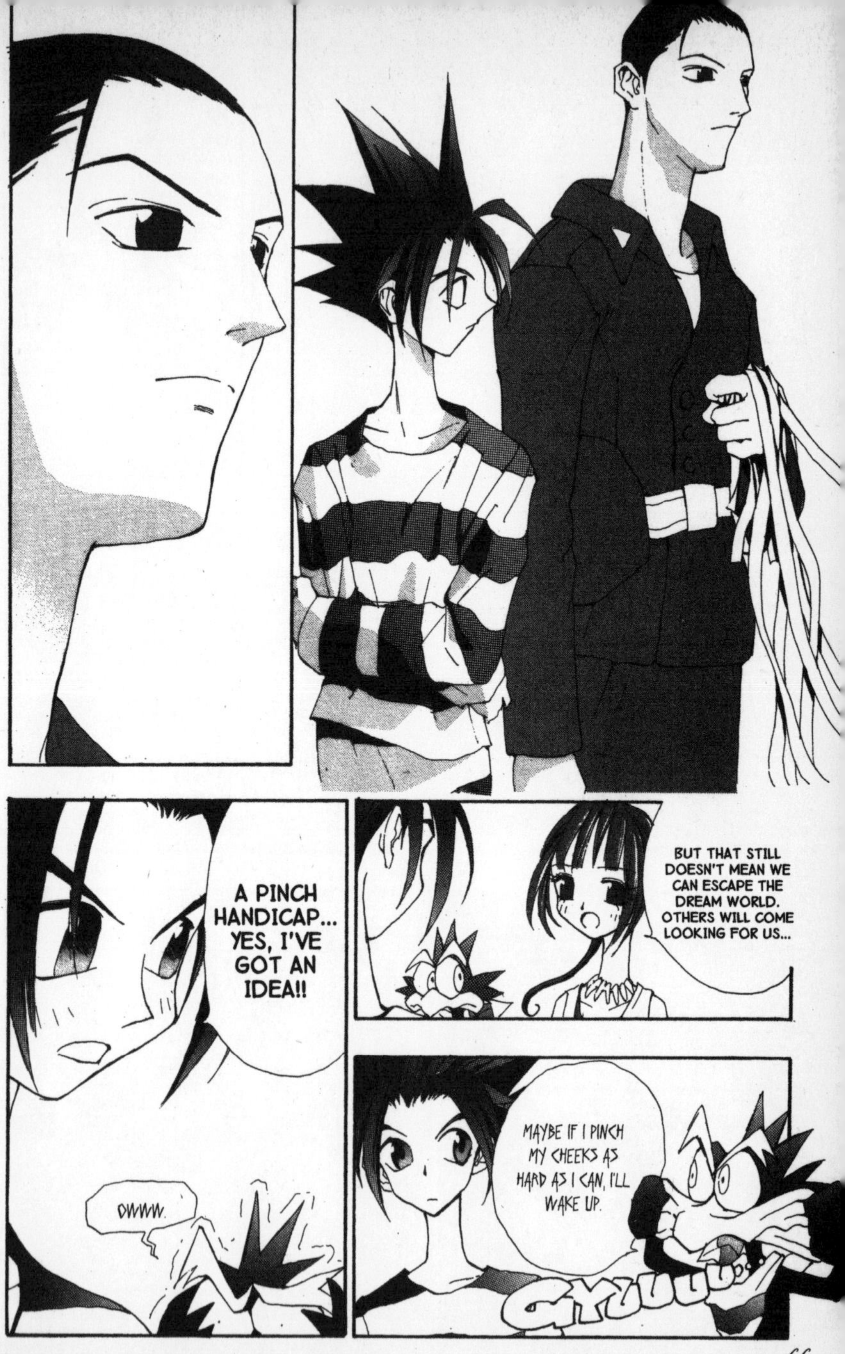
BUT THAT STILL DOESN'T MEAN WE CAN ESCAPE THE DREAM WORLD. OTHERS WILL COME LOOKING FOR US...
MAYBE IF I PINCH MY CHEEKS AS HARD AS I CAN, I'LL WAKE UP.
GYUUUU
A PINCH HANDICAP... YES, I'VE GOT AN IDEA!!
OWWW.

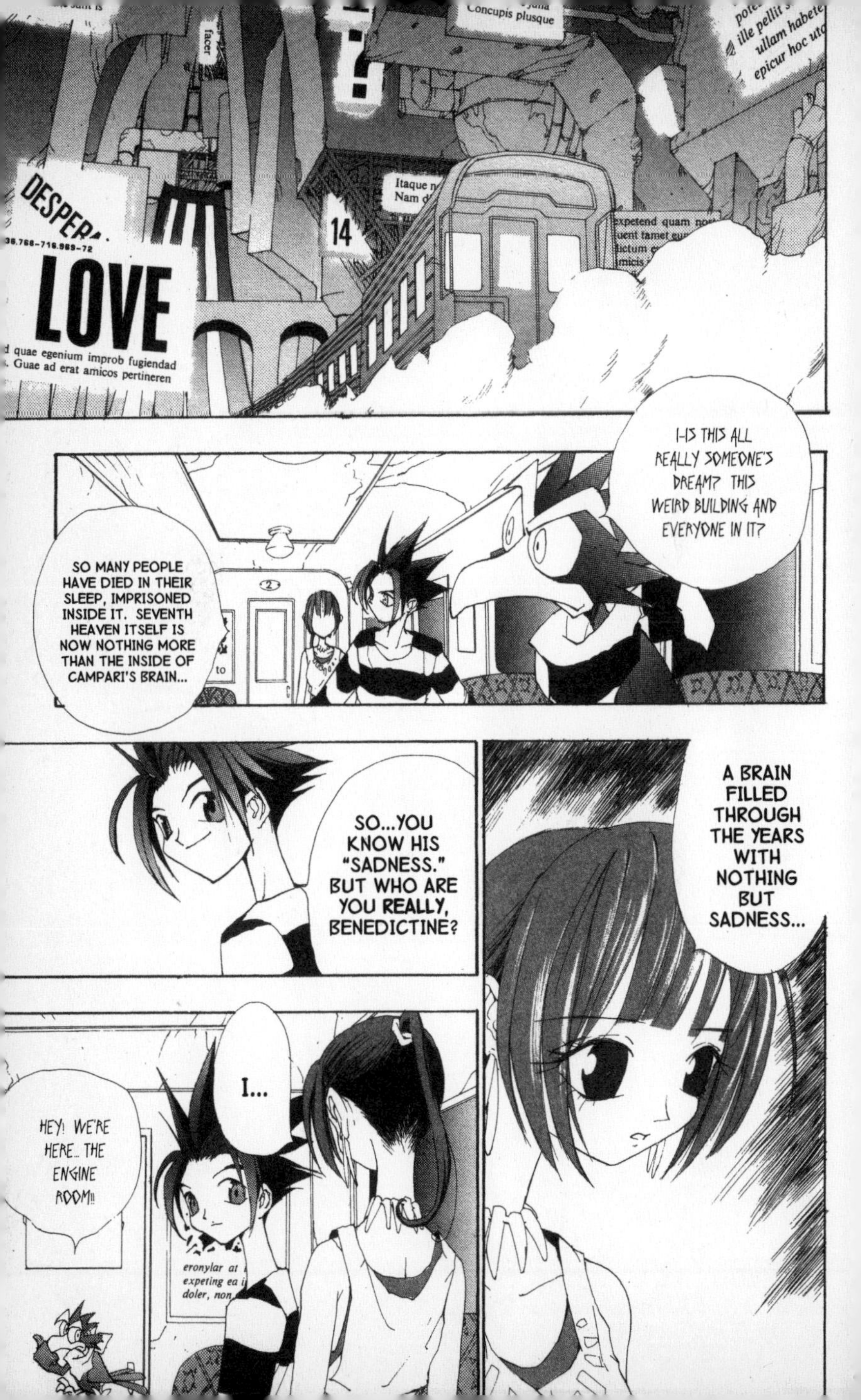
Concupis plusque
LOVE
14
Guae ad erat amicos pertineren
I-IS THIS ALL REALLY SOMEONE'S DREAM? THIS WEIRD BUILDING AND EVERYONE IN IT?
SO MANY PEOPLE HAVE DIED IN THEIR SLEEP, IMPRISONED INSIDE IT. SEVENTH HEAVEN ITSELF IS NOW NOTHING MORE THAN THE INSIDE OF CAMPARI'S BRAIN...
A BRAIN FILLED THROUGH THE YEARS WITH NOTHING BUT SADNESS...
SO...YOU KNOW HIS "SADNESS." BUT WHO ARE YOU REALLY, BENEDICTINE?
I...
HEY! WE'RE HERE... THE ENGINE ROOM!!

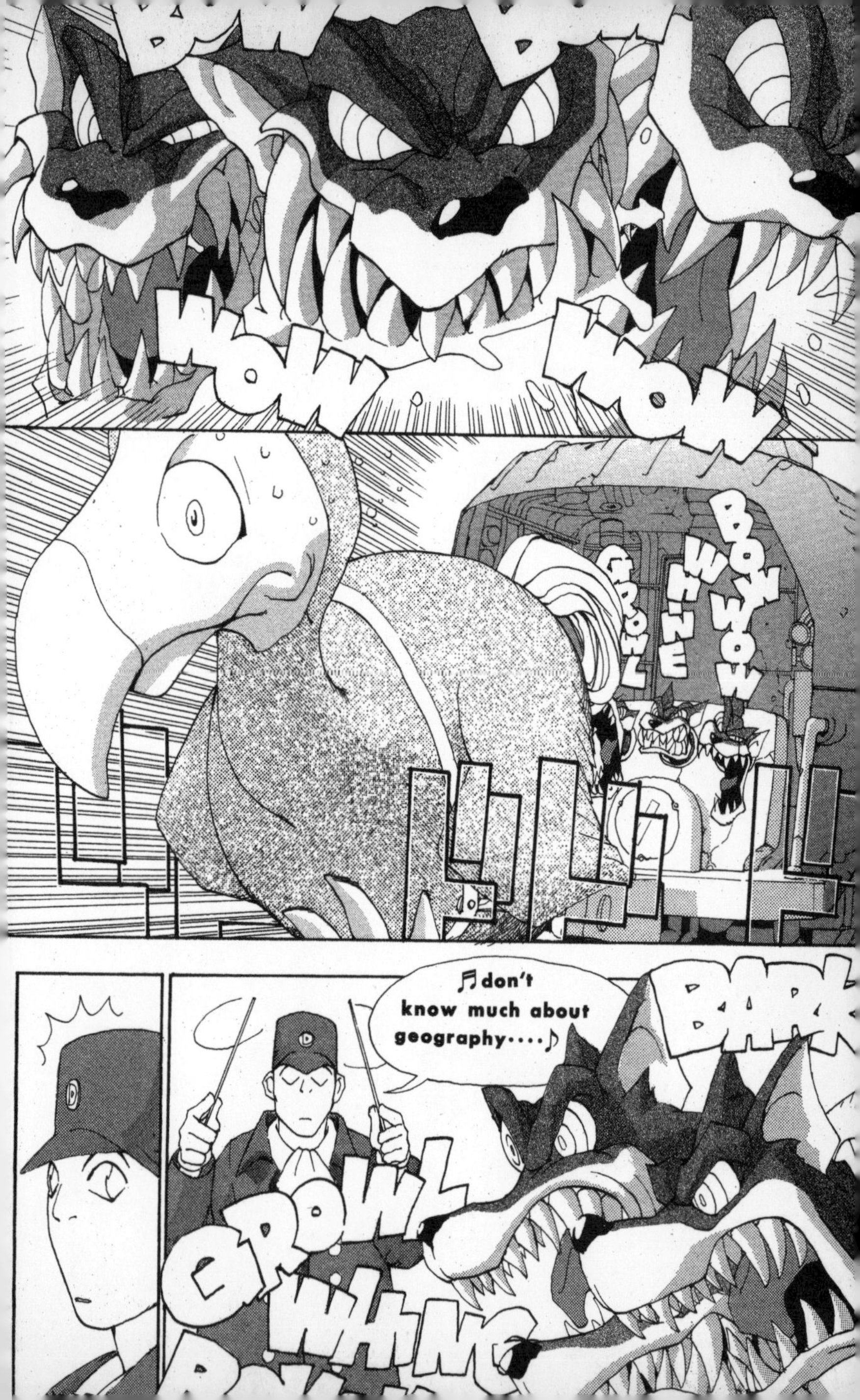
WOW
WOW
BOW WOW WOW
WHINE
GROWL
♬don't know much about geography....♪
BARK
GROWL

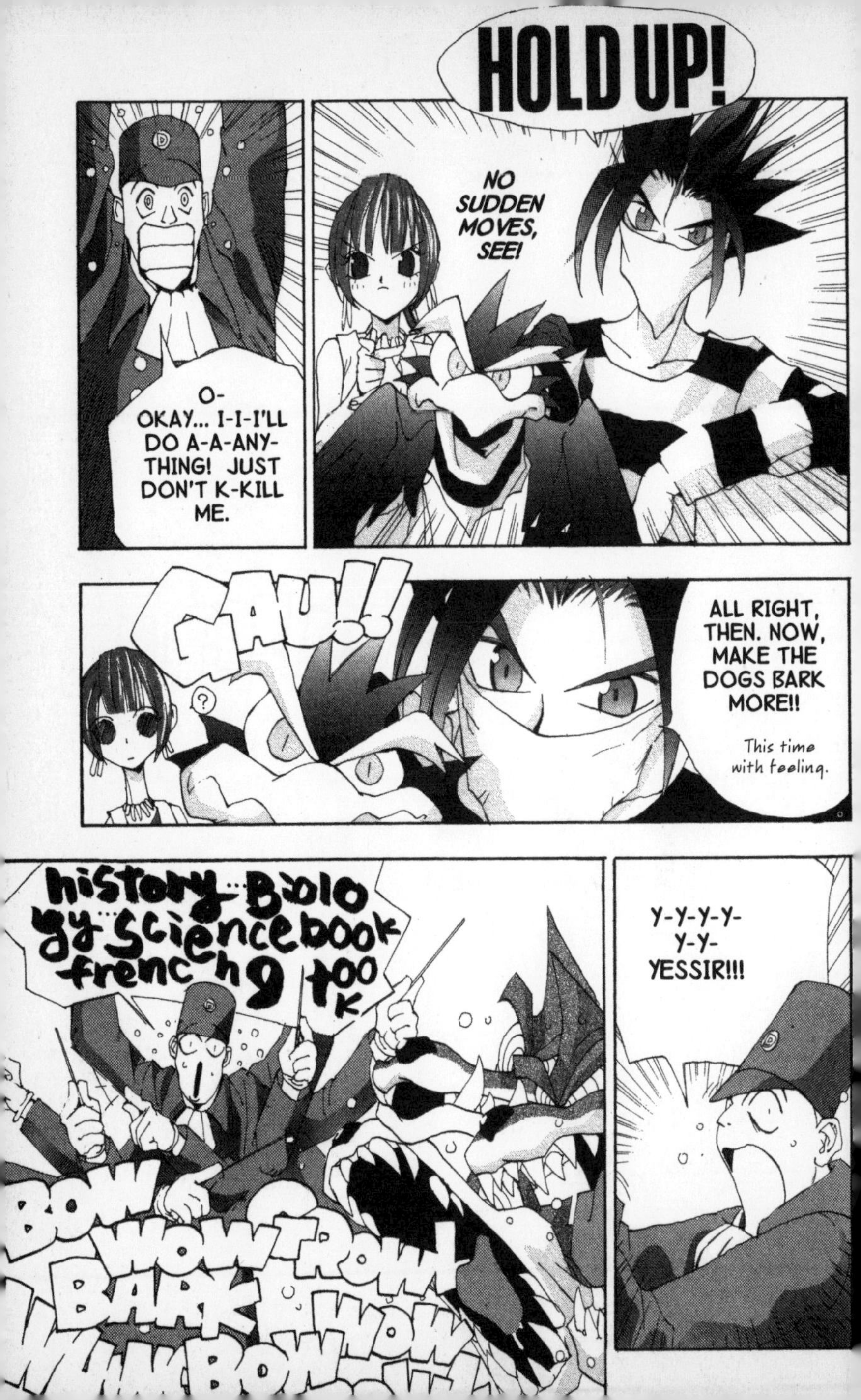
HOLD UP!
NO SUDDEN MOVES, SEE!
O- OKAY... I-I-I'LL DO A-A-ANY-THING! JUST DON'T K-KILL ME.
ALL RIGHT, THEN. NOW, MAKE THE DOGS BARK MORE!!
This time with feeling.
GAU!!
Y-Y-Y-Y- Y-Y- YESSIR!!!
history... Biolo gy... Science book french 9 too k
BOW WOW ROW
BARK! WOW
BOW

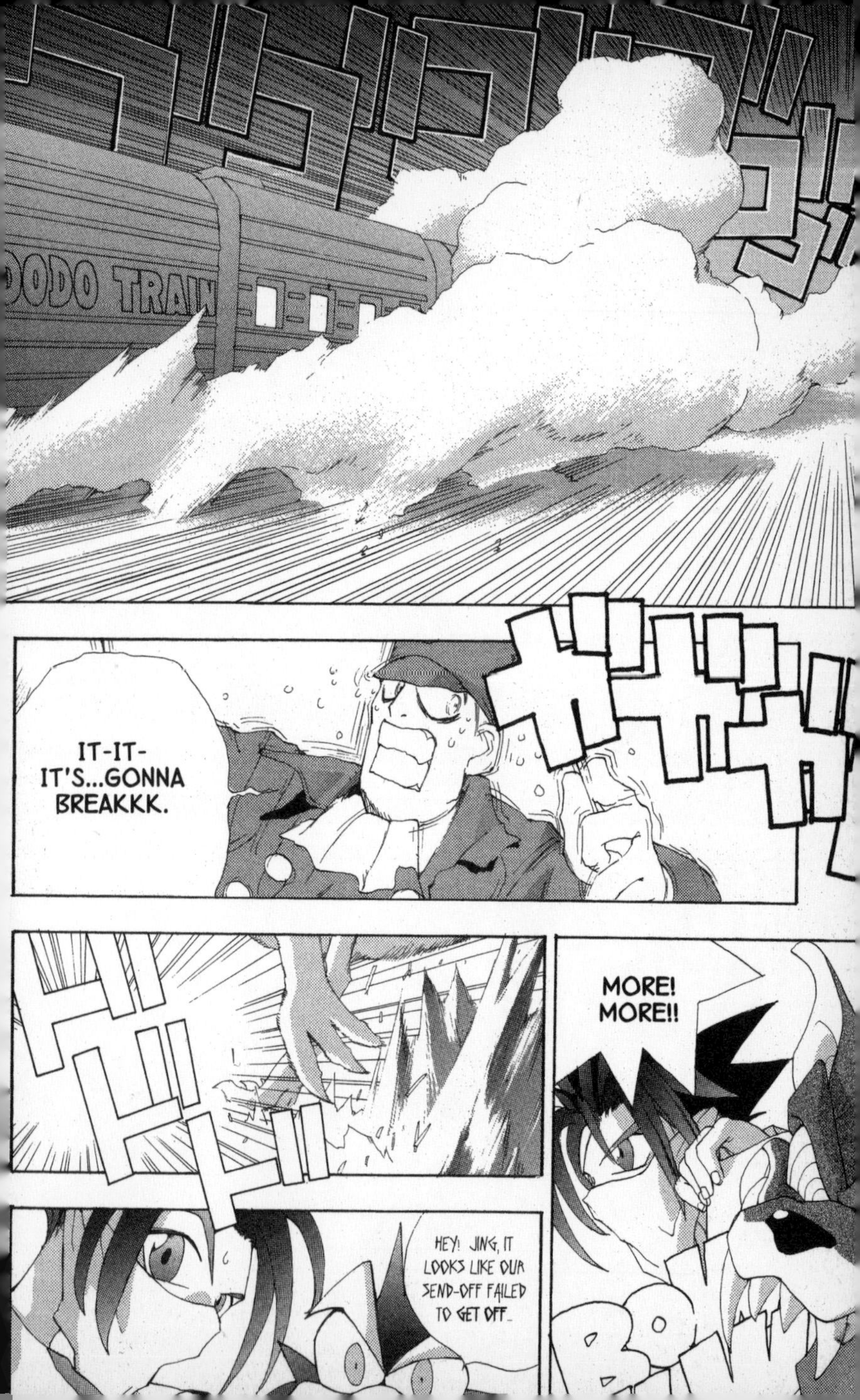
DODO TRAIN
IT-IT- IT'S...GONNA BREAKKK.
MORE! MORE!!
HEY! JING, IT LOOKS LIKE OUR SEND-OFF FAILED TO GET OFF...

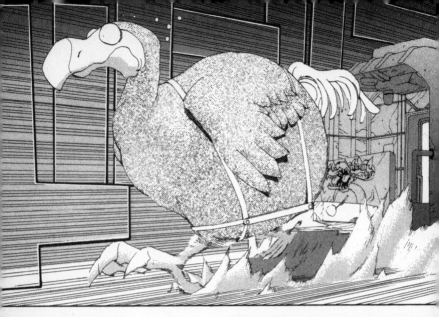

LOOK-- AT THE TOP!! IT'S NOT JUST BREAKING, IT'S BEING TORN APART!!
EVERYONE!! JUMP ON THE BIRD'S BACK!!
H-H-HOLD ON THERE, JING!! I KNOW YOU RELY ON ME AND ALL, BUT TWO HUMANS IS A BIT...
NOT YOU! THIS GUY!!!!

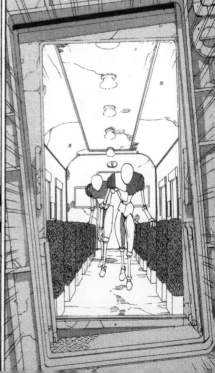

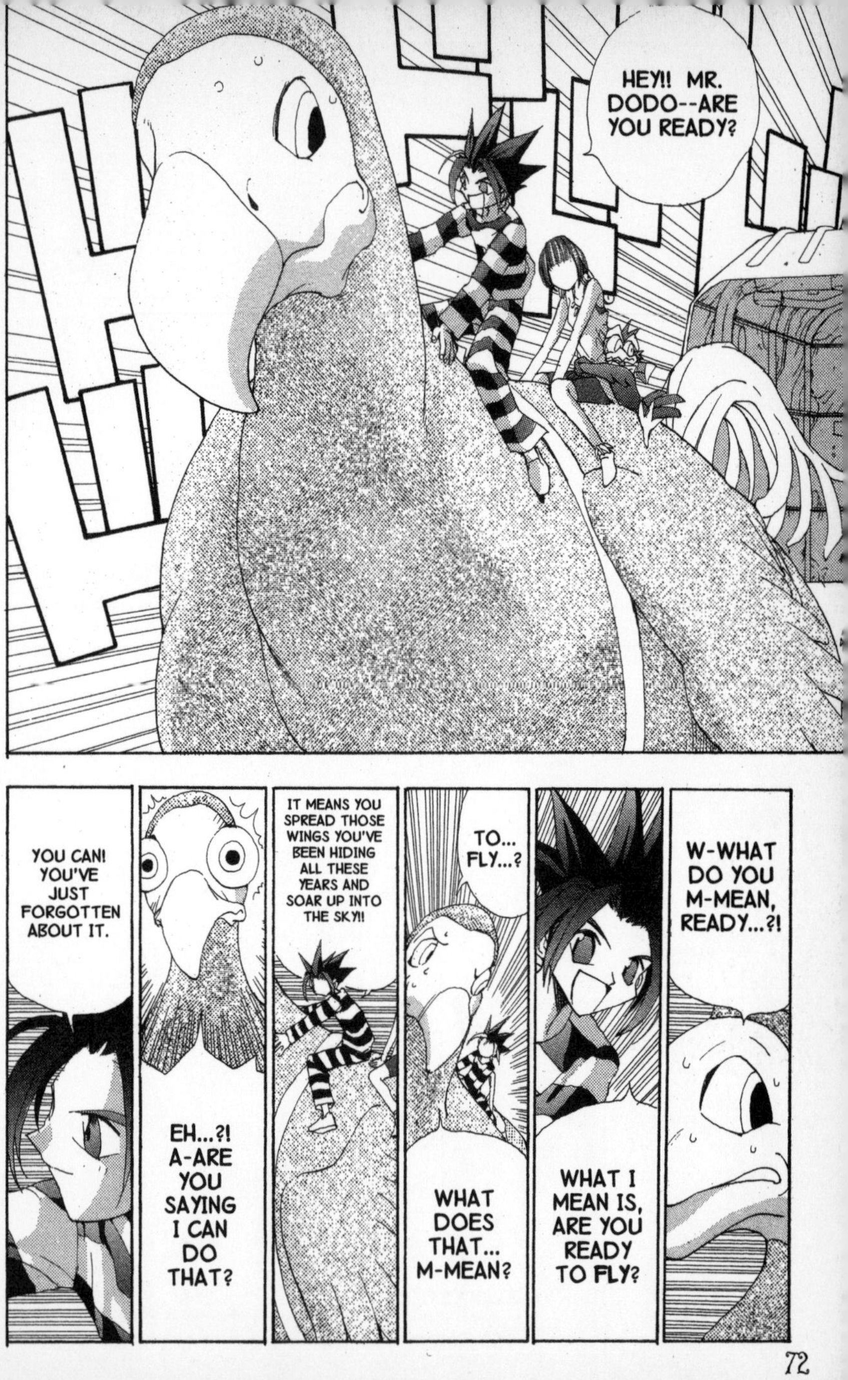
HEY!! MR. DODO--ARE YOU READY?
W-WHAT DO YOU M-MEAN, READY...?!
WHAT I MEAN IS, ARE YOU READY TO FLY?
TO... FLY...?
WHAT DOES THAT... M-MEAN?
IT MEANS YOU SPREAD THOSE WINGS YOU'VE BEEN HIDING ALL THESE YEARS AND SOAR UP INTO THE SKY!!
EH...?! A-ARE YOU SAYING I CAN DO THAT?
YOU CAN! YOU'VE JUST FORGOTTEN ABOUT IT.

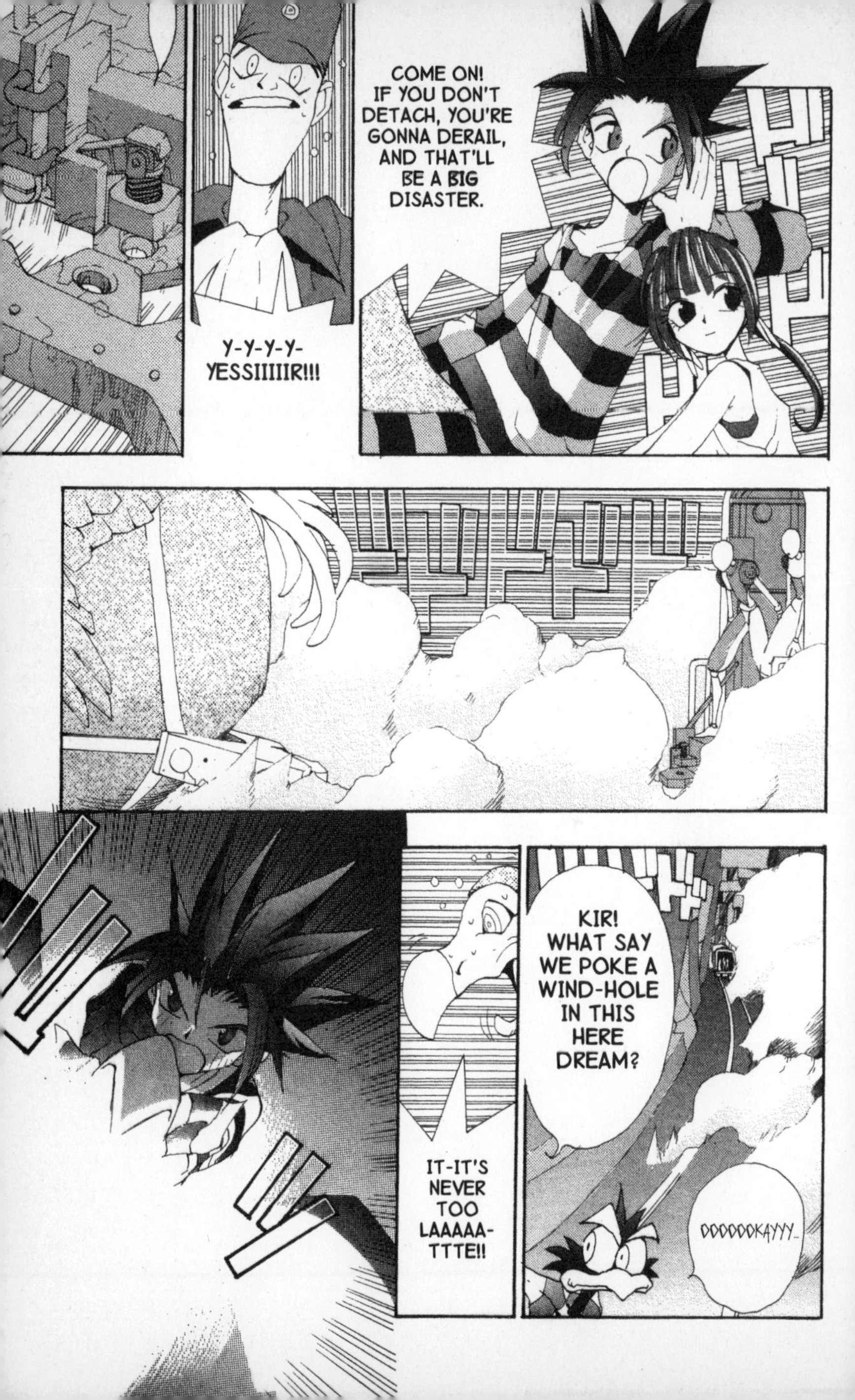
COME ON! IF YOU DON'T DETACH, YOU'RE GONNA DERAIL, AND THAT'LL BE A BIG DISASTER.
Y-Y-Y-Y-YESSIIIIIR!!!
KIR! WHAT SAY WE POKE A WIND-HOLE IN THIS HERE DREAM?
OOOOOOKAYYY...
IT-IT'S NEVER TOO LAAAAA-TTTE!!

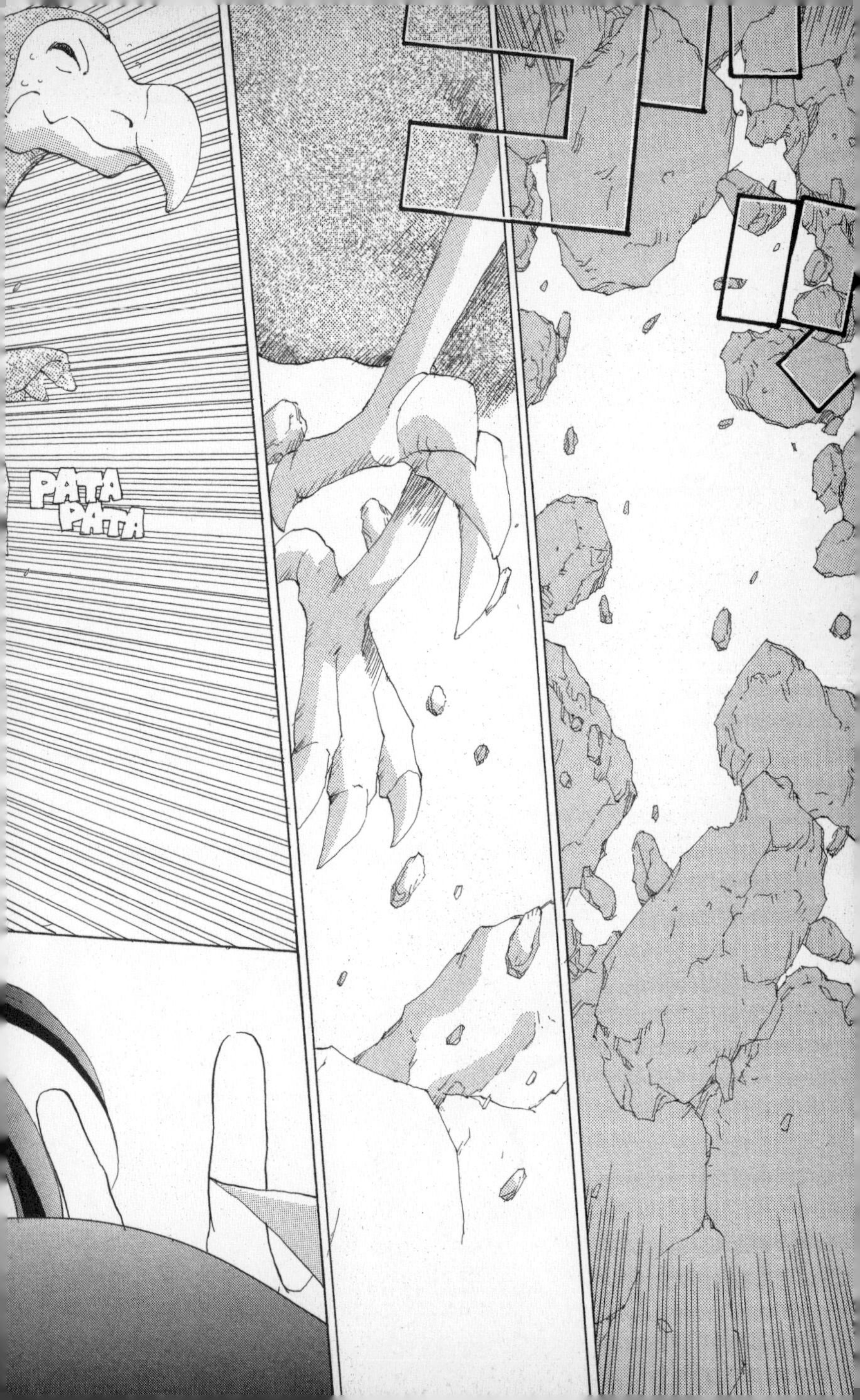
PATA PATA

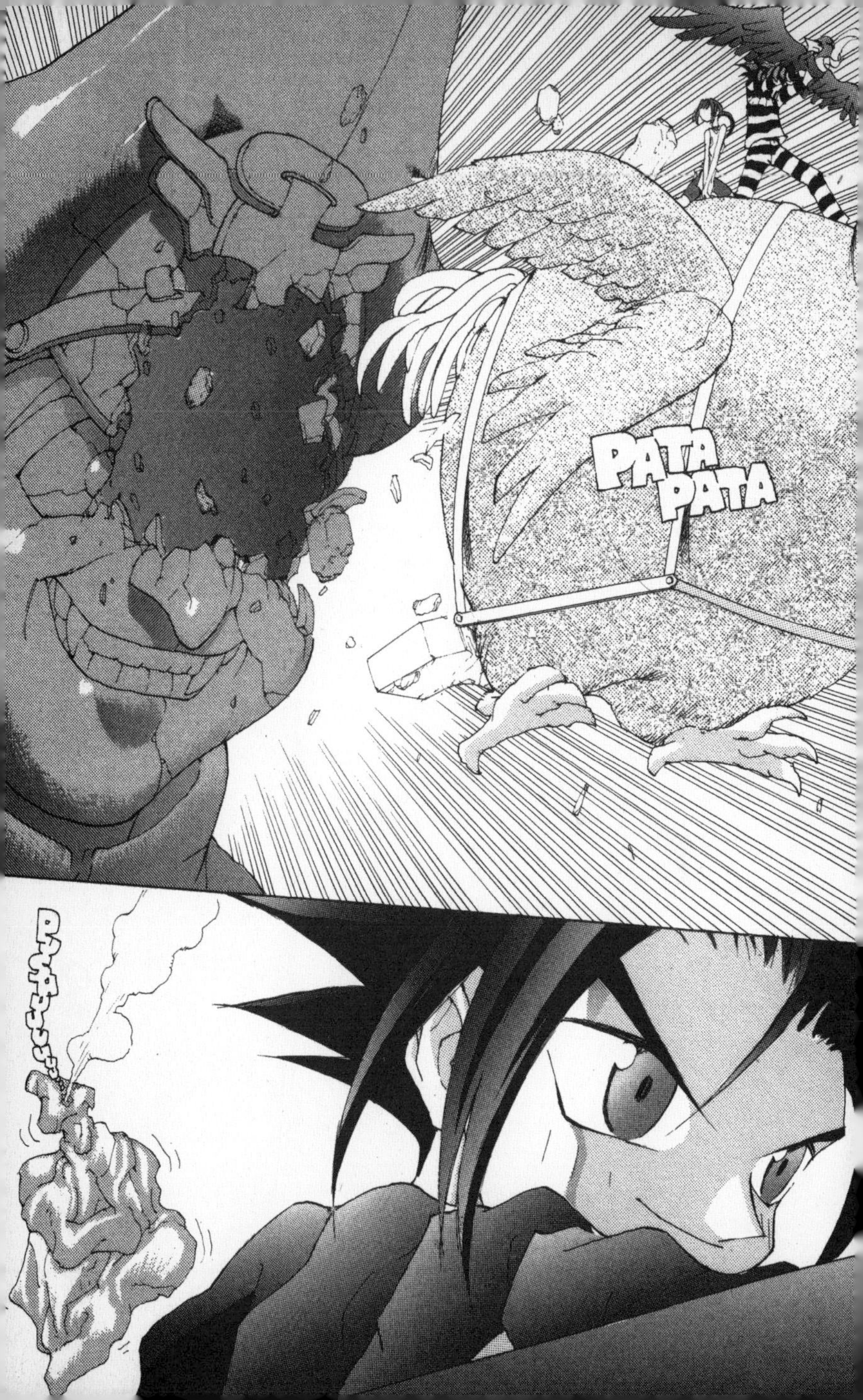
PATA PATA
PSSSSSSSS

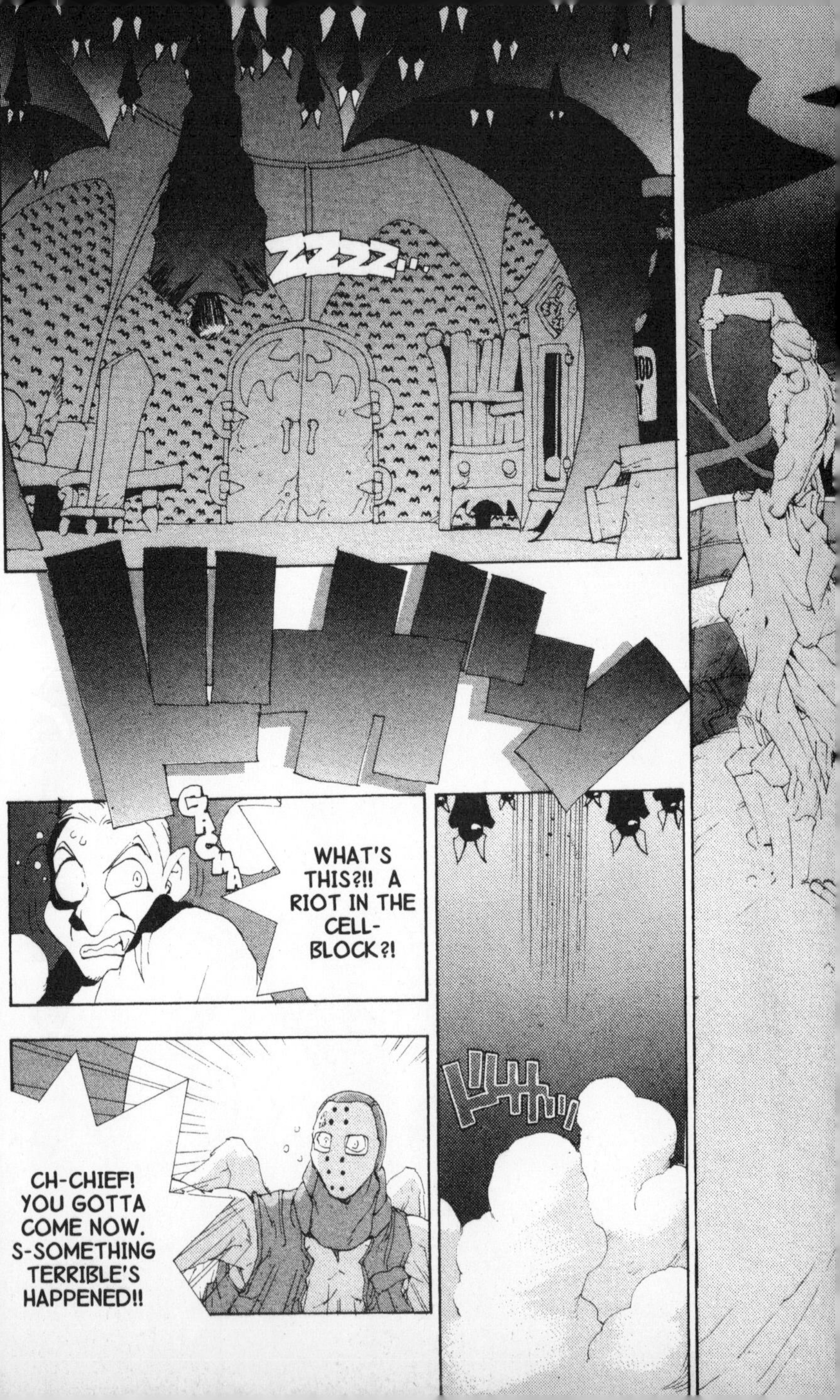
ZZZZ...
GACHA
WHAT'S THIS?!! A RIOT IN THE CELL-BLOCK?!
CH-CHIEF! YOU GOTTA COME NOW. S-SOMETHING TERRIBLE'S HAPPENED!!

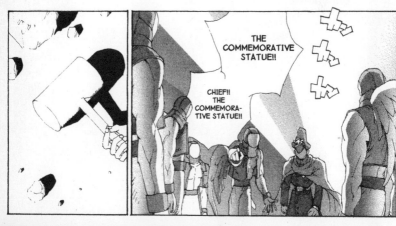

THE
COMMEMORATIVE
STATUE!!

CHIEF!!
THE
COMMEMORA-
TIVE STATUE!!

WH...
WHAT...?!

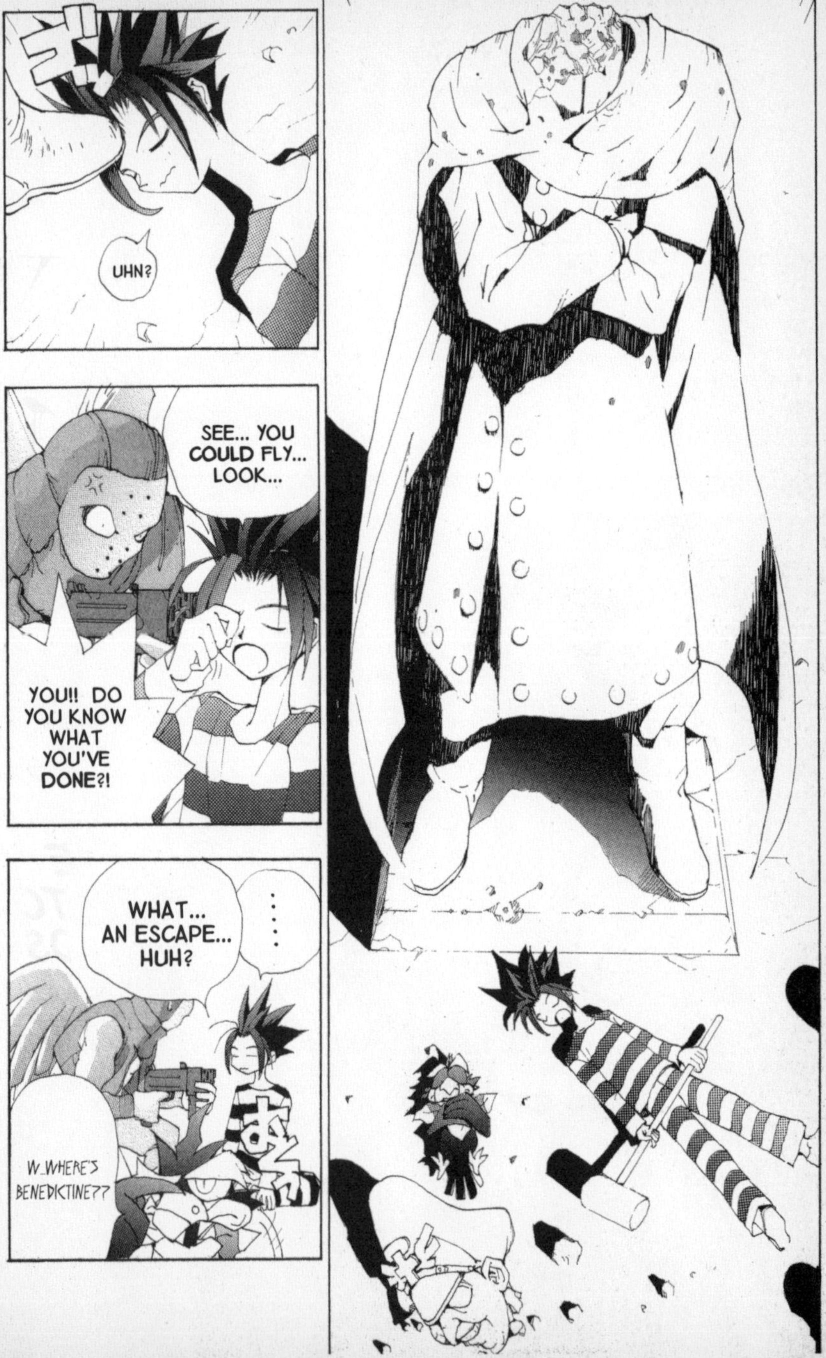
UHN?
SEE... YOU COULD FLY... LOOK...
YOU!! DO YOU KNOW WHAT YOU'VE DONE?!
.....
WHAT... AN ESCAPE... HUH?
W_WHERE'S BENEDICTINE??

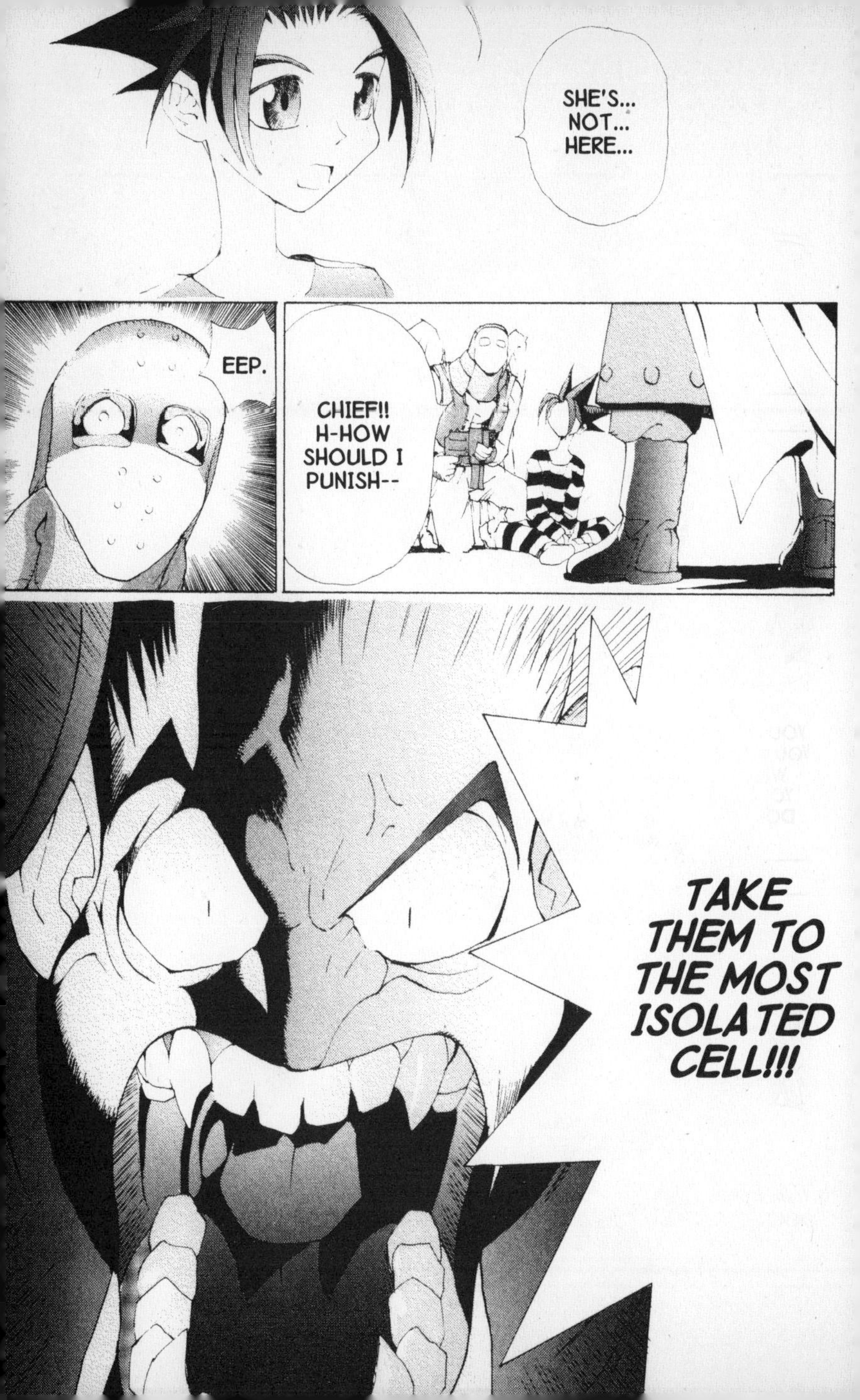
SHE'S... NOT... HERE...
CHIEF!! H-HOW SHOULD I PUNISH--
EEP.
TAKE THEM TO THE MOST ISOLATED CELL!!!

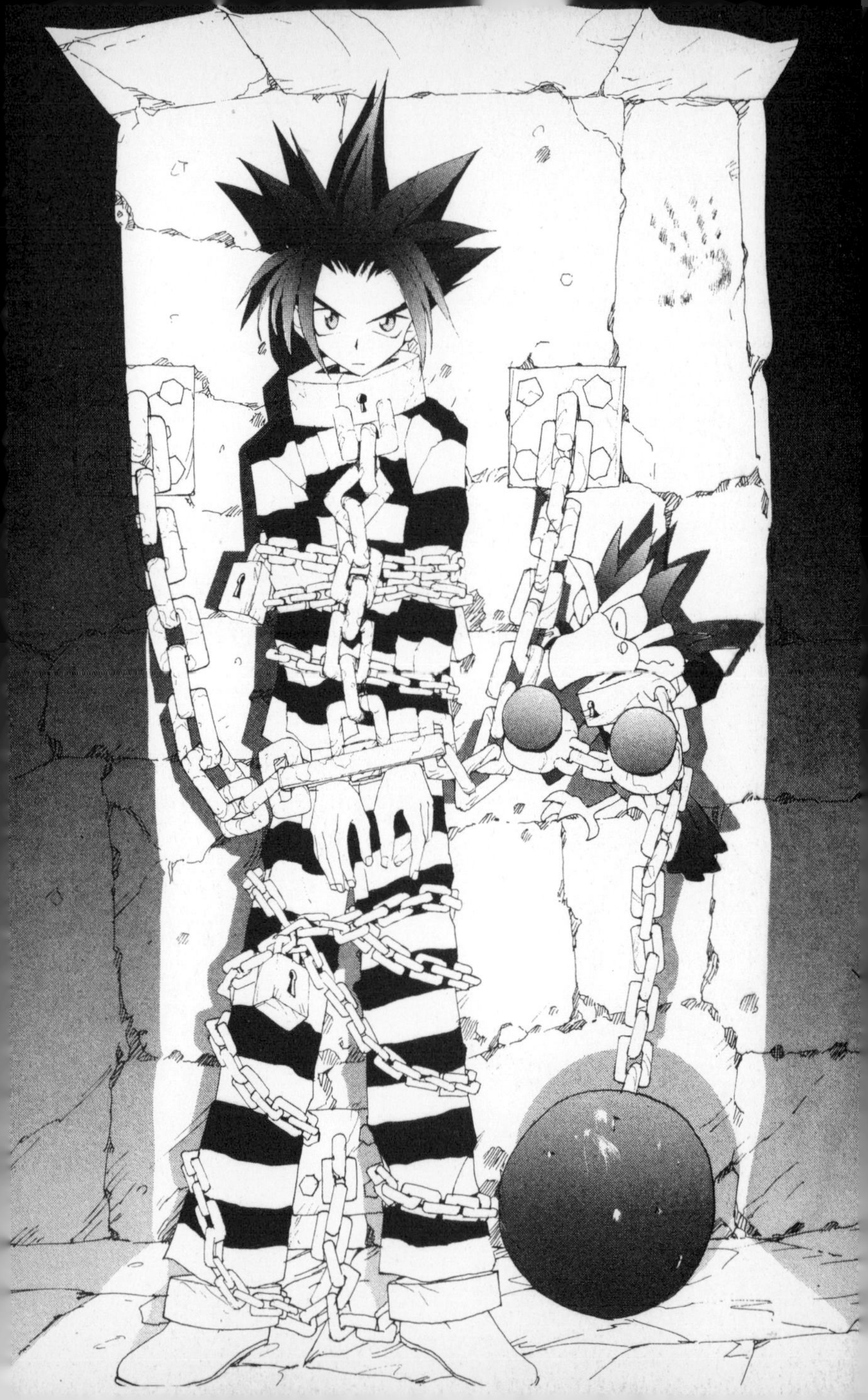

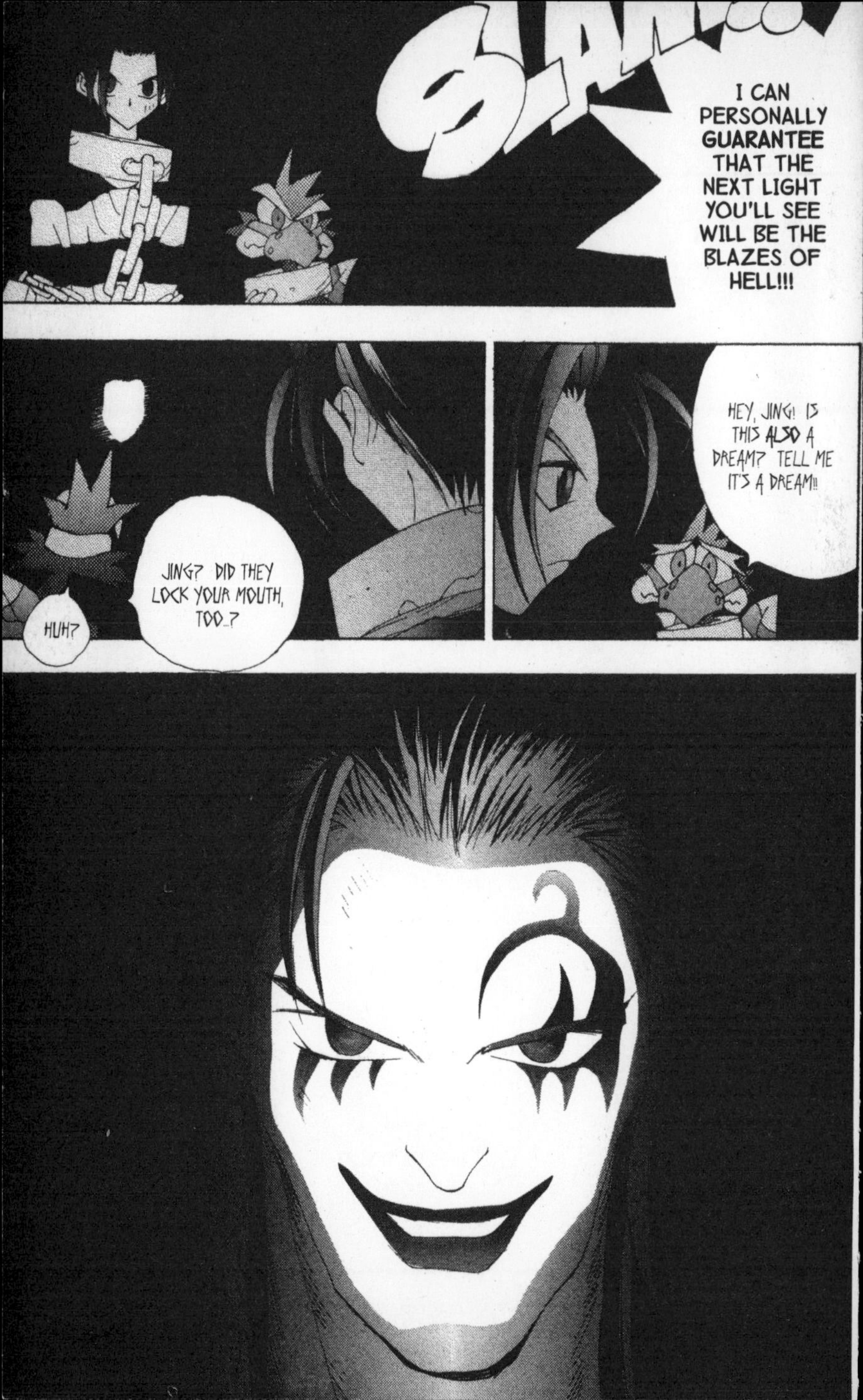
SLAM
I CAN PERSONALLY GUARANTEE THAT THE NEXT LIGHT YOU'LL SEE WILL BE THE BLAZES OF HELL!!!
HEY, JING! IS THIS ALSO A DREAM? TELL ME IT'S A DREAM!!
JING? DID THEY LOCK YOUR MOUTH, TOO..?
HUH?

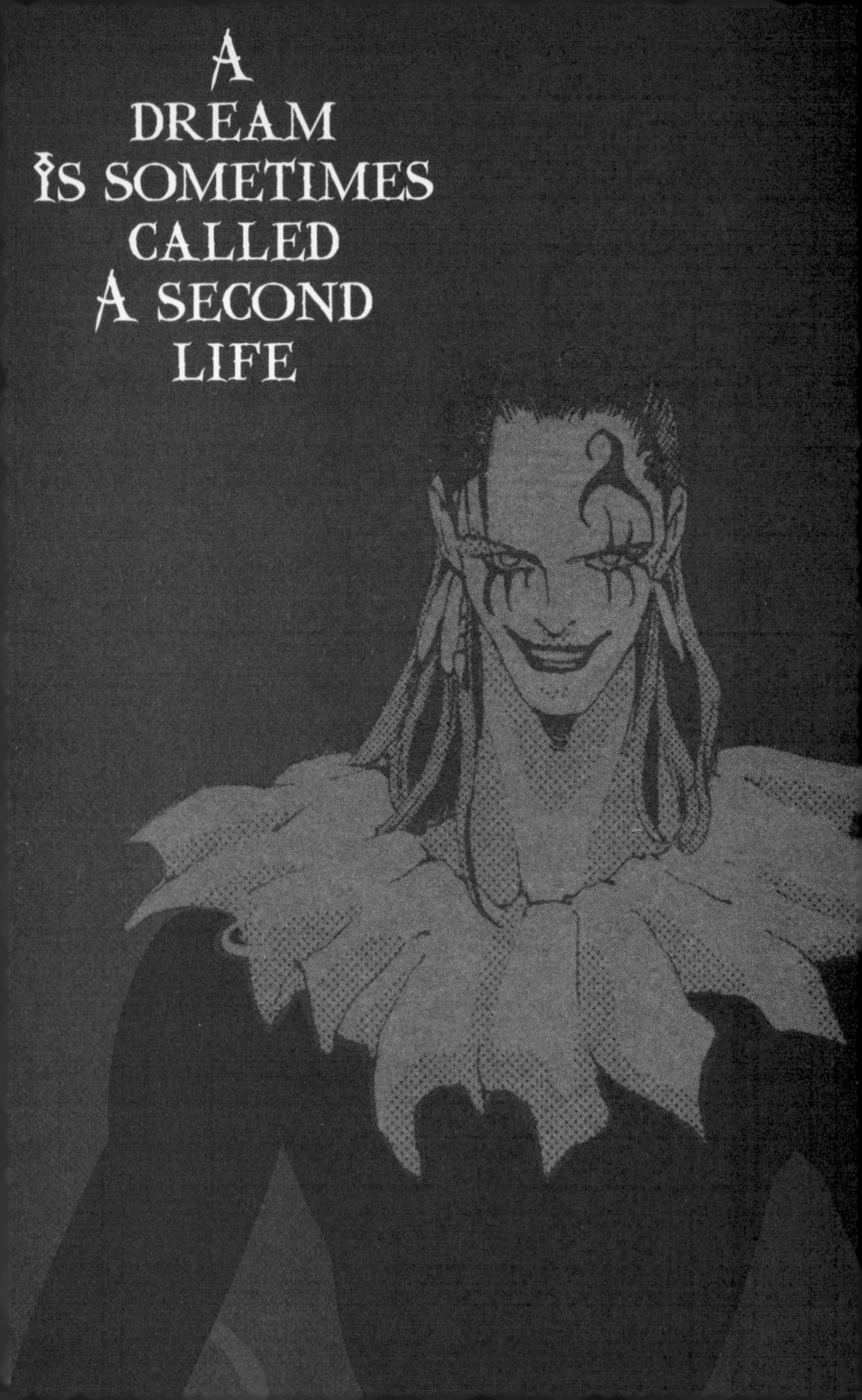
A DREAM IS SOMETIMES CALLED A SECOND LIFE

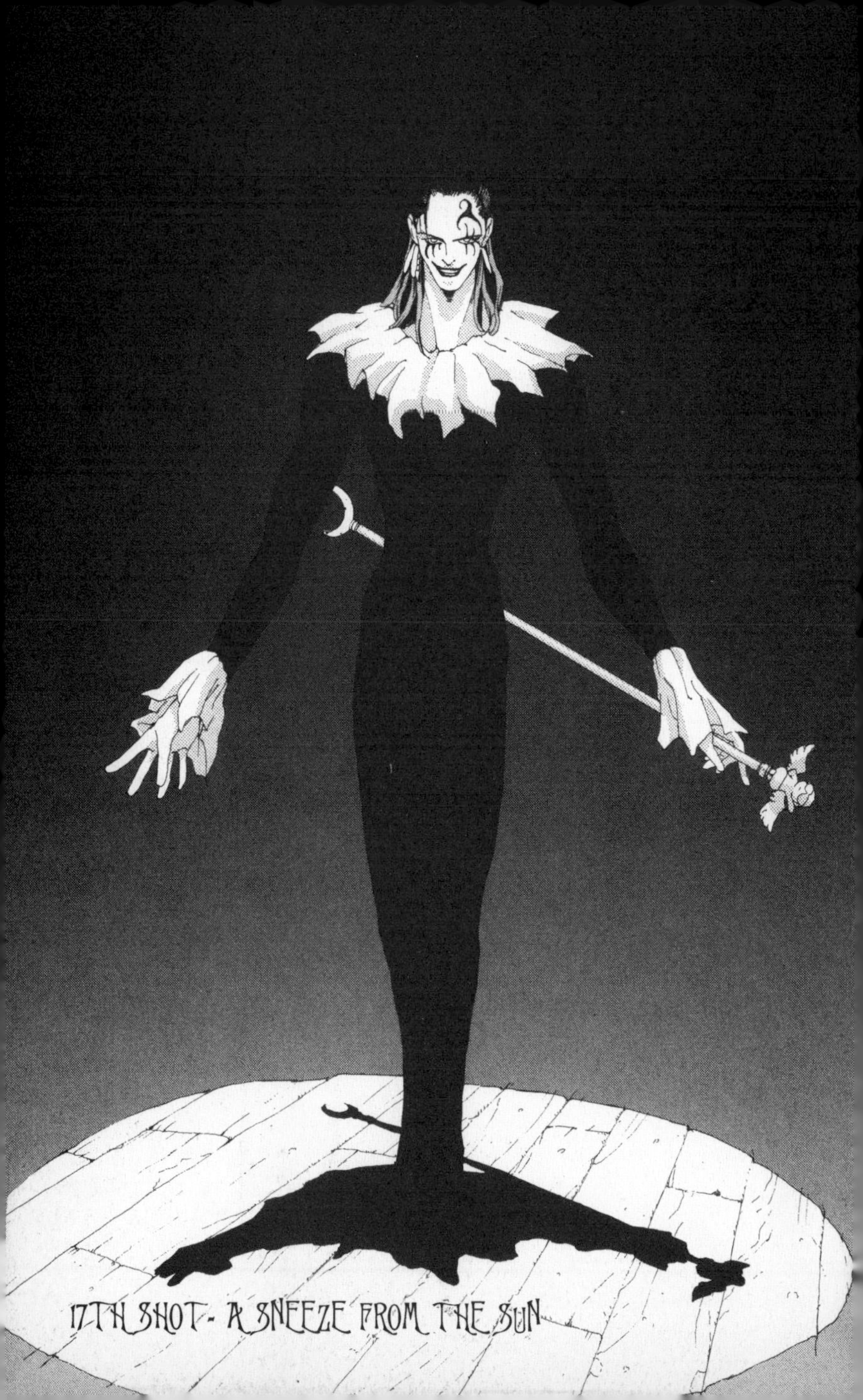
17TH SHOT - A SNEEZE FROM THE SUN

IF THIS WERE TRUE...WOULD NOT THAT WHICH WE CALL "LIFE" BECOME MERELY THE OPENING ACT OF A DREAM...

...AND AN EXTREMELY BORING ACT BESIDES?

OR...!!

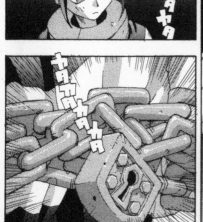

AS WITH LIFE, WOULD IT NOT BE CONSIDERED MERELY A DREAM WE SEE WHILST PASSING INTO THAT SOUND SLEEP KNOWN AS "DEATH"?!

SWING''

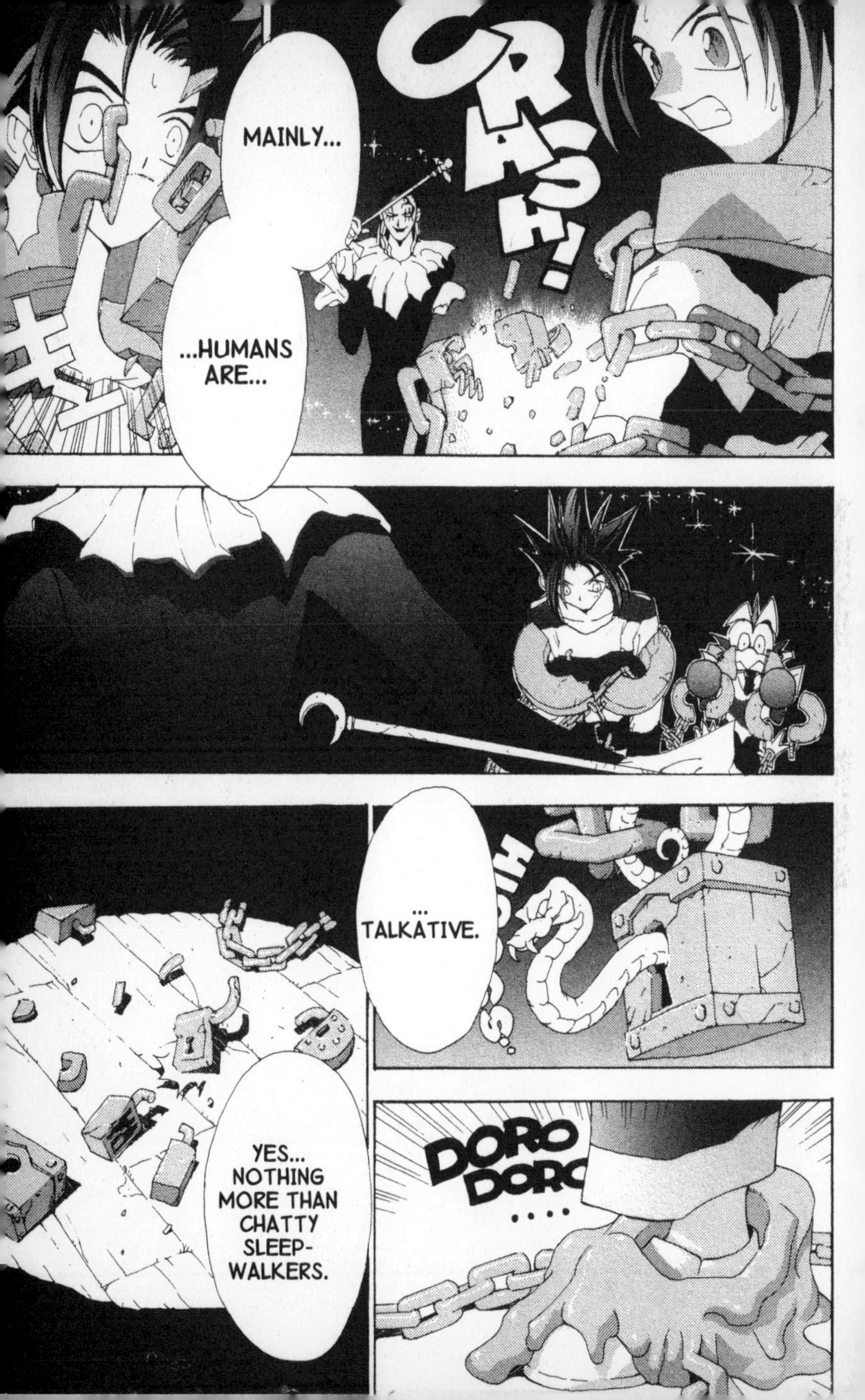
CRASH!
MAINLY...
...HUMANS ARE...
... TALKATIVE.
DORO DORO ....
YES... NOTHING MORE THAN CHATTY SLEEP-WALKERS.

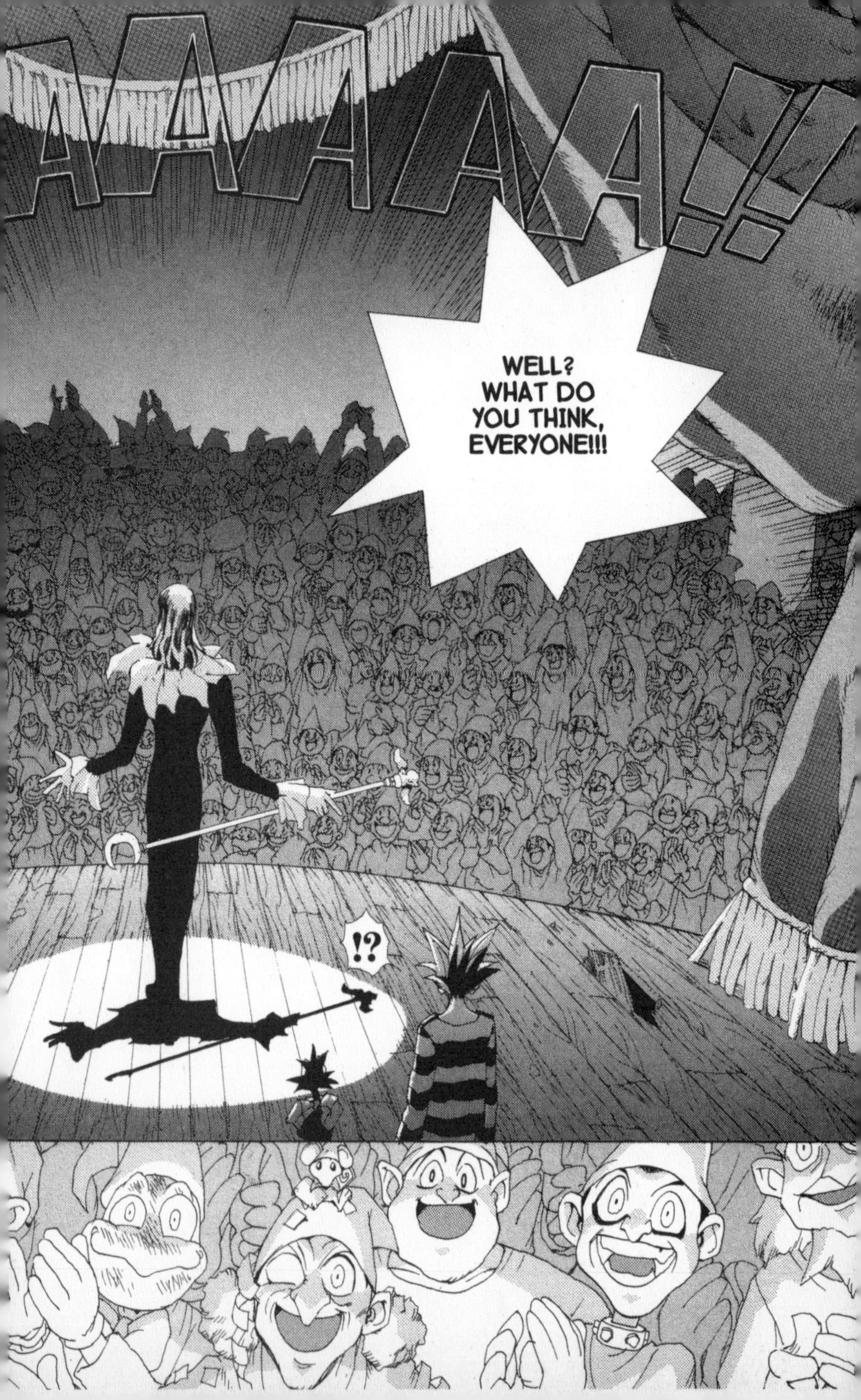
AAAAAA!!!
WELL? WHAT DO YOU THINK, EVERYONE!!!
!?

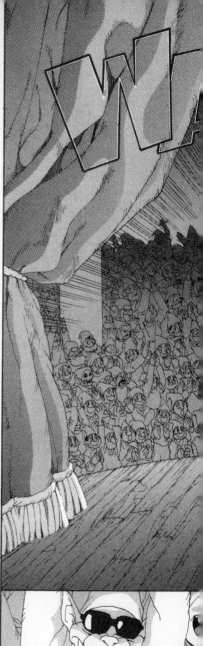

LADIES AND GENTLEMEN-- ONE MORE ROUND OF APPLAUSE FOR THE COURA- GEOUS LAD AND HIS TRUSTY SIDEKICK!!

THEN AGAIN, IT IS SOMETIMES SAID THAT TOO MUCH COURAGE CAN BE A NUISANCE...

...AND THAT EVEN MAGIC TRICKS ARE SOMETIMES EXECUTED IMPERFECTLY...

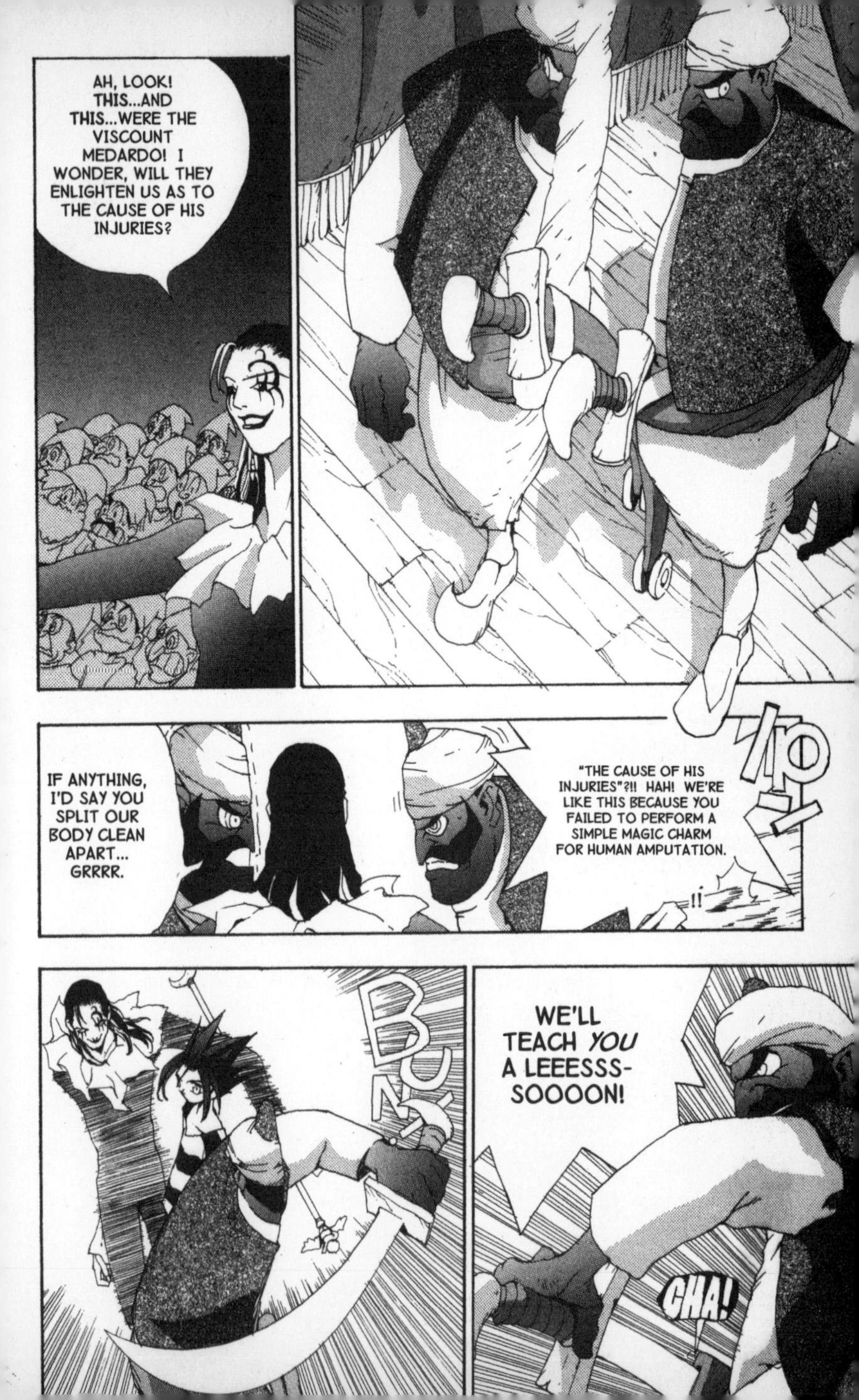
AH, LOOK! THIS...AND THIS...WERE THE VISCOUNT MEDARDO! I WONDER, WILL THEY ENLIGHTEN US AS TO THE CAUSE OF HIS INJURIES?
"THE CAUSE OF HIS INJURIES"?!! HAH! WE'RE LIKE THIS BECAUSE YOU FAILED TO PERFORM A SIMPLE MAGIC CHARM FOR HUMAN AMPUTATION.
!!
IF ANYTHING, I'D SAY YOU SPLIT OUR BODY CLEAN APART... GRRRR.
WE'LL TEACH *YOU* A LEEESSS-SOOOON!
CHA!
BUN

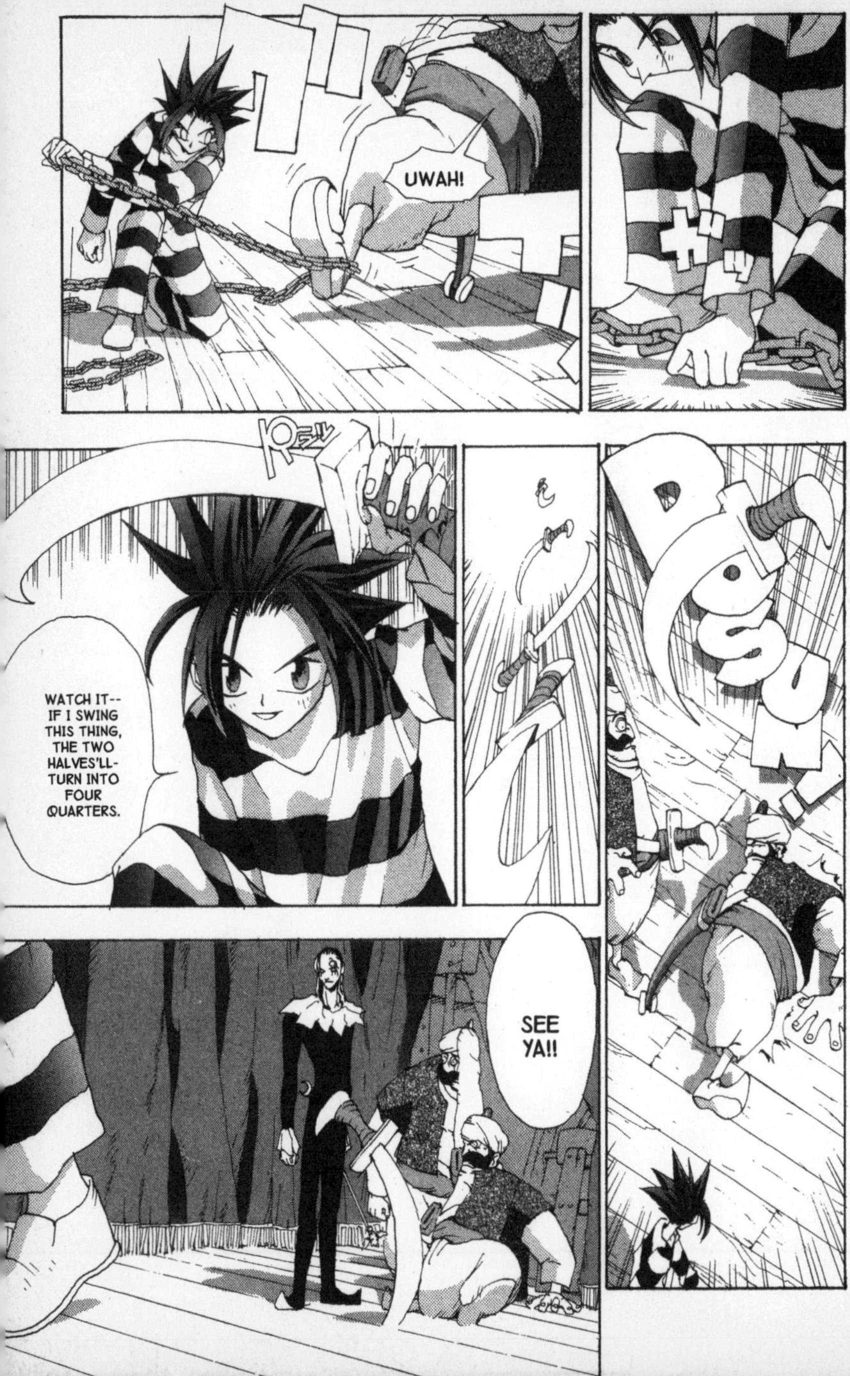
UWAH!
WATCH IT-- IF I SWING THIS THING, THE TWO HALVES'LL-TURN INTO FOUR QUARTERS.
SEE YA!!

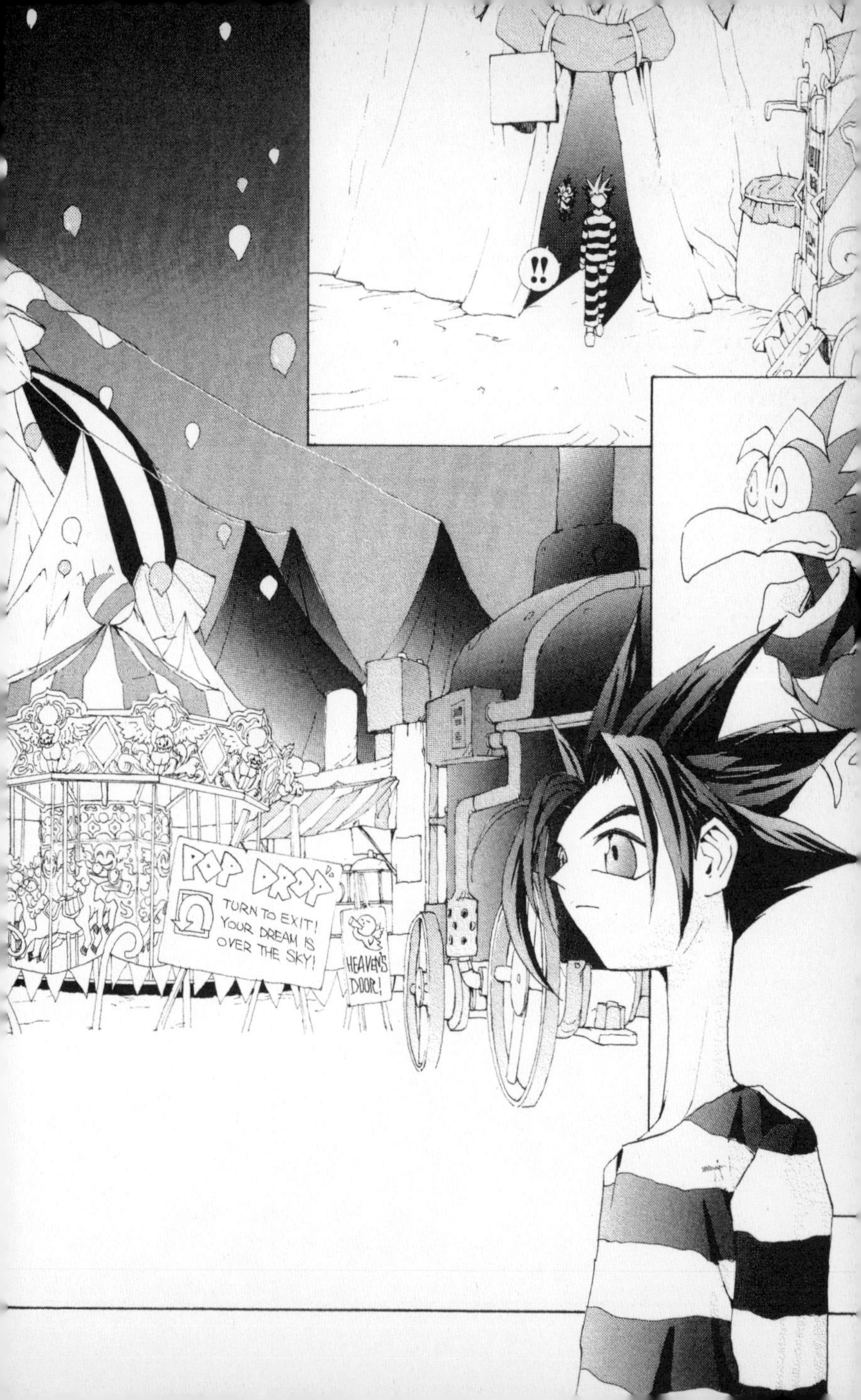
!!
POP DROP
TURN TO EXIT!
YOUR DREAM IS
OVER THE SKY!
HEAVEN'S
DOOR!

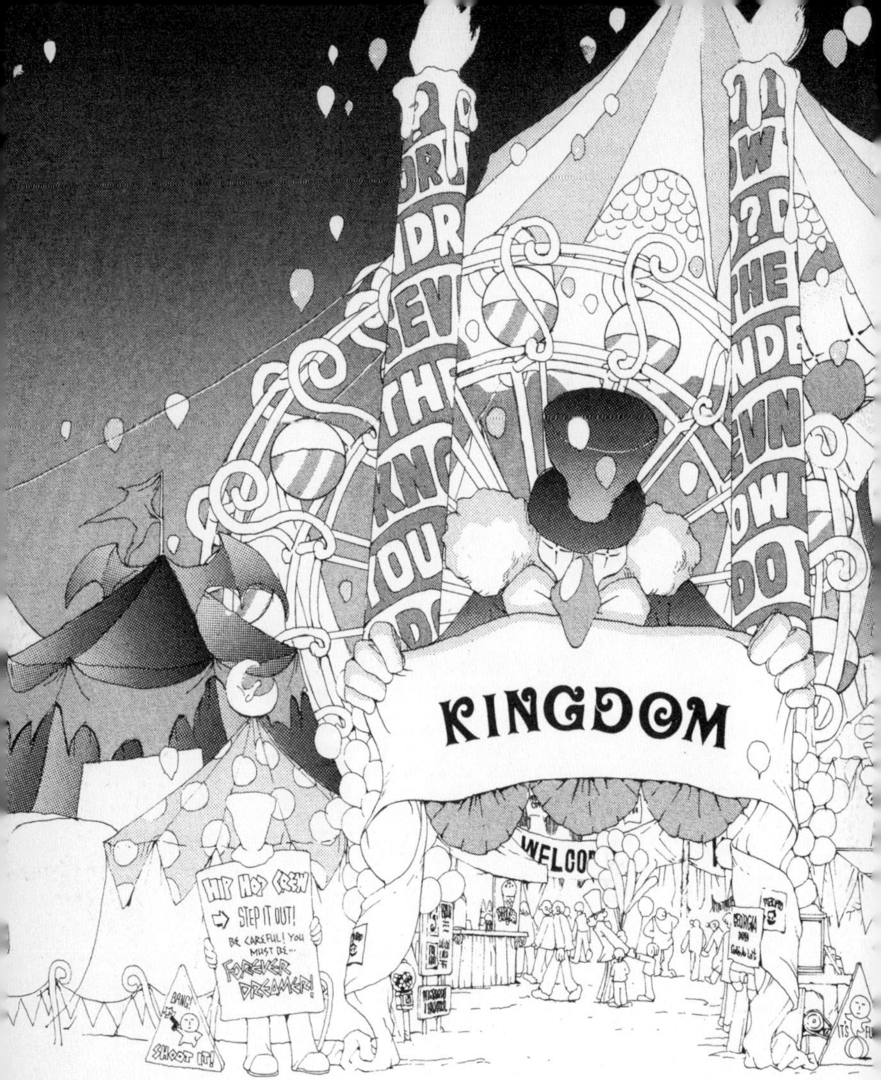
KINGDOM
HIP HOP CREW
STEP IT OUT!
BE CAREFUL! YOU MUST BE...
FOREVER DREAMER!
BANG!
SHOOT IT!

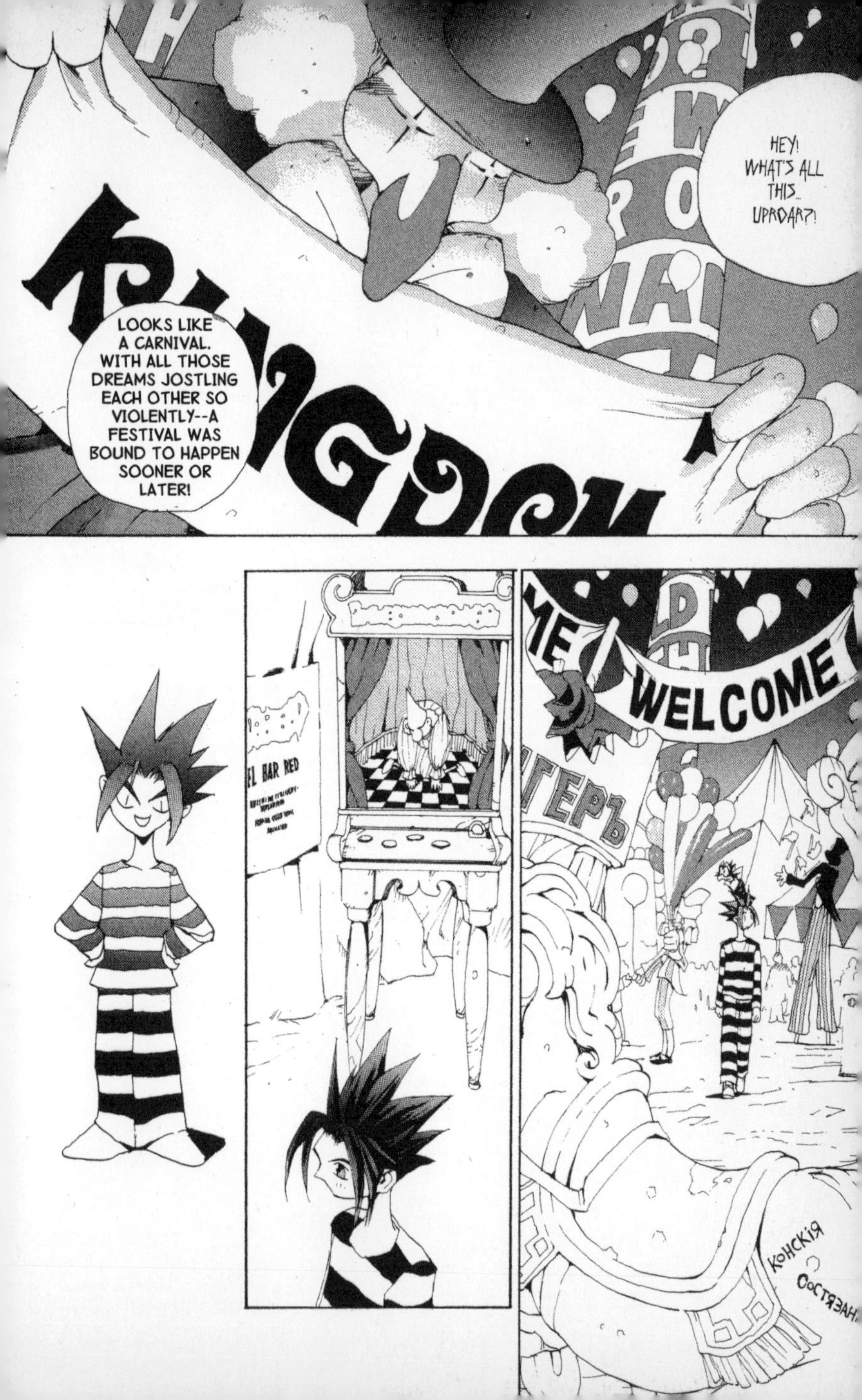
HEY! WHAT'S ALL THIS... UPROAR?!
LOOKS LIKE A CARNIVAL. WITH ALL THOSE DREAMS JOSTLING EACH OTHER SO VIOLENTLY--A FESTIVAL WAS BOUND TO HAPPEN SOONER OR LATER!
WELCOME
КОНСКІЯ

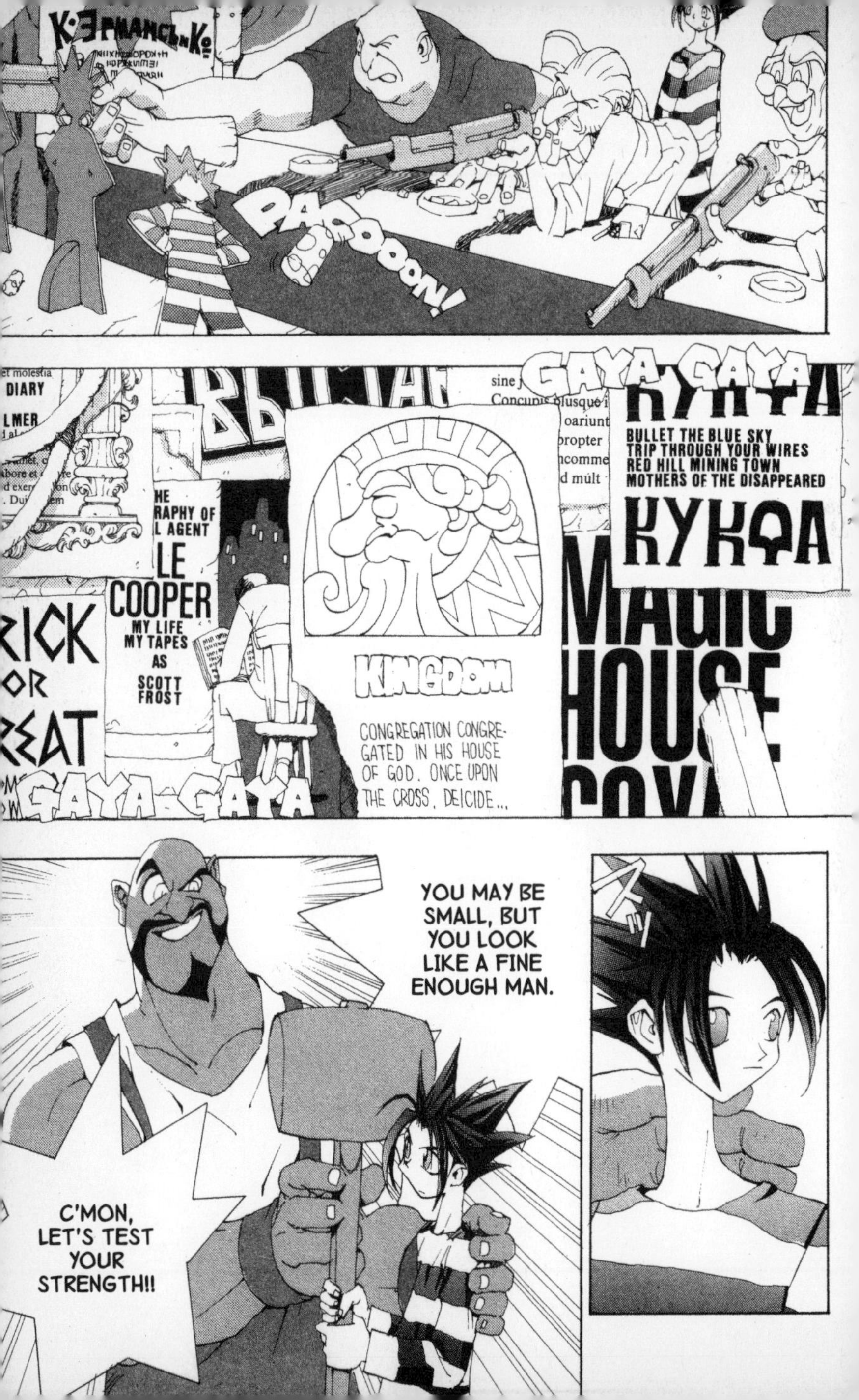
DAGOOOON!
GAYA GAYA
BULLET THE BLUE SKY
TRIP THROUGH YOUR WIRES
RED HILL MINING TOWN
MOTHERS OF THE DISAPPEARED
KYKQA
KINGDOM
CONGREGATION CONGREGATED IN HIS HOUSE OF GOD. ONCE UPON THE CROSS, DEICIDE...
COOPER
MY LIFE
MY TAPES
AS
SCOTT
FROST
DIARY
GAYA-GAYA
YOU MAY BE SMALL, BUT YOU LOOK LIKE A FINE ENOUGH MAN.
C'MON, LET'S TEST YOUR STRENGTH!!

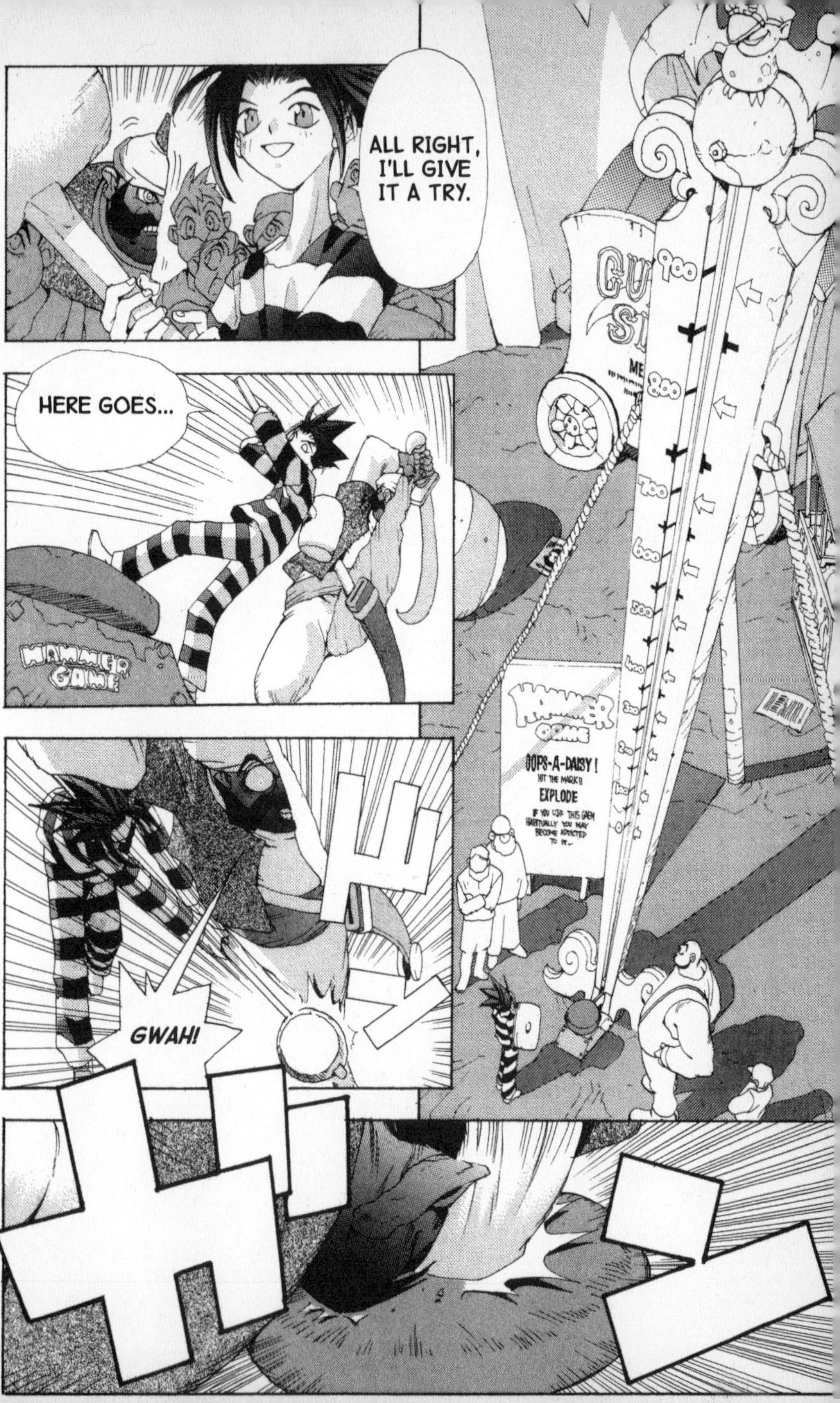
HAMMER GAME
OOPS-A-DAISY!
HIT THE MARK!!
EXPLODE
IF YOU USE THIS GAEM HABITUALLY YOU MAY BECOME ADDICTED TO IT...
ALL RIGHT, I'LL GIVE IT A TRY.
HERE GOES...
HAMMER GAME
GWAH!

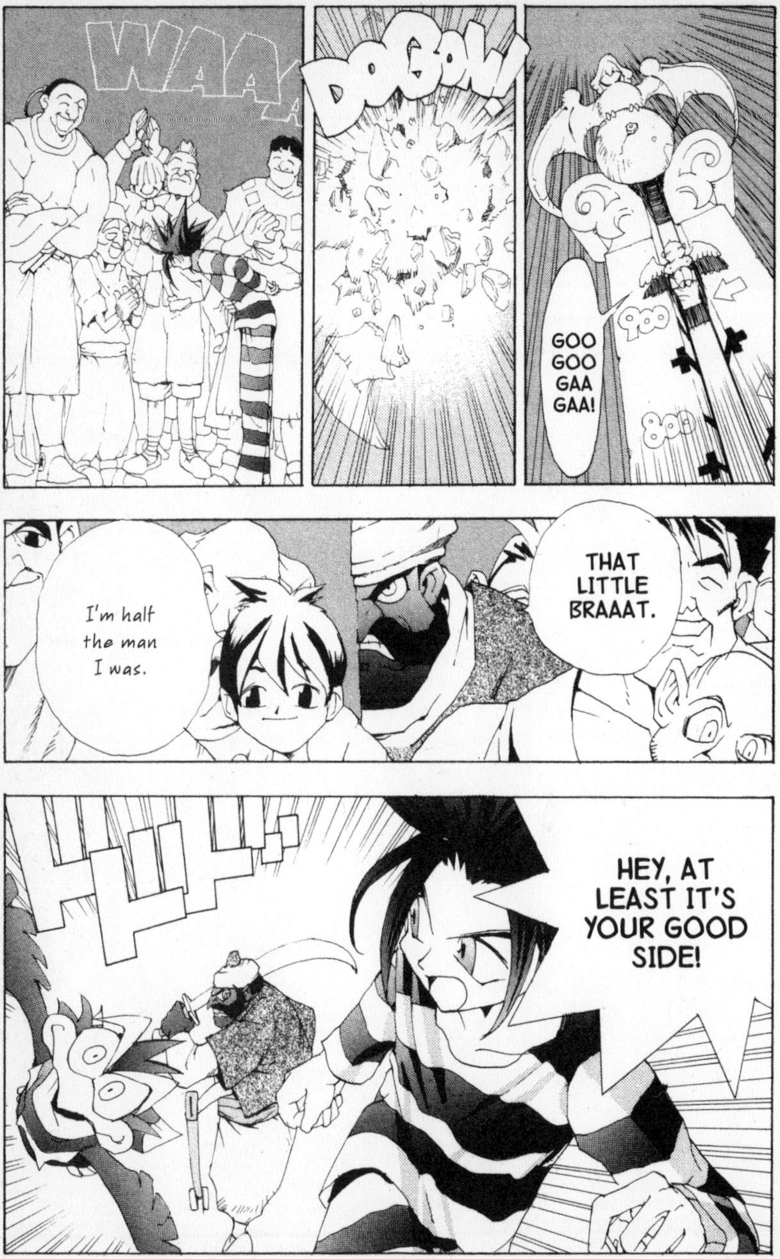
GOO GOO GAA GAA!
DOGOW!
WAA
THAT LITTLE BRAAAT.
I'm half the man I was.
HEY, AT LEAST IT'S YOUR GOOD SIDE!

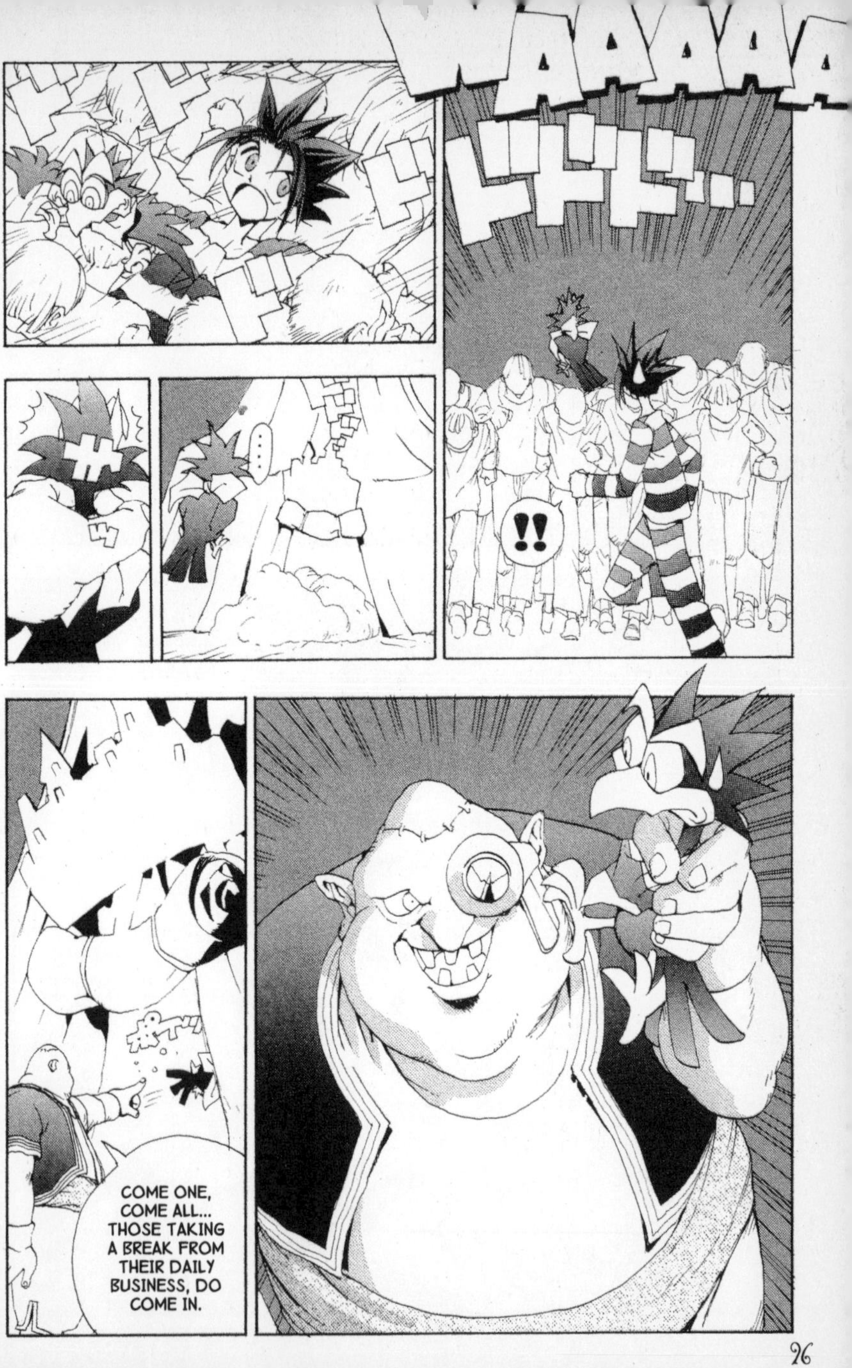
!!
COME ONE, COME ALL... THOSE TAKING A BREAK FROM THEIR DAILY BUSINESS, DO COME IN.

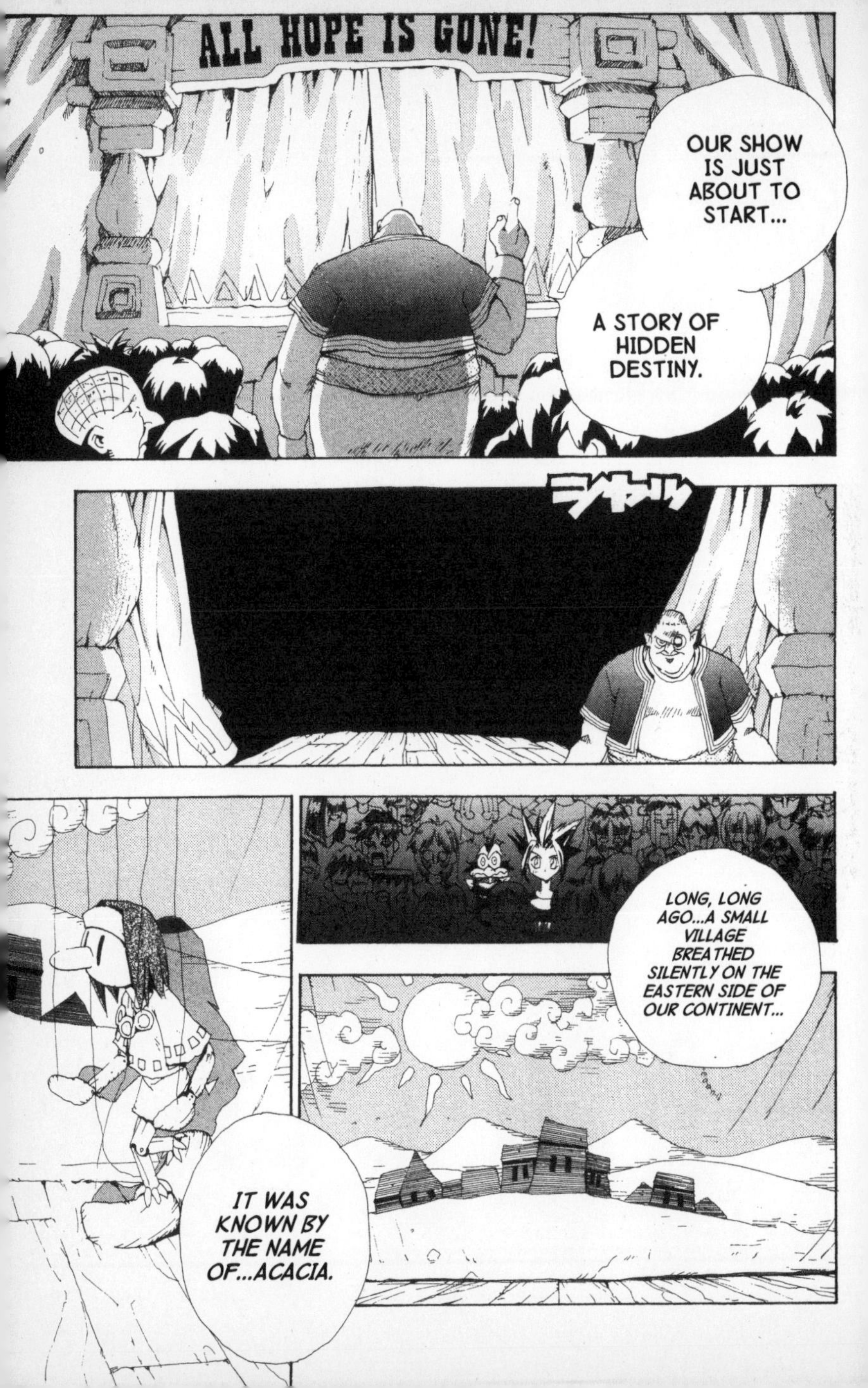
ALL HOPE IS GONE!
OUR SHOW IS JUST ABOUT TO START...
A STORY OF HIDDEN DESTINY.
LONG, LONG AGO...A SMALL VILLAGE BREATHED SILENTLY ON THE EASTERN SIDE OF OUR CONTINENT...
IT WAS KNOWN BY THE NAME OF...ACACIA.

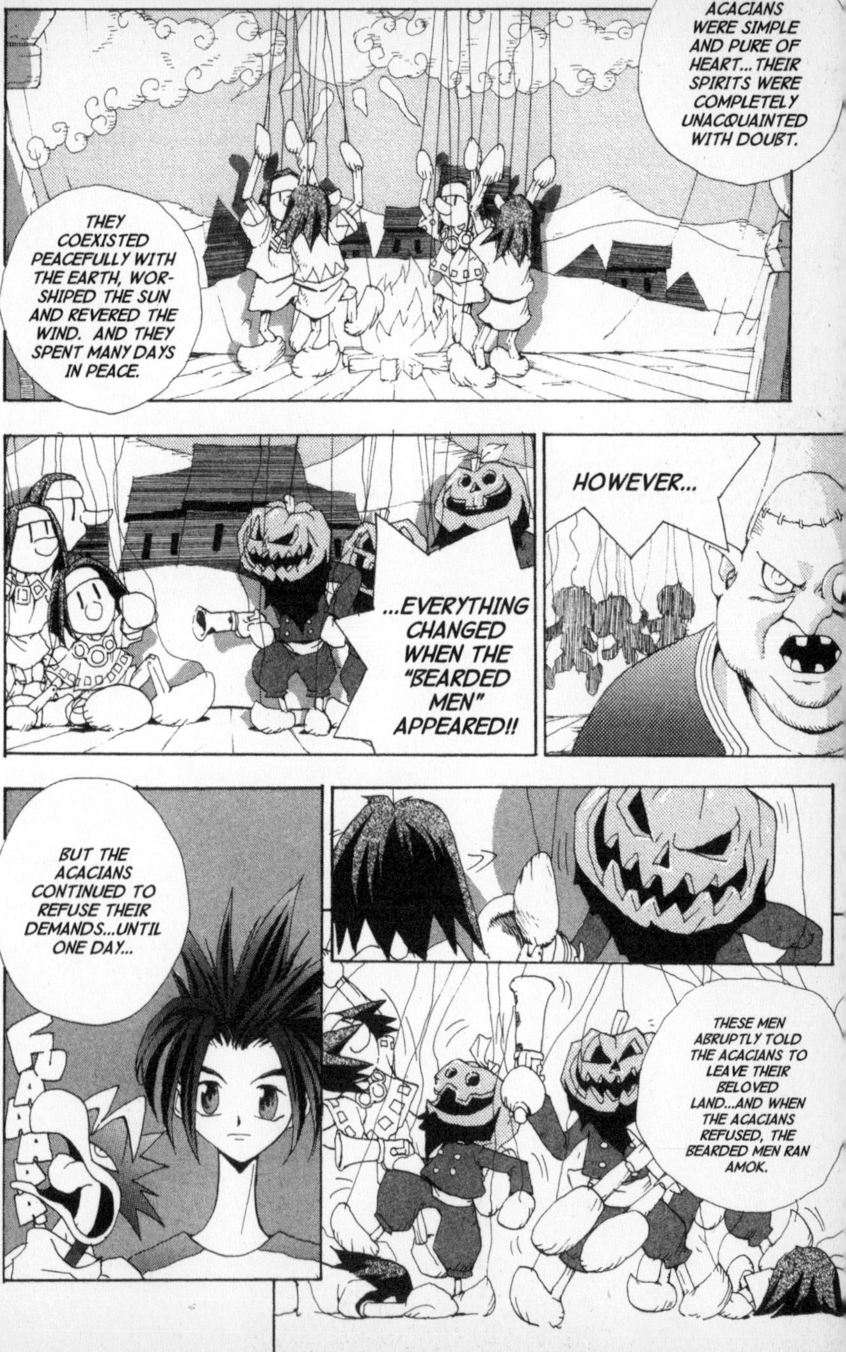

THE ACACIANS WERE SIMPLE AND PURE OF HEART...THEIR SPIRITS WERE COMPLETELY UNACQUAINTED WITH DOUBT.
THEY COEXISTED PEACEFULLY WITH THE EARTH, WOR-SHIPED THE SUN AND REVERED THE WIND. AND THEY SPENT MANY DAYS IN PEACE.
HOWEVER...
...EVERYTHING CHANGED WHEN THE "BEARDED MEN" APPEARED!!
THESE MEN ABRUPTLY TOLD THE ACACIANS TO LEAVE THEIR BELOVED LAND...AND WHEN THE ACACIANS REFUSED, THE BEARDED MEN RAN AMOK.
BUT THE ACACIANS CONTINUED TO REFUSE THEIR DEMANDS...UNTIL ONE DAY...

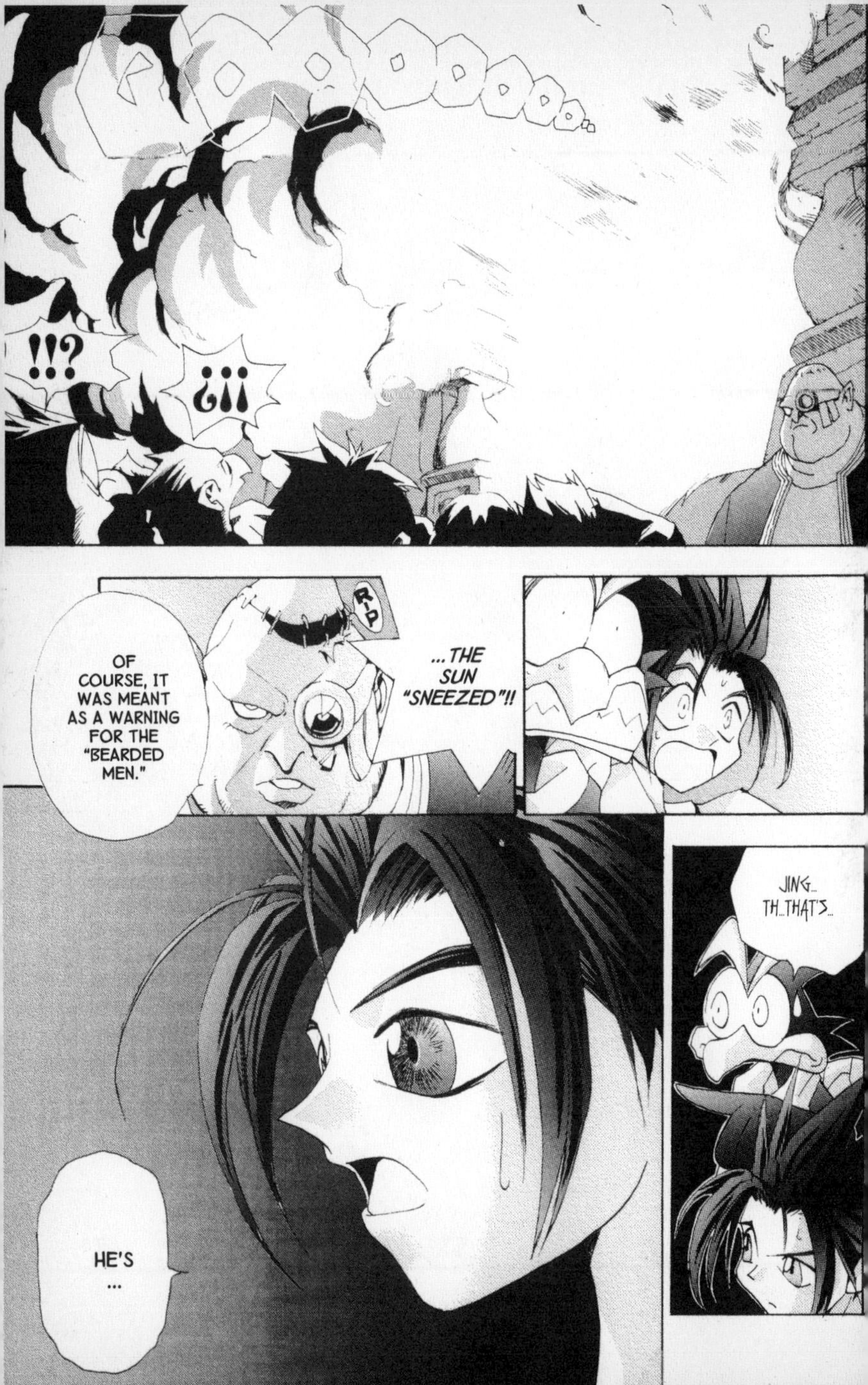
POOOOOOOO..
¿¡¡
!!?
RIP
...THE SUN "SNEEZED"!!
OF COURSE, IT WAS MEANT AS A WARNING FOR THE "BEARDED MEN."
JING... TH...THAT'S...
HE'S ...

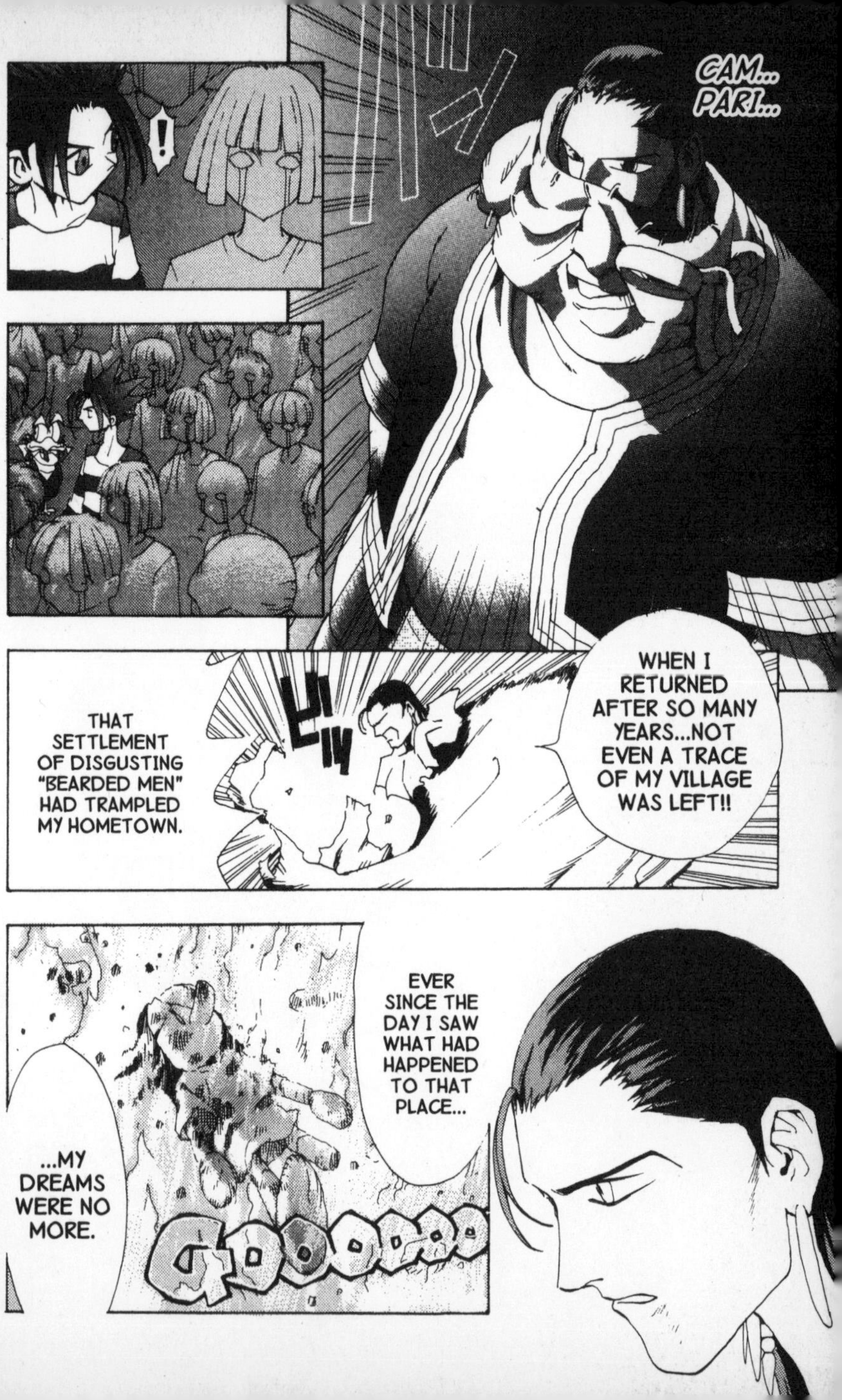
CAM... PARI...
!
WHEN I RETURNED AFTER SO MANY YEARS...NOT EVEN A TRACE OF MY VILLAGE WAS LEFT!!
THAT SETTLEMENT OF DISGUSTING "BEARDED MEN" HAD TRAMPLED MY HOMETOWN.
EVER SINCE THE DAY I SAW WHAT HAD HAPPENED TO THAT PLACE...
...MY DREAMS WERE NO MORE.

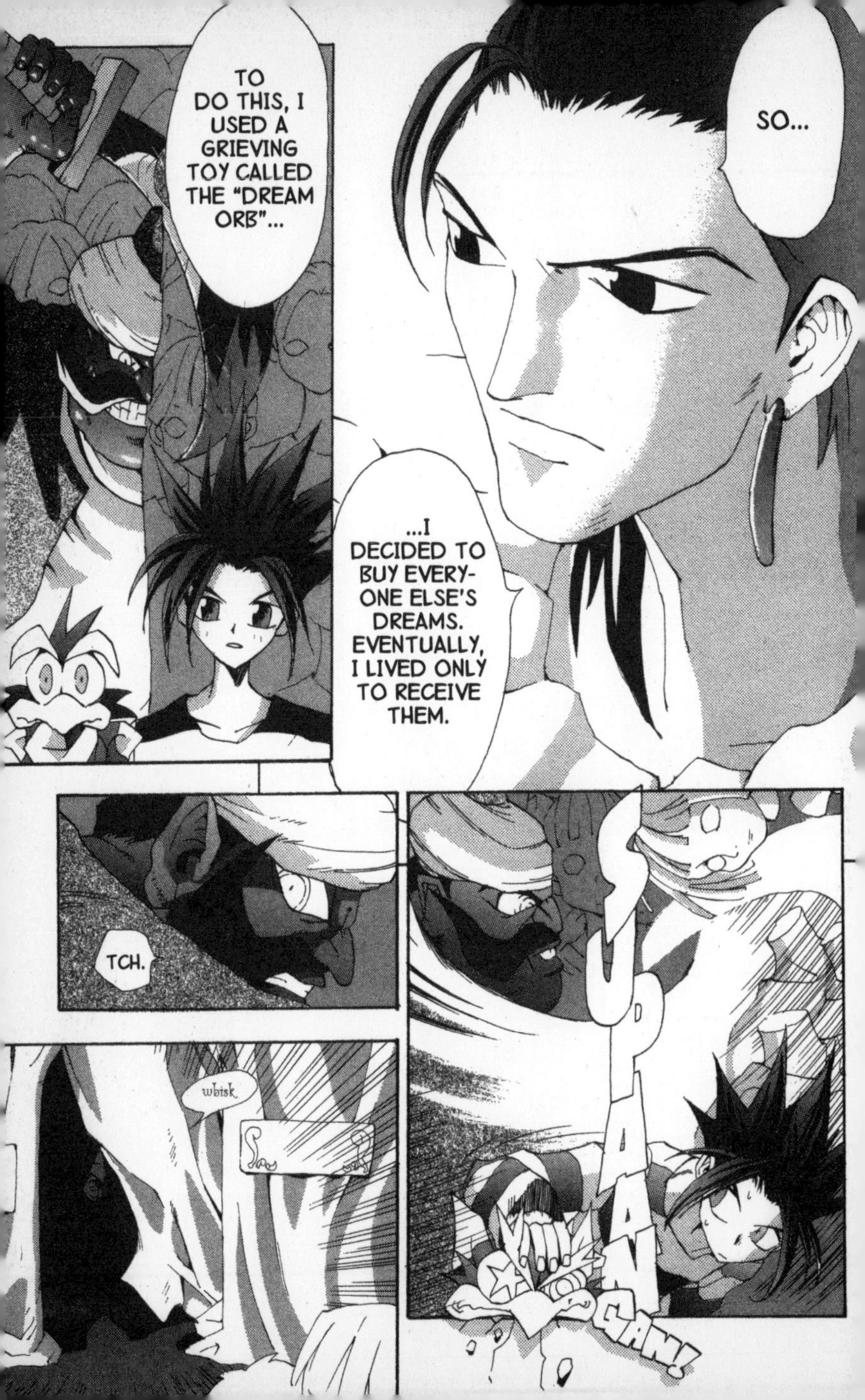
SO...
...I DECIDED TO BUY EVERY-ONE ELSE'S DREAMS. EVENTUALLY, I LIVED ONLY TO RECEIVE THEM.
TO DO THIS, I USED A GRIEVING TOY CALLED THE "DREAM ORB"...
GAN!
TCH.
whisk

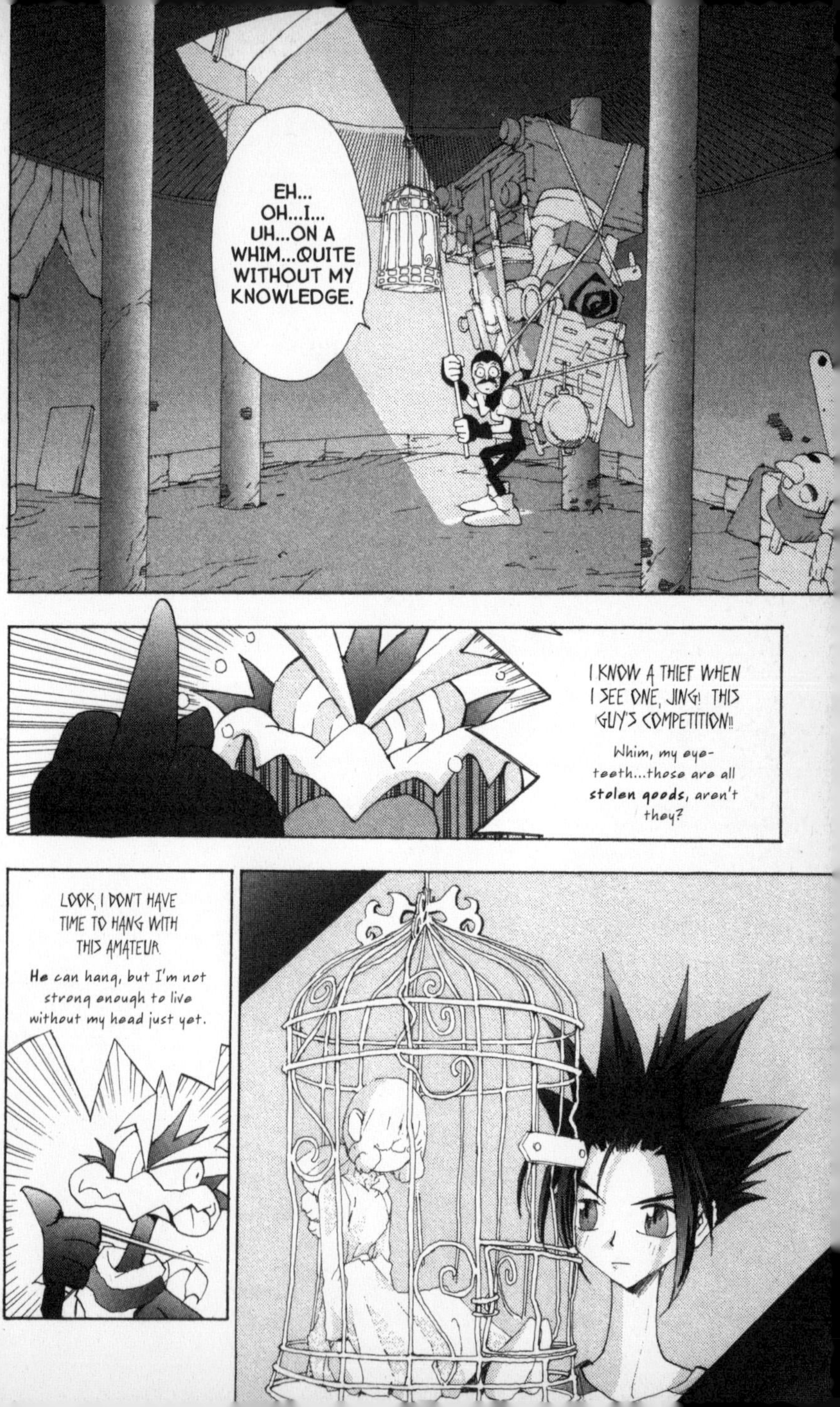
EH... OH...I... UH...ON A WHIM...QUITE WITHOUT MY KNOWLEDGE.
I KNOW A THIEF WHEN I SEE ONE, JING! THIS GUY'S COMPETITION!!
Whim, my eye-teeth...those are all stolen goods, aren't they?
LOOK, I DON'T HAVE TIME TO HANG WITH THIS AMATEUR.
He can hang, but I'm not strong enough to live without my head just yet.

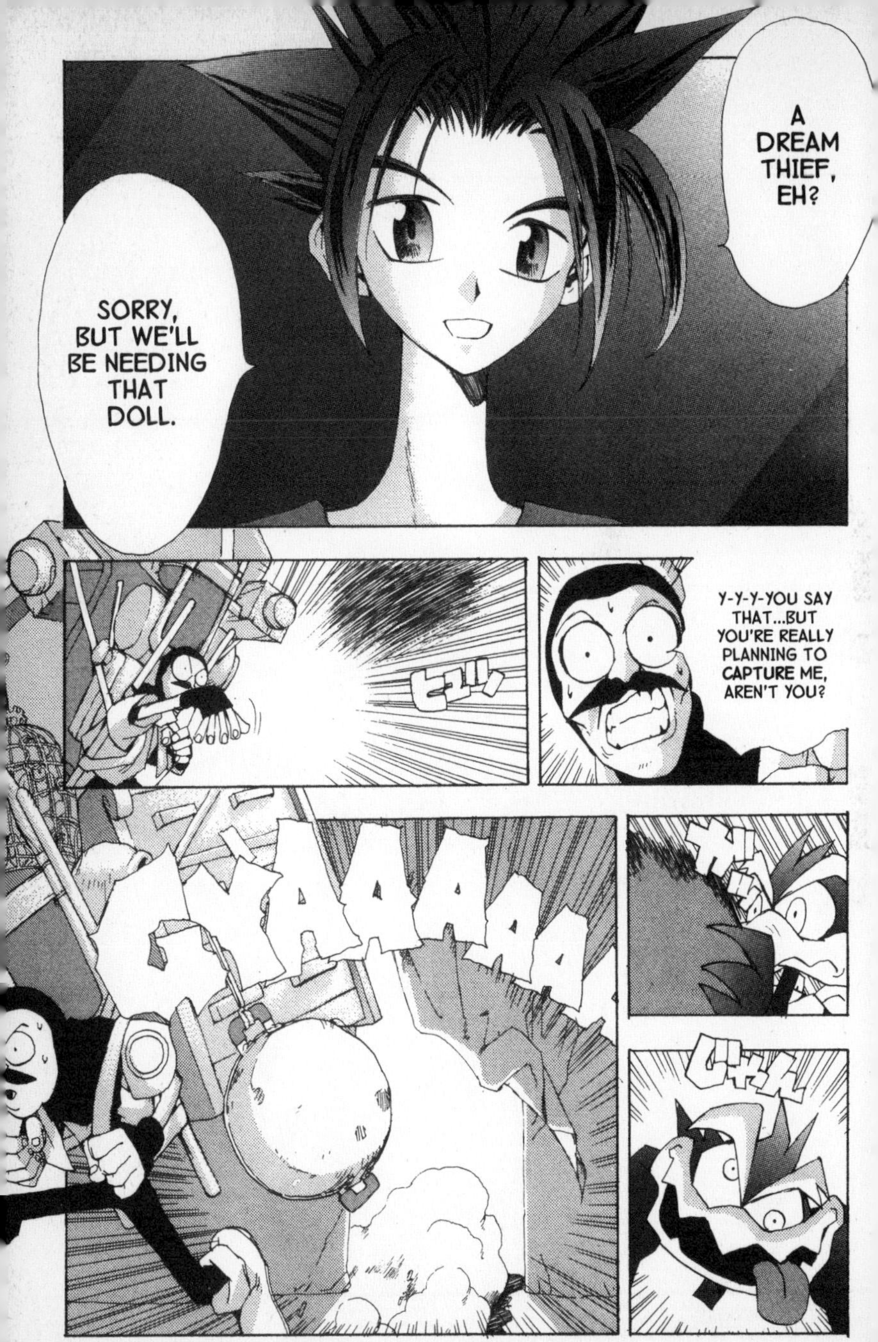
A DREAM THIEF, EH?
SORRY, BUT WE'LL BE NEEDING THAT DOLL.
Y-Y-Y-YOU SAY THAT...BUT YOU'RE REALLY PLANNING TO CAPTURE ME, AREN'T YOU?
YAAAAA

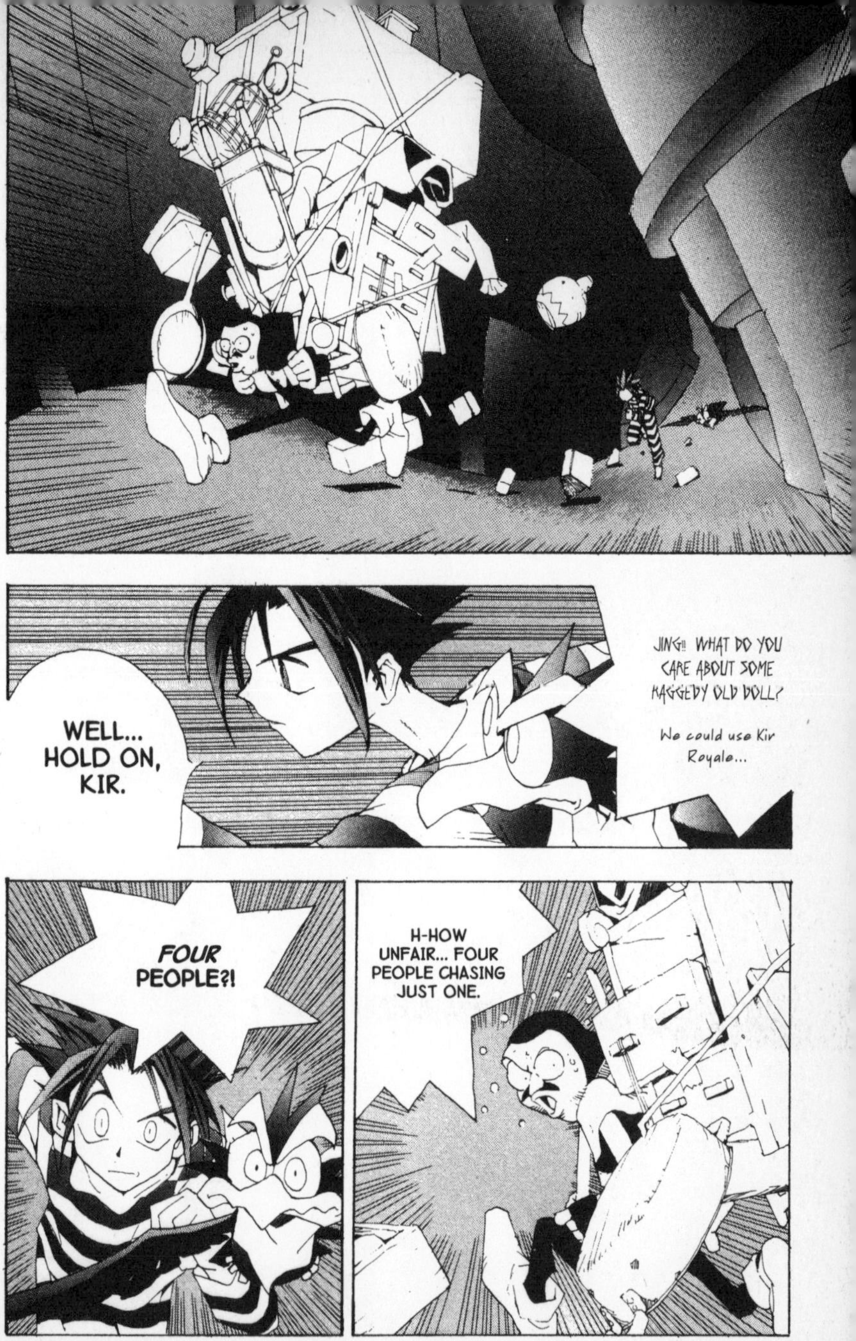
JING!! WHAT DO YOU CARE ABOUT SOME RAGGEDY OLD DOLL?
We could use Kir Royale...
WELL... HOLD ON, KIR.
H-HOW UNFAIR... FOUR PEOPLE CHASING JUST ONE.
FOUR PEOPLE?!

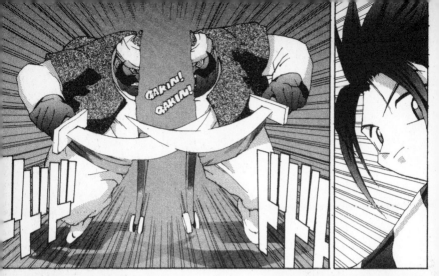

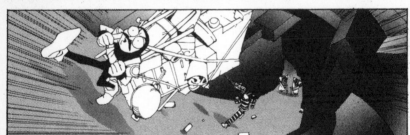

HE'S GETTING AWAY! I'M GOING AFTER HIM.

WHERE ARE YOU GOING, EXACTLY?!?!?!

P-P-PARDON MEEEEEE!!

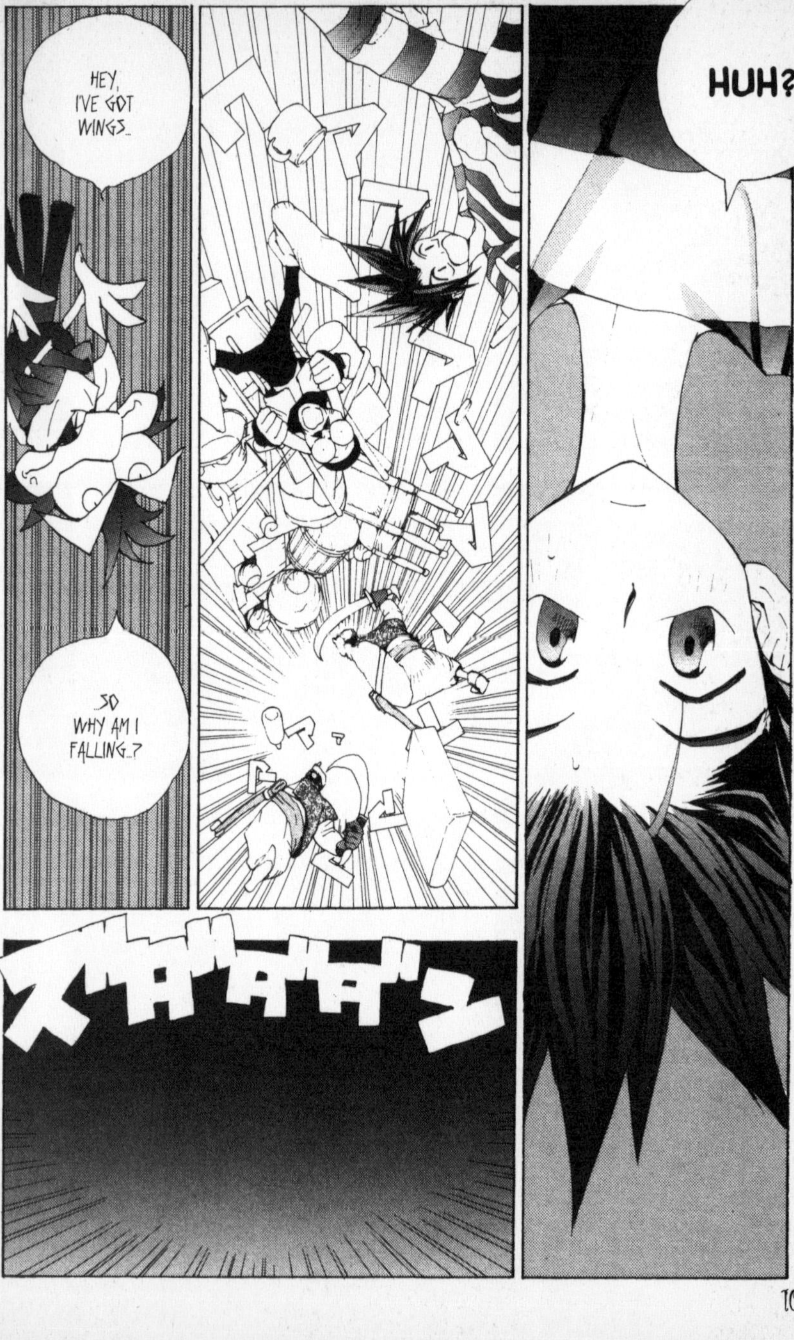

HUH?!
HEY, I'VE GOT WINGS...
...SO WHY AM I FALLING...?

WAAAHH!

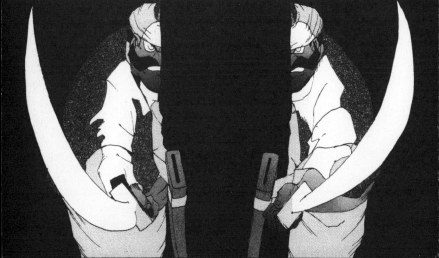

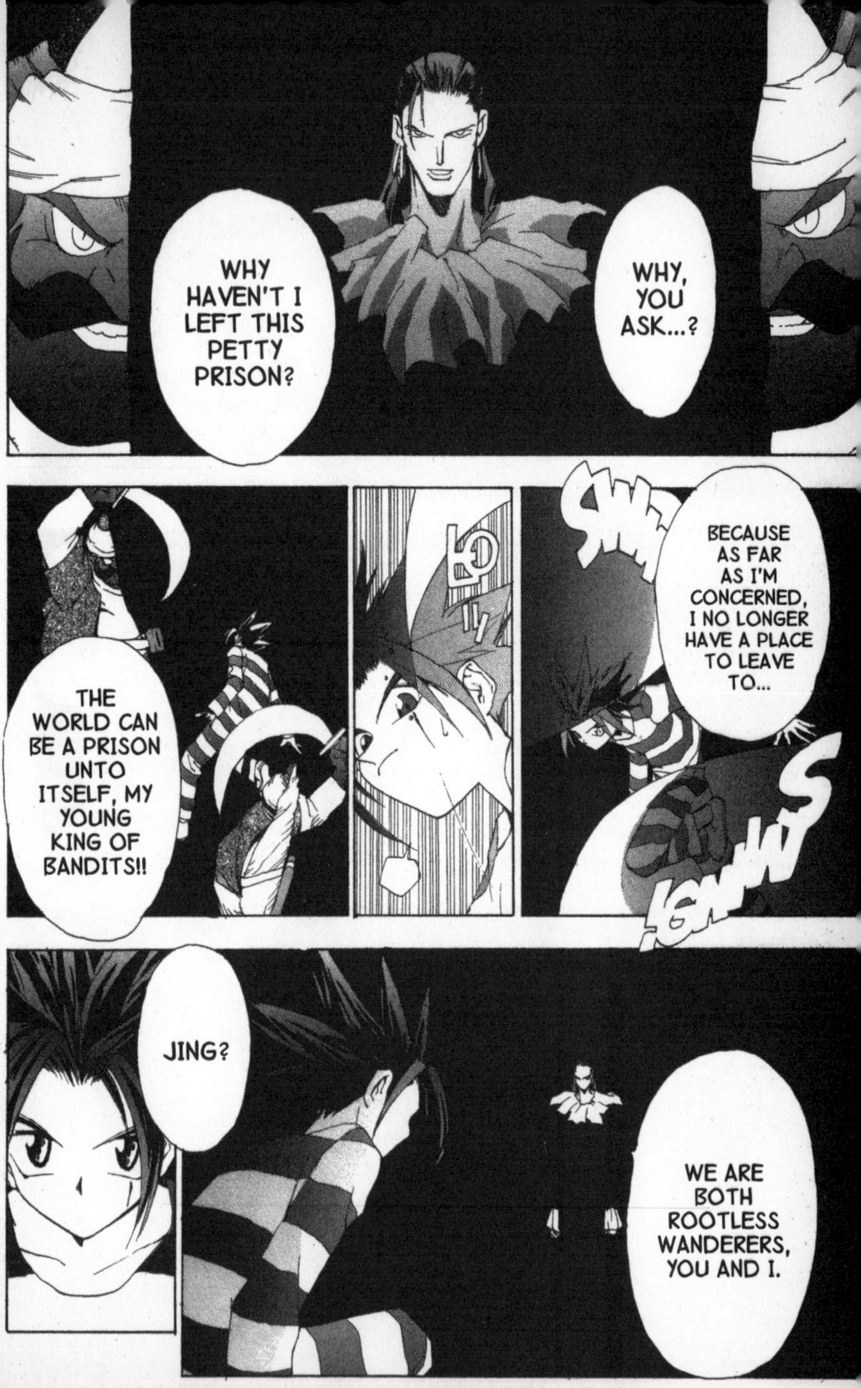
WHY HAVEN'T I LEFT THIS PETTY PRISON?
WHY, YOU ASK...?
BECAUSE AS FAR AS I'M CONCERNED, I NO LONGER HAVE A PLACE TO LEAVE TO...
THE WORLD CAN BE A PRISON UNTO ITSELF, MY YOUNG KING OF BANDITS!!
WE ARE BOTH ROOTLESS WANDERERS, YOU AND I.
JING?

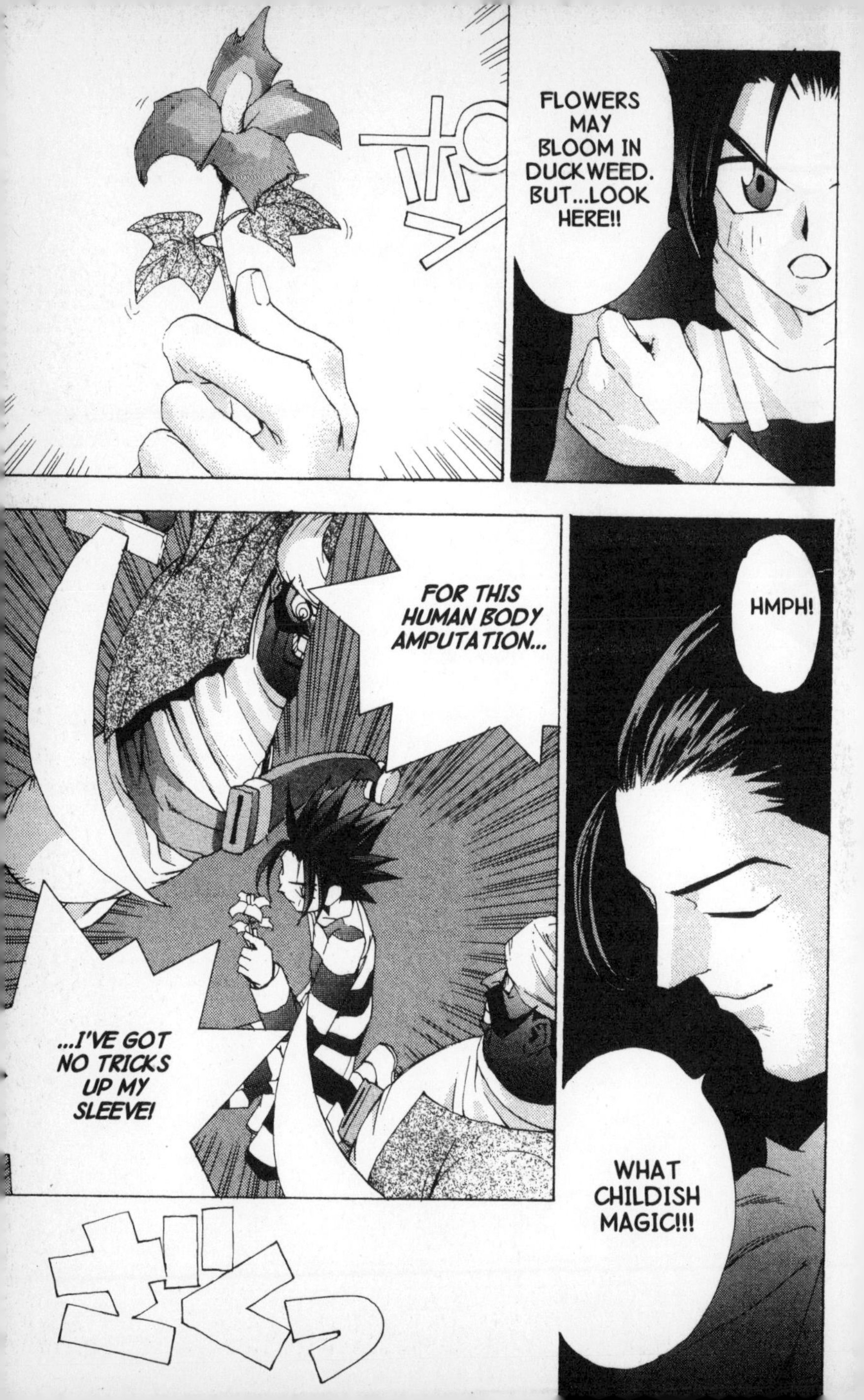
FLOWERS MAY BLOOM IN DUCKWEED. BUT...LOOK HERE!!
HMPH!
WHAT CHILDISH MAGIC!!!
FOR THIS HUMAN BODY AMPUTATION...
...I'VE GOT NO TRICKS UP MY SLEEVE!

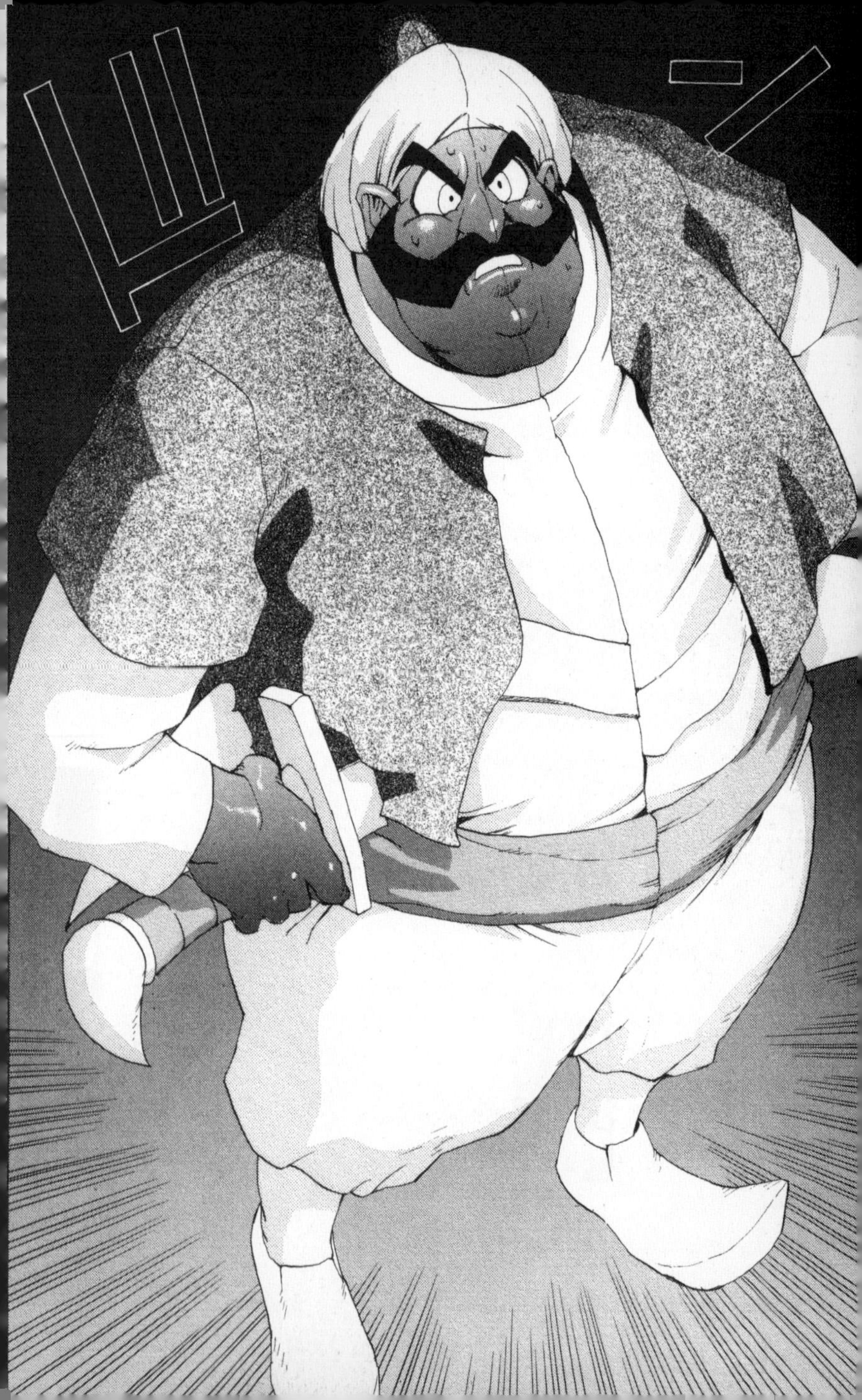

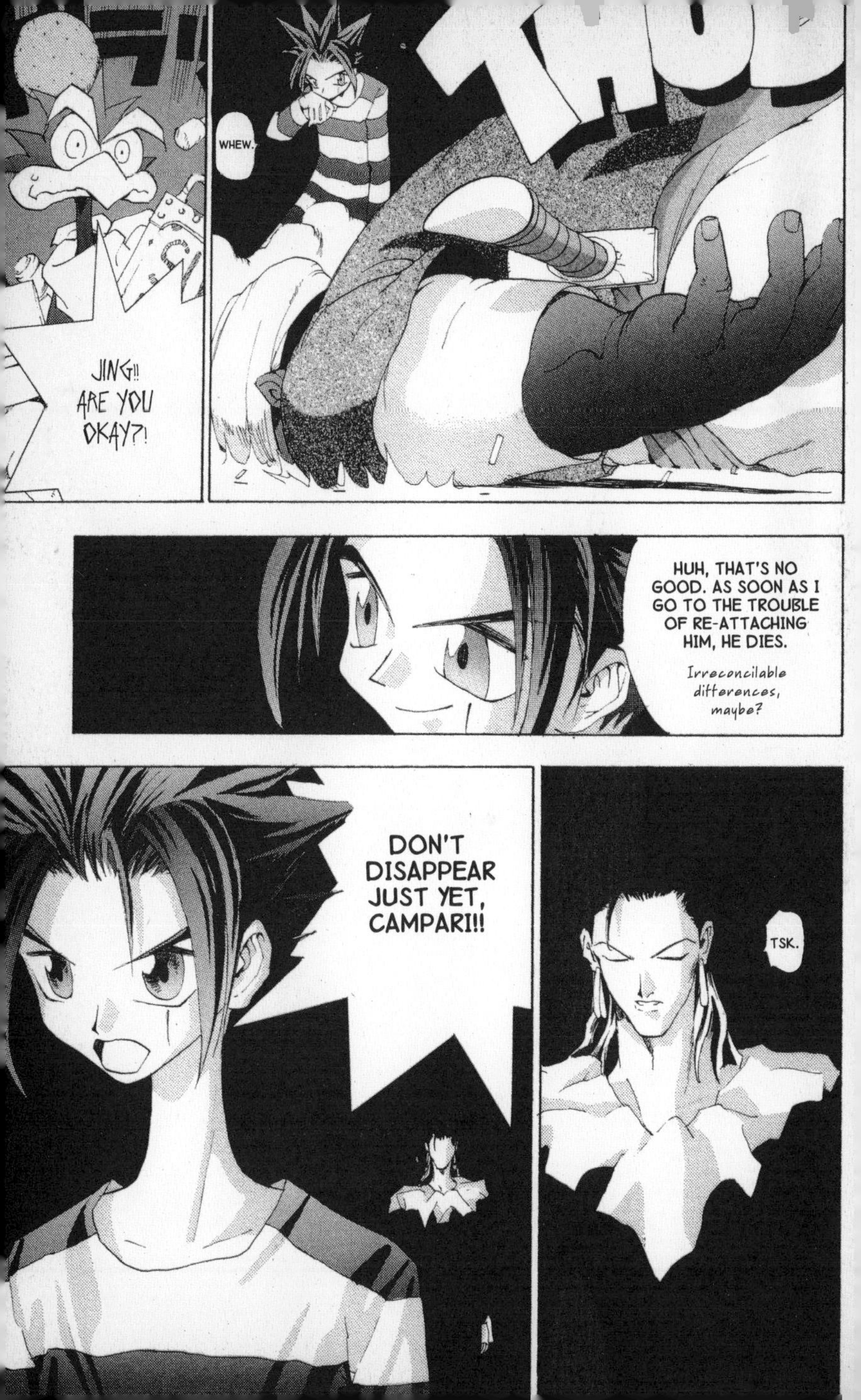
WHEW.
JING!! ARE YOU OKAY?!
HUH, THAT'S NO GOOD. AS SOON AS I GO TO THE TROUBLE OF RE-ATTACHING HIM, HE DIES.
Irreconcilable differences, maybe?
TSK.
DON'T DISAPPEAR JUST YET, CAMPARI!!

OH...
AND...

WAIT TILL YOU SEE MY MAGIC... THEN DECIDE!!

GARA GARA

AND ...NOTHING.

HEY, JING...CAN YOU ACTUALLY DO MAGIC?

MMM.

Estimado lector:
Le quedamos muy
agradecidos por adquirir
este libro el cual
deseamos responda
completamente a sus
necesidades.
Si desea recibir el
catálogo gratuitamente,
por favor rellene sus
personales e indique sus
temas de catálogos en
su interés.

Dear reader:
Thank you for buying this
book. We hope it answers
your convenience.
If you wish to receive a
free copy of our catalog,
please fill out your
personal and
indicate your
think....

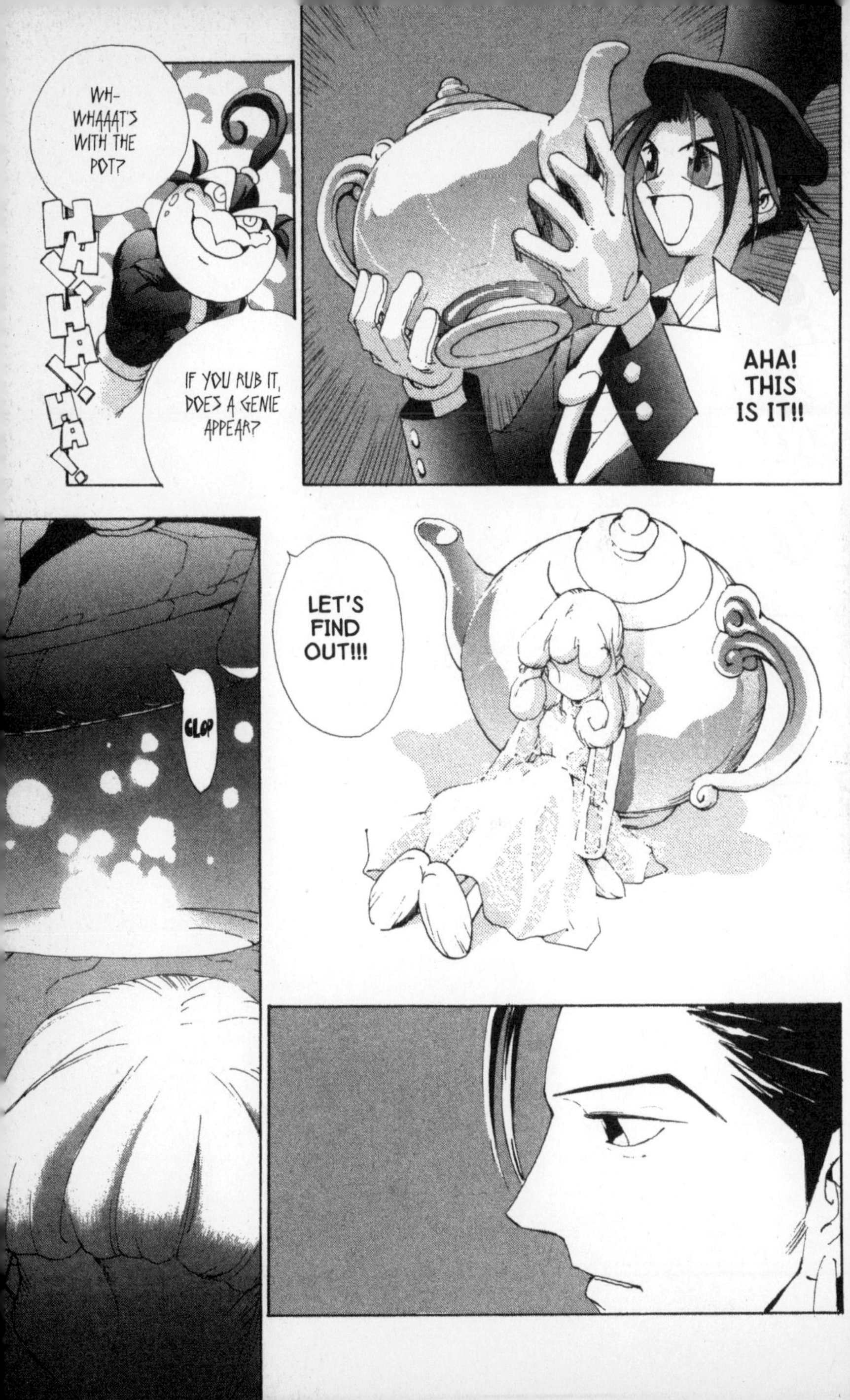
AHA! THIS IS IT!!
WH- WHAAAT'S WITH THE POT?
HA! HA! HA!
IF YOU RUB IT, DOES A GENIE APPEAR?
LET'S FIND OUT!!!
GLOP

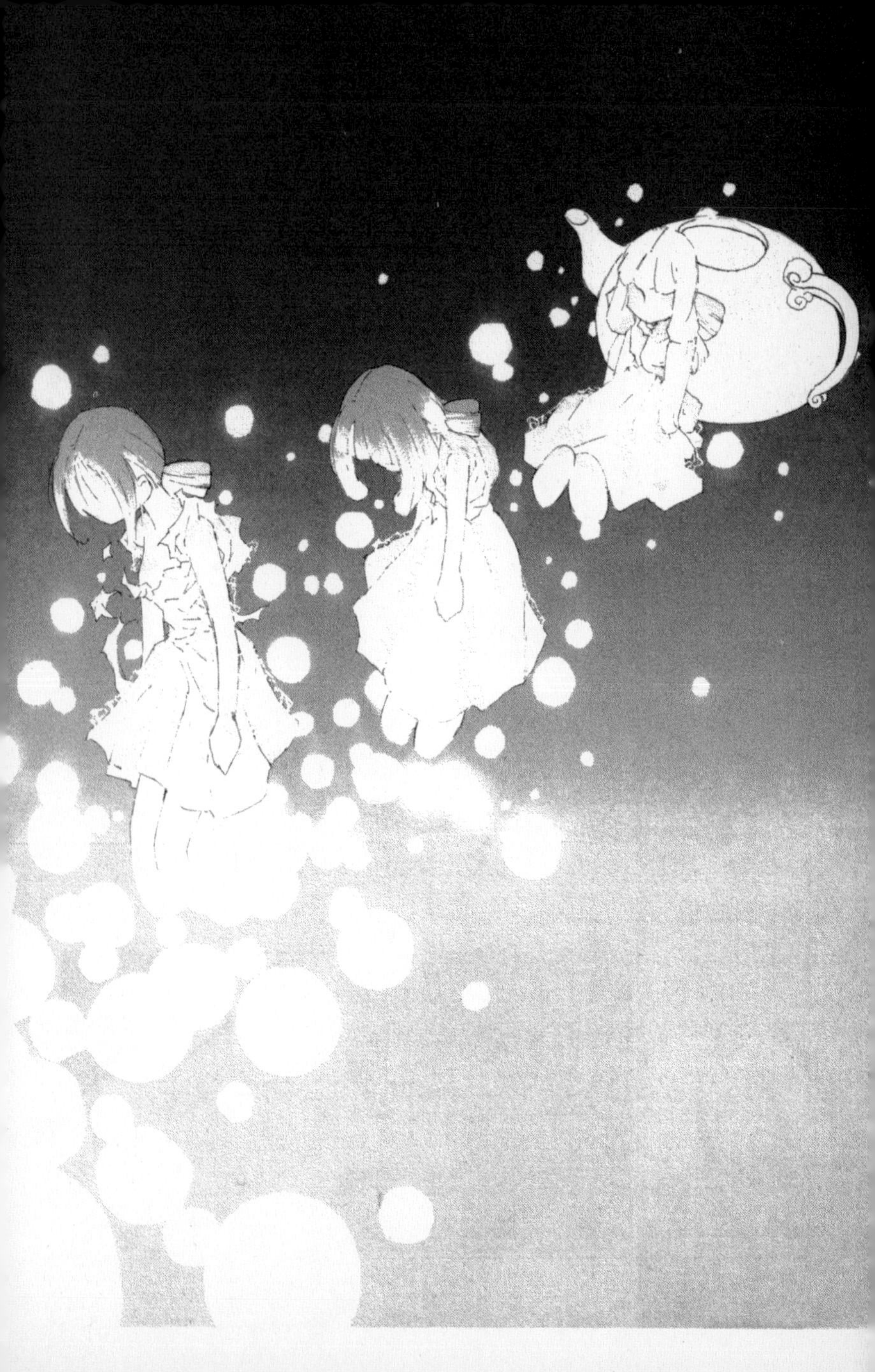

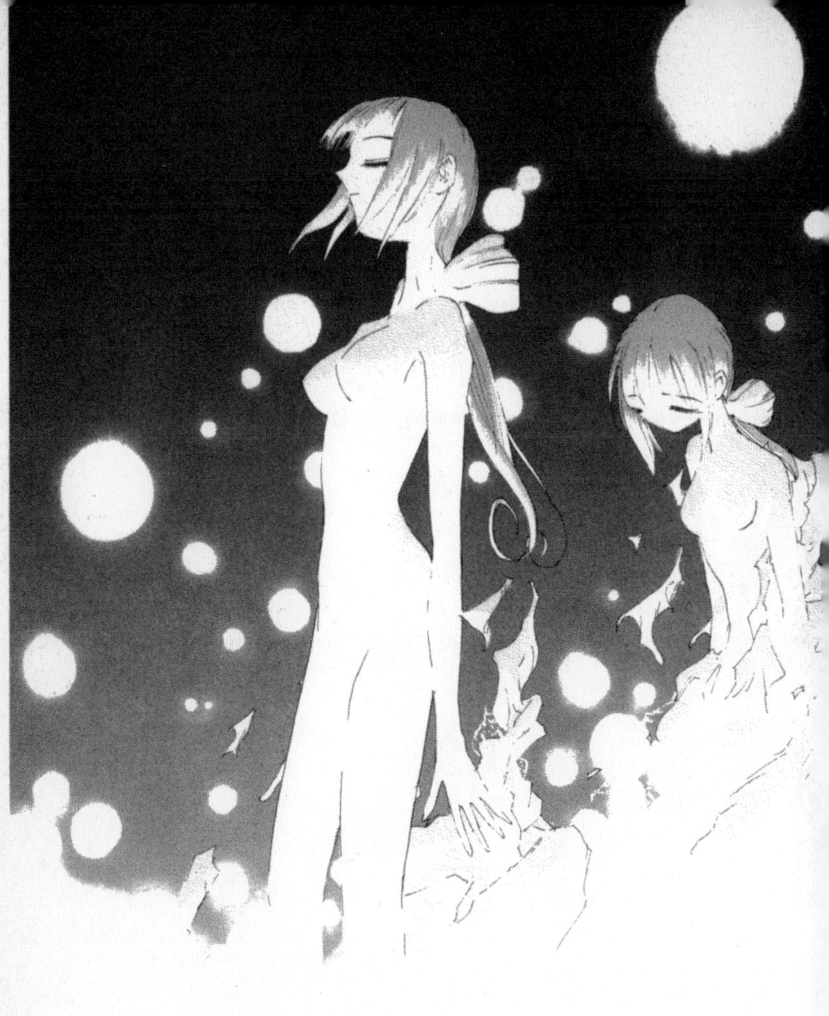

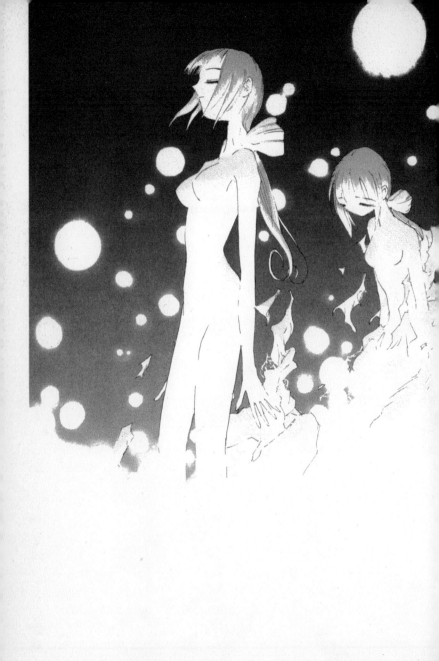

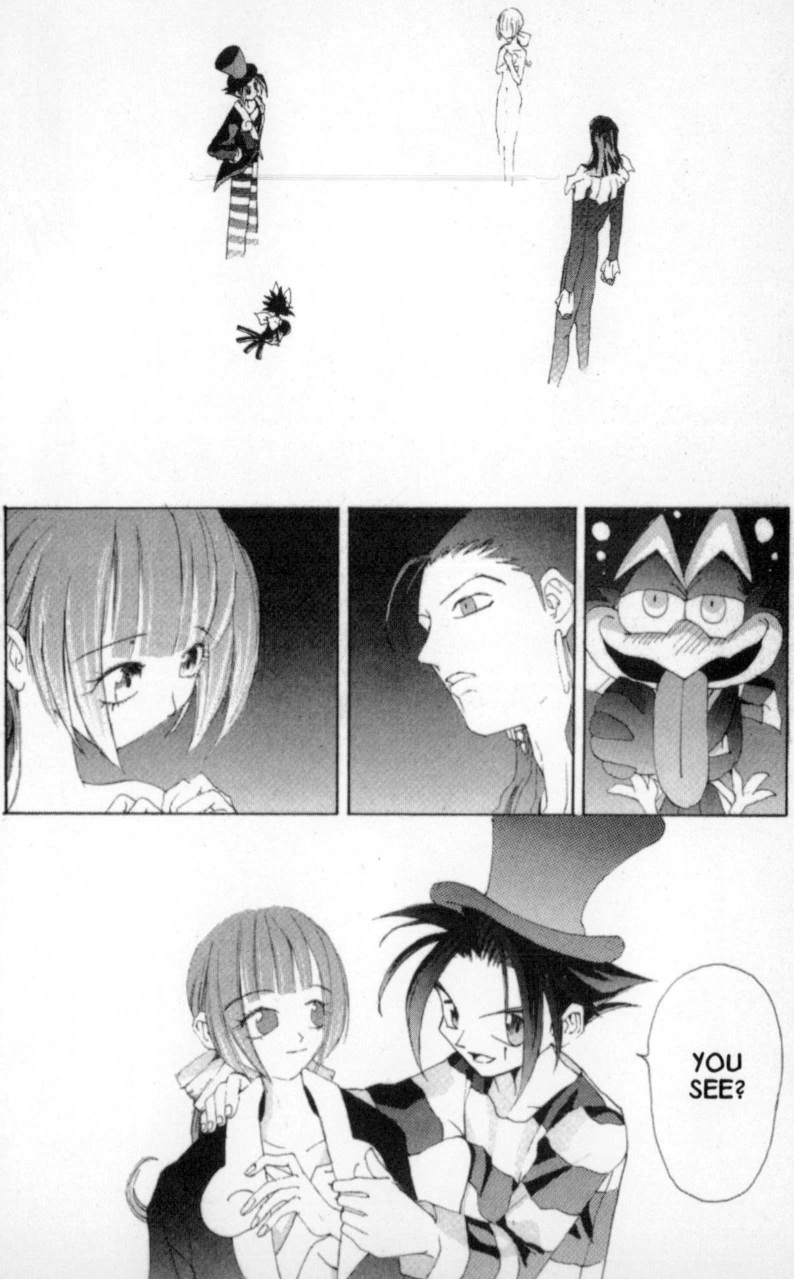
YOU
SEE?

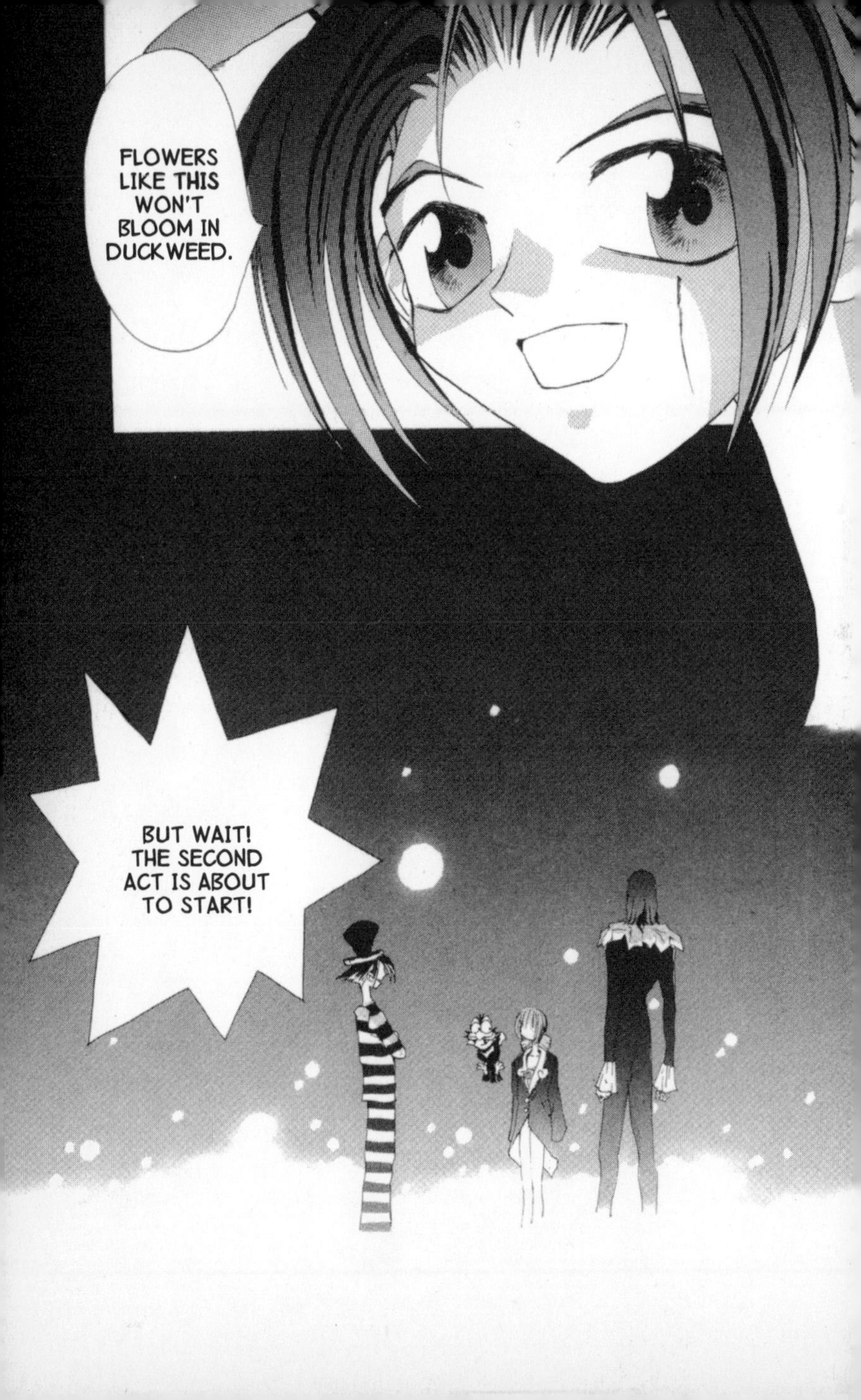
FLOWERS LIKE THIS WON'T BLOOM IN DUCKWEED.
BUT WAIT! THE SECOND ACT IS ABOUT TO START!

O Children sown from fertile soil,
With your Acacian eyes so blue...
No wonder that the sky above
Is always there within your view!
To stumble with eyes looking down
Is just an ordinary trip,
But while you're looking at the stars
It's such a graceful, wondrous slip!

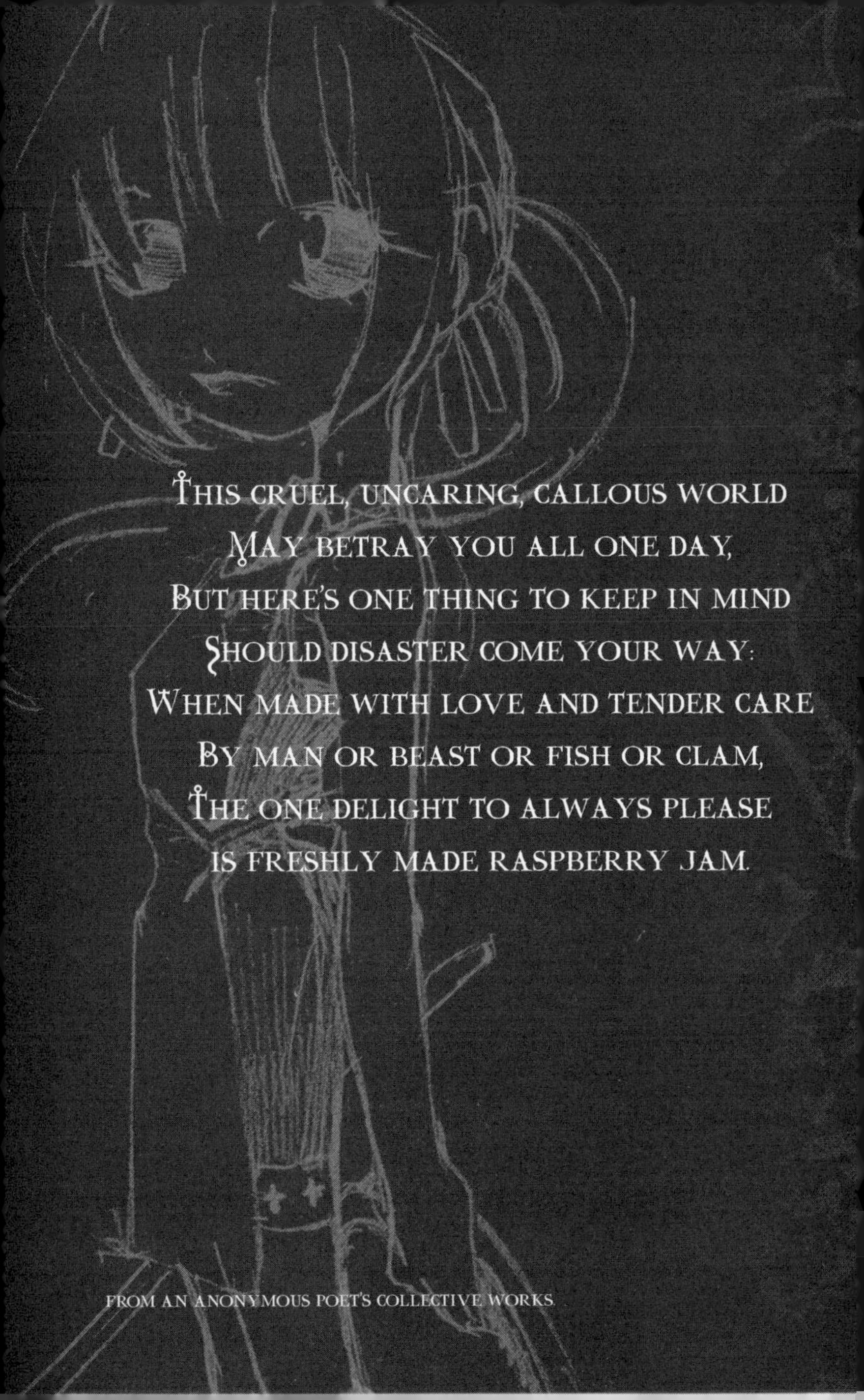

This cruel, uncaring, callous world
May betray you all one day,
But here's one thing to keep in mind
Should disaster come your way:
When made with love and tender care
By man or beast or fish or clam,
The one delight to always please
Is freshly made raspberry jam.

FROM AN ANONYMOUS POET'S COLLECTIVE WORKS.

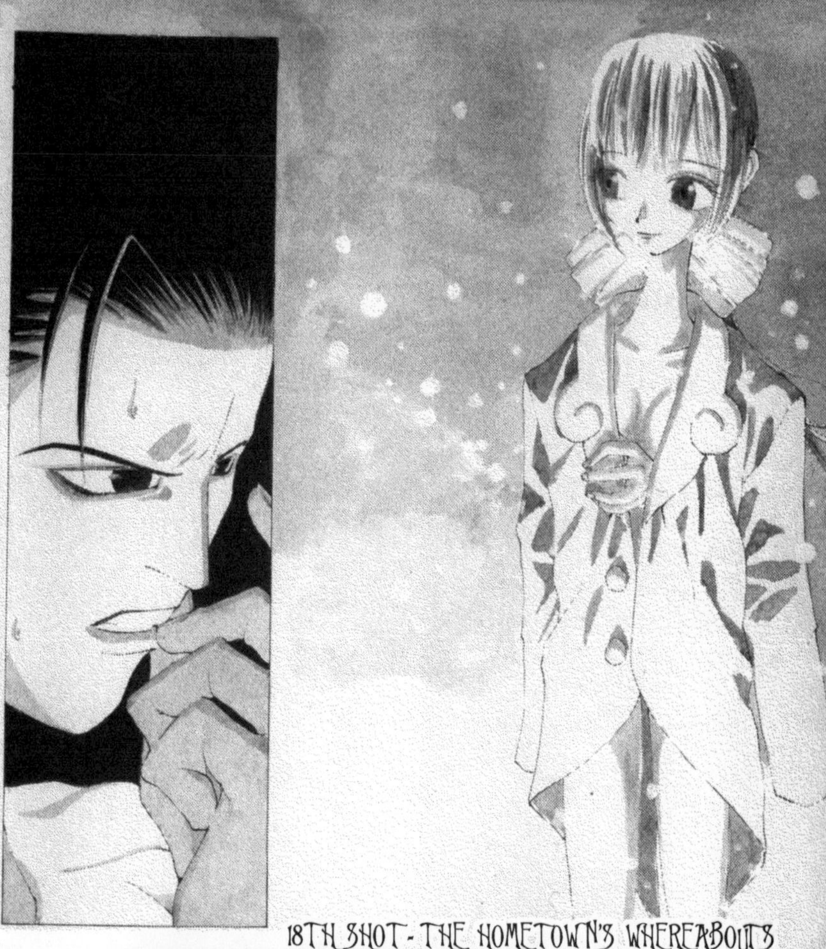

18TH SHOT - THE HOMETOWN'S WHEREABOUTS

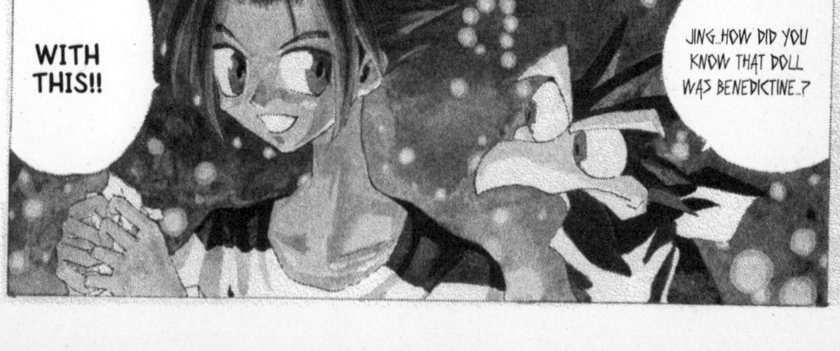
JING...HOW DID YOU KNOW THAT DOLL WAS BENEDICTINE...?
WITH THIS!!

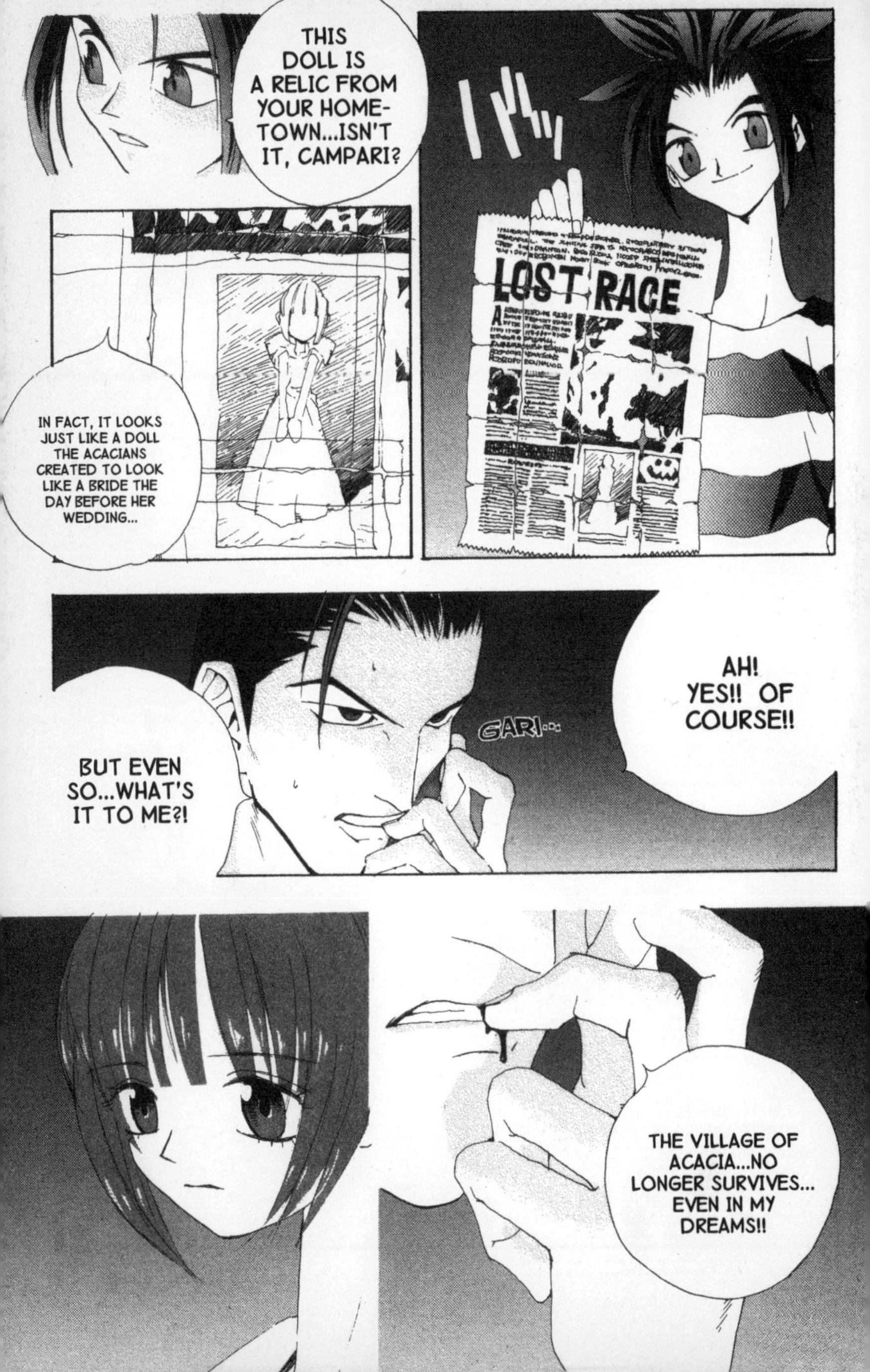
LOST RACE
THIS DOLL IS A RELIC FROM YOUR HOME-TOWN...ISN'T IT, CAMPARI?
IN FACT, IT LOOKS JUST LIKE A DOLL THE ACACIANS CREATED TO LOOK LIKE A BRIDE THE DAY BEFORE HER WEDDING...
AH! YES!! OF COURSE!!
GARI...
BUT EVEN SO...WHAT'S IT TO ME?!
THE VILLAGE OF ACACIA...NO LONGER SURVIVES... EVEN IN MY DREAMS!!

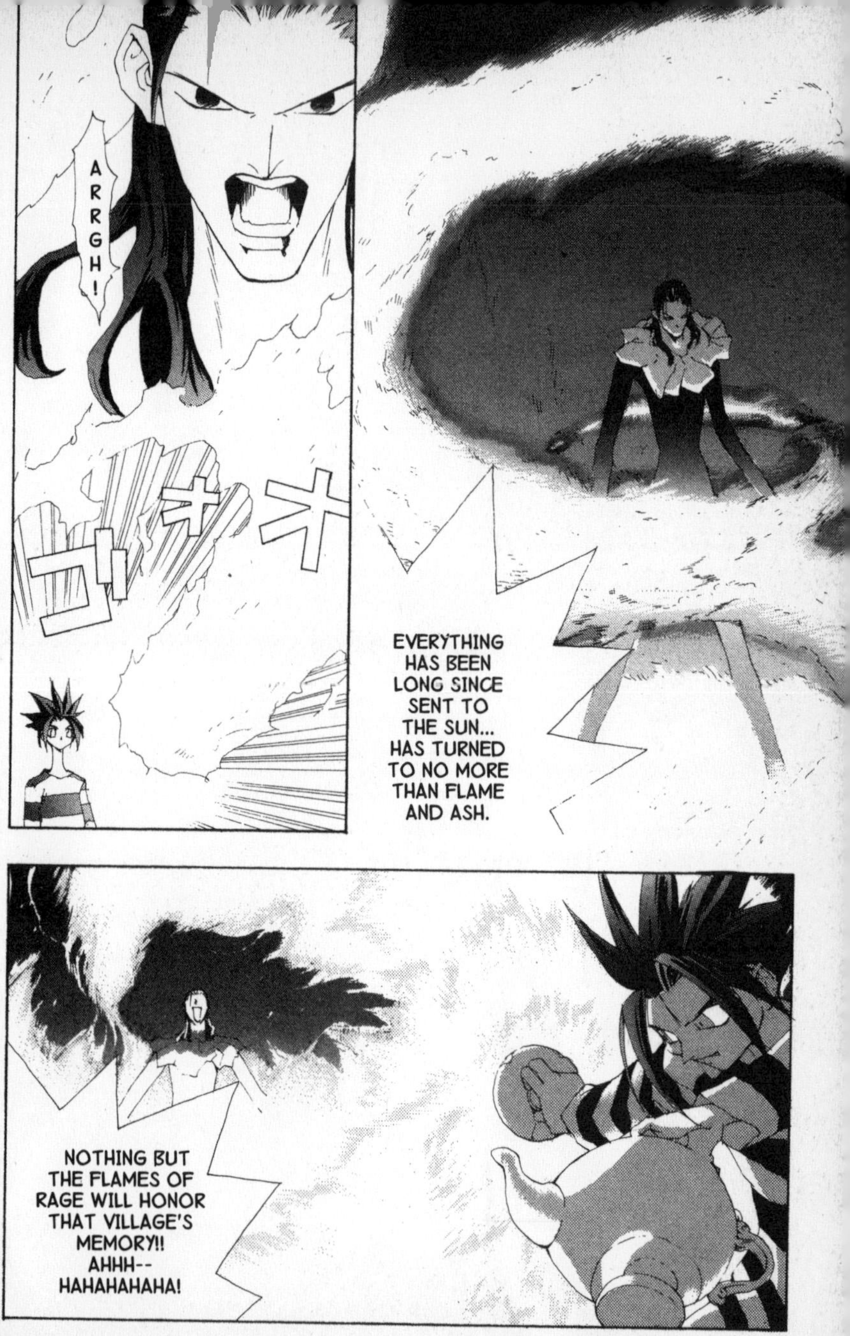
EVERYTHING HAS BEEN LONG SINCE SENT TO THE SUN... HAS TURNED TO NO MORE THAN FLAME AND ASH.
ARRGH!
ゴオオ
NOTHING BUT THE FLAMES OF RAGE WILL HONOR THAT VILLAGE'S MEMORY!! AHHH-- HAHAHAHAHA!

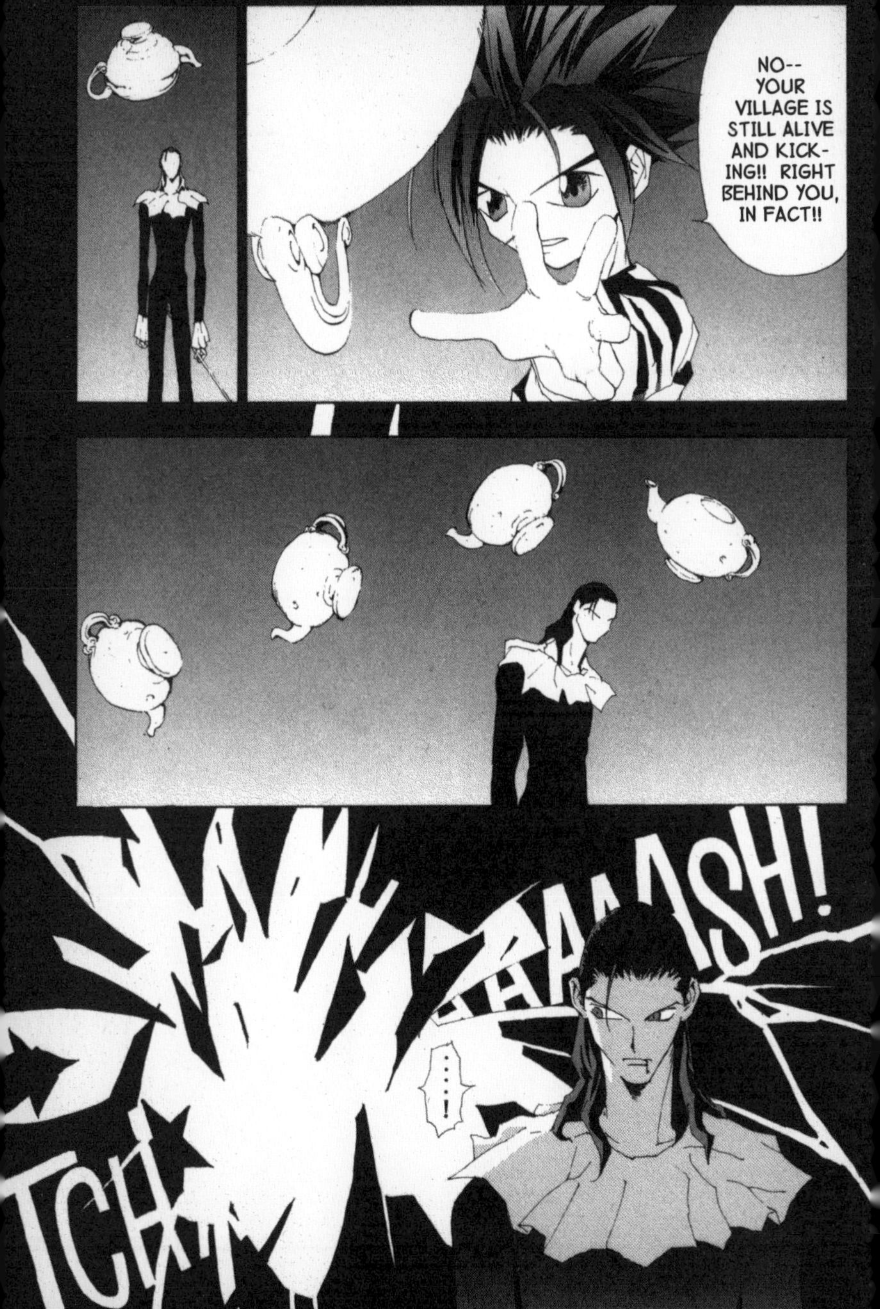
NO-- YOUR VILLAGE IS STILL ALIVE AND KICKING!! RIGHT BEHIND YOU, IN FACT!!
TCH
...!
RAAASH!

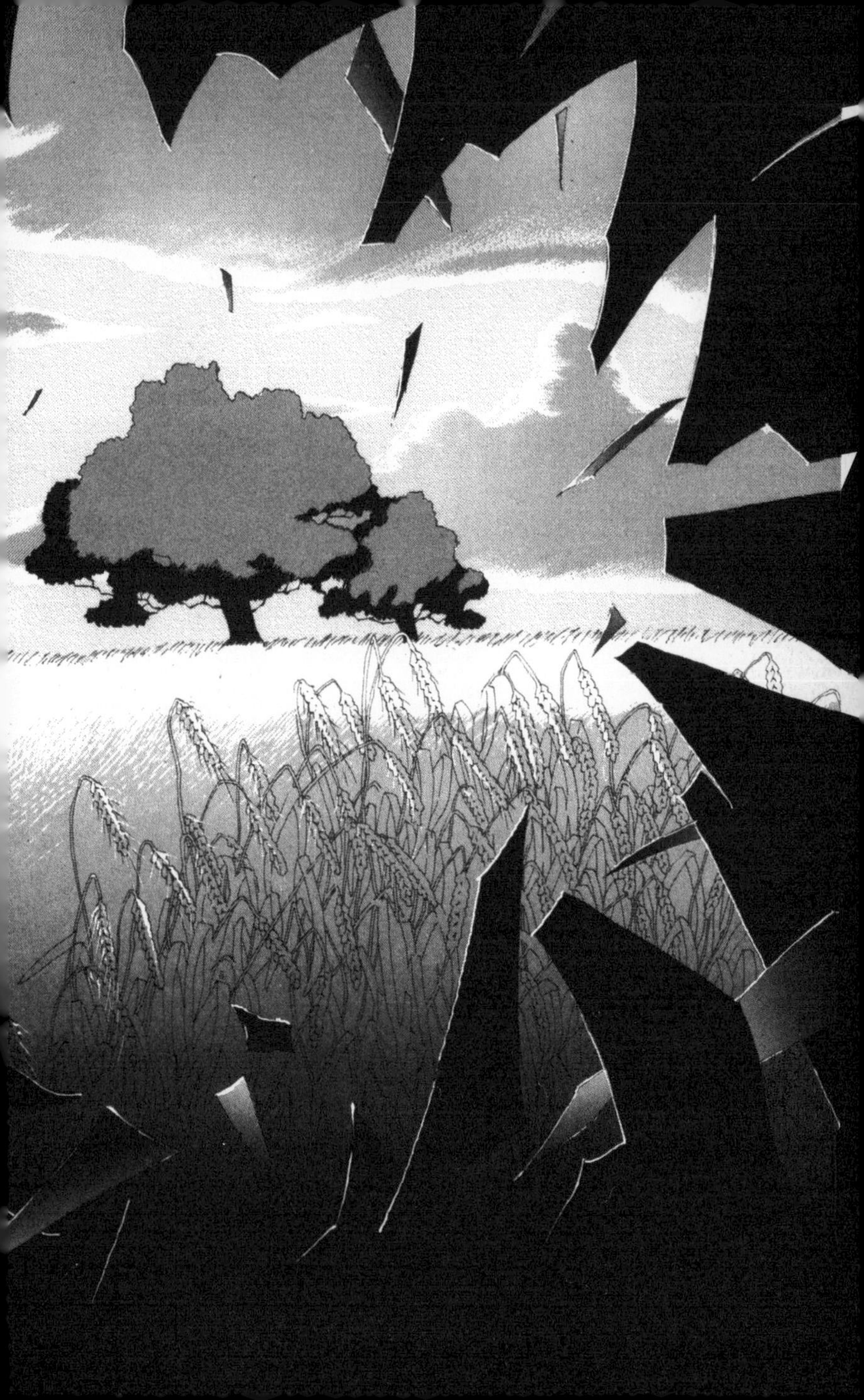

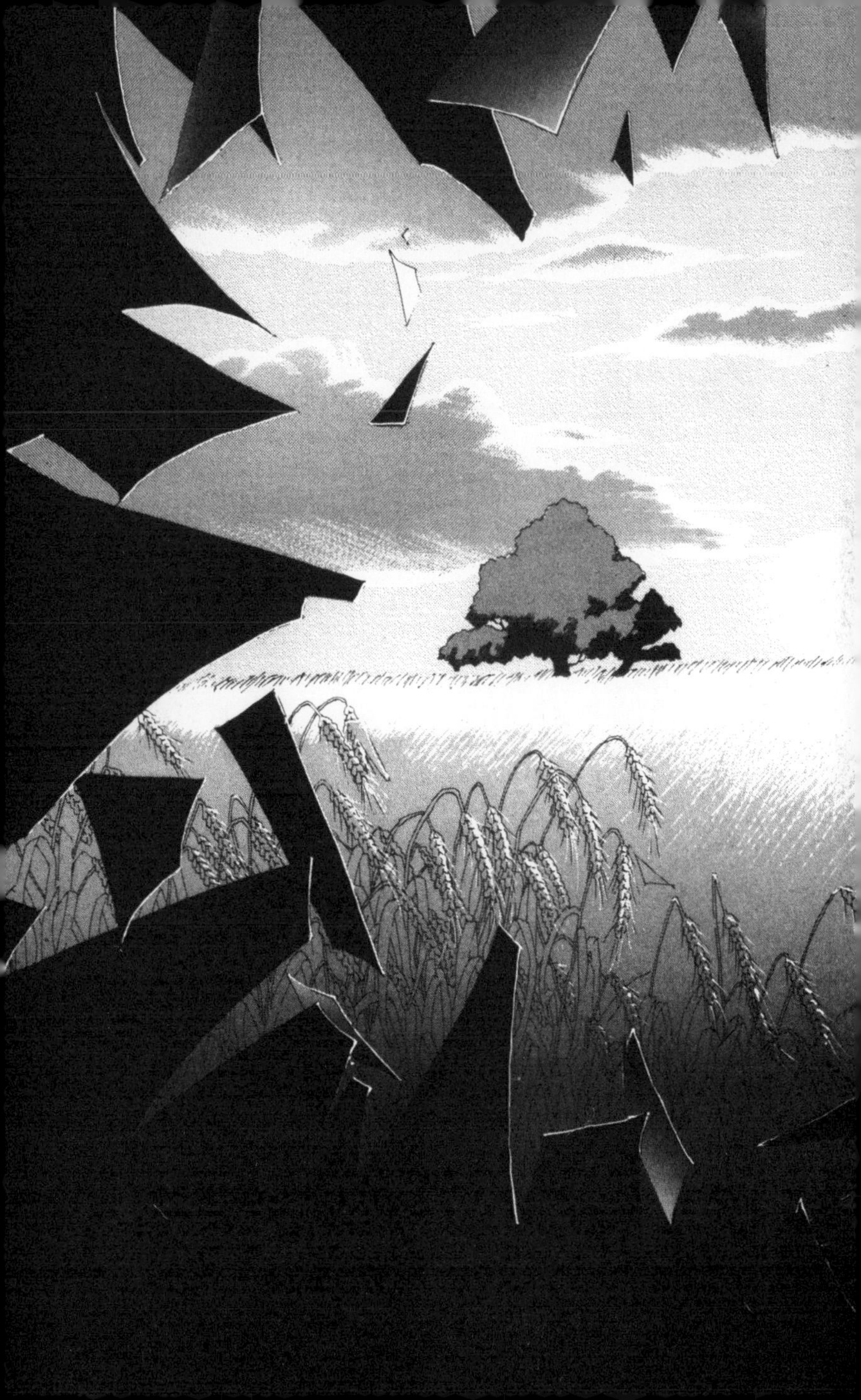

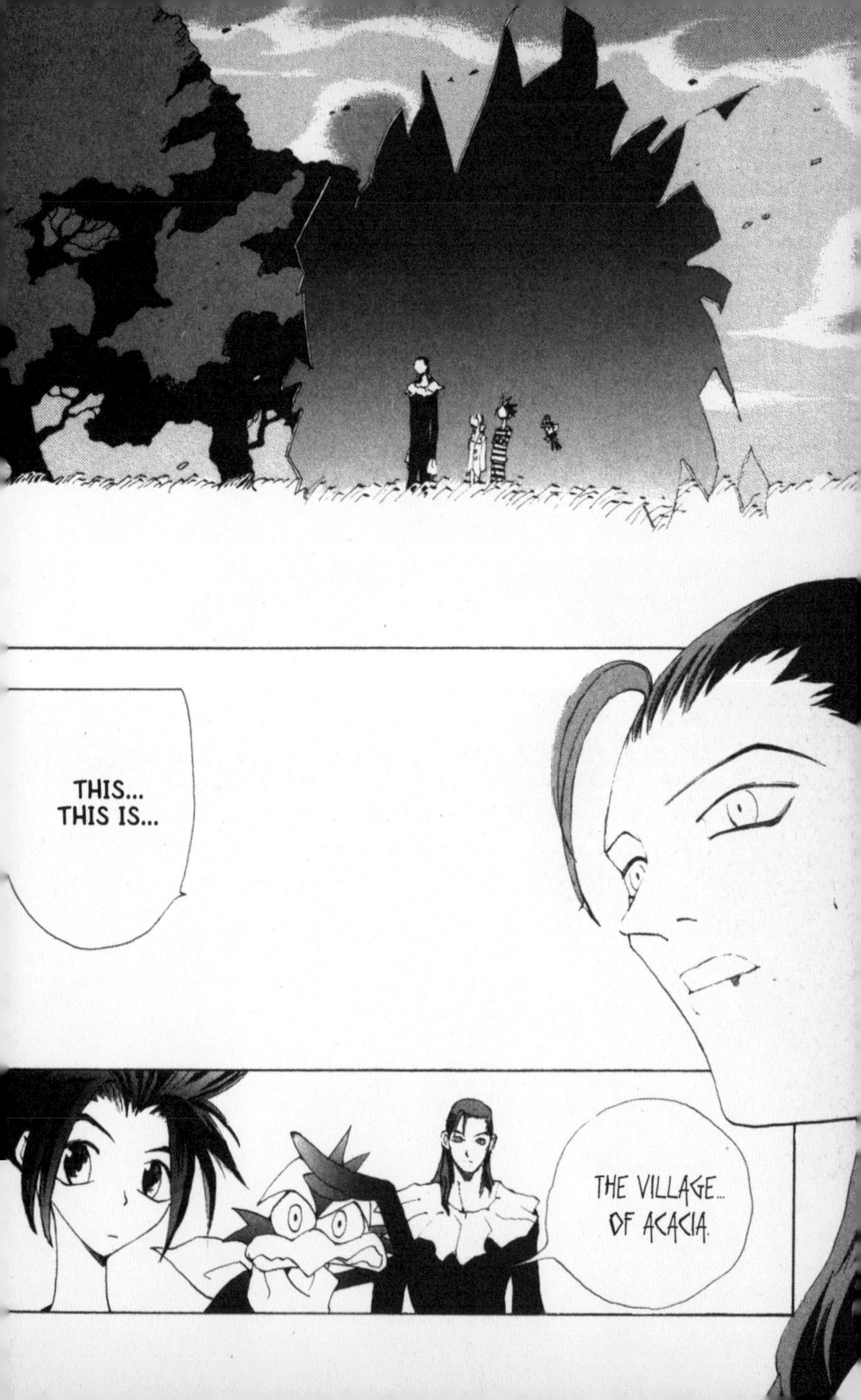
THIS... THIS IS...
THE VILLAGE... OF ACACIA.

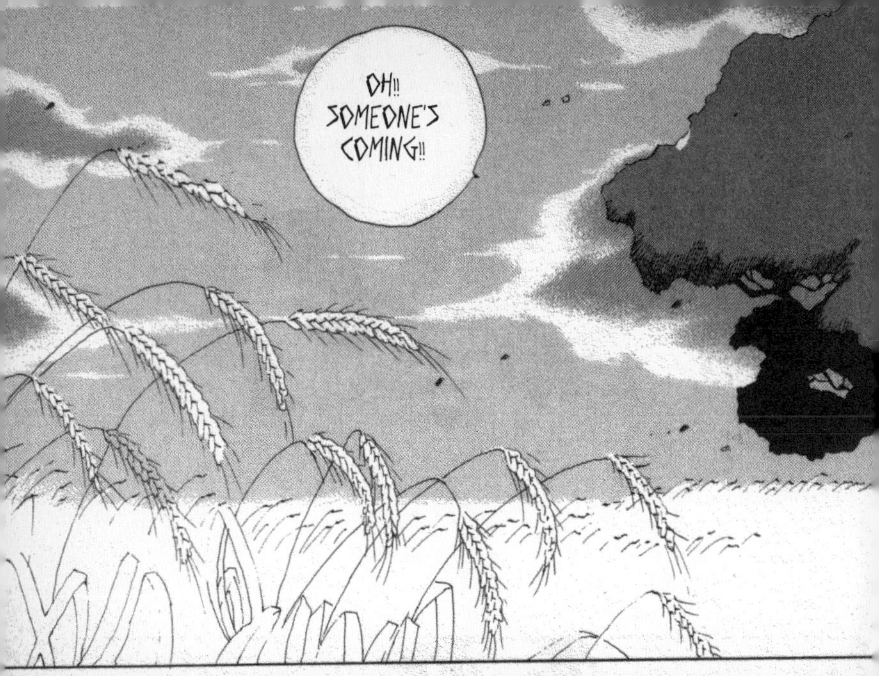
OH!! SOMEONE'S COMING!!
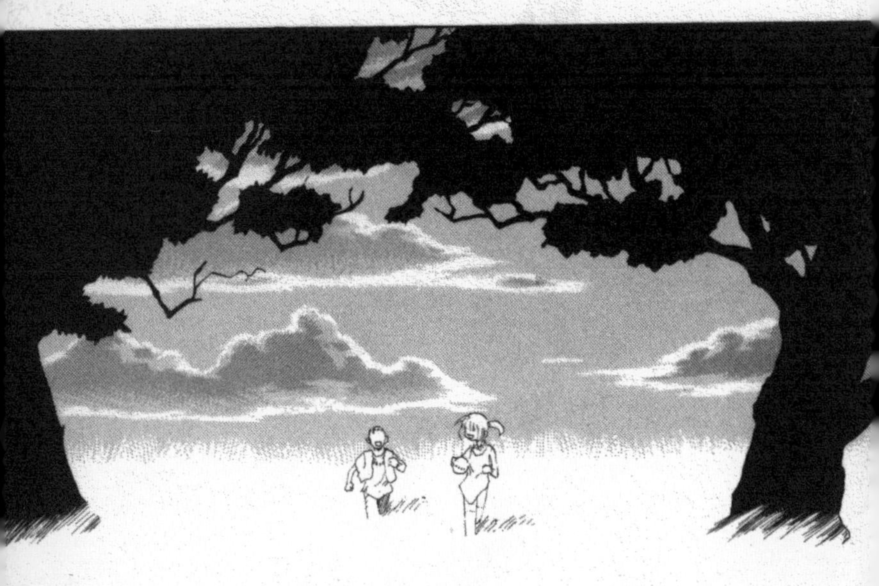

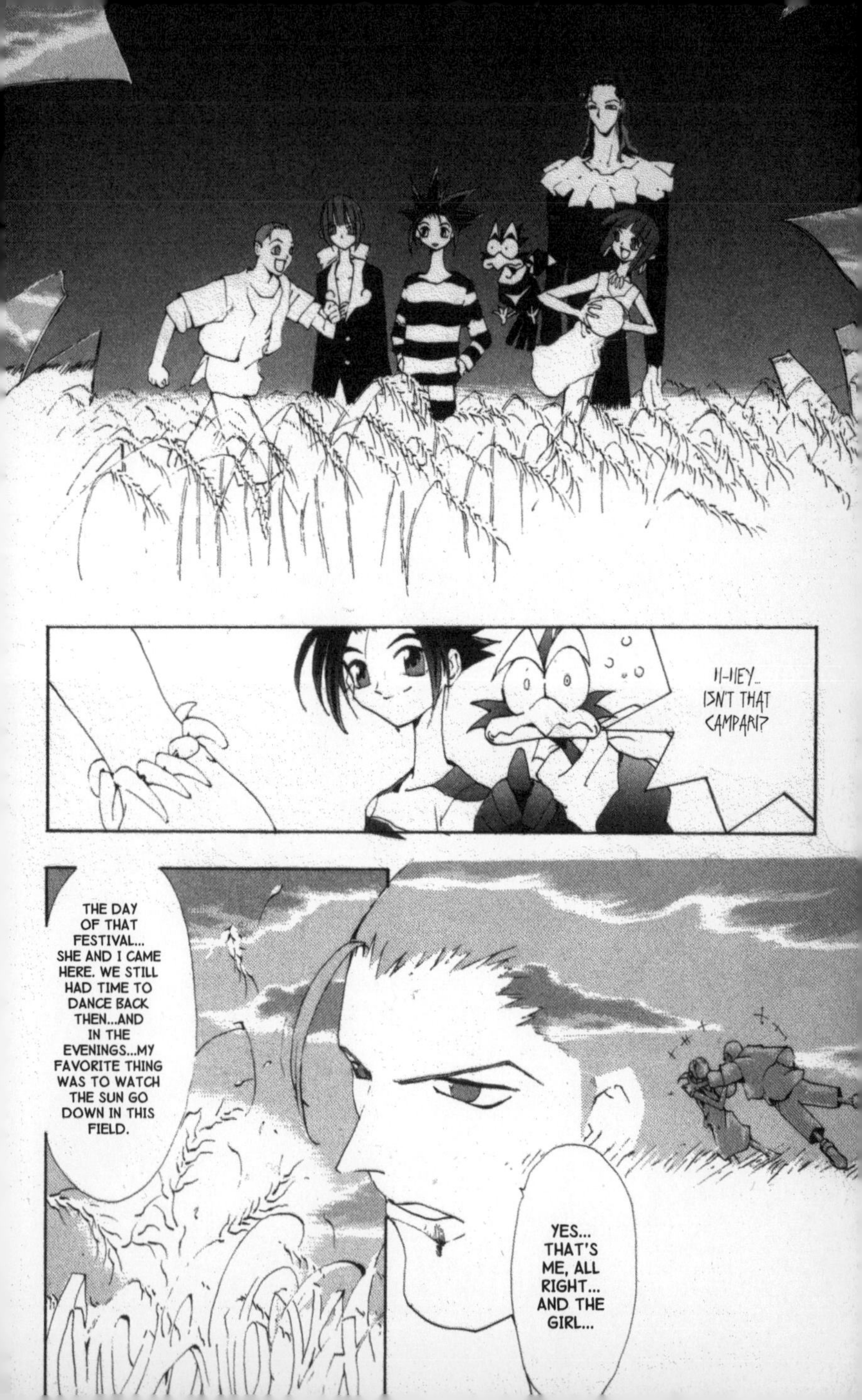
H-HEY.. ISN'T THAT CAMPARI?
YES... THAT'S ME, ALL RIGHT... AND THE GIRL...
THE DAY OF THAT FESTIVAL... SHE AND I CAME HERE. WE STILL HAD TIME TO DANCE BACK THEN...AND IN THE EVENINGS...MY FAVORITE THING WAS TO WATCH THE SUN GO DOWN IN THIS FIELD.

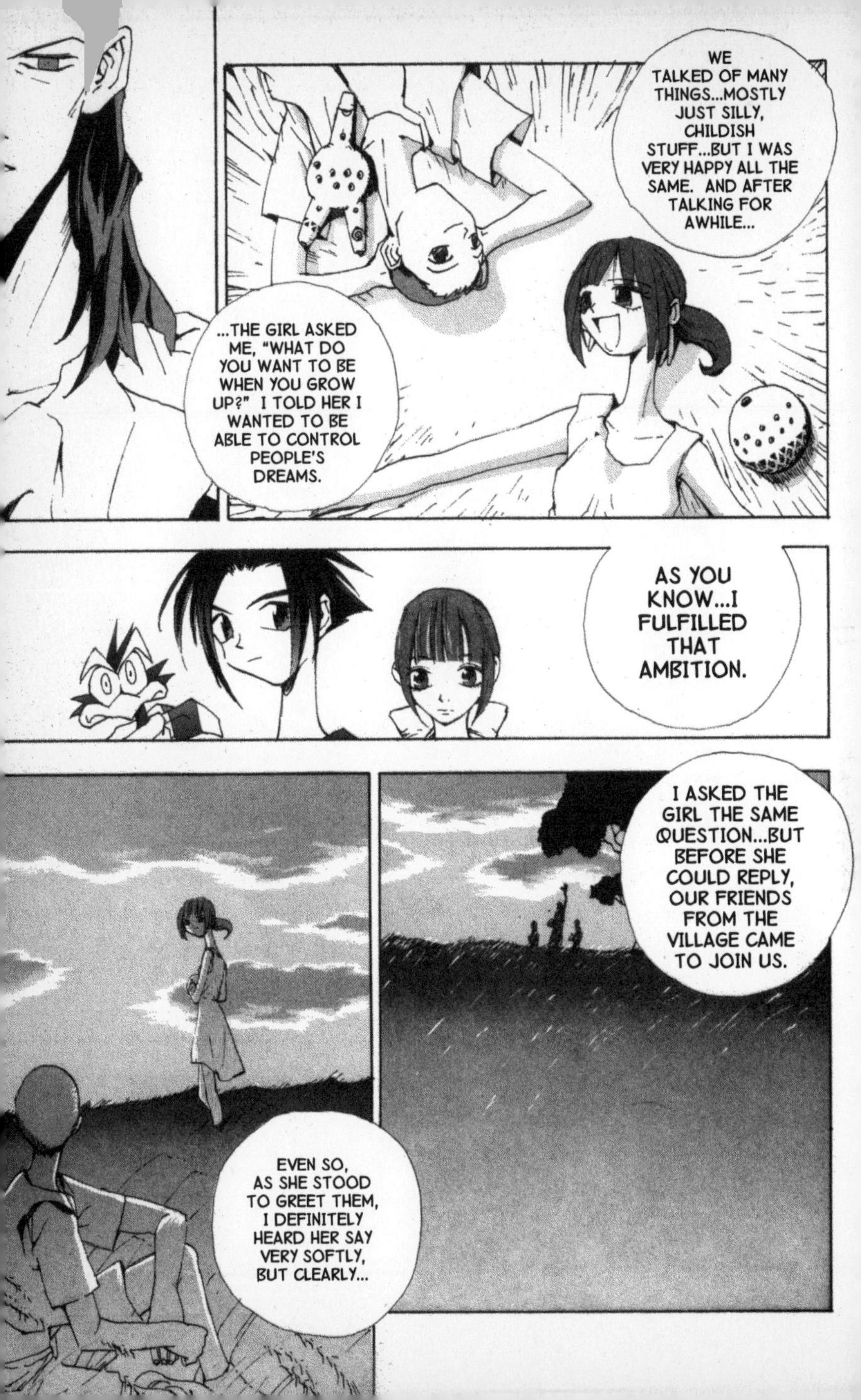
WE TALKED OF MANY THINGS...MOSTLY JUST SILLY, CHILDISH STUFF...BUT I WAS VERY HAPPY ALL THE SAME. AND AFTER TALKING FOR AWHILE...
...THE GIRL ASKED ME, "WHAT DO YOU WANT TO BE WHEN YOU GROW UP?" I TOLD HER I WANTED TO BE ABLE TO CONTROL PEOPLE'S DREAMS.
AS YOU KNOW...I FULFILLED THAT AMBITION.
I ASKED THE GIRL THE SAME QUESTION...BUT BEFORE SHE COULD REPLY, OUR FRIENDS FROM THE VILLAGE CAME TO JOIN US.
EVEN SO, AS SHE STOOD TO GREET THEM, I DEFINITELY HEARD HER SAY VERY SOFTLY, BUT CLEARLY...

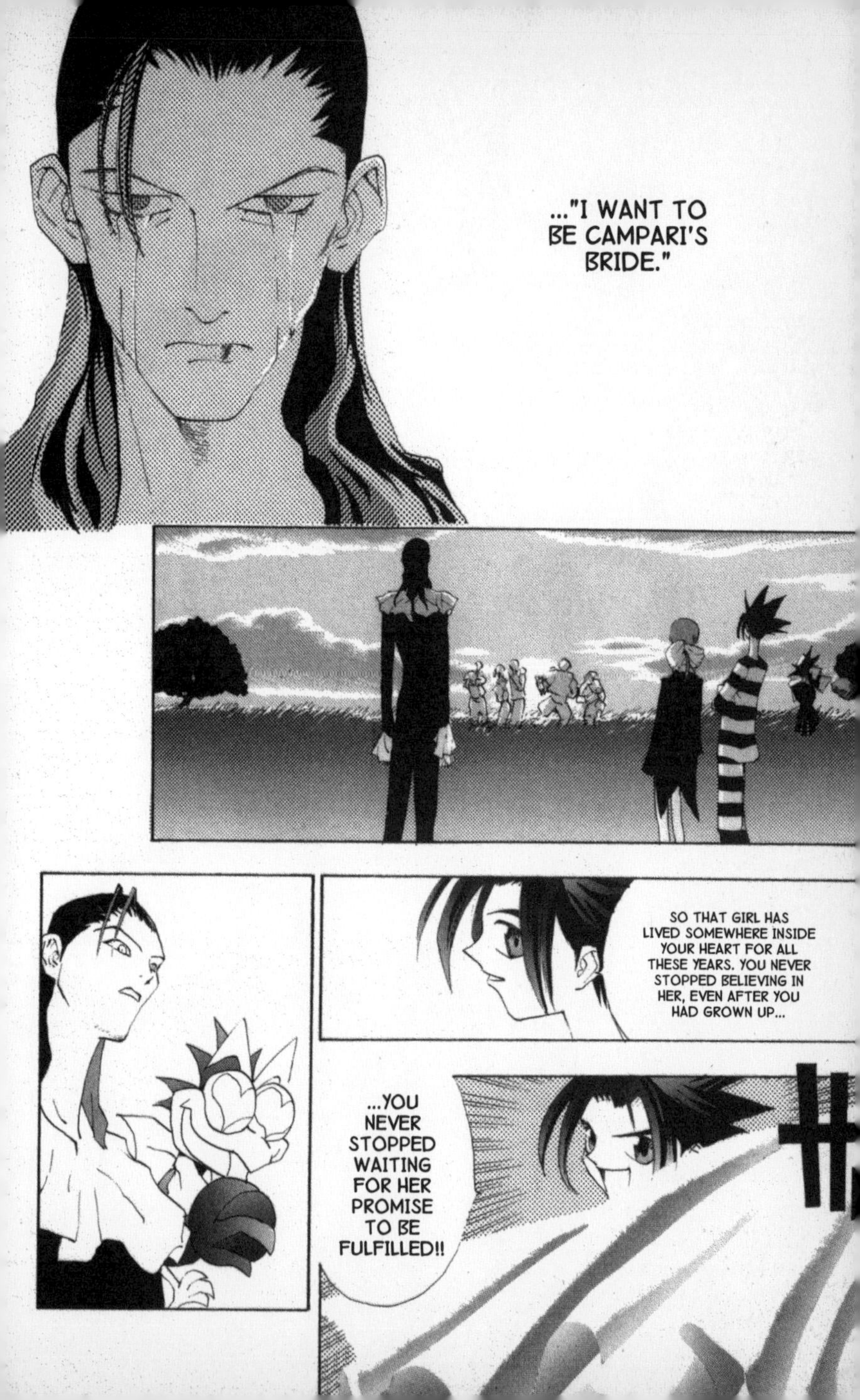
..."I WANT TO BE CAMPARI'S BRIDE."
SO THAT GIRL HAS LIVED SOMEWHERE INSIDE YOUR HEART FOR ALL THESE YEARS. YOU NEVER STOPPED BELIEVING IN HER, EVEN AFTER YOU HAD GROWN UP...
...YOU NEVER STOPPED WAITING FOR HER PROMISE TO BE FULFILLED!!

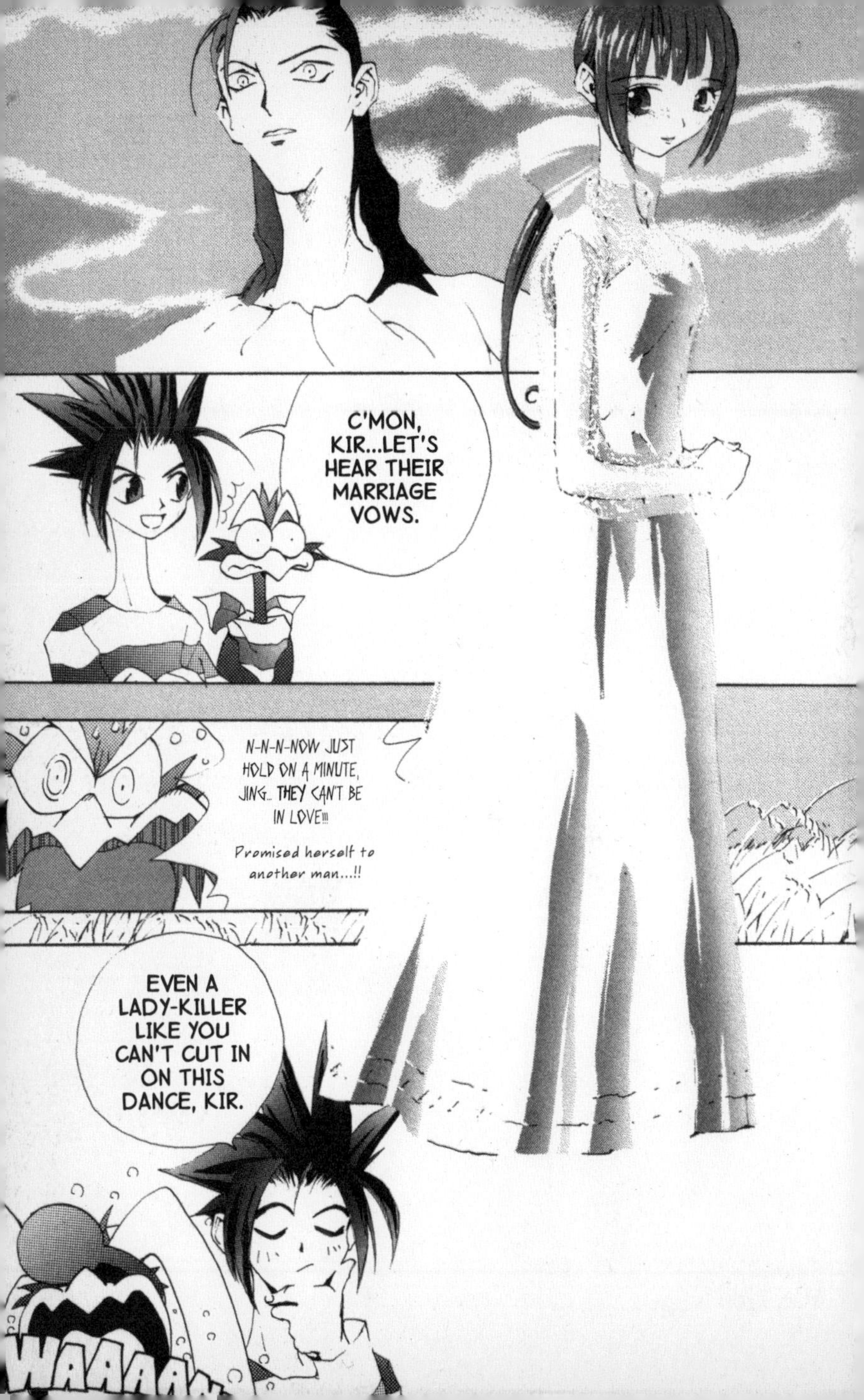

C'MON, KIR...LET'S HEAR THEIR MARRIAGE VOWS.
N-N-N-NOW JUST HOLD ON A MINUTE, JING... THEY CAN'T BE IN LOVE!!!
Promised herself to another man...!!
EVEN A LADY-KILLER LIKE YOU CAN'T CUT IN ON THIS DANCE, KIR.
WAAAAN

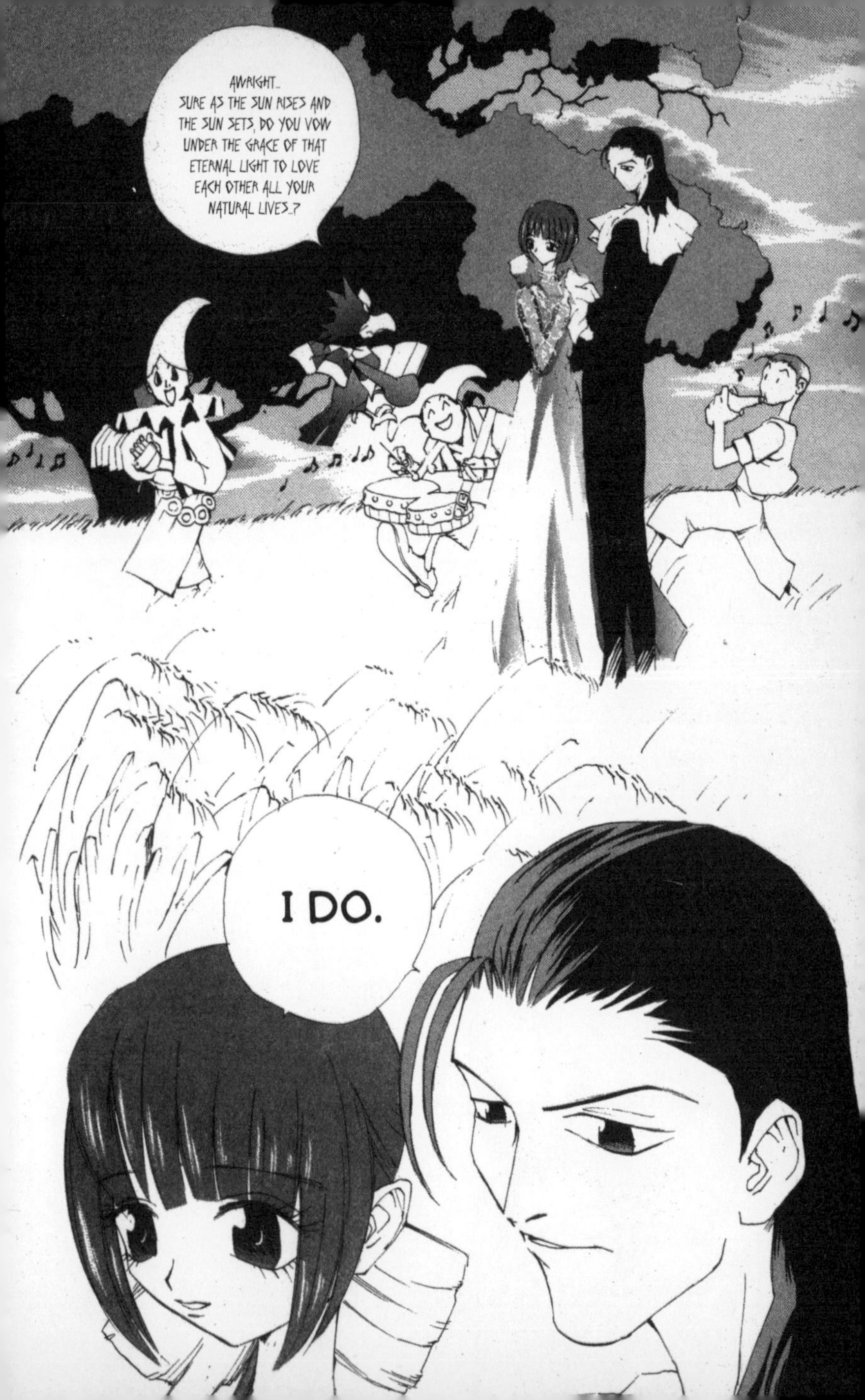
AWRIGHT... SURE AS THE SUN RISES AND THE SUN SETS, DO YOU VOW UNDER THE GRACE OF THAT ETERNAL LIGHT TO LOVE EACH OTHER ALL YOUR NATURAL LIVES...?
I DO.

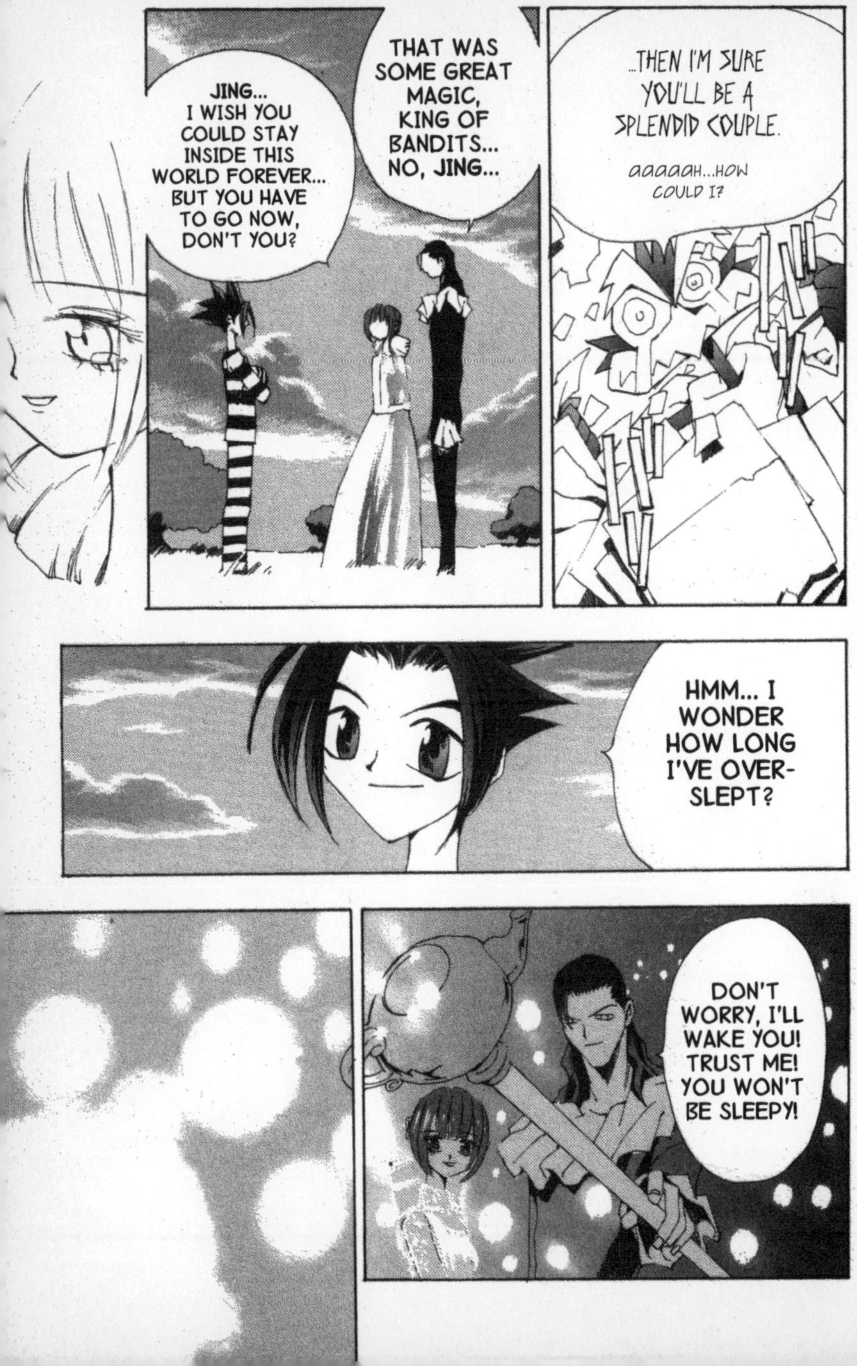
...THEN I'M SURE YOU'LL BE A SPLENDID COUPLE.
aaaaah...HOW COULD I?
THAT WAS SOME GREAT MAGIC, KING OF BANDITS... NO, JING...
JING... I WISH YOU COULD STAY INSIDE THIS WORLD FOREVER... BUT YOU HAVE TO GO NOW, DON'T YOU?
HMM... I WONDER HOW LONG I'VE OVER-SLEPT?
DON'T WORRY, I'LL WAKE YOU! TRUST ME! YOU WON'T BE SLEEPY!

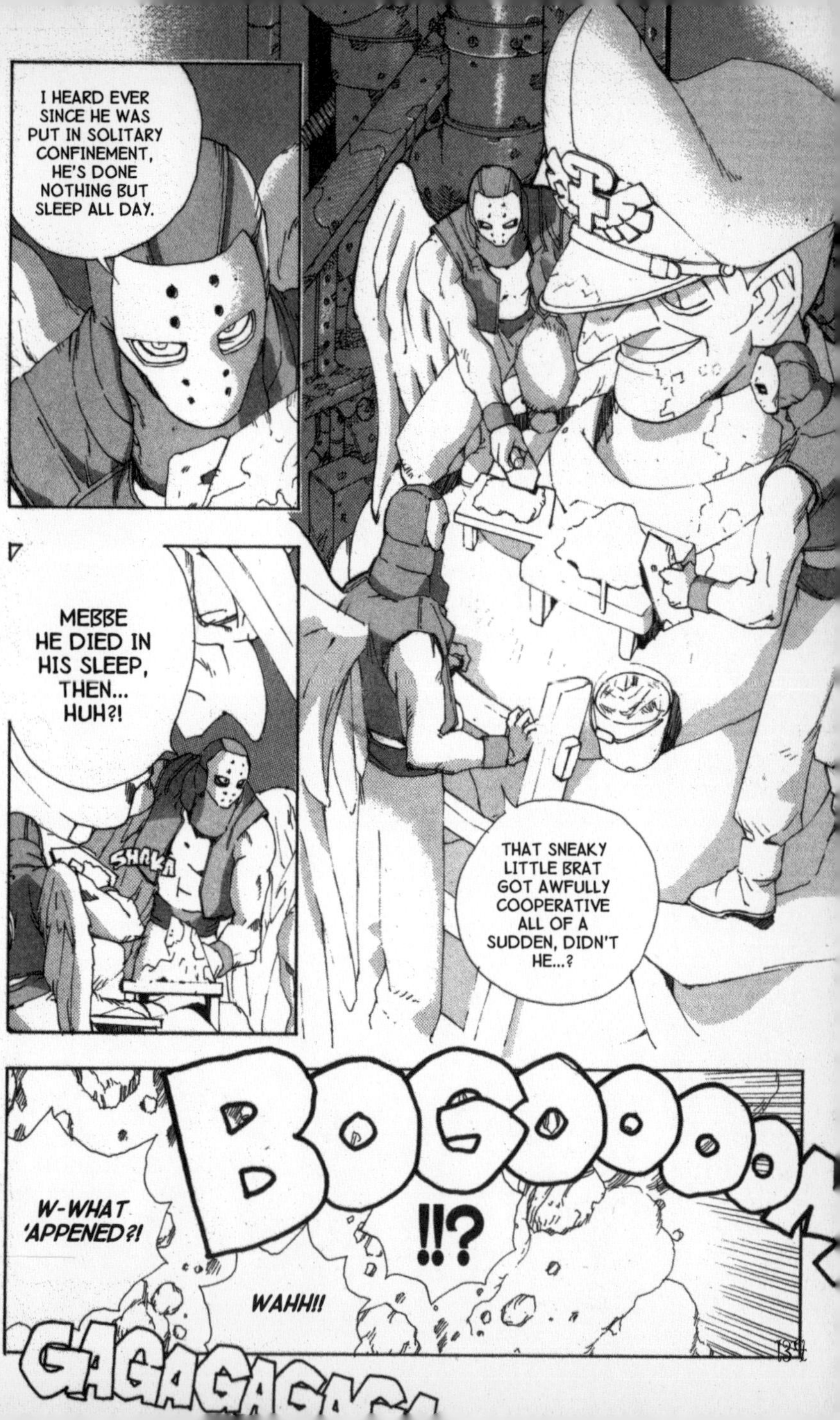

THAT SNEAKY LITTLE BRAT GOT AWFULLY COOPERATIVE ALL OF A SUDDEN, DIDN'T HE...?
I HEARD EVER SINCE HE WAS PUT IN SOLITARY CONFINEMENT, HE'S DONE NOTHING BUT SLEEP ALL DAY.
MEBBE HE DIED IN HIS SLEEP, THEN... HUH?!
SHAKA
BOGOOOOON
!!?
W-WHAT 'APPENED?!
WAHH!!
GAGAGAGAGA

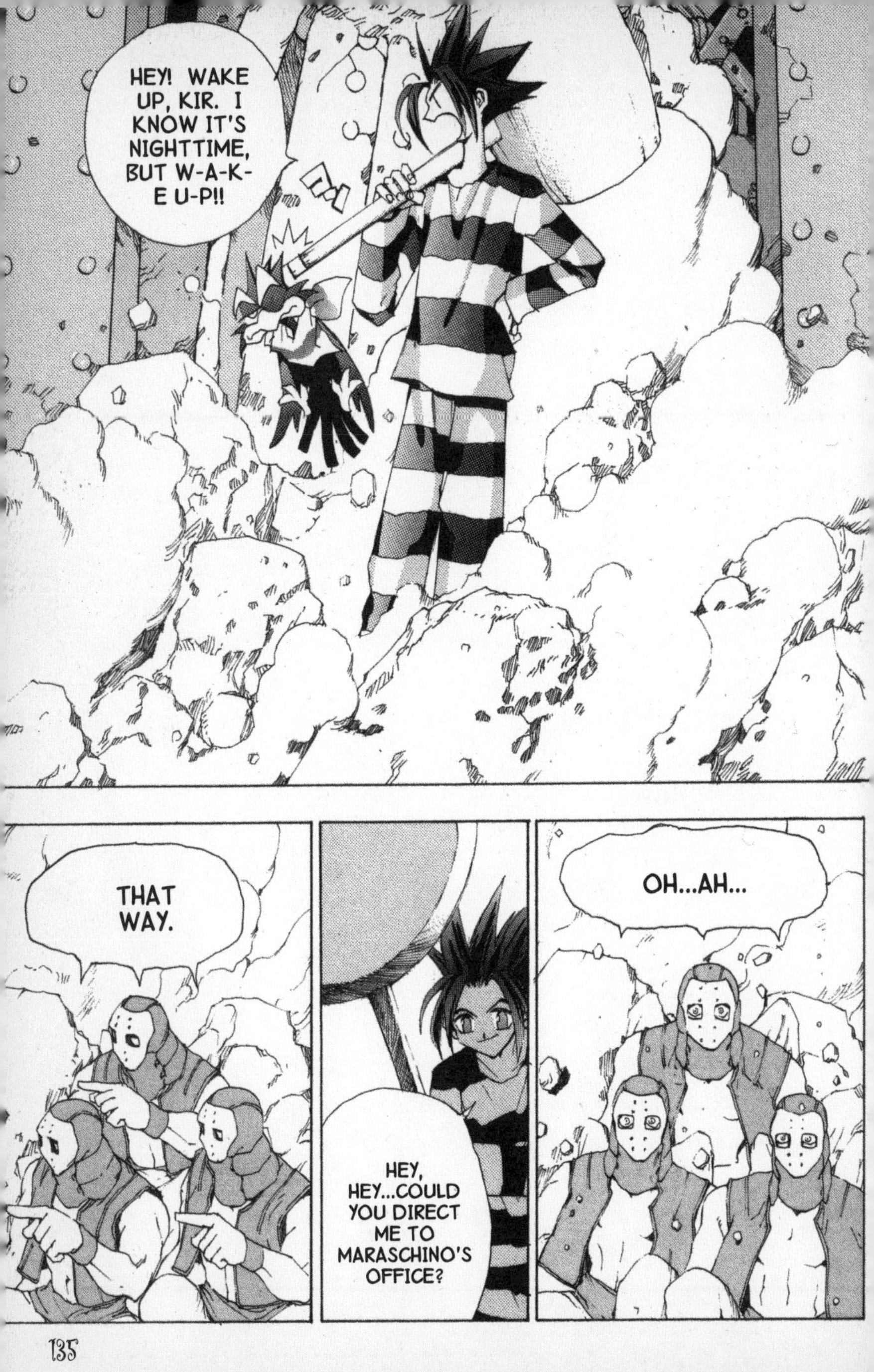
HEY! WAKE UP, KIR. I KNOW IT'S NIGHTTIME, BUT W-A-K-E U-P!!
OH...AH...
HEY, HEY...COULD YOU DIRECT ME TO MARASCHINO'S OFFICE?
THAT WAY.

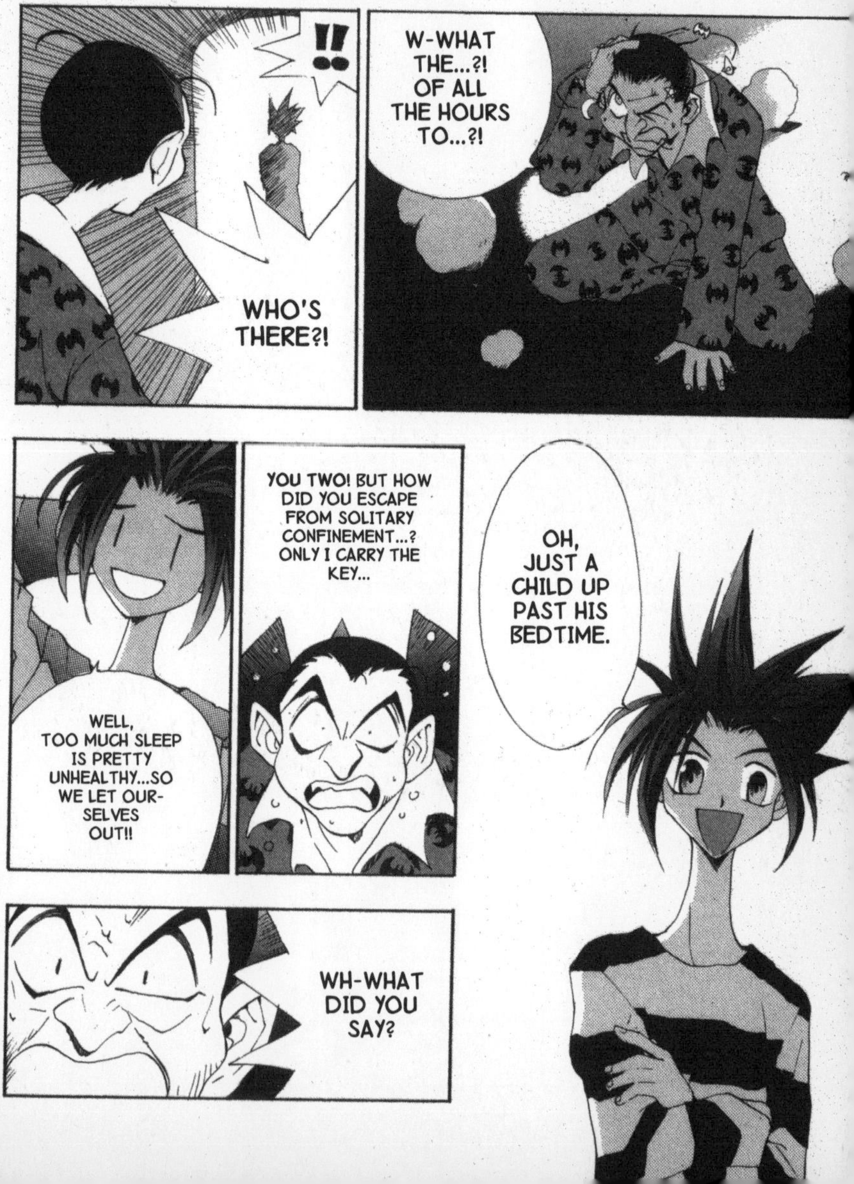
W-WHAT THE...?! OF ALL THE HOURS TO...?!
!!
WHO'S THERE?!
OH, JUST A CHILD UP PAST HIS BEDTIME.
YOU TWO! BUT HOW DID YOU ESCAPE FROM SOLITARY CONFINEMENT...? ONLY I CARRY THE KEY...
WELL, TOO MUCH SLEEP IS PRETTY UNHEALTHY...SO WE LET OUR-SELVES OUT!!
WH-WHAT DID YOU SAY?

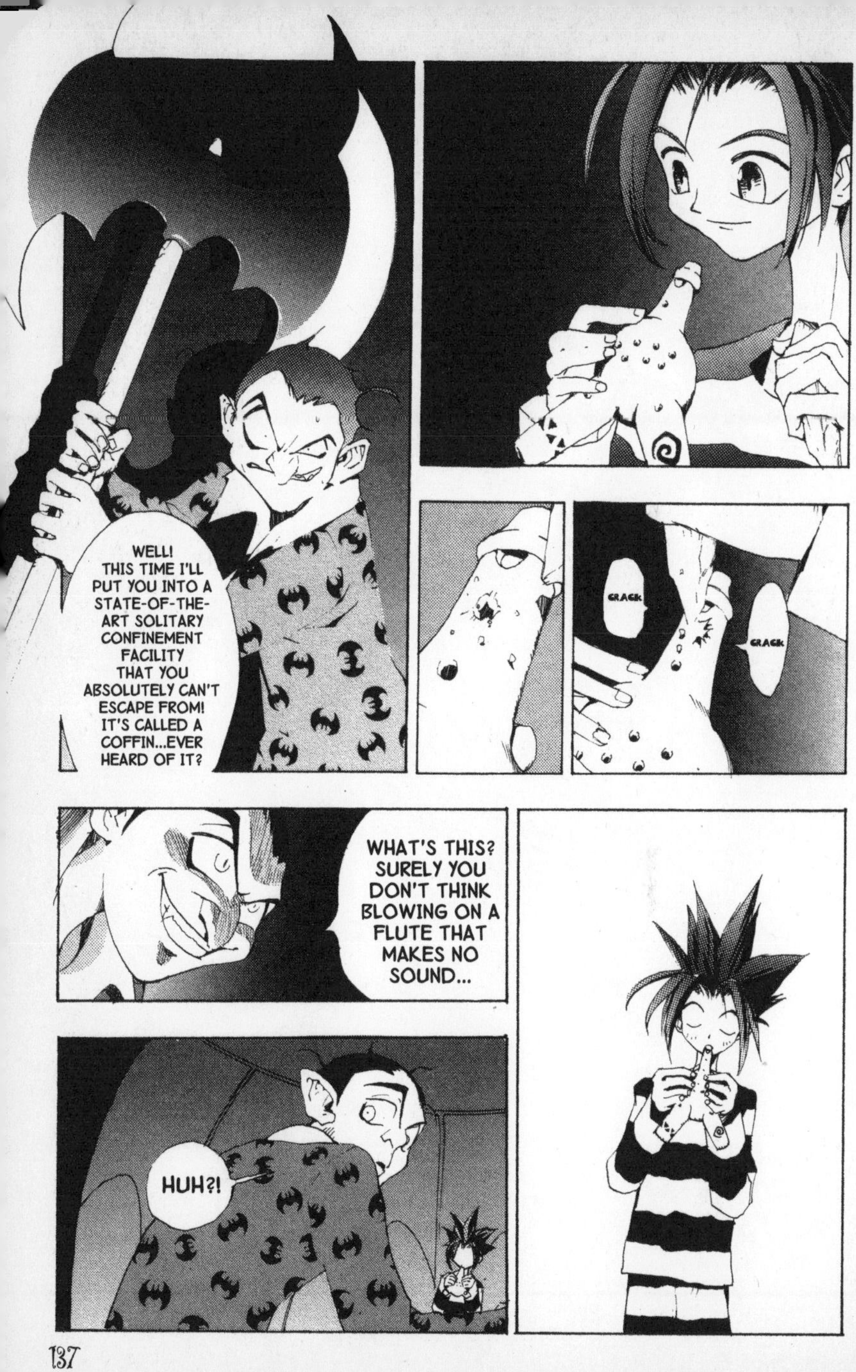
CRACK
CRACK
WELL! THIS TIME I'LL PUT YOU INTO A STATE-OF-THE-ART SOLITARY CONFINEMENT FACILITY THAT YOU ABSOLUTELY CAN'T ESCAPE FROM! IT'S CALLED A COFFIN...EVER HEARD OF IT?
WHAT'S THIS? SURELY YOU DON'T THINK BLOWING ON A FLUTE THAT MAKES NO SOUND...
HUH?!

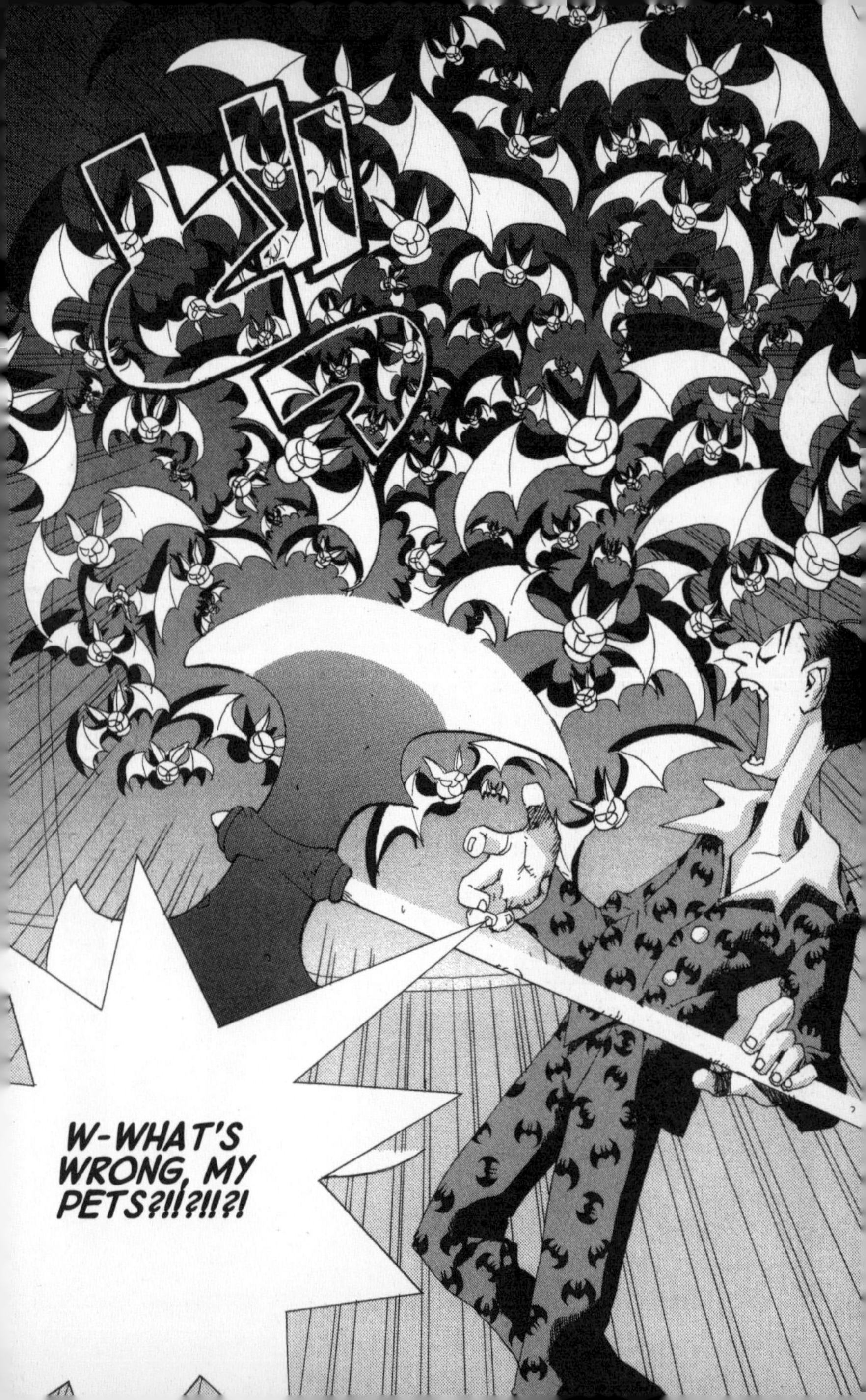
W-WHAT'S WRONG, MY PETS?!!?!!?!

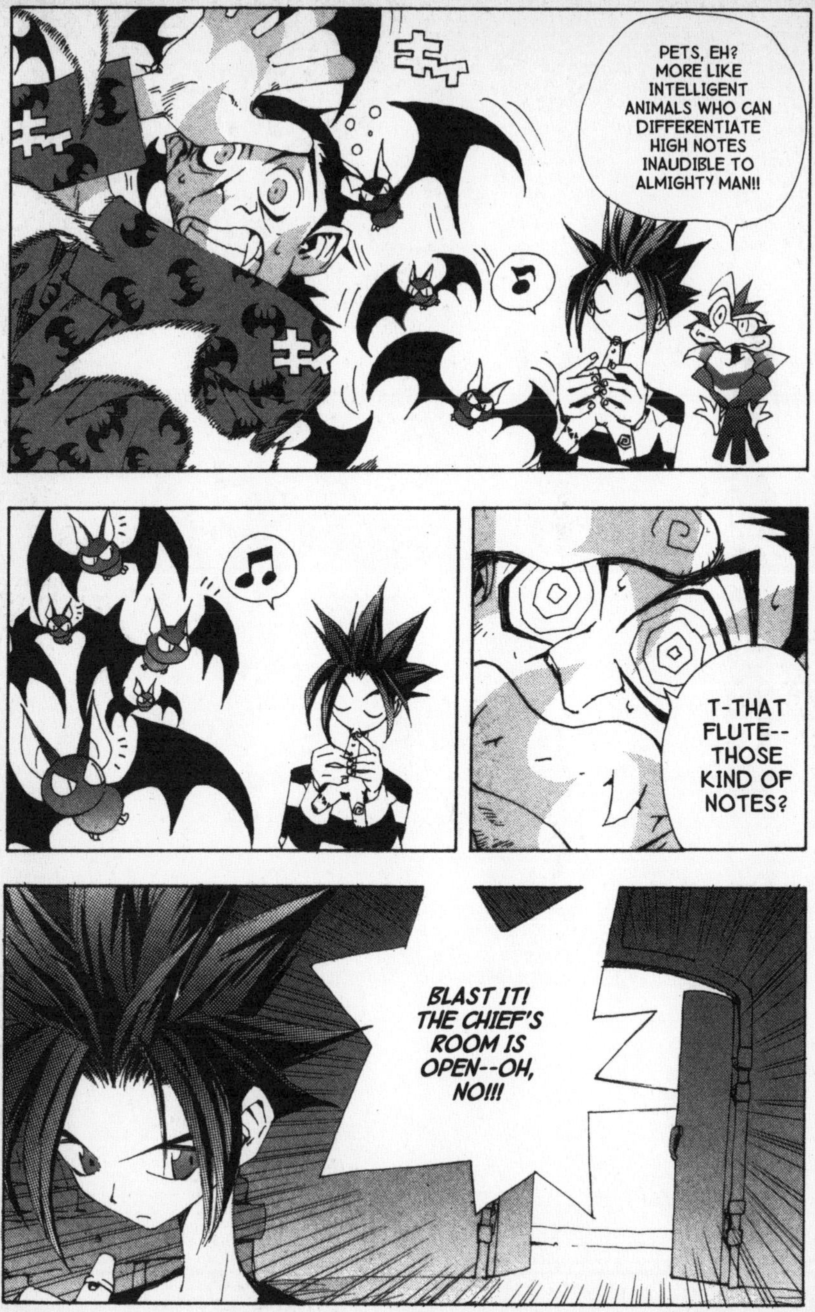
PETS, EH? MORE LIKE INTELLIGENT ANIMALS WHO CAN DIFFERENTIATE HIGH NOTES INAUDIBLE TO ALMIGHTY MAN!!
キィ
キィ
キィ
T-THAT FLUTE-- THOSE KIND OF NOTES?
BLAST IT! THE CHIEF'S ROOM IS OPEN--OH, NO!!!

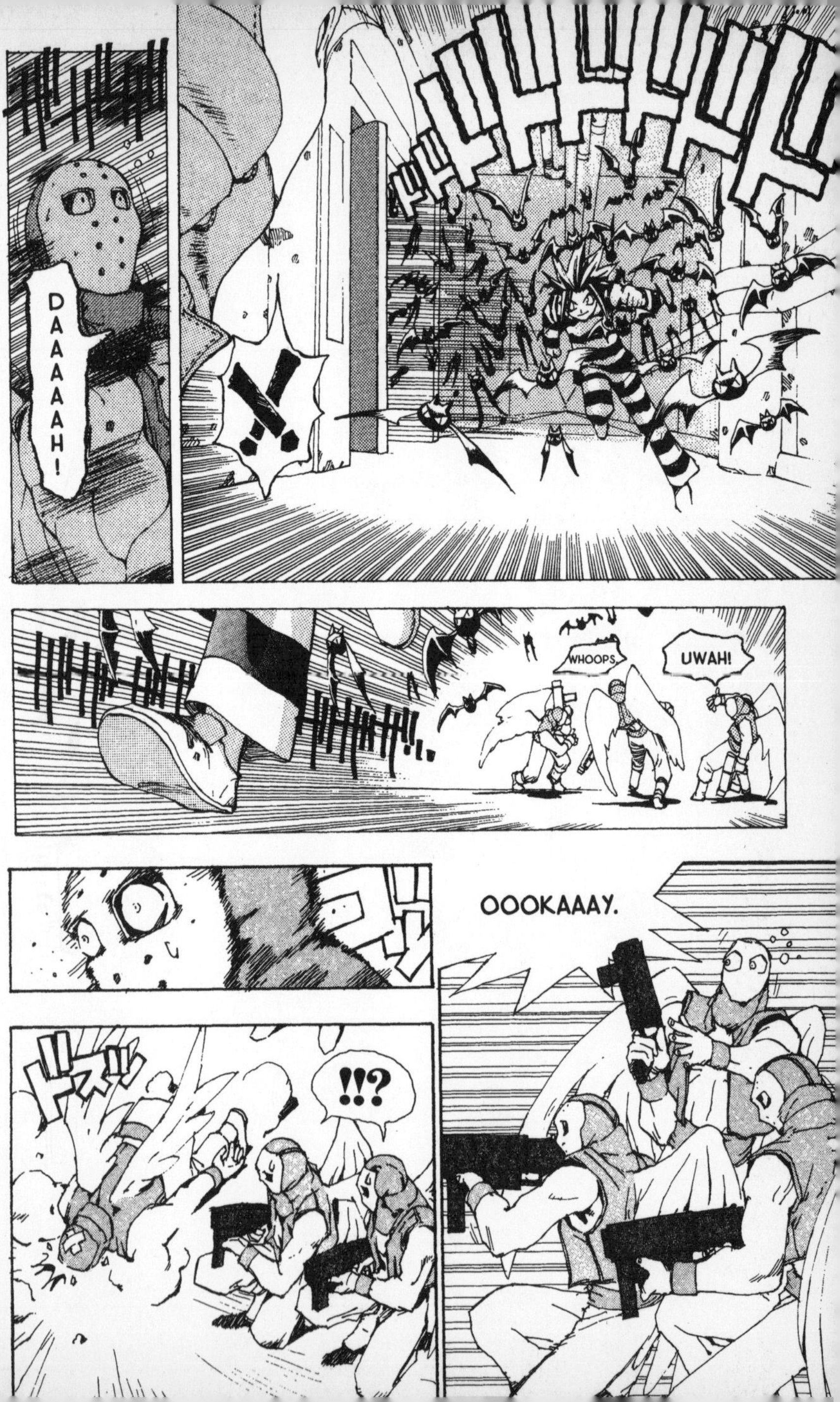
!
DAAAAAAH!
UWAH!
WHOOPS.
OOOKAAAY.
!!?

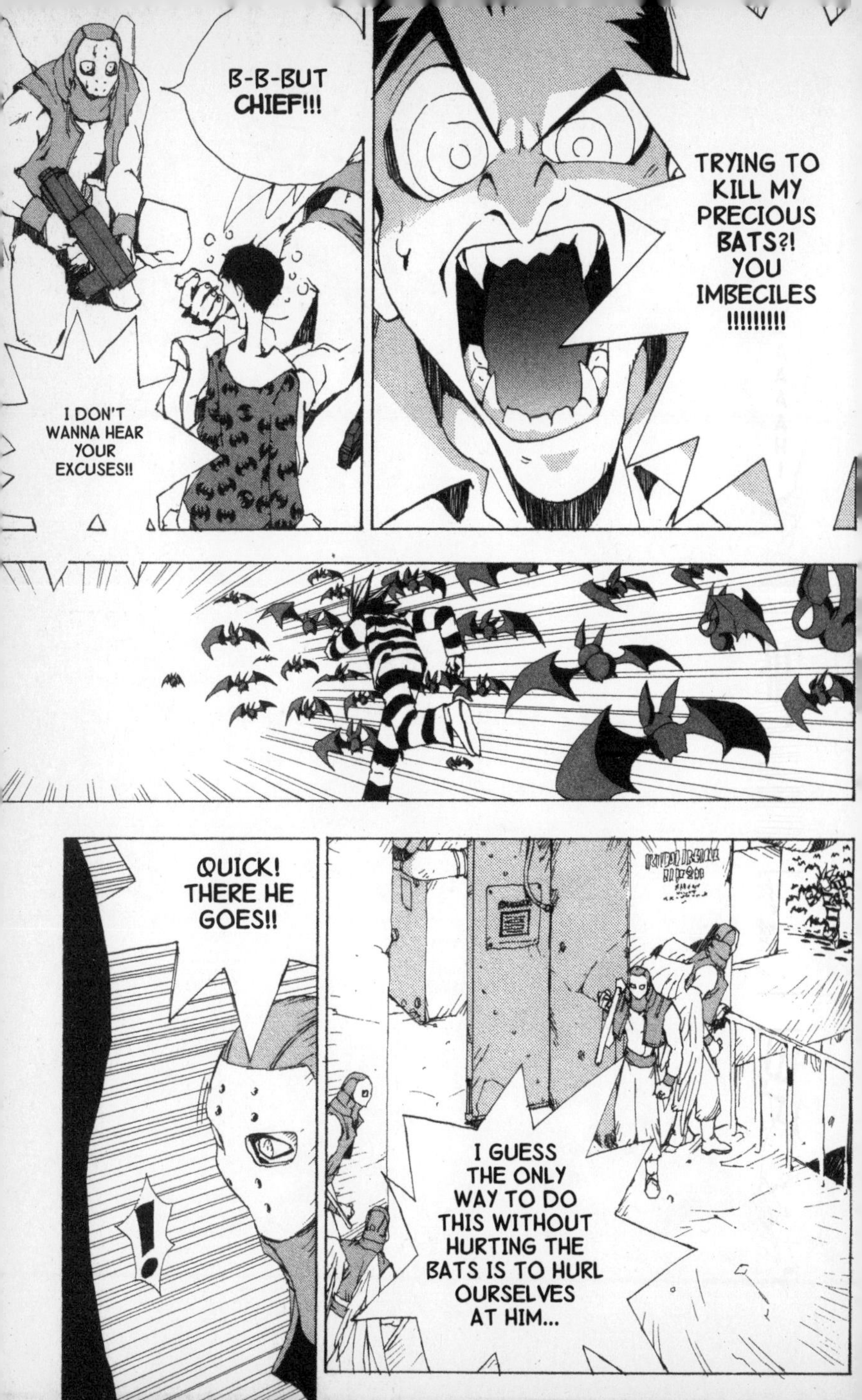
TRYING TO KILL MY PRECIOUS BATS?! YOU IMBECILES !!!!!!!!!
B-B-BUT CHIEF!!!
I DON'T WANNA HEAR YOUR EXCUSES!!
I GUESS THE ONLY WAY TO DO THIS WITHOUT HURTING THE BATS IS TO HURL OURSELVES AT HIM...
QUICK! THERE HE GOES!!
!

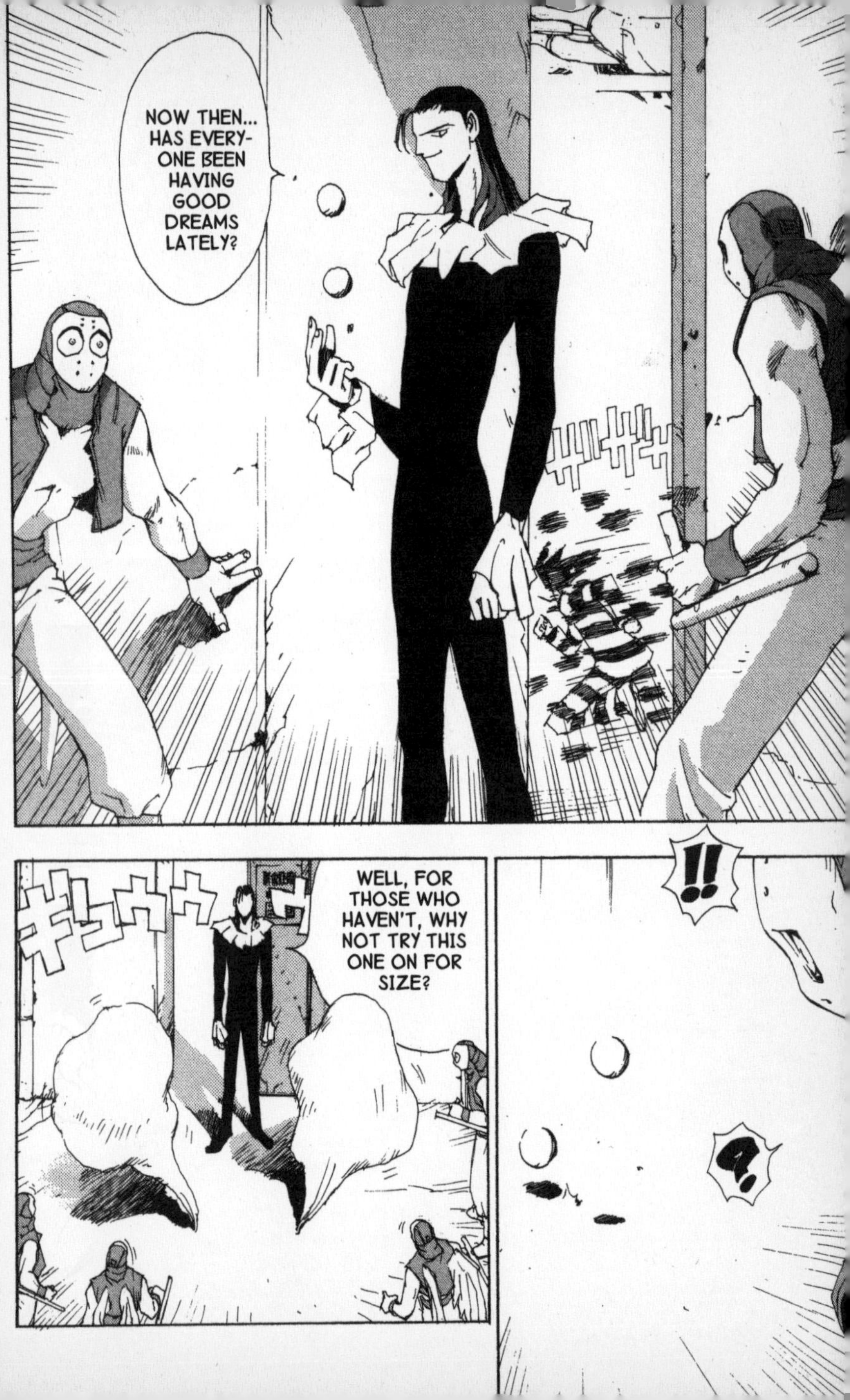
NOW THEN... HAS EVERY-ONE BEEN HAVING GOOD DREAMS LATELY?
!!
WELL, FOR THOSE WHO HAVEN'T, WHY NOT TRY THIS ONE ON FOR SIZE?

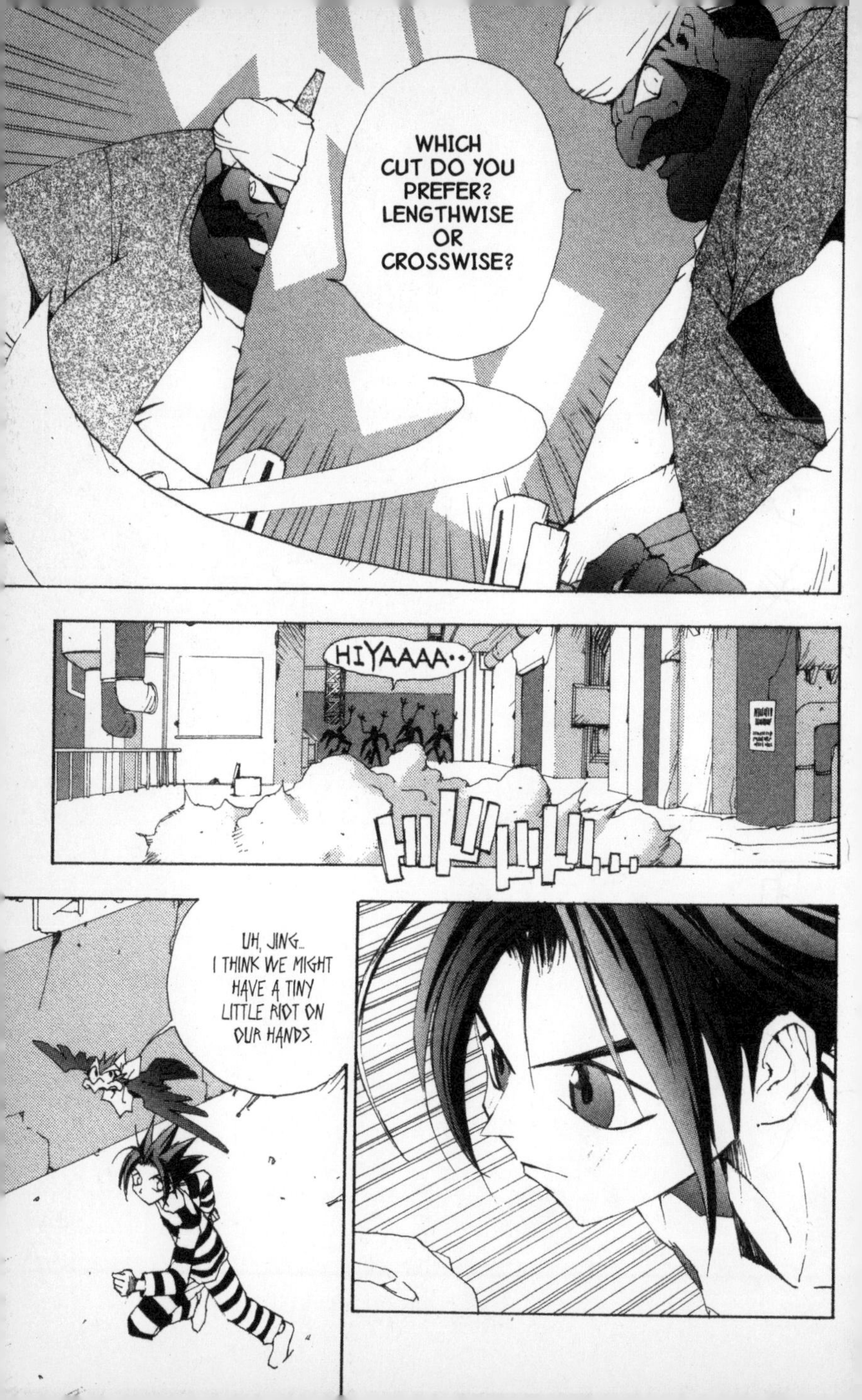
WHICH CUT DO YOU PREFER? LENGTHWISE OR CROSSWISE?
HIYAAAA..
UH, JING... I THINK WE MIGHT HAVE A TINY LITTLE RIOT ON OUR HANDS.

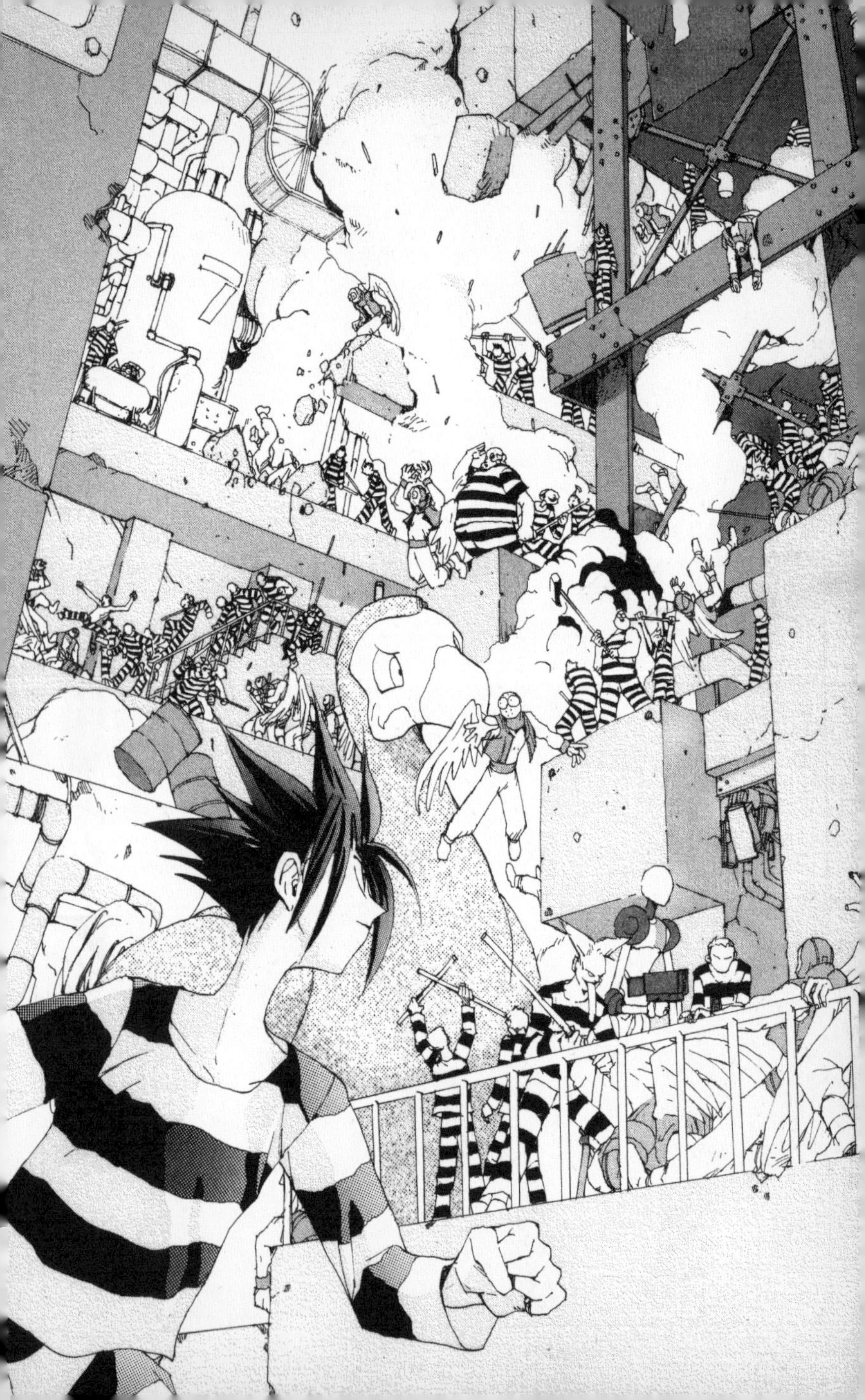
7

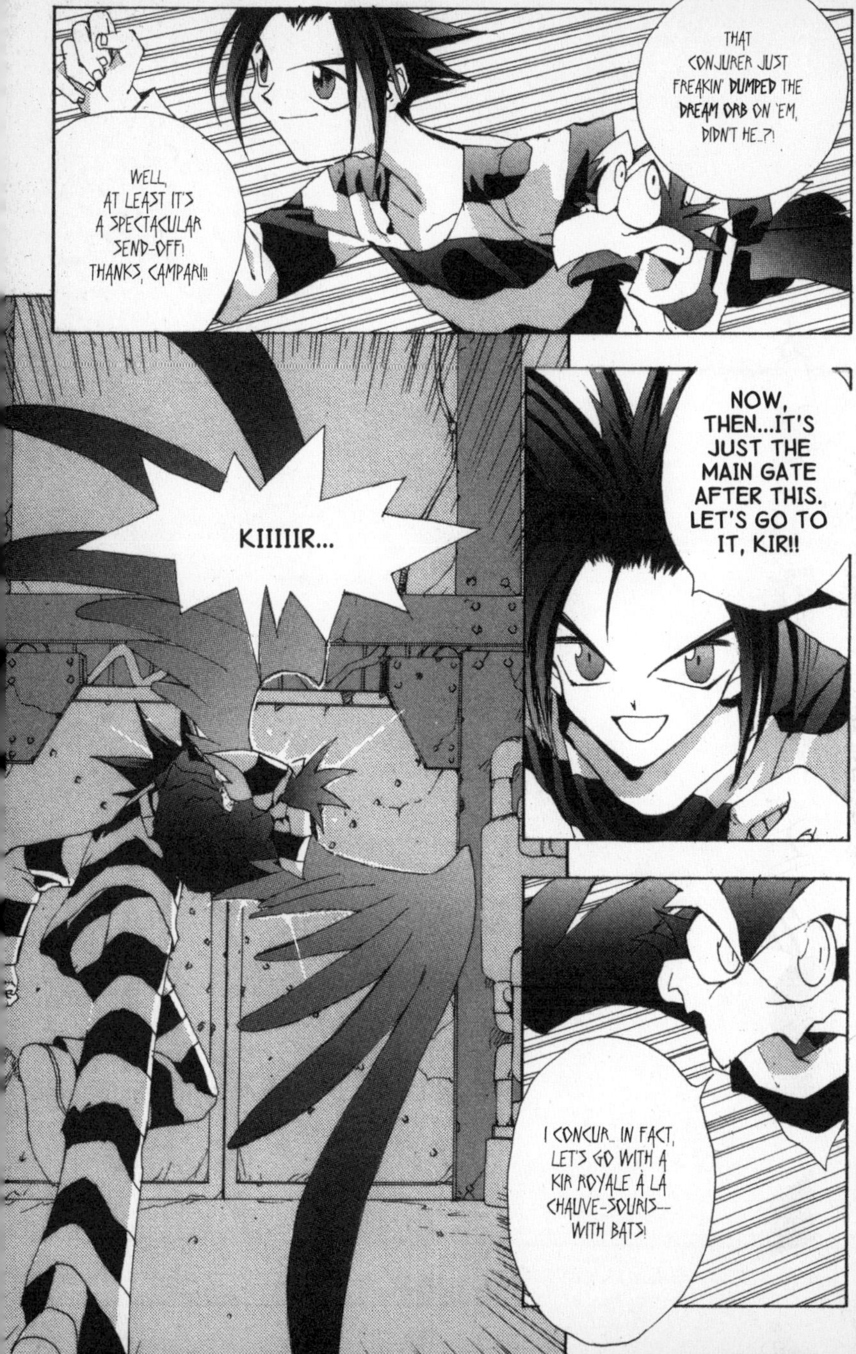
THAT CONJURER JUST FREAKIN' **DUMPED** THE **DREAM ORB** ON 'EM, DIDN'T HE..?!
WELL, AT LEAST IT'S A SPECTACULAR SEND-OFF! THANKS, CAMPARI!!
NOW, THEN...IT'S JUST THE MAIN GATE AFTER THIS. LET'S GO TO IT, KIR!!
I CONCUR.. IN FACT, LET'S GO WITH A KIR ROYALE À LA CHAUVE-SOURIS-- WITH BATS!
KIIIIIR...

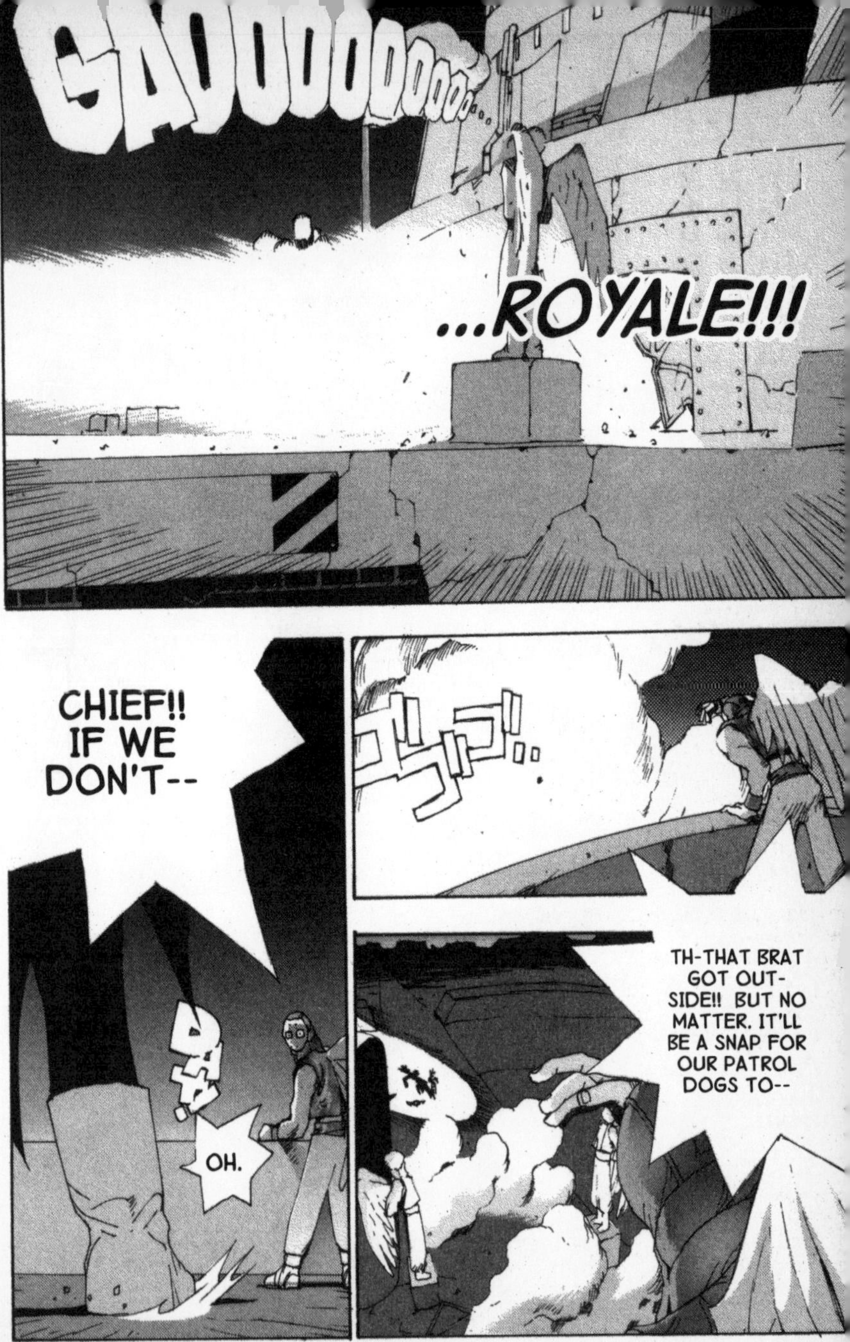
GAOOOOOOOO...
...ROYALE!!!
TH-THAT BRAT GOT OUT-SIDE!! BUT NO MATTER. IT'LL BE A SNAP FOR OUR PATROL DOGS TO--
CHIEF!! IF WE DON'T--
OH.

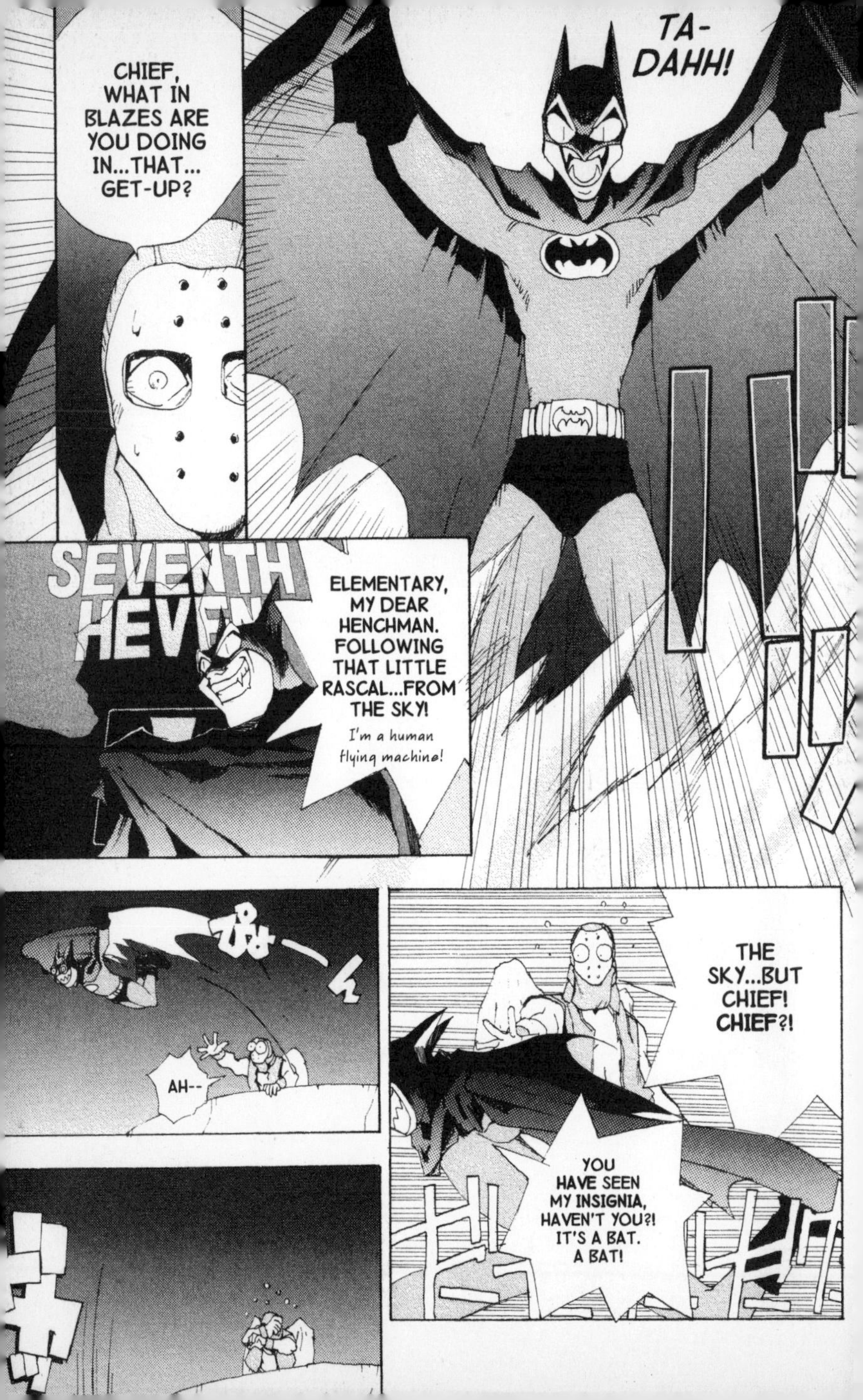
TA-DAHH!
CHIEF, WHAT IN BLAZES ARE YOU DOING IN...THAT... GET-UP?
SEVENTH
ELEMENTARY, MY DEAR HENCHMAN. FOLLOWING THAT LITTLE RASCAL...FROM THE SKY!
I'm a human flying machine!
THE SKY...BUT CHIEF! CHIEF?!
YOU HAVE SEEN MY INSIGNIA, HAVEN'T YOU?! IT'S A BAT. A BAT!
AH--

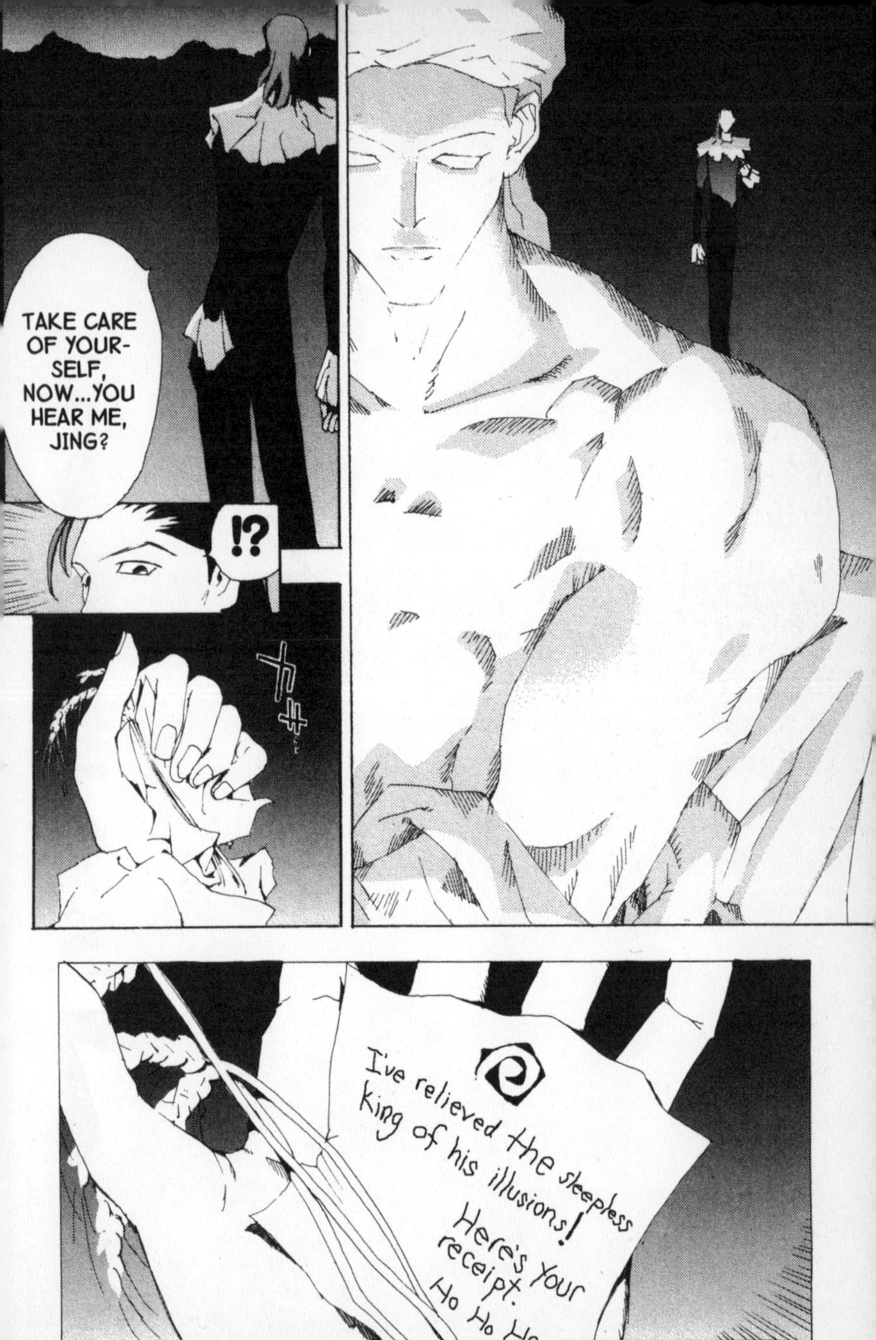
TAKE CARE OF YOUR-SELF, NOW...YOU HEAR ME, JING?
!?
I've relieved the sleepless King of his illusions!
Here's your receipt.
Ho Ho Ho

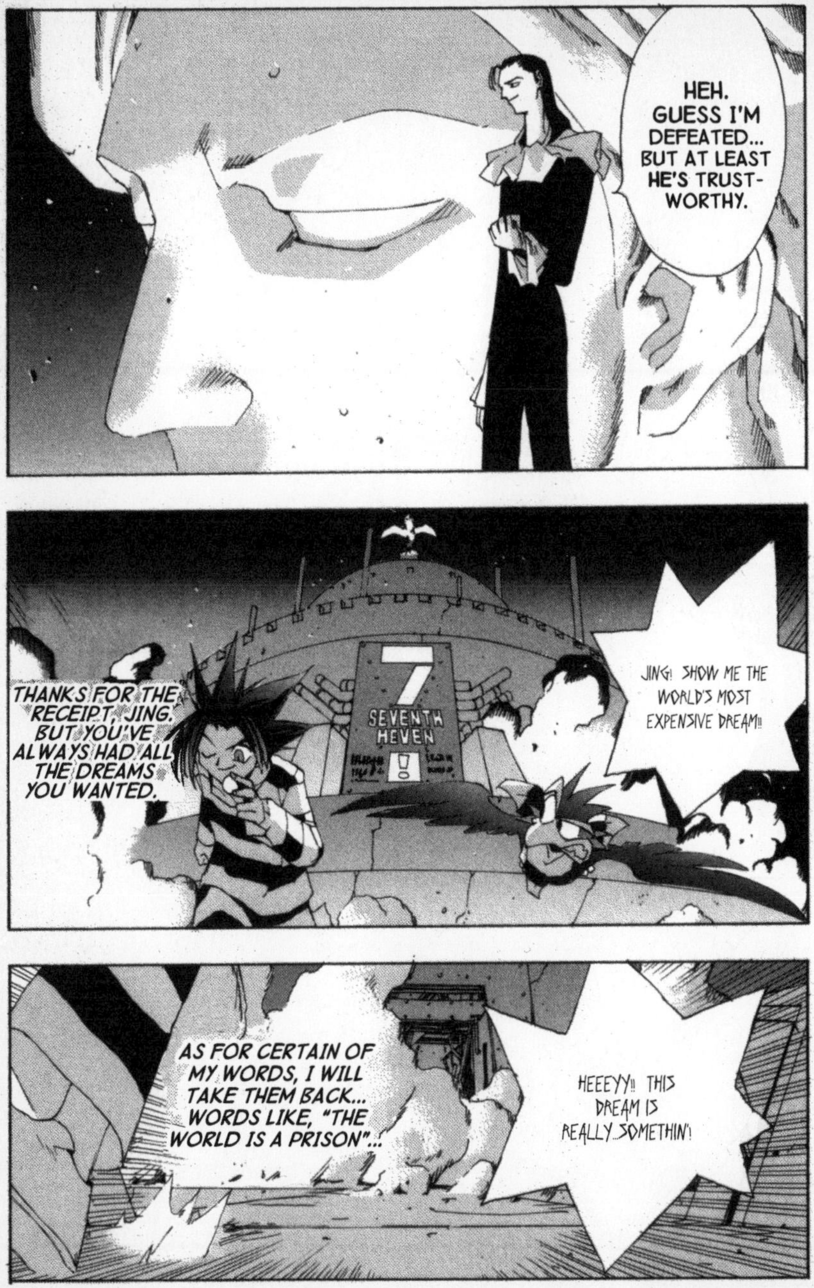
HEH. GUESS I'M DEFEATED... BUT AT LEAST HE'S TRUST-WORTHY.
JING! SHOW ME THE WORLD'S MOST EXPENSIVE DREAM!!
7 SEVENTH HEVEN
THANKS FOR THE RECEIPT, JING. BUT YOU'VE ALWAYS HAD ALL THE DREAMS YOU WANTED.
HEEEYY!! THIS DREAM IS REALLY...SOMETHIN'!
AS FOR CERTAIN OF MY WORDS, I WILL TAKE THEM BACK... WORDS LIKE, "THE WORLD IS A PRISON"...

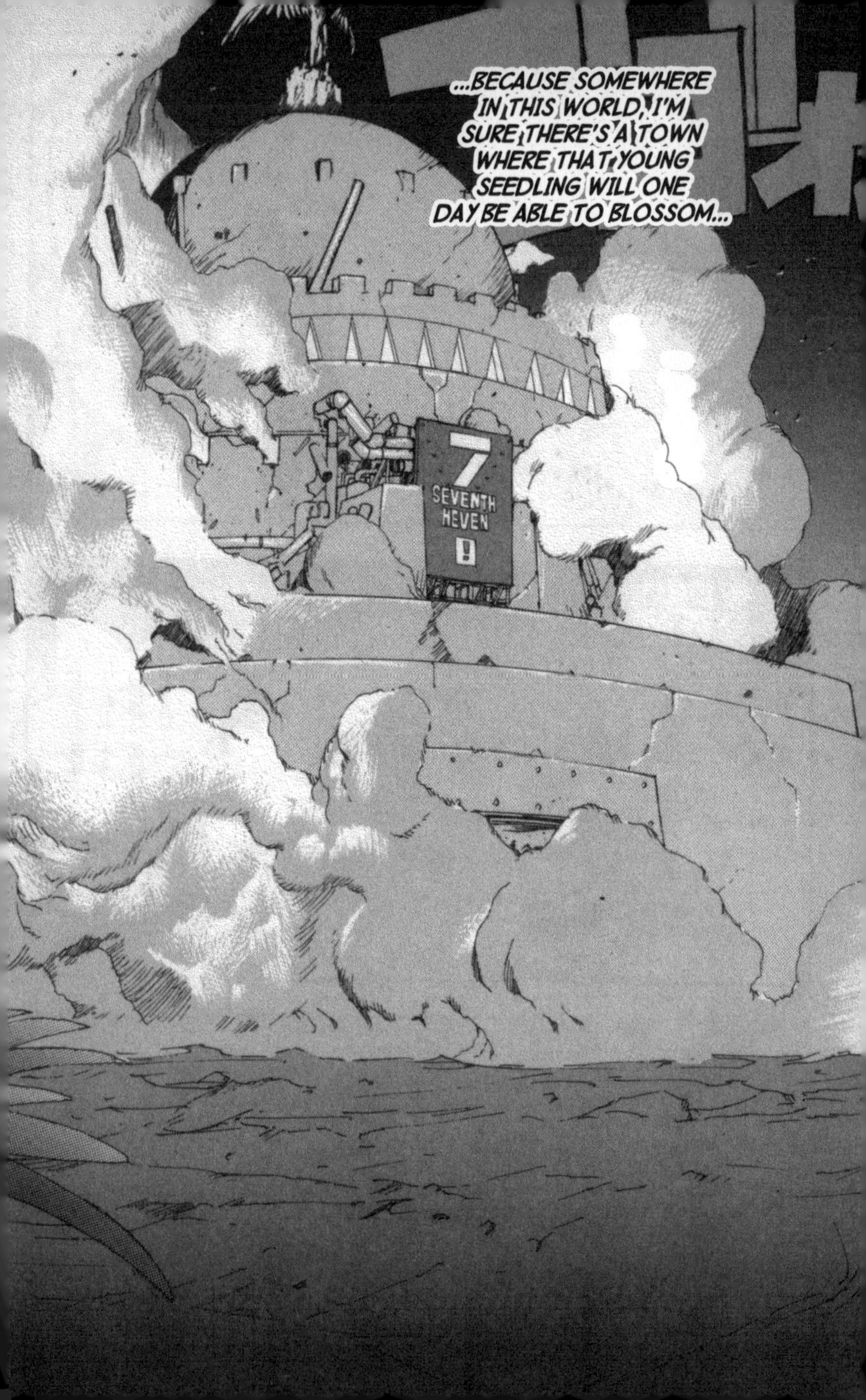
...BECAUSE SOMEWHERE IN THIS WORLD, I'M SURE THERE'S A TOWN WHERE THAT YOUNG SEEDLING WILL ONE DAY BE ABLE TO BLOSSOM...
7
SEVENTH HEVEN
!

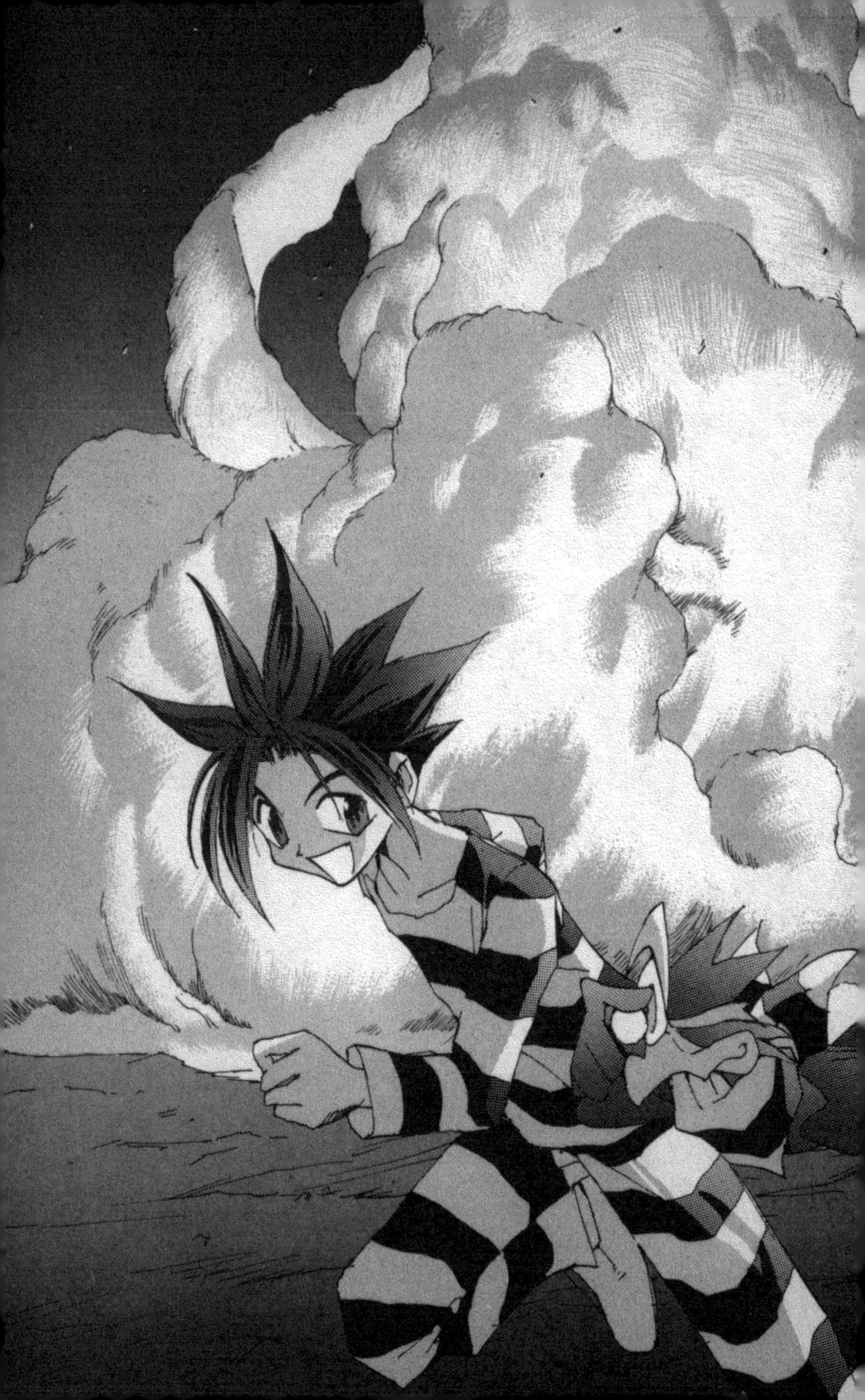

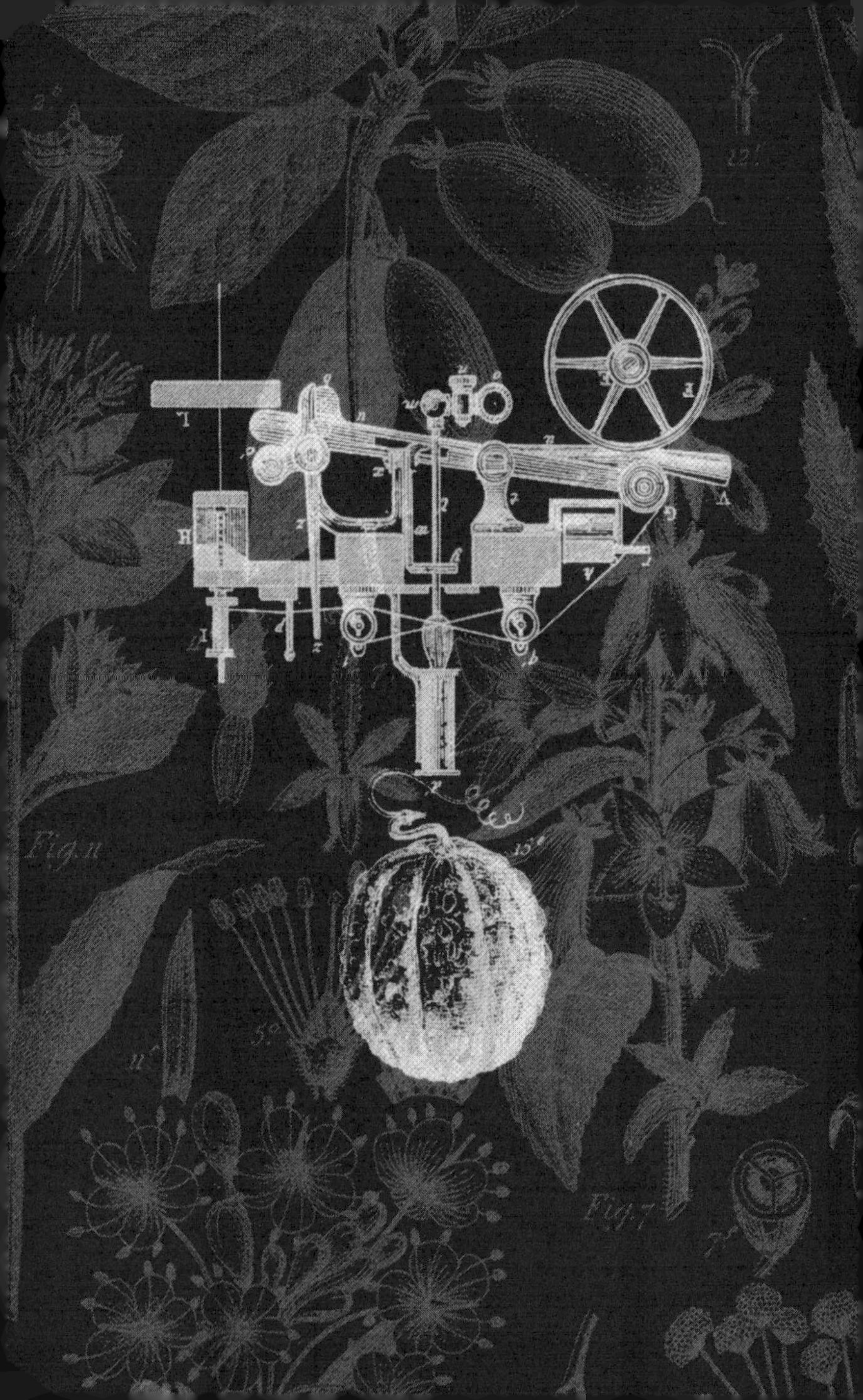
Fig.n
Fig.7

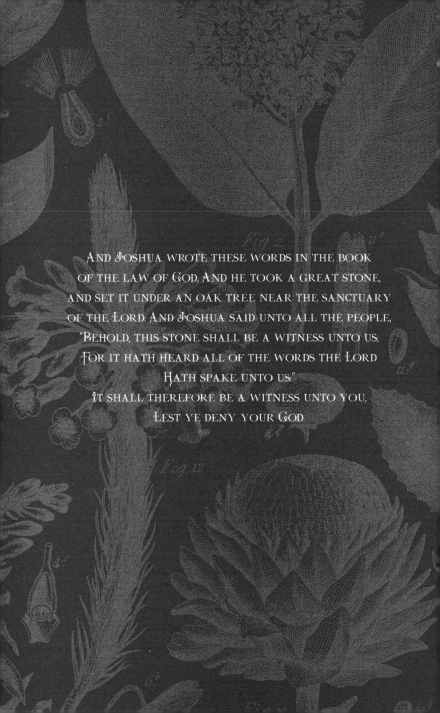

AND JOSHUA WROTE THESE WORDS IN THE BOOK
OF THE LAW OF GOD, AND HE TOOK A GREAT STONE,
AND SET IT UNDER AN OAK TREE NEAR THE SANCTUARY
OF THE LORD. AND JOSHUA SAID UNTO ALL THE PEOPLE,
"BEHOLD, THIS STONE SHALL BE A WITNESS UNTO US;
FOR IT HATH HEARD ALL OF THE WORDS THE LORD
HATH SPAKE UNTO US."
IT SHALL THEREFORE BE A WITNESS UNTO YOU,
LEST YE DENY YOUR GOD.

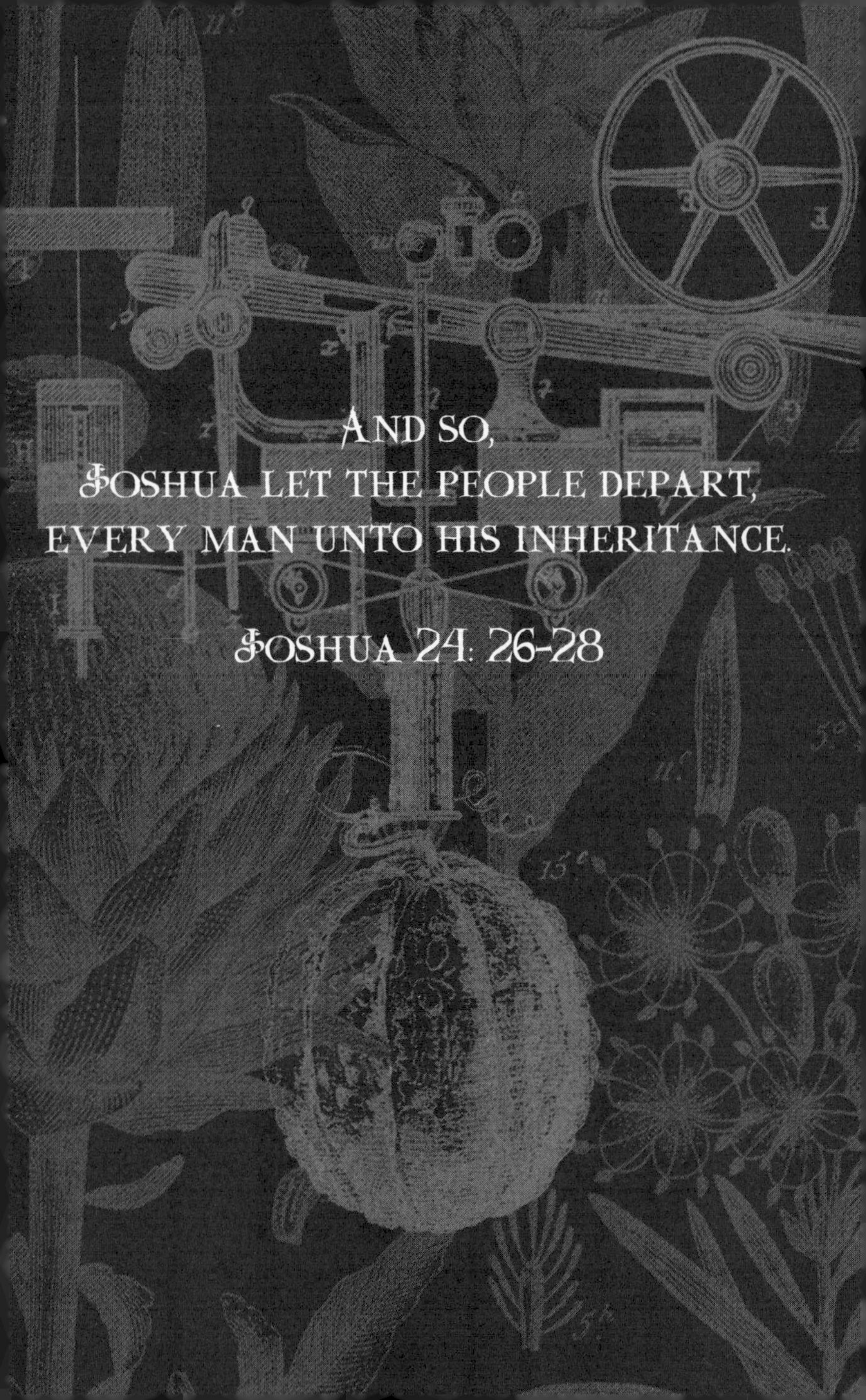

And so,
Joshua let the people depart,
every man unto his inheritance.

Joshua 24: 26-28

EXTRA SHOT 1
AMARCORD / FIRST VOLUME
BATATATA
UP, HUT!!
LEFT AND RIGHT, HUT, HUT!!
DOWN, HUT!!

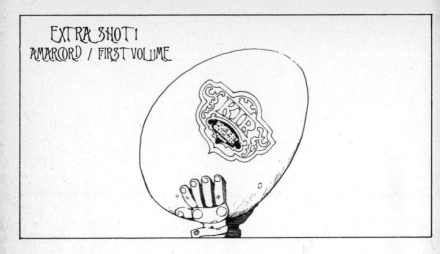

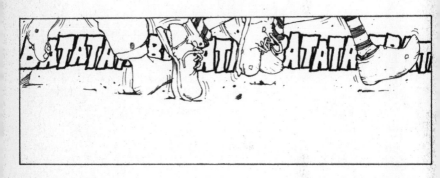

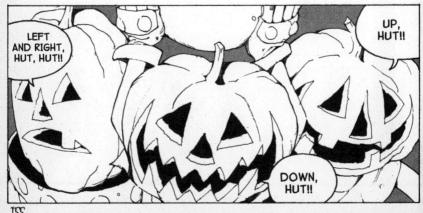

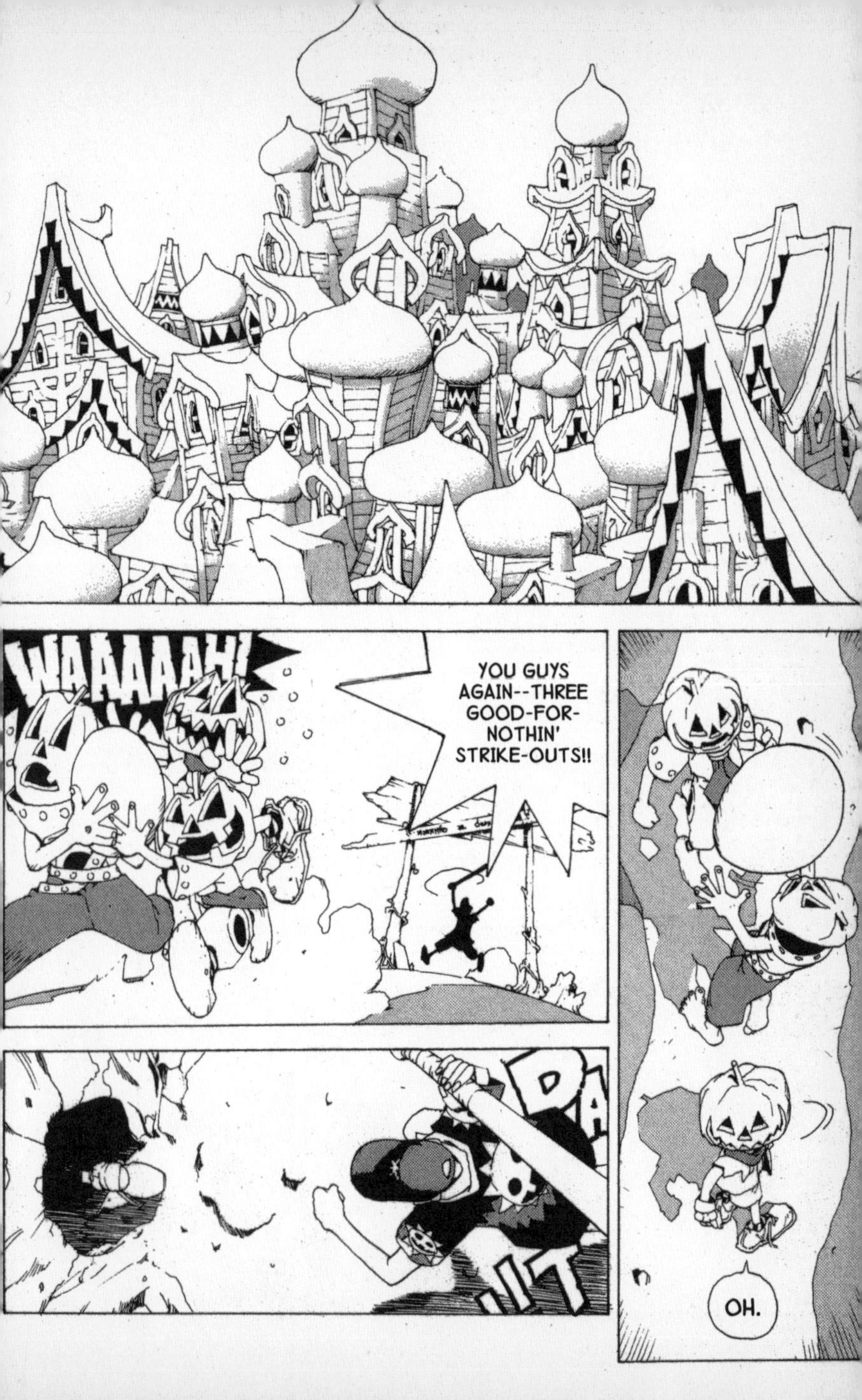
OH.
WAAAAAH!
YOU GUYS AGAIN--THREE GOOD-FOR-NOTHIN' STRIKE-OUTS!!

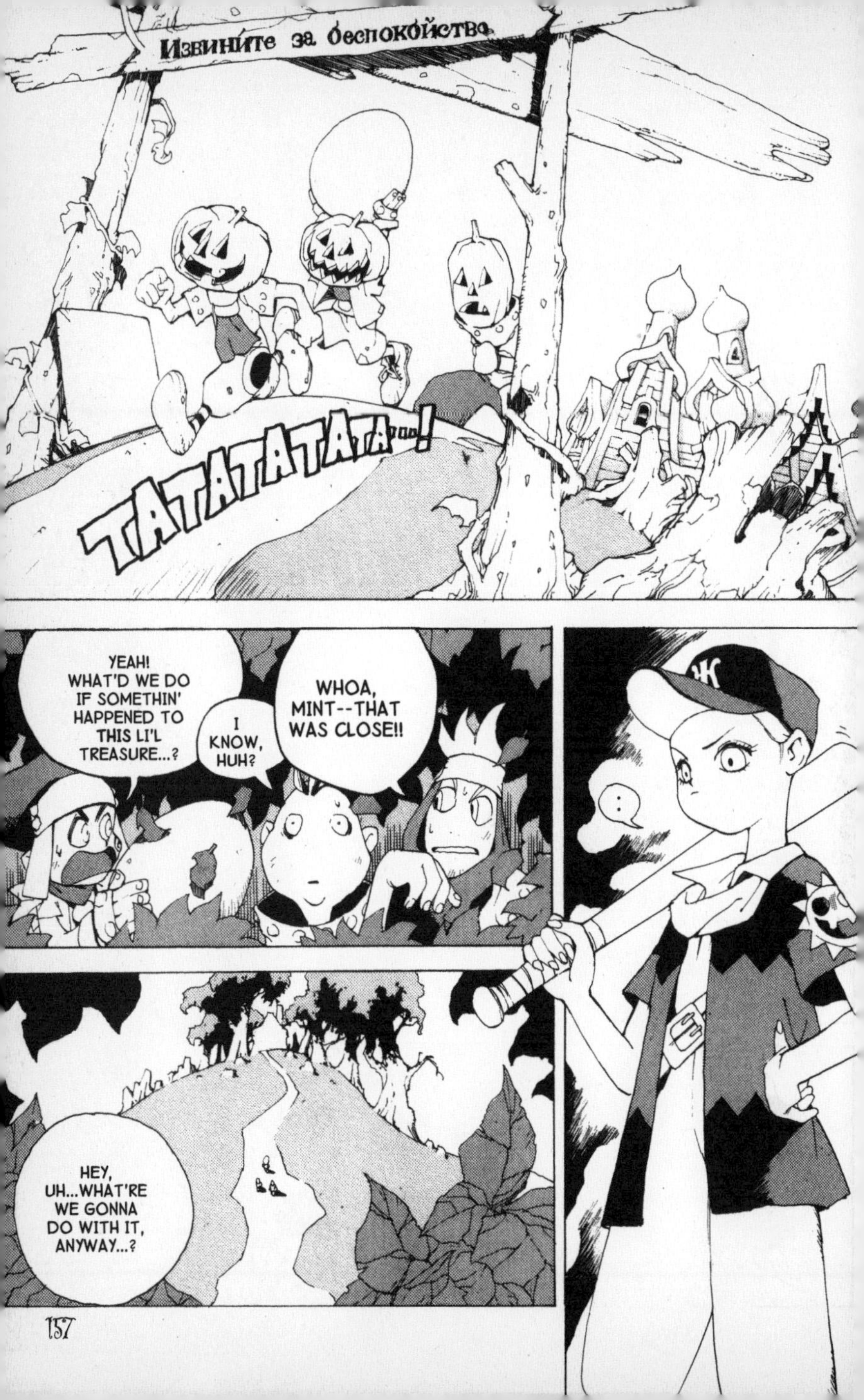
Извините за беспокойство
TATATATATA...!
...
WHOA, MINT--THAT WAS CLOSE!!
I KNOW, HUH?
YEAH! WHAT'D WE DO IF SOMETHIN' HAPPENED TO THIS LI'L TREASURE...?
HEY, UH...WHAT'RE WE GONNA DO WITH IT, ANYWAY...?

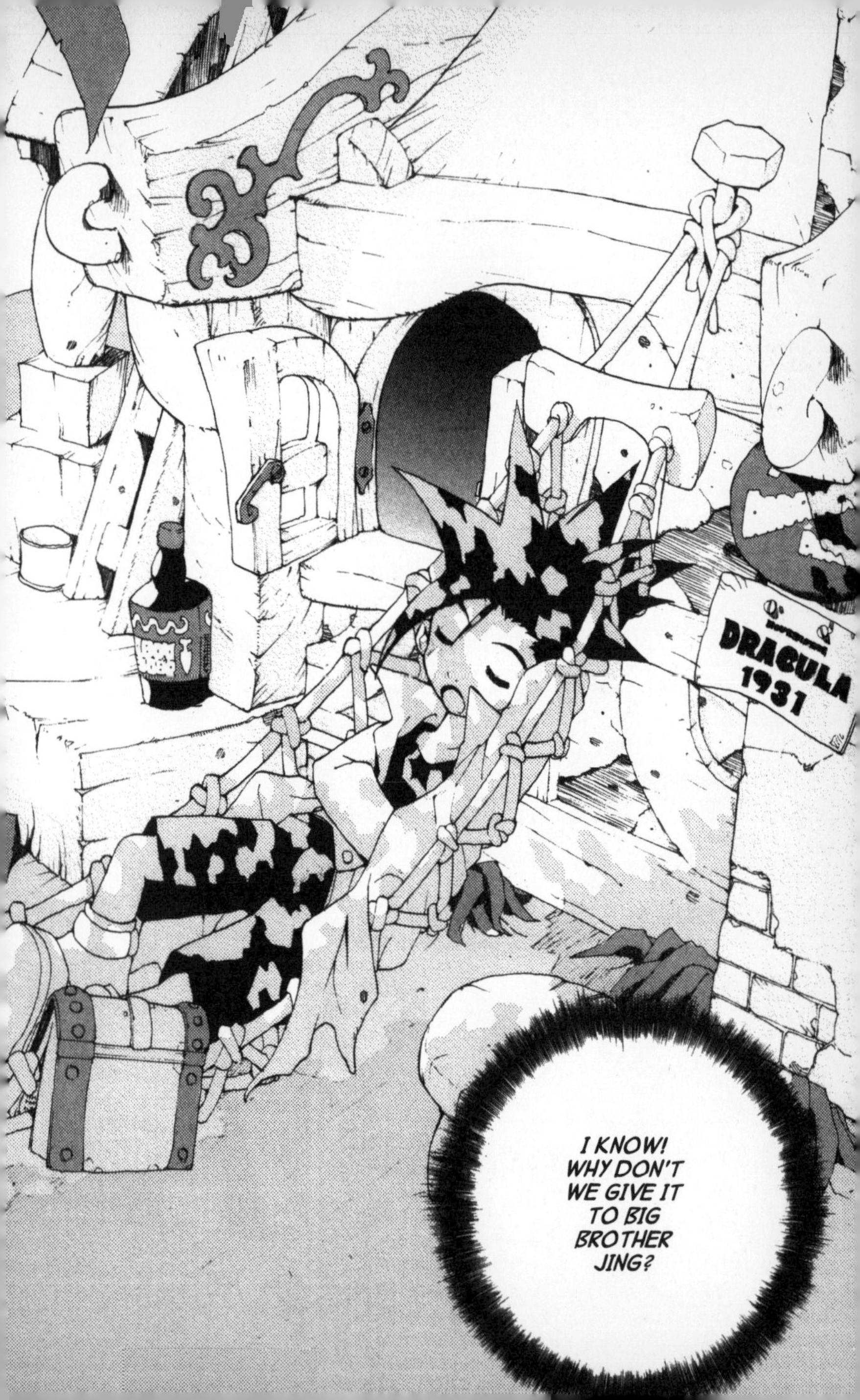
DRACULA
1931
I KNOW! WHY DON'T WE GIVE IT TO BIG BROTHER JING?

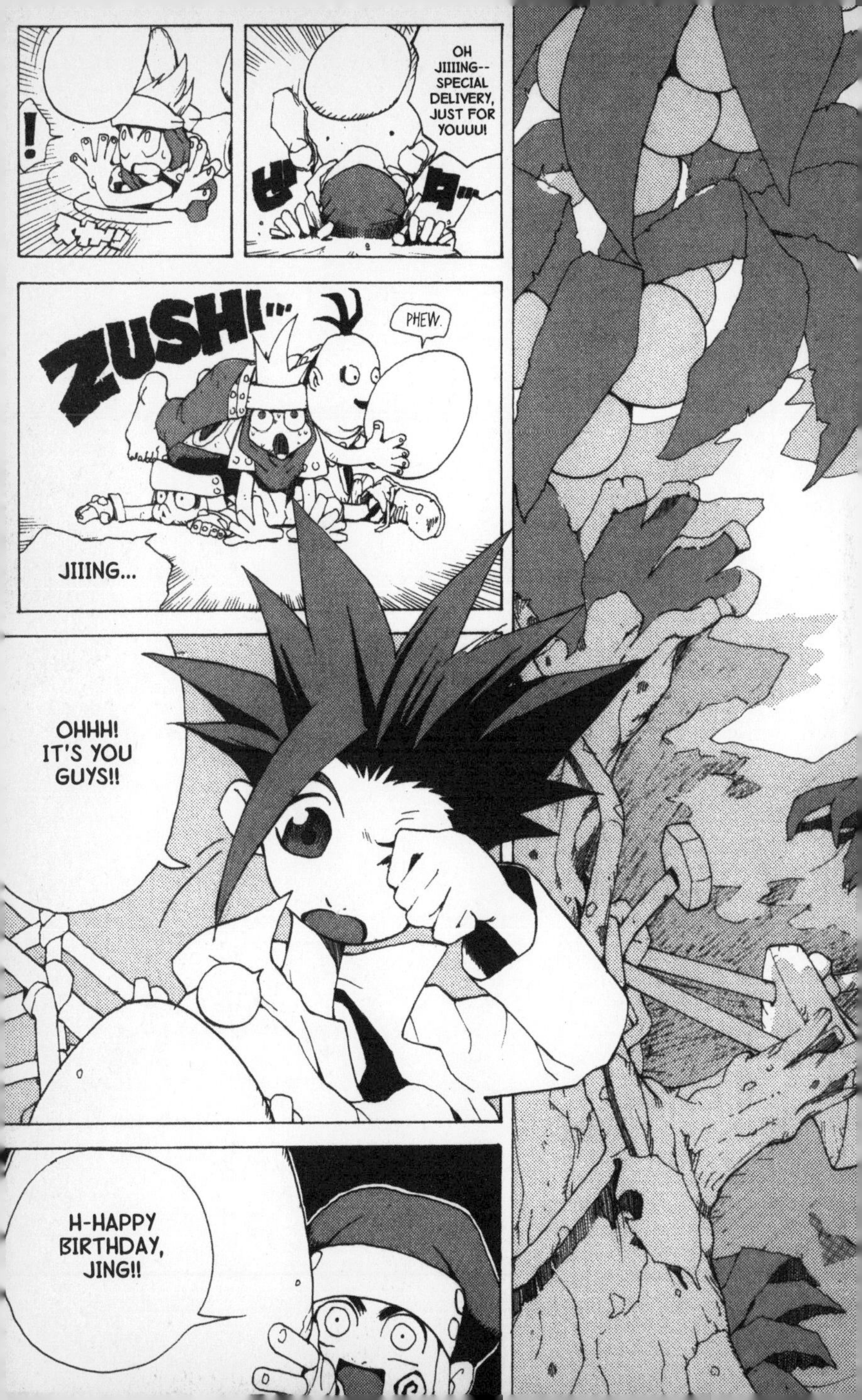
OH JIIING-- SPECIAL DELIVERY, JUST FOR YOUUU!
!
PHEW.
ZUSHI!"
JIIING...
OHHH! IT'S YOU GUYS!!
H-HAPPY BIRTHDAY, JING!!

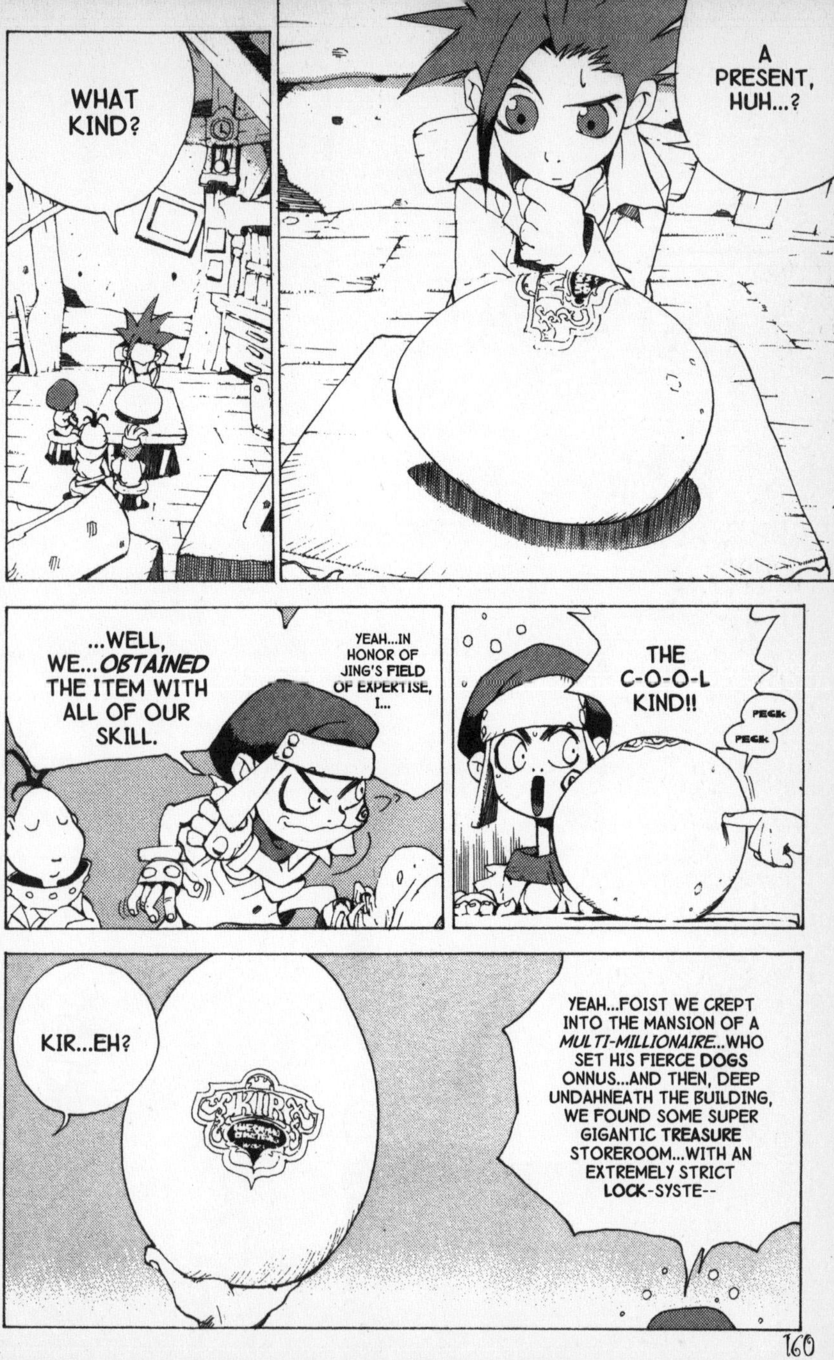
A PRESENT, HUH...?
WHAT KIND?
THE C-O-O-L KIND!!
PECK
PECK
YEAH...IN HONOR OF JING'S FIELD OF EXPERTISE, I...
...WELL, WE...*OBTAINED* THE ITEM WITH ALL OF OUR SKILL.
YEAH...FOIST WE CREPT INTO THE MANSION OF A *MULTI-MILLIONAIRE*...WHO SET HIS FIERCE DOGS ONNUS...AND THEN, DEEP UNDAHNEATH THE BUILDING, WE FOUND SOME SUPER GIGANTIC TREASURE STOREROOM...WITH AN EXTREMELY STRICT LOCK-SYSTE--
KIR...EH?

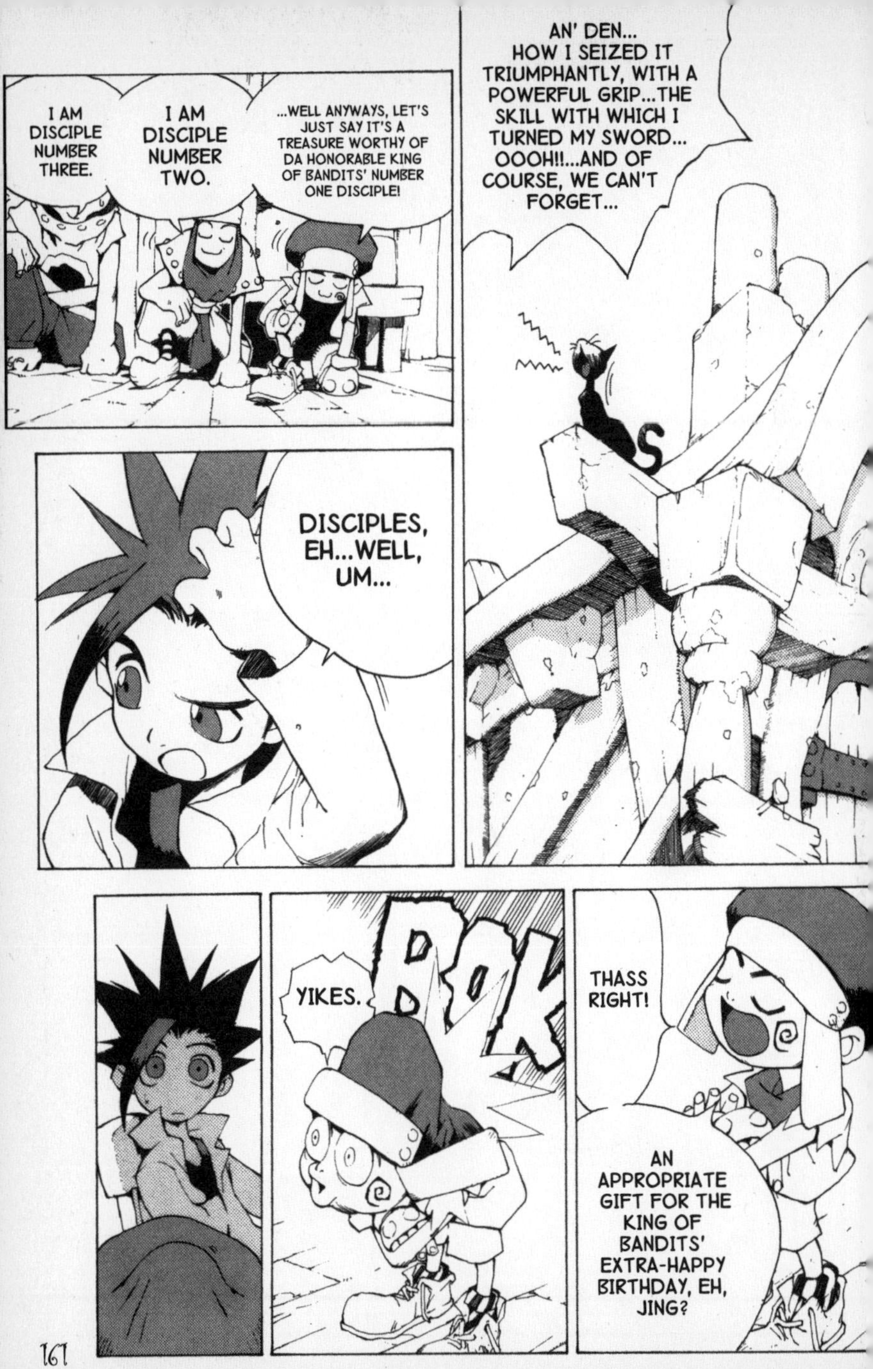
AN' DEN... HOW I SEIZED IT TRIUMPHANTLY, WITH A POWERFUL GRIP...THE SKILL WITH WHICH I TURNED MY SWORD... OOOH!!...AND OF COURSE, WE CAN'T FORGET...
...WELL ANYWAYS, LET'S JUST SAY IT'S A TREASURE WORTHY OF DA HONORABLE KING OF BANDITS' NUMBER ONE DISCIPLE!
I AM DISCIPLE NUMBER TWO.
I AM DISCIPLE NUMBER THREE.
DISCIPLES, EH...WELL, UM...
THASS RIGHT!
AN APPROPRIATE GIFT FOR THE KING OF BANDITS' EXTRA-HAPPY BIRTHDAY, EH, JING?
BOK
YIKES.

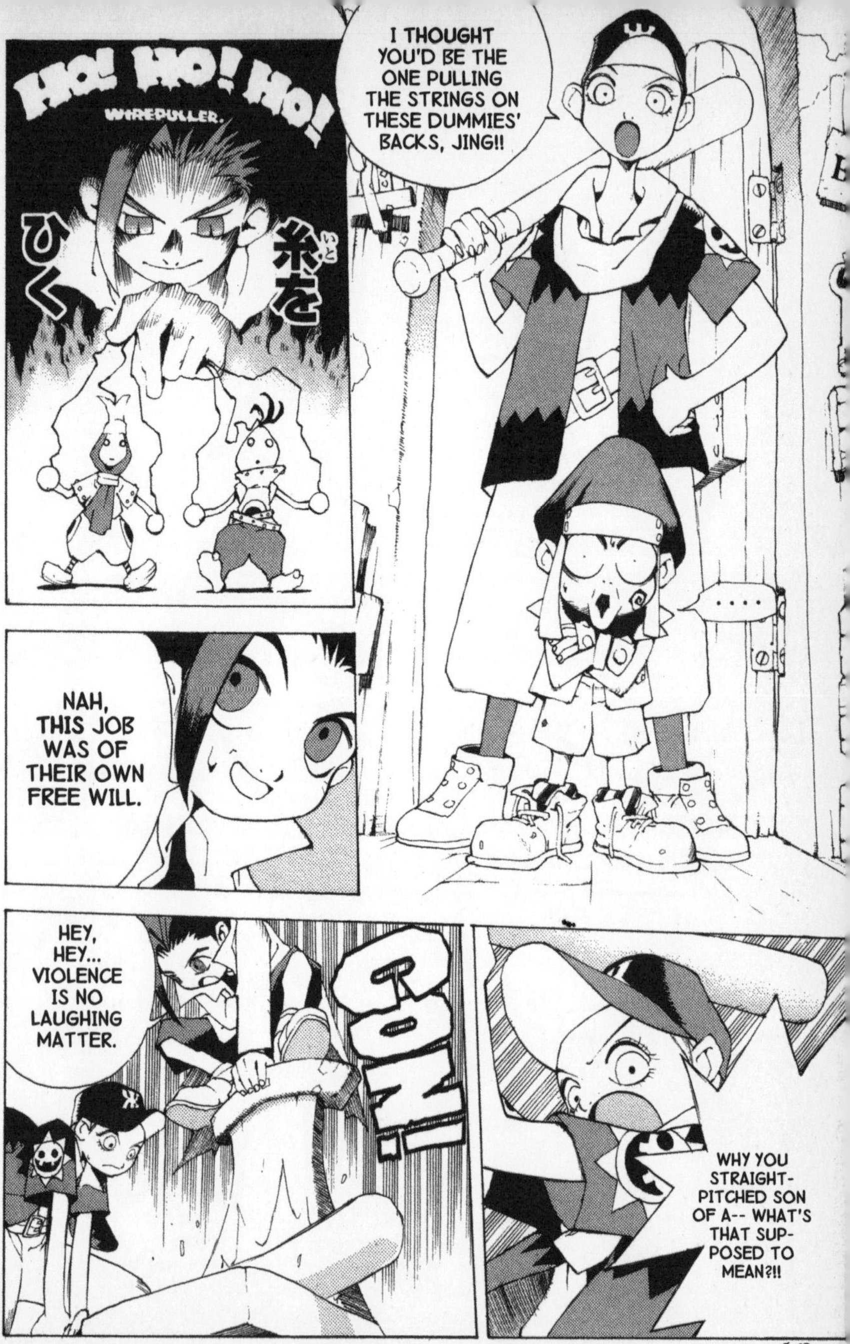
I THOUGHT YOU'D BE THE ONE PULLING THE STRINGS ON THESE DUMMIES' BACKS, JING!!
....
HO! HO! HO!
WIREPULLER.
糸をひく
NAH, THIS JOB WAS OF THEIR OWN FREE WILL.
WHY YOU STRAIGHT-PITCHED SON OF A-- WHAT'S THAT SUP-POSED TO MEAN?!!
HEY, HEY... VIOLENCE IS NO LAUGHING MATTER.
CON!!

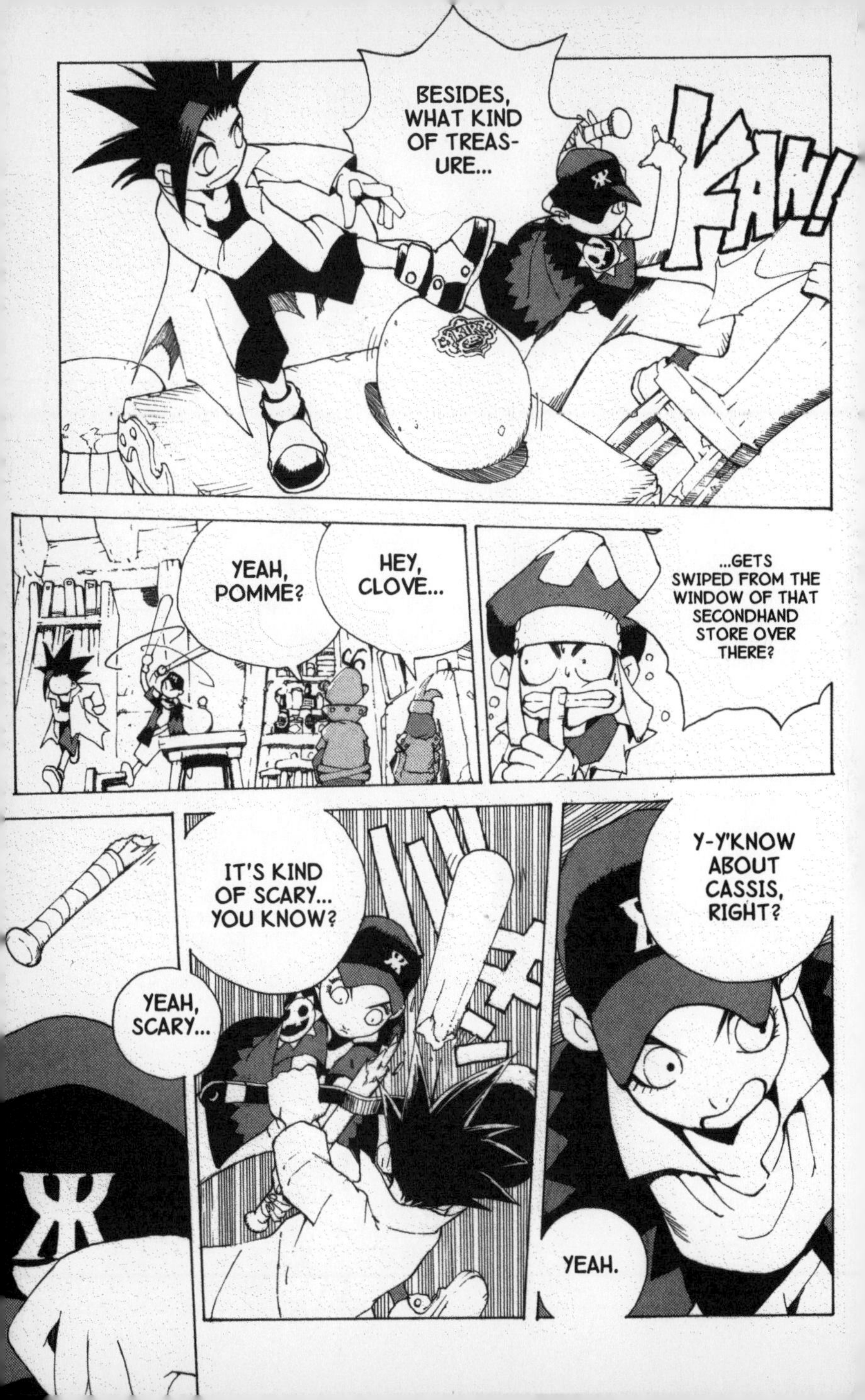
BESIDES, WHAT KIND OF TREASURE...
KAW!!
...GETS SWIPED FROM THE WINDOW OF THAT SECONDHAND STORE OVER THERE?
HEY, CLOVE...
YEAH, POMME?
Y-Y'KNOW ABOUT CASSIS, RIGHT?
YEAH.
IT'S KIND OF SCARY... YOU KNOW?
YEAH, SCARY...

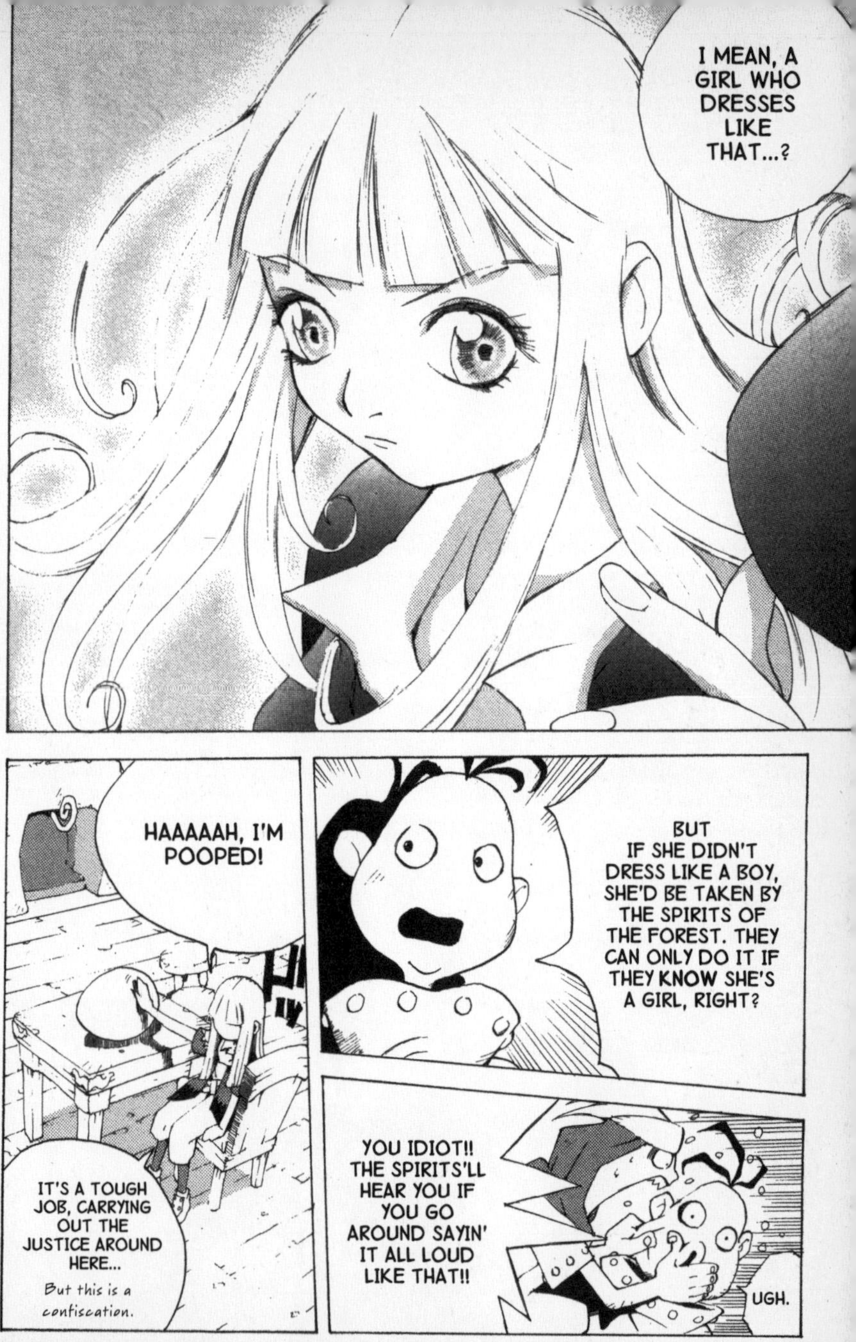
I MEAN, A GIRL WHO DRESSES LIKE THAT...?
BUT IF SHE DIDN'T DRESS LIKE A BOY, SHE'D BE TAKEN BY THE SPIRITS OF THE FOREST. THEY CAN ONLY DO IT IF THEY KNOW SHE'S A GIRL, RIGHT?
YOU IDIOT!! THE SPIRITS'LL HEAR YOU IF YOU GO AROUND SAYIN' IT ALL LOUD LIKE THAT!!
UGH.
HAAAAAH, I'M POOPED!
IT'S A TOUGH JOB, CARRYING OUT THE JUSTICE AROUND HERE...
But this is a confiscation.

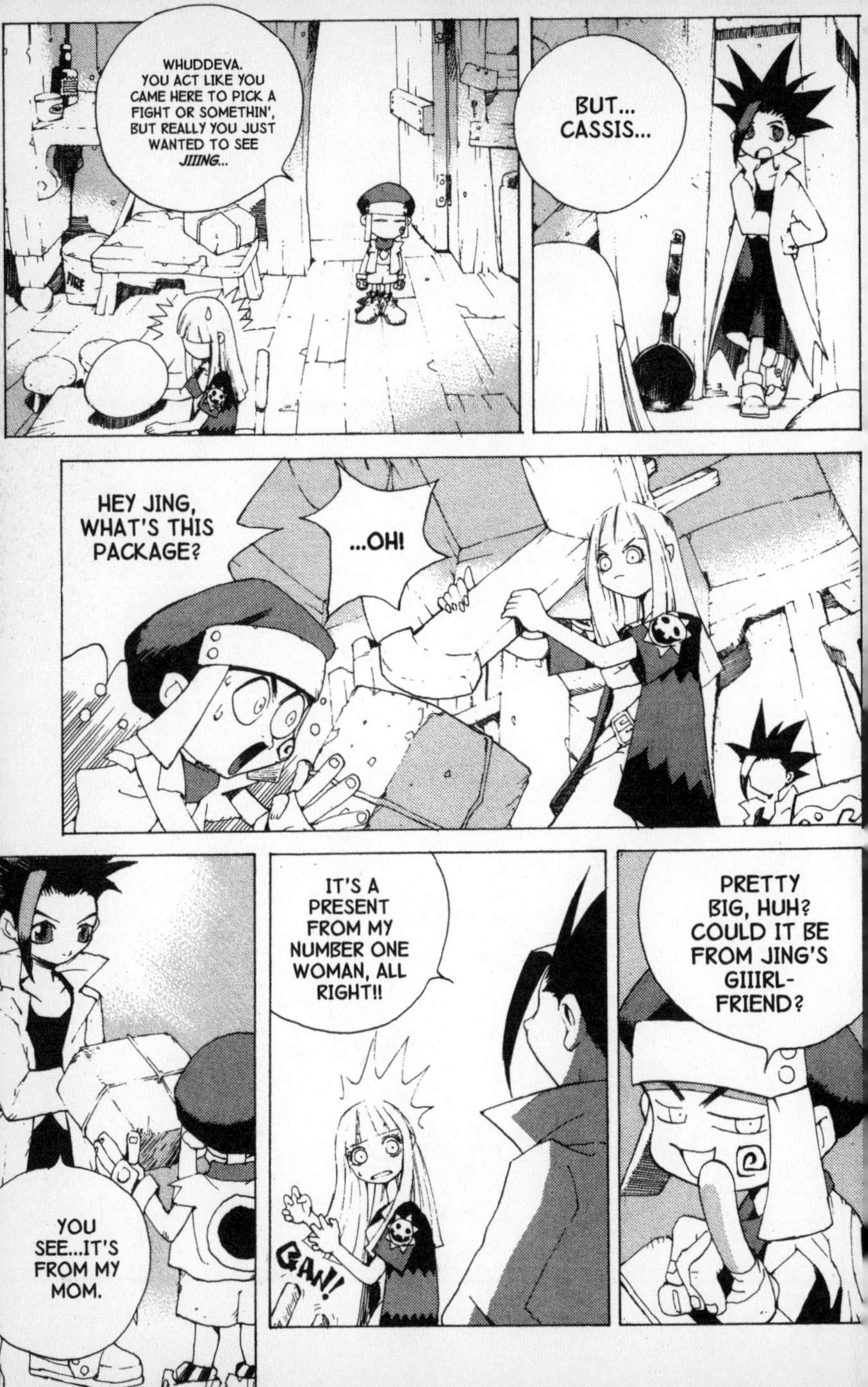
BUT... CASSIS...
WHUDDEVA. YOU ACT LIKE YOU CAME HERE TO PICK A FIGHT OR SOMETHIN', BUT REALLY YOU JUST WANTED TO SEE *JIIING*...
HEY JING, WHAT'S THIS PACKAGE?
...OH!
PRETTY BIG, HUH? COULD IT BE FROM JING'S GIIIRL-FRIEND?
IT'S A PRESENT FROM MY NUMBER ONE WOMAN, ALL RIGHT!!
GAN!
YOU SEE...IT'S FROM MY MOM.

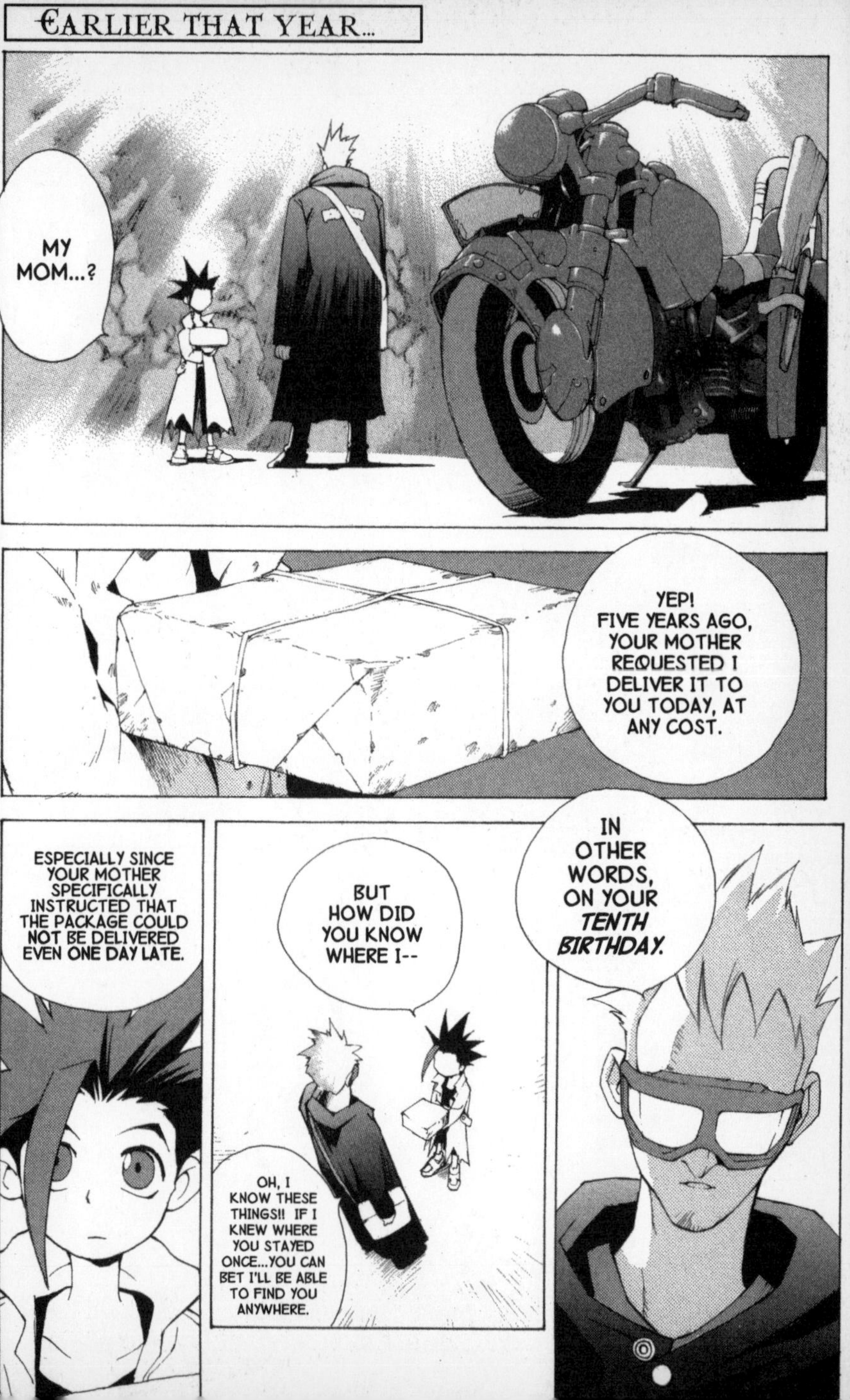
EARLIER THAT YEAR...
MY MOM...?
YEP! FIVE YEARS AGO, YOUR MOTHER REQUESTED I DELIVER IT TO YOU TODAY, AT ANY COST.
IN OTHER WORDS, ON YOUR *TENTH BIRTHDAY.*
BUT HOW DID YOU KNOW WHERE I--
OH, I KNOW THESE THINGS!! IF I KNEW WHERE YOU STAYED ONCE...YOU CAN BET I'LL BE ABLE TO FIND YOU ANYWHERE.
ESPECIALLY SINCE YOUR MOTHER SPECIFICALLY INSTRUCTED THAT THE PACKAGE COULD NOT BE DELIVERED EVEN ONE DAY LATE.

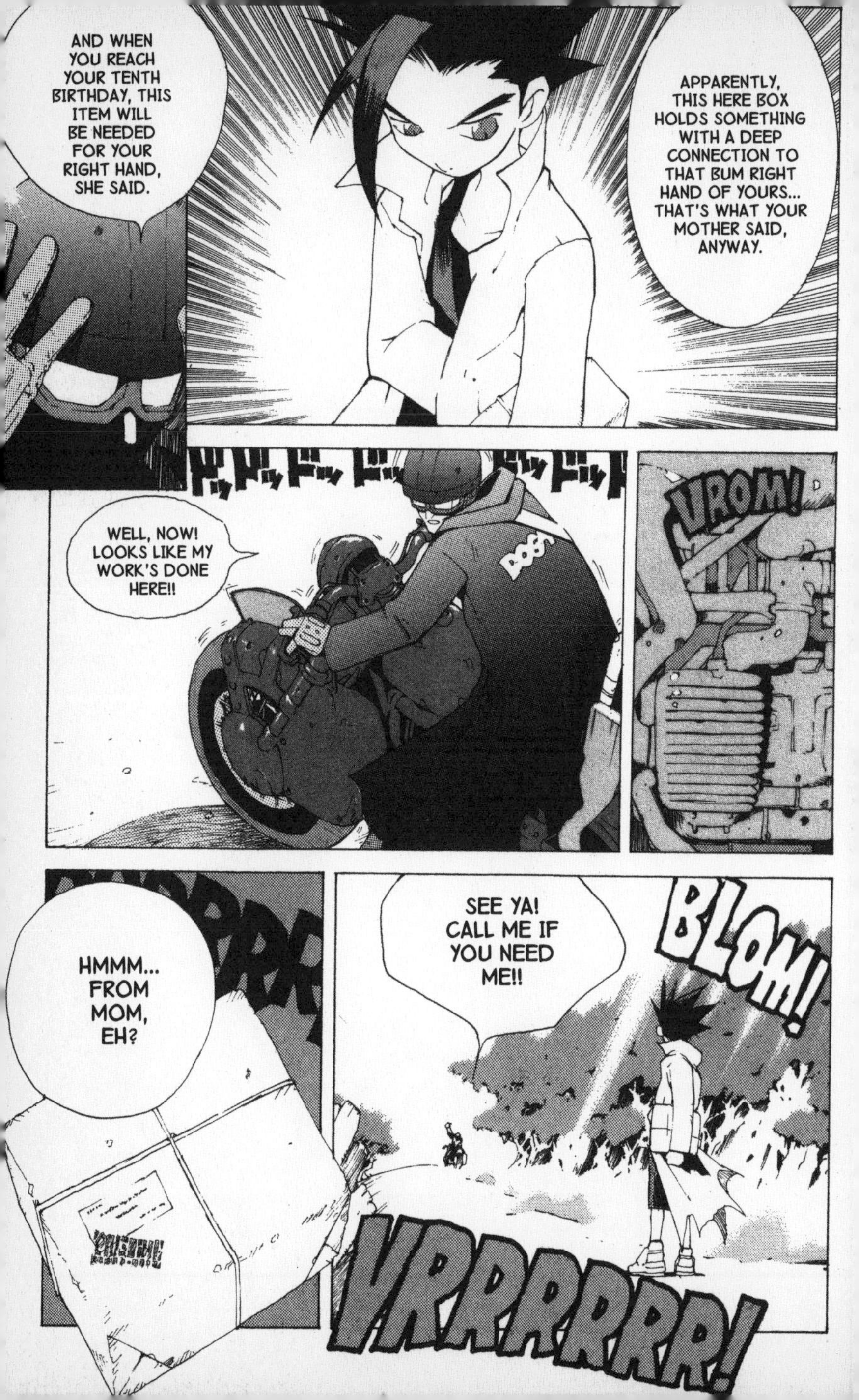
APPARENTLY, THIS HERE BOX HOLDS SOMETHING WITH A DEEP CONNECTION TO THAT BUM RIGHT HAND OF YOURS... THAT'S WHAT YOUR MOTHER SAID, ANYWAY.
AND WHEN YOU REACH YOUR TENTH BIRTHDAY, THIS ITEM WILL BE NEEDED FOR YOUR RIGHT HAND, SHE SAID.
VROM!
WELL, NOW! LOOKS LIKE MY WORK'S DONE HERE!!
BOSS
SEE YA! CALL ME IF YOU NEED ME!!
BLOM!
VRRRRRR!
HMMM... FROM MOM, EH?

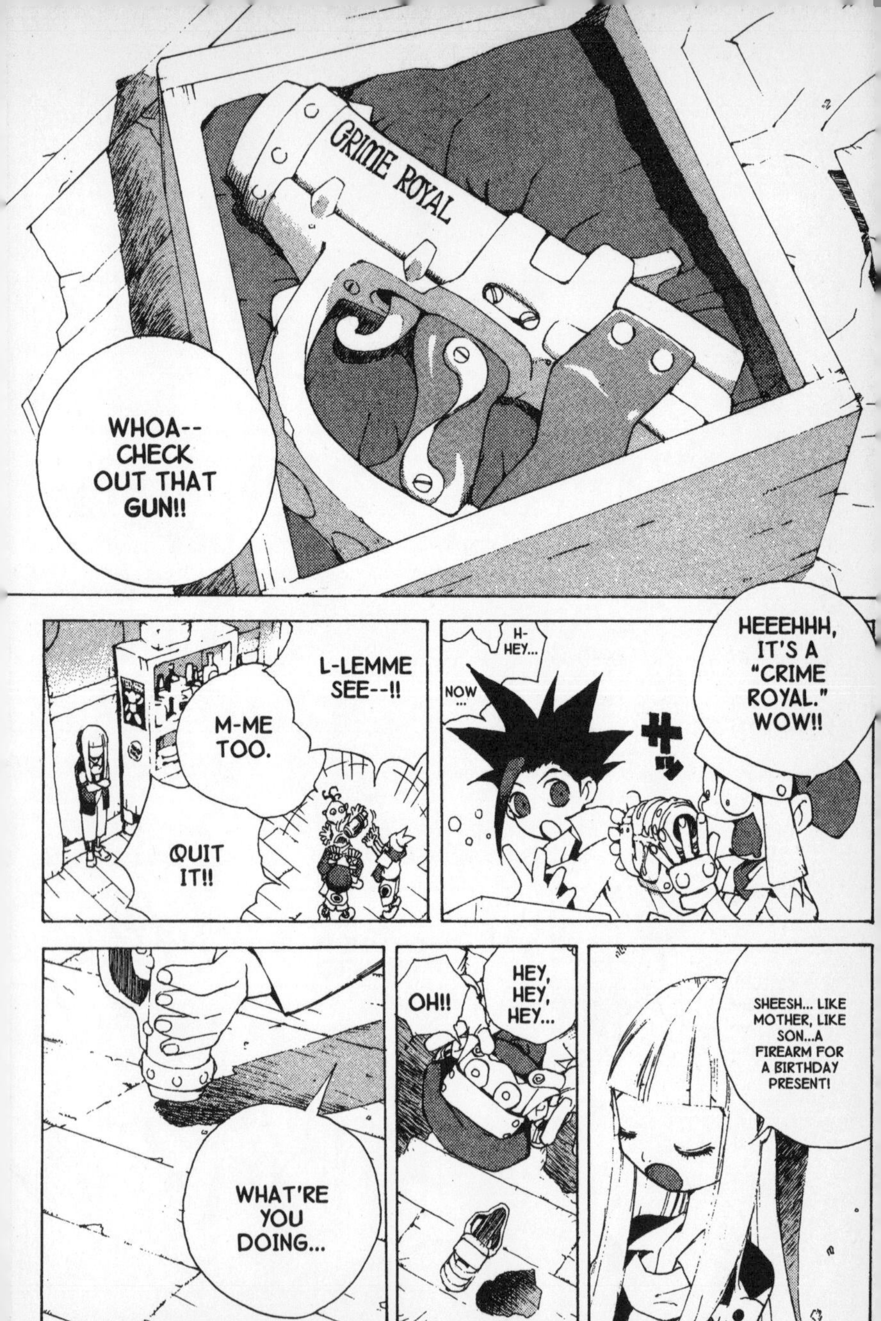
GRIME ROYAL
WHOA--CHECK OUT THAT GUN!!
HEEEEHHH, IT'S A "CRIME ROYAL." WOW!!
サッ
H-HEY...
NOW...
L-LEMME SEE--!!
M-ME TOO.
QUIT IT!!
SHEESH... LIKE MOTHER, LIKE SON...A FIREARM FOR A BIRTHDAY PRESENT!
HEY, HEY, HEY...
OH!!
WHAT'RE YOU DOING...

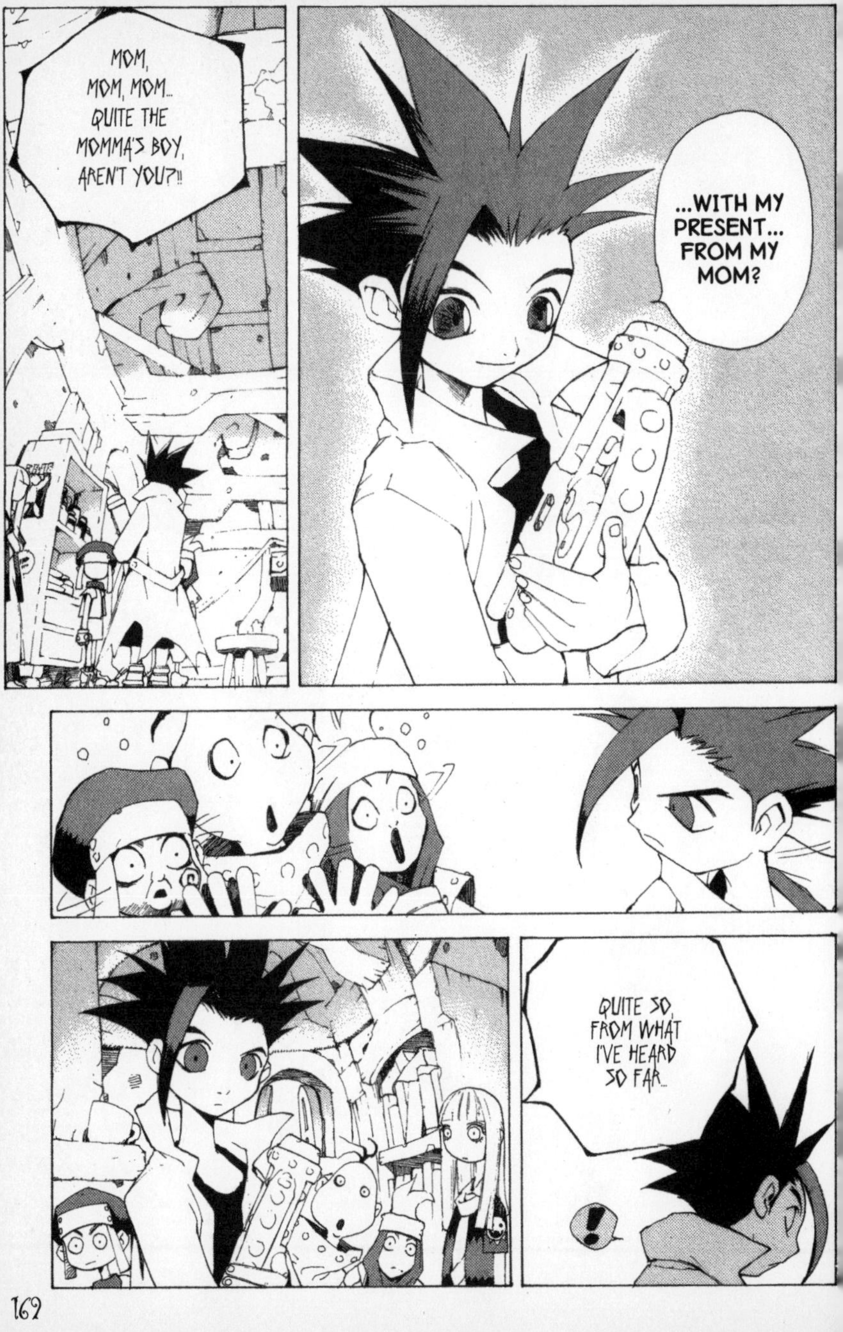
...WITH MY PRESENT... FROM MY MOM?
MOM, MOM, MOM... QUITE THE MOMMA'S BOY, AREN'T YOU?!!
QUITE SO, FROM WHAT I'VE HEARD SO FAR...
!

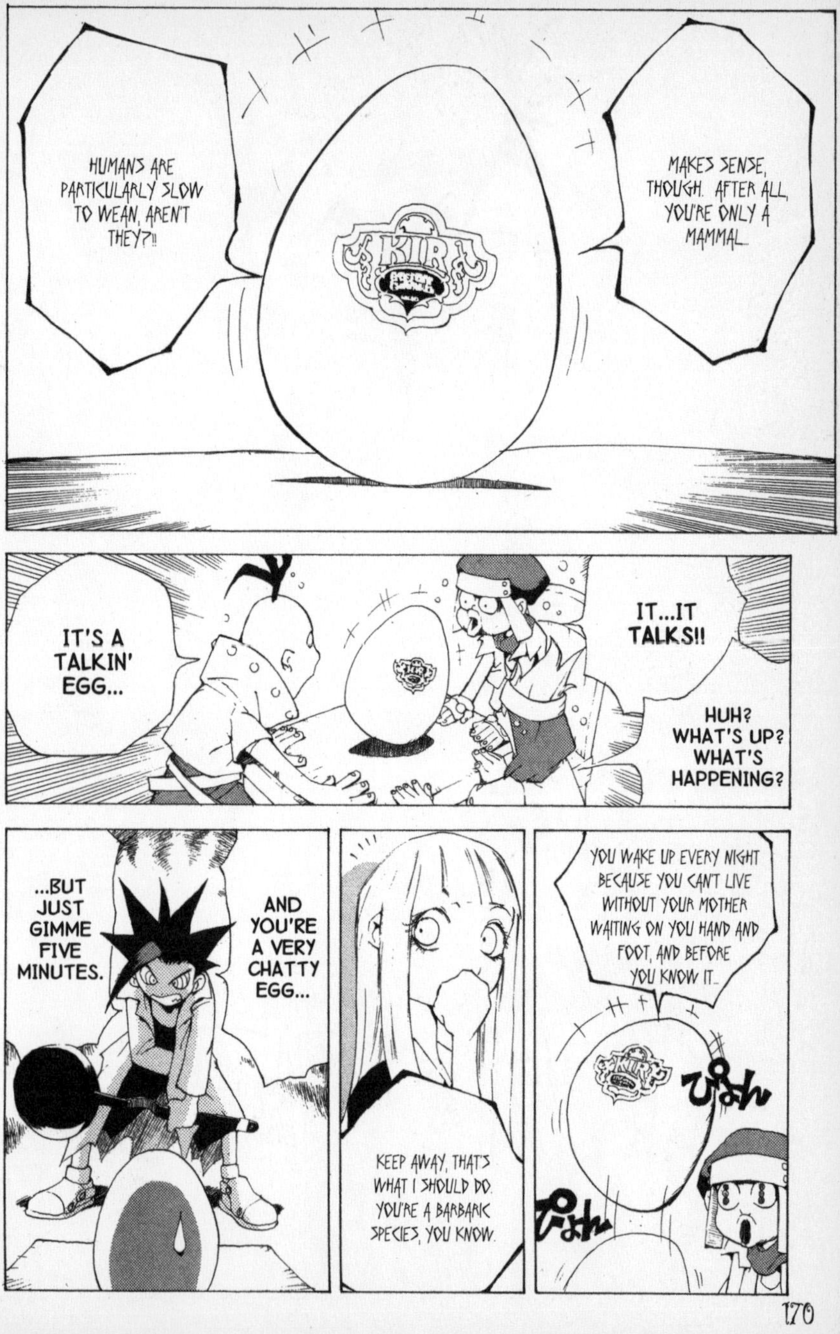
MAKES SENSE, THOUGH. AFTER ALL, YOU'RE ONLY A MAMMAL...
HUMANS ARE PARTICULARLY SLOW TO WEAN, AREN'T THEY?!!
IT...IT TALKS!!
IT'S A TALKIN' EGG...
HUH? WHAT'S UP? WHAT'S HAPPENING?
YOU WAKE UP EVERY NIGHT BECAUSE YOU CAN'T LIVE WITHOUT YOUR MOTHER WAITING ON YOU HAND AND FOOT, AND BEFORE YOU KNOW IT...
ぴょん
ぴょん
KEEP AWAY, THAT'S WHAT I SHOULD DO. YOU'RE A BARBARIC SPECIES, YOU KNOW.
AND YOU'RE A VERY CHATTY EGG...
...BUT JUST GIMME FIVE MINUTES.

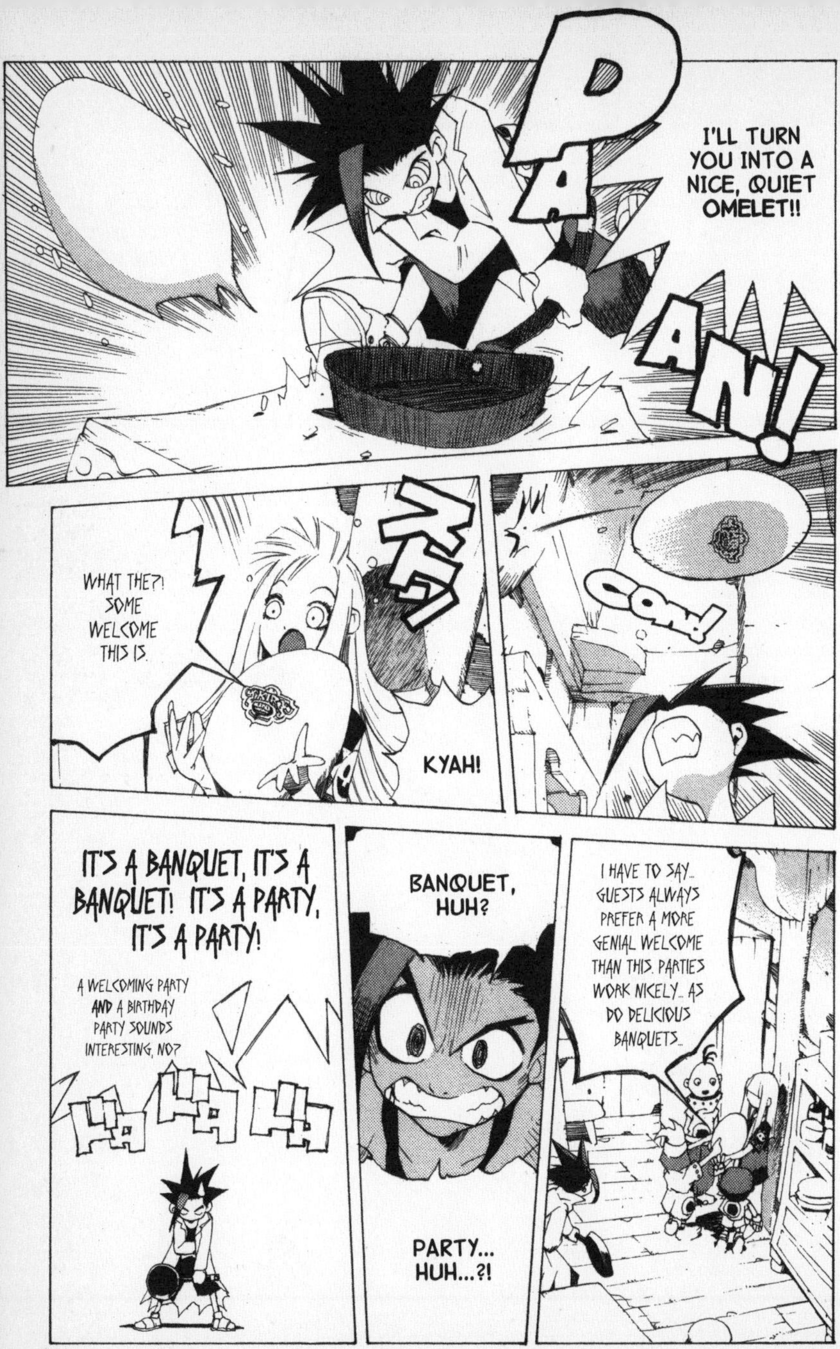
PAN!
I'LL TURN YOU INTO A NICE, QUIET OMELET!!
CON!
KYAH!
WHAT THE?! SOME WELCOME THIS IS.
I HAVE TO SAY... GUESTS ALWAYS PREFER A MORE GENIAL WELCOME THAN THIS. PARTIES WORK NICELY... AS DO DELICIOUS BANQUETS...
BANQUET, HUH?
PARTY... HUH...?!
IT'S A BANQUET, IT'S A BANQUET! IT'S A PARTY, IT'S A PARTY!
A WELCOMING PARTY AND A BIRTHDAY PARTY SOUNDS INTERESTING, NO?

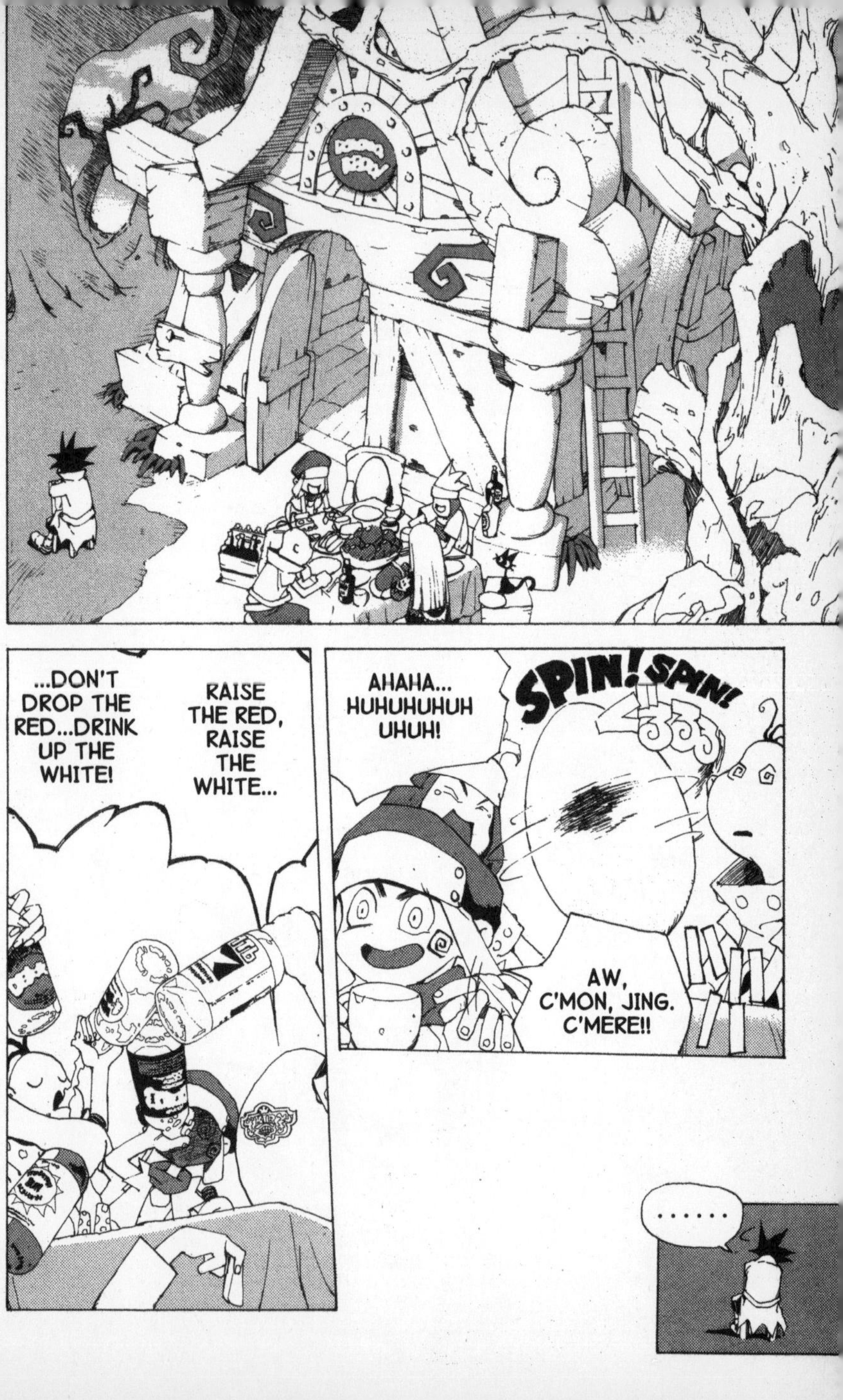
SPIN! SPIN!
AHAHA... HUHUHUHUH UHUH!
AW, C'MON, JING. C'MERE!!
RAISE THE RED, RAISE THE WHITE...
...DON'T DROP THE RED...DRINK UP THE WHITE!
......

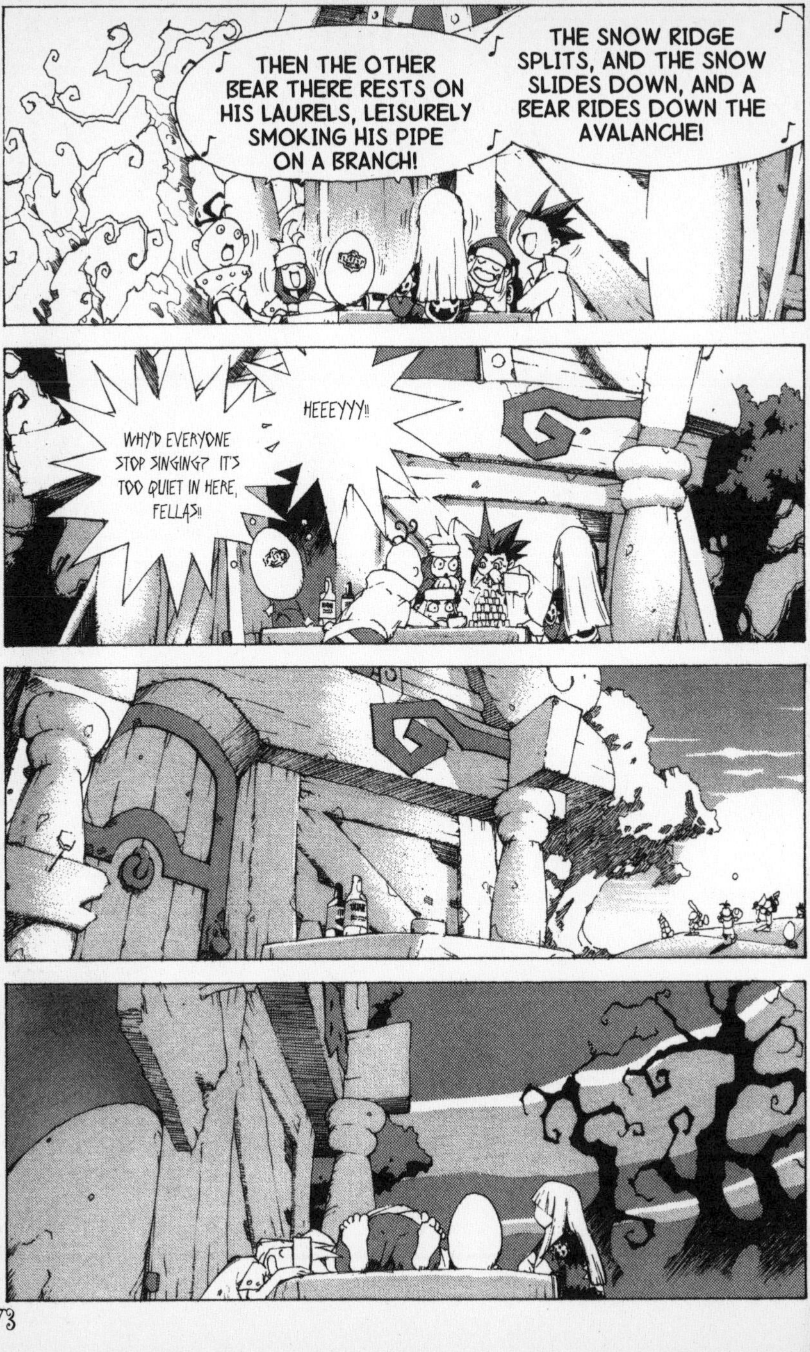
THE SNOW RIDGE SPLITS, AND THE SNOW SLIDES DOWN, AND A BEAR RIDES DOWN THE AVALANCHE!
THEN THE OTHER BEAR THERE RESTS ON HIS LAURELS, LEISURELY SMOKING HIS PIPE ON A BRANCH!
HEEEYYY!!
WHY'D EVERYONE STOP SINGING? IT'S TOO QUIET IN HERE, FELLAS!!

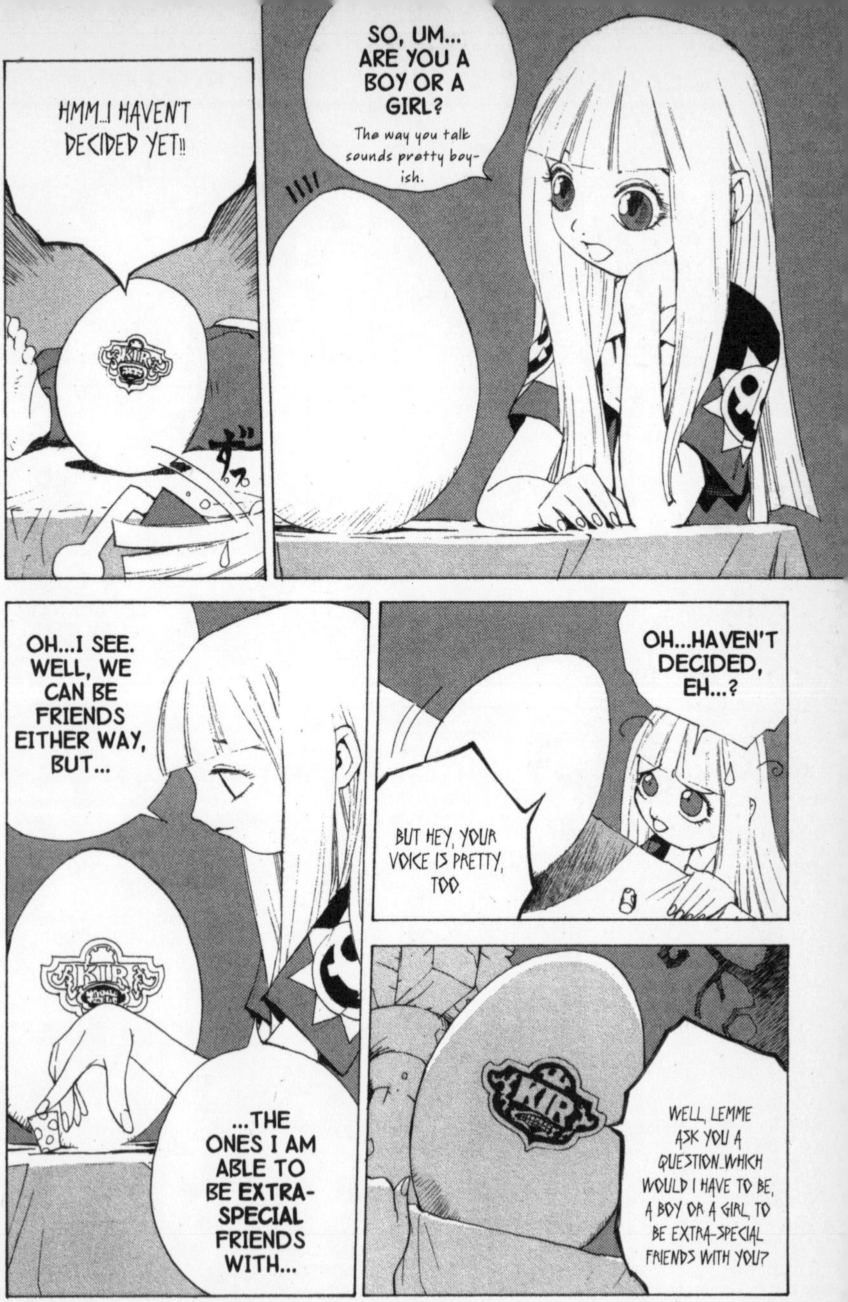
SO, UM... ARE YOU A BOY OR A GIRL?
The way you talk sounds pretty boy-ish.
HMM...I HAVEN'T DECIDED YET!!
OH...HAVEN'T DECIDED, EH...?
BUT HEY, YOUR VOICE IS PRETTY, TOO.
WELL, LEMME ASK YOU A QUESTION...WHICH WOULD I HAVE TO BE, A BOY OR A GIRL, TO BE EXTRA-SPECIAL FRIENDS WITH YOU?
OH...I SEE. WELL, WE CAN BE FRIENDS EITHER WAY, BUT...
...THE ONES I AM ABLE TO BE EXTRA-SPECIAL FRIENDS WITH...

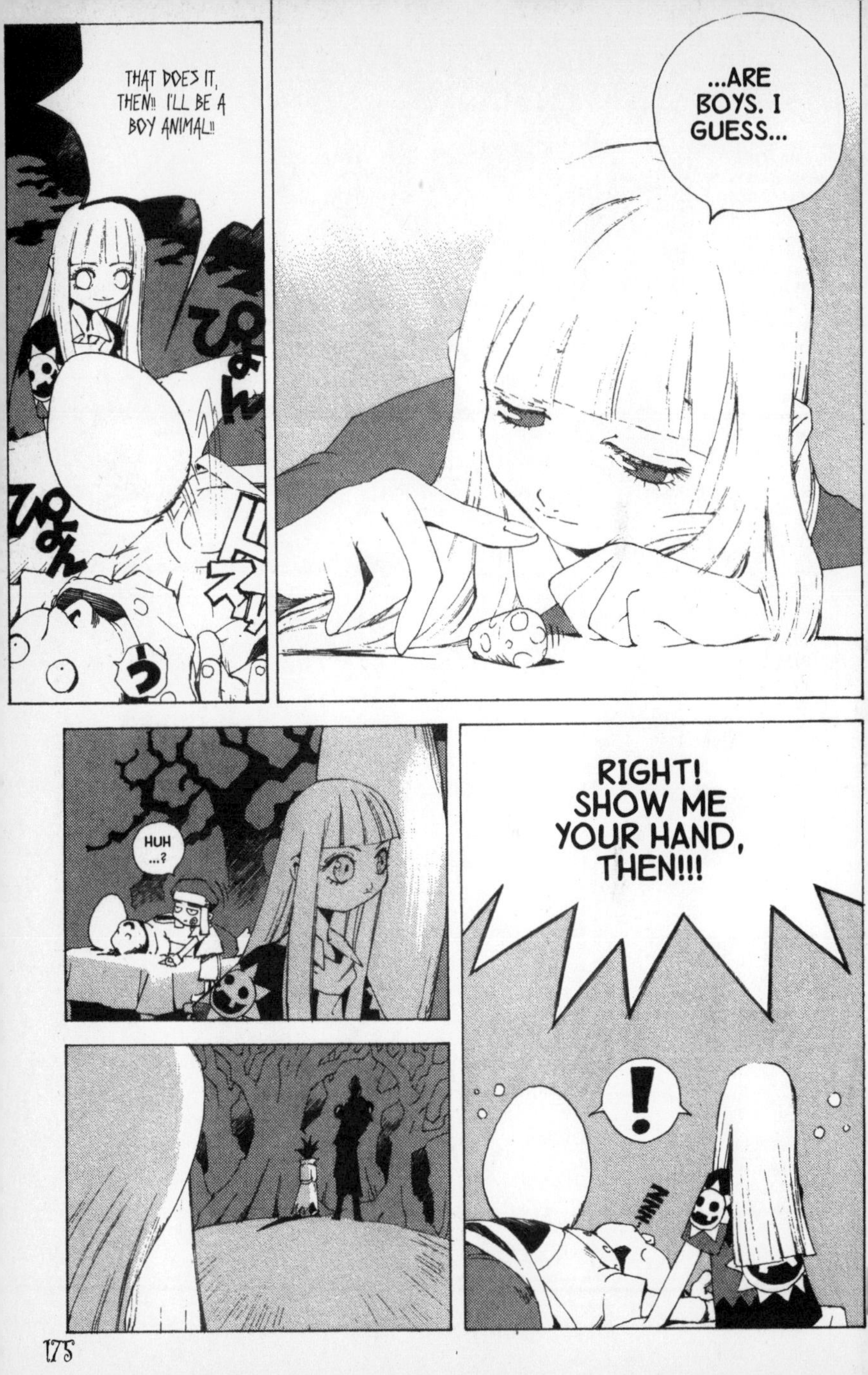
...ARE BOYS. I GUESS...
THAT DOES IT, THEN!! I'LL BE A BOY ANIMAL!!
ぴょん
ぴょん
RIGHT! SHOW ME YOUR HAND, THEN!!!
!
NNH...
HUH ...?

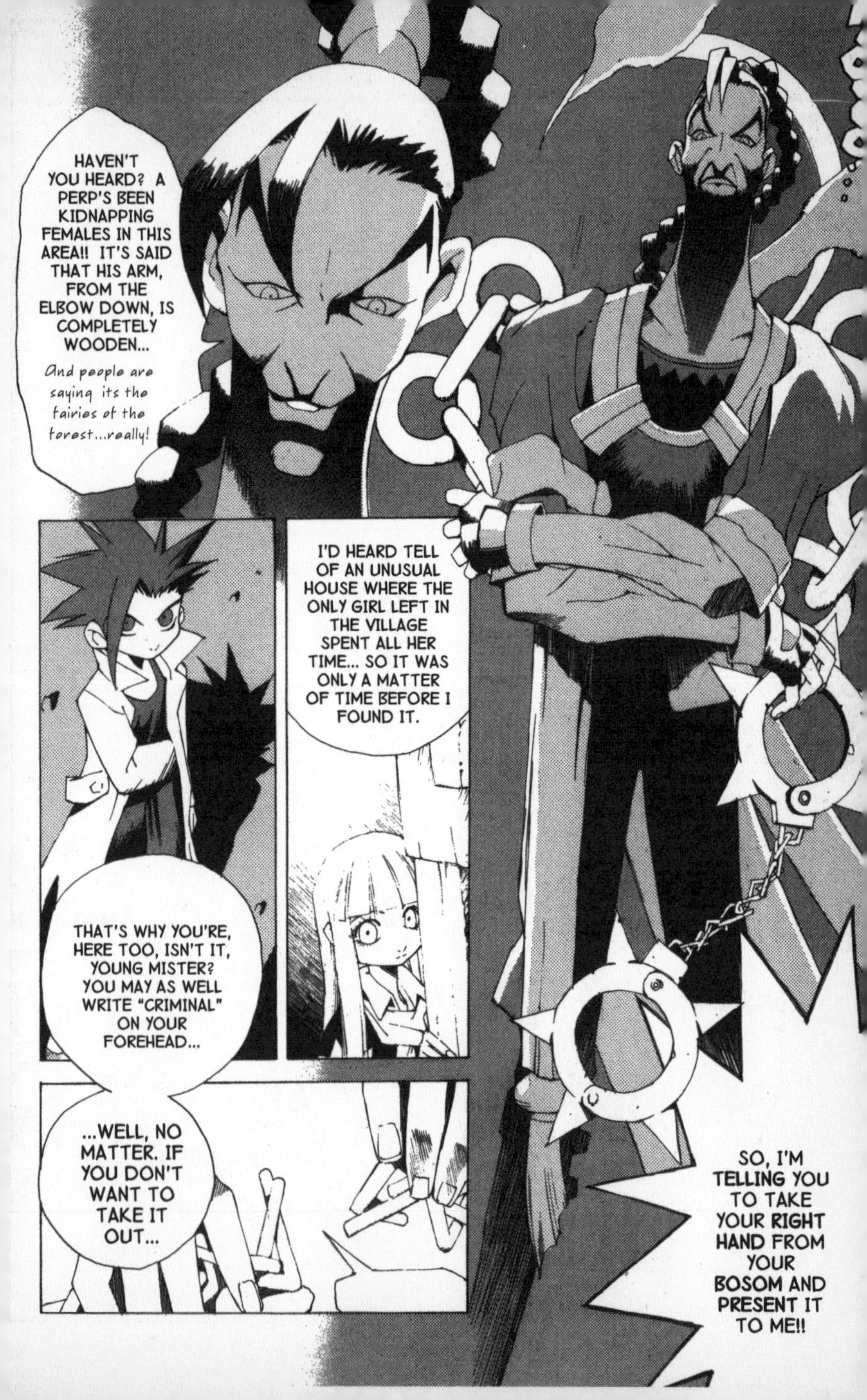
HAVEN'T YOU HEARD? A PERP'S BEEN KIDNAPPING FEMALES IN THIS AREA!! IT'S SAID THAT HIS ARM, FROM THE ELBOW DOWN, IS COMPLETELY WOODEN...
And people are saying its the fairies of the forest...really!
I'D HEARD TELL OF AN UNUSUAL HOUSE WHERE THE ONLY GIRL LEFT IN THE VILLAGE SPENT ALL HER TIME... SO IT WAS ONLY A MATTER OF TIME BEFORE I FOUND IT.
THAT'S WHY YOU'RE, HERE TOO, ISN'T IT, YOUNG MISTER? YOU MAY AS WELL WRITE "CRIMINAL" ON YOUR FOREHEAD...
...WELL, NO MATTER. IF YOU DON'T WANT TO TAKE IT OUT...
SO, I'M TELLING YOU TO TAKE YOUR RIGHT HAND FROM YOUR BOSOM AND PRESENT IT TO ME!!

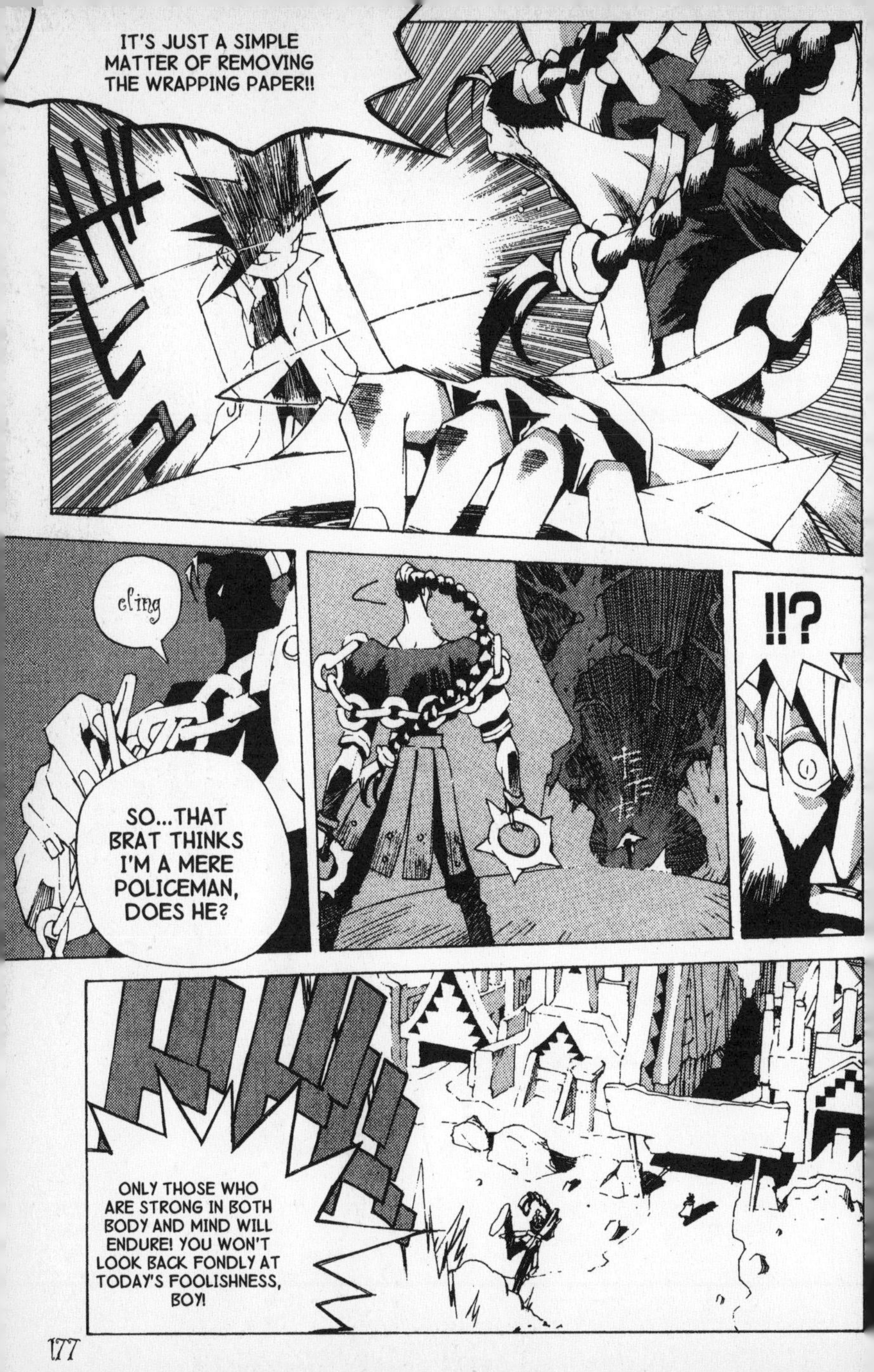
IT'S JUST A SIMPLE MATTER OF REMOVING THE WRAPPING PAPER!!
!!?
cling
SO...THAT BRAT THINKS I'M A MERE POLICEMAN, DOES HE?
ONLY THOSE WHO ARE STRONG IN BOTH BODY AND MIND WILL ENDURE! YOU WON'T LOOK BACK FONDLY AT TODAY'S FOOLISHNESS, BOY!

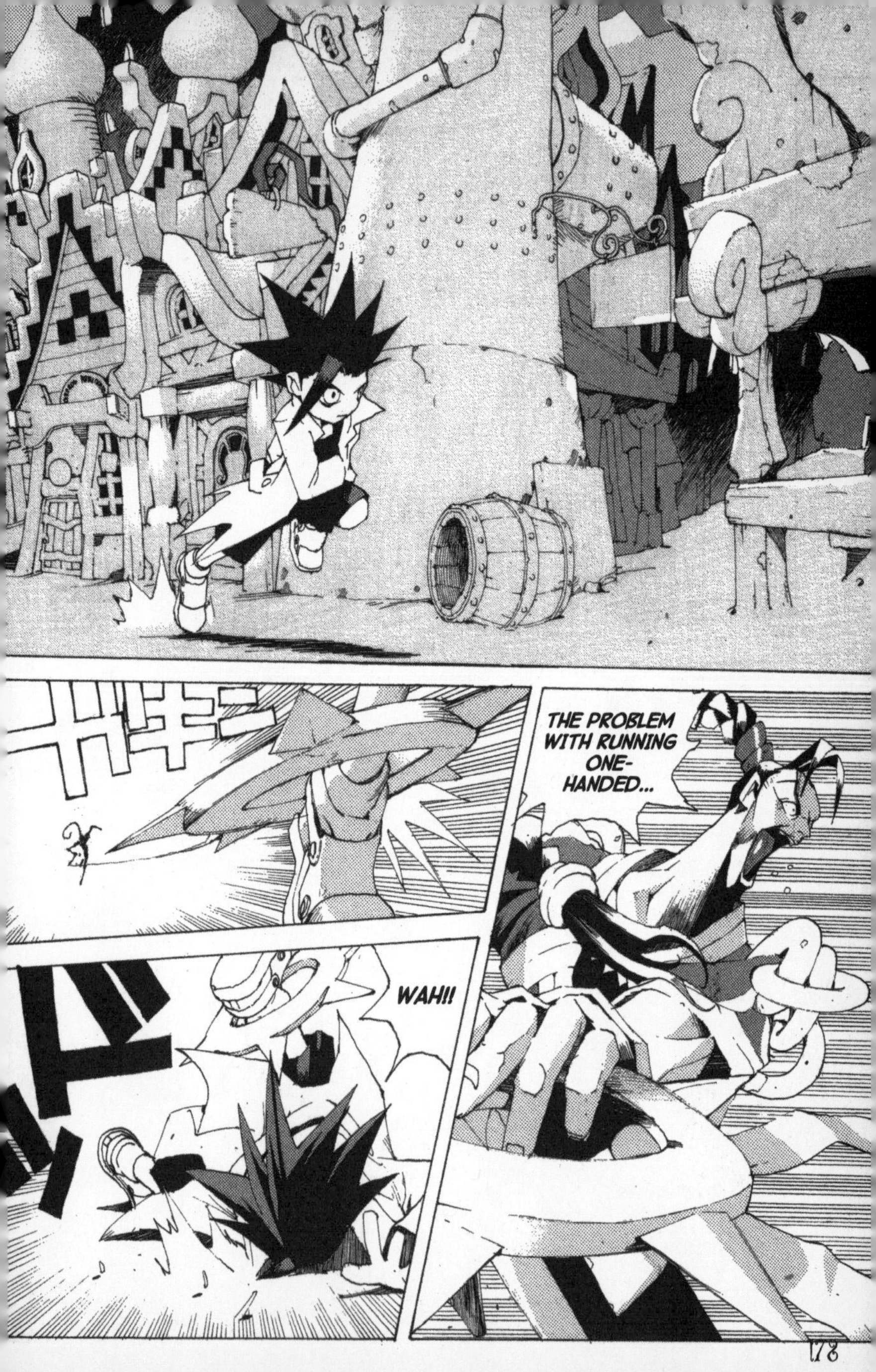
THE PROBLEM WITH RUNNING ONE-HANDED...
WAH!!

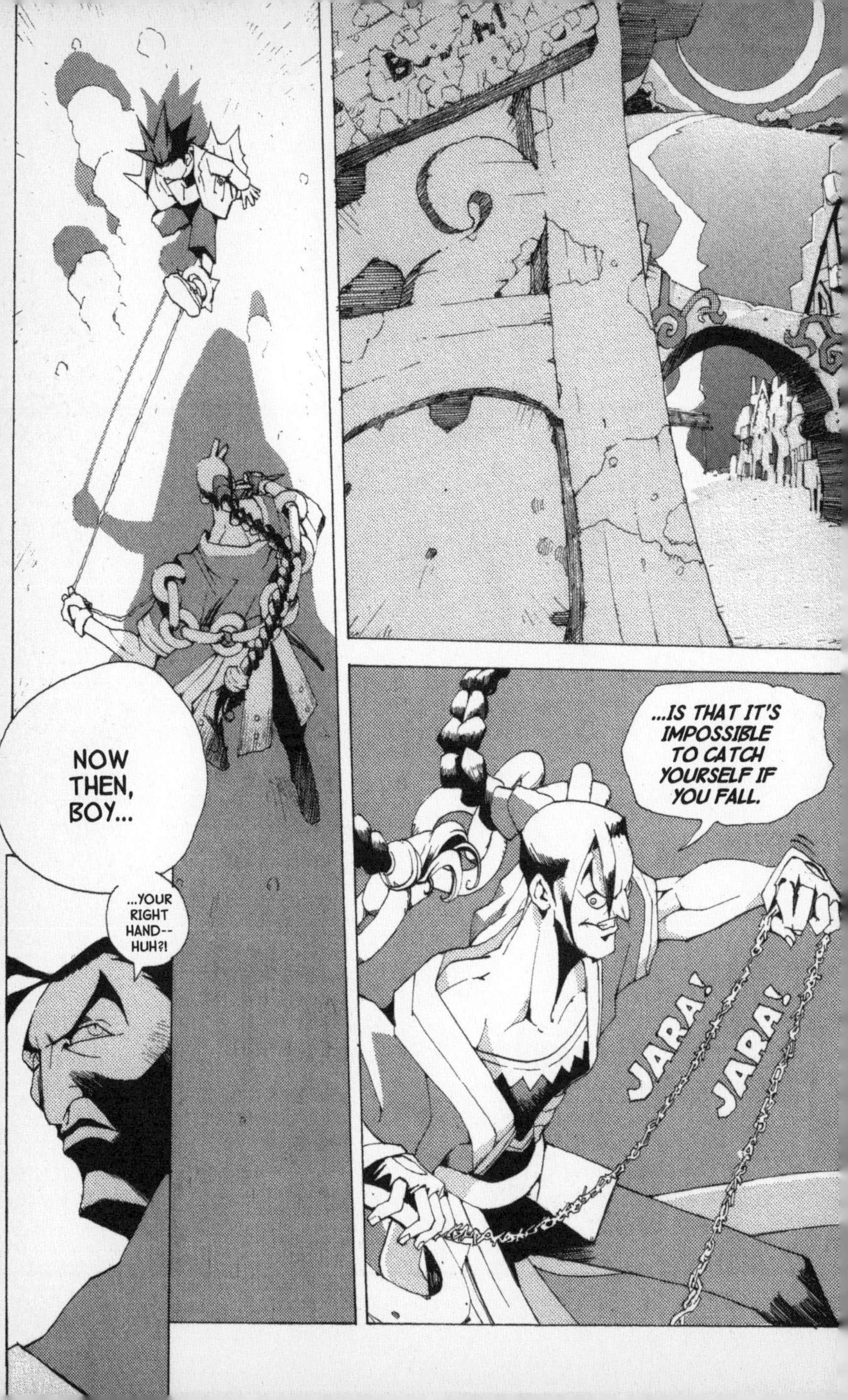
...IS THAT IT'S IMPOSSIBLE TO CATCH YOURSELF IF YOU FALL.
JARA! JARA!
NOW THEN, BOY...
...YOUR RIGHT HAND-- HUH?!

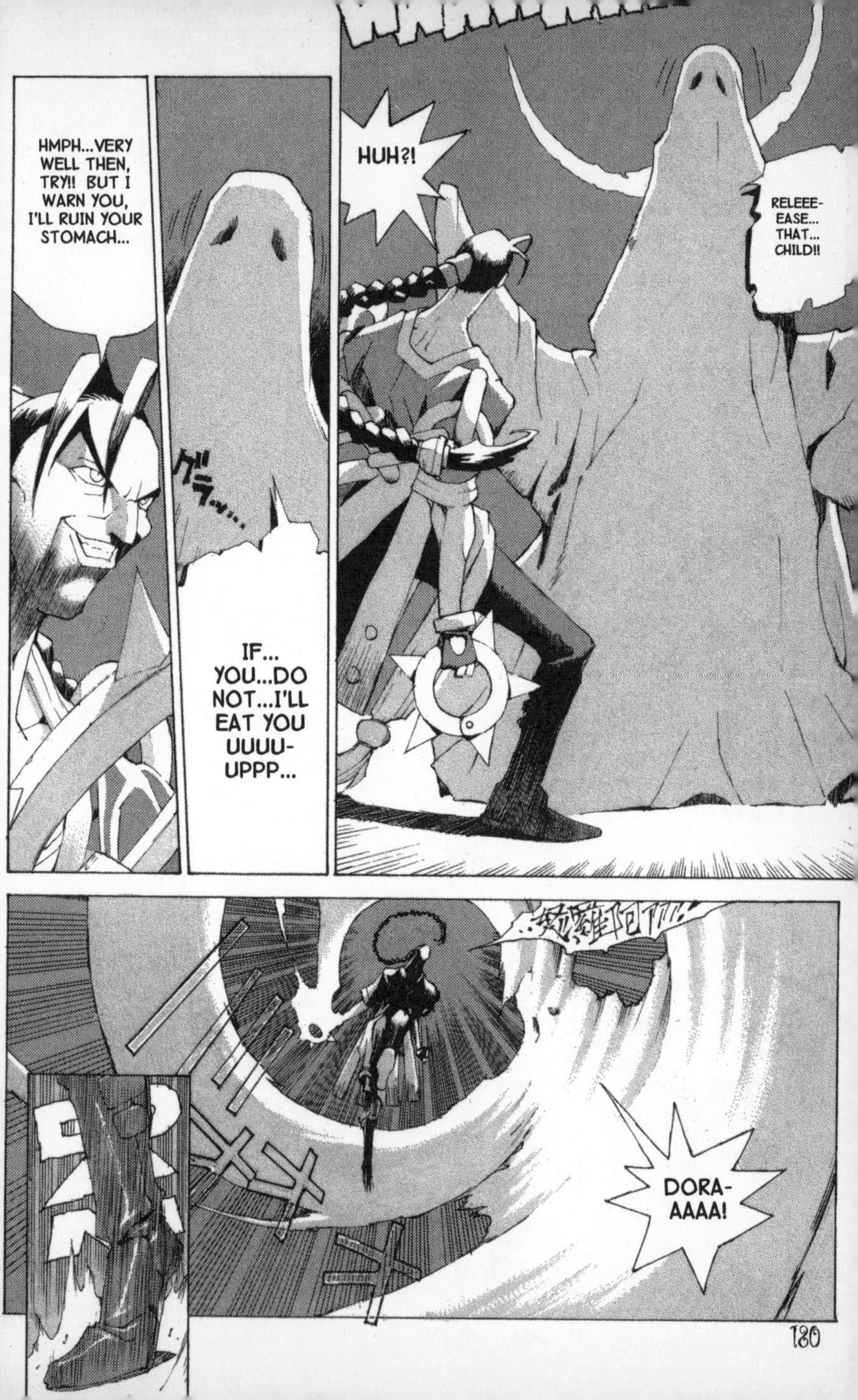
RELEEE-EASE... THAT... CHILD!!
HUH?!
IF... YOU...DO NOT...I'LL EAT YOU UUUU-UPPP...
HMPH...VERY WELL THEN, TRY!! BUT I WARN YOU, I'LL RUIN YOUR STOMACH...
DORA-AAAA!

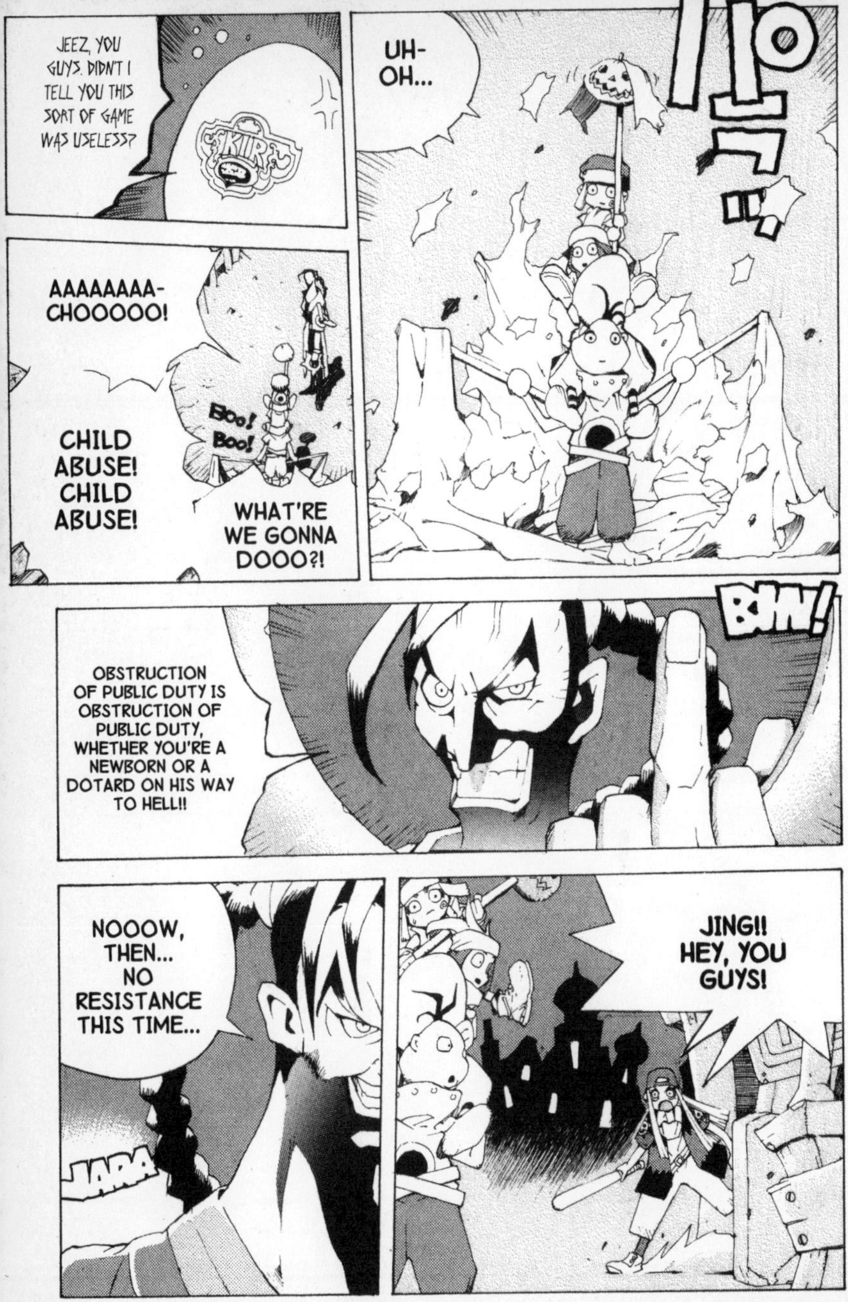
UH-
OH...
JEEZ, YOU GUYS. DIDN'T I TELL YOU THIS SORT OF GAME WAS USELESS?
KIR
AAAAAAAA-CHOOOOO!
BOO! BOO!
CHILD ABUSE! CHILD ABUSE!
WHAT'RE WE GONNA DOOO?!
BOW!
OBSTRUCTION OF PUBLIC DUTY IS OBSTRUCTION OF PUBLIC DUTY, WHETHER YOU'RE A NEWBORN OR A DOTARD ON HIS WAY TO HELL!!
JING!! HEY, YOU GUYS!
NOOOW, THEN... NO RESISTANCE THIS TIME...
JARA

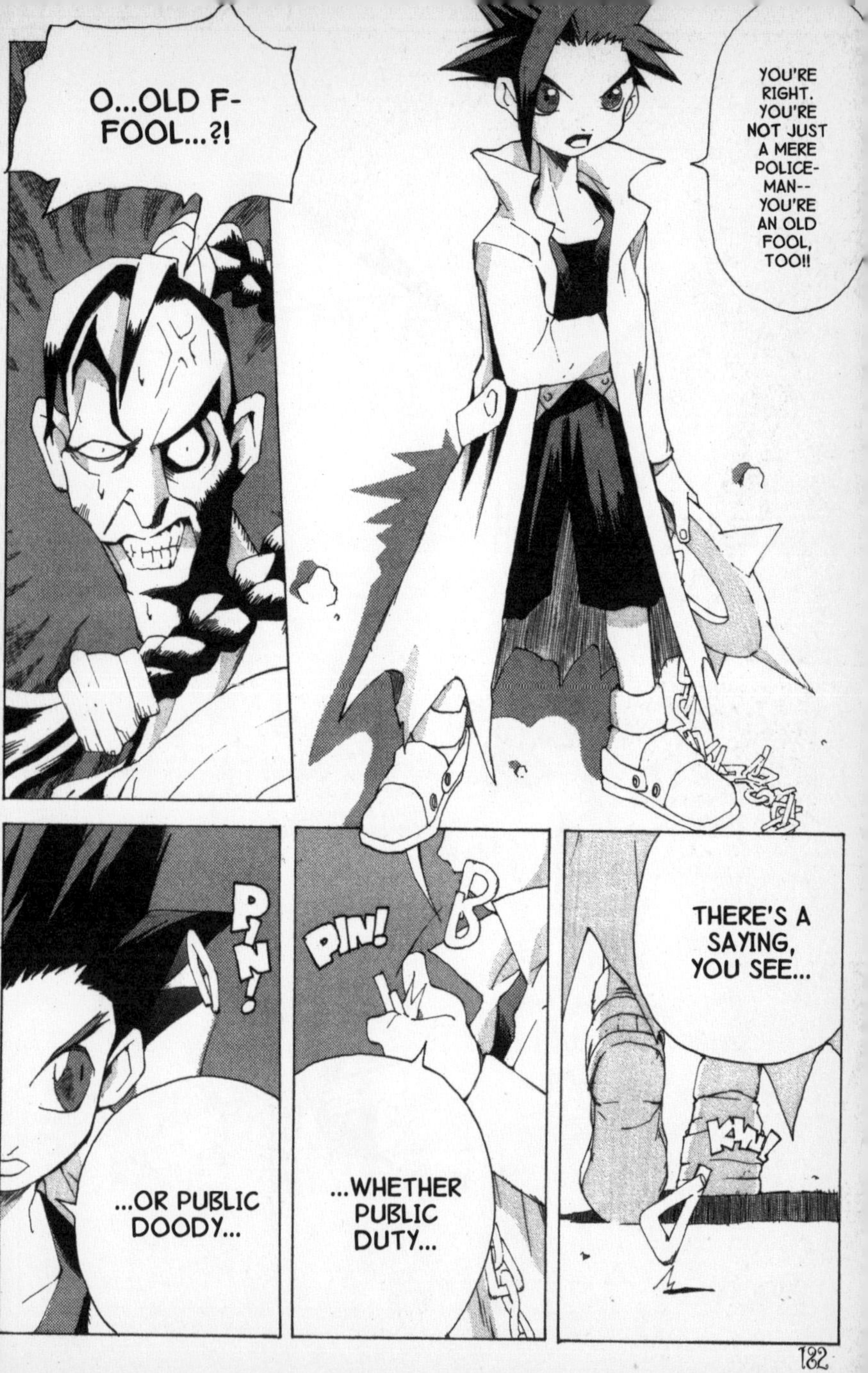
YOU'RE RIGHT. YOU'RE NOT JUST A MERE POLICE-MAN-- YOU'RE AN OLD FOOL, TOO!!
O...OLD F-FOOL...?!
THERE'S A SAYING, YOU SEE...
PIN!
...WHETHER PUBLIC DUTY...
PIN!
...OR PUBLIC DOODY...

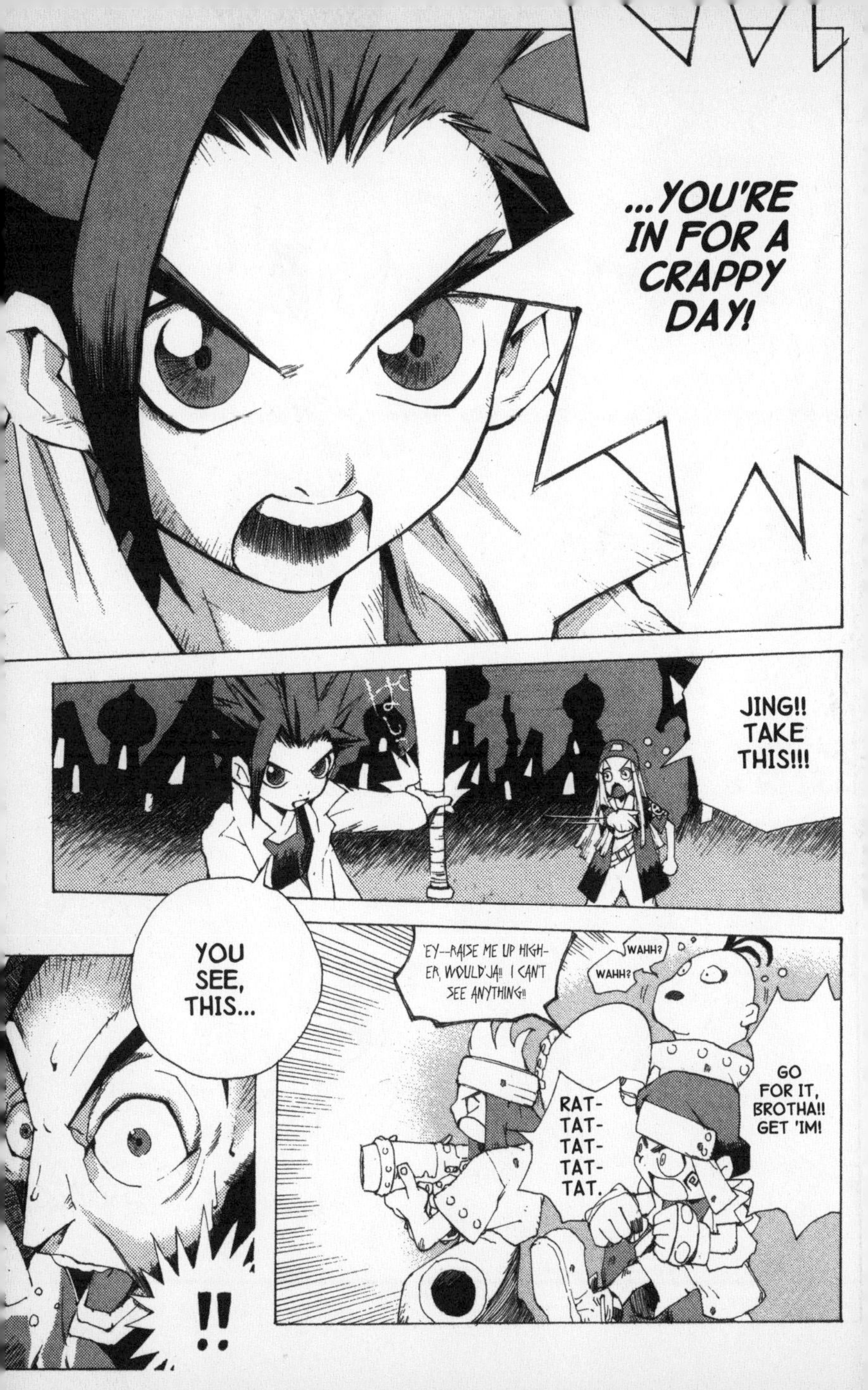
...YOU'RE IN FOR A CRAPPY DAY!
JING!! TAKE THIS!!!
WAHH?
WAHH?
'EY--RAISE ME UP HIGH-ER, WOULD'JA!! I CAN'T SEE ANYTHING!!
GO FOR IT, BROTHA!! GET 'IM!
RAT-TAT-TAT-TAT-TAT.
YOU SEE, THIS...
!!

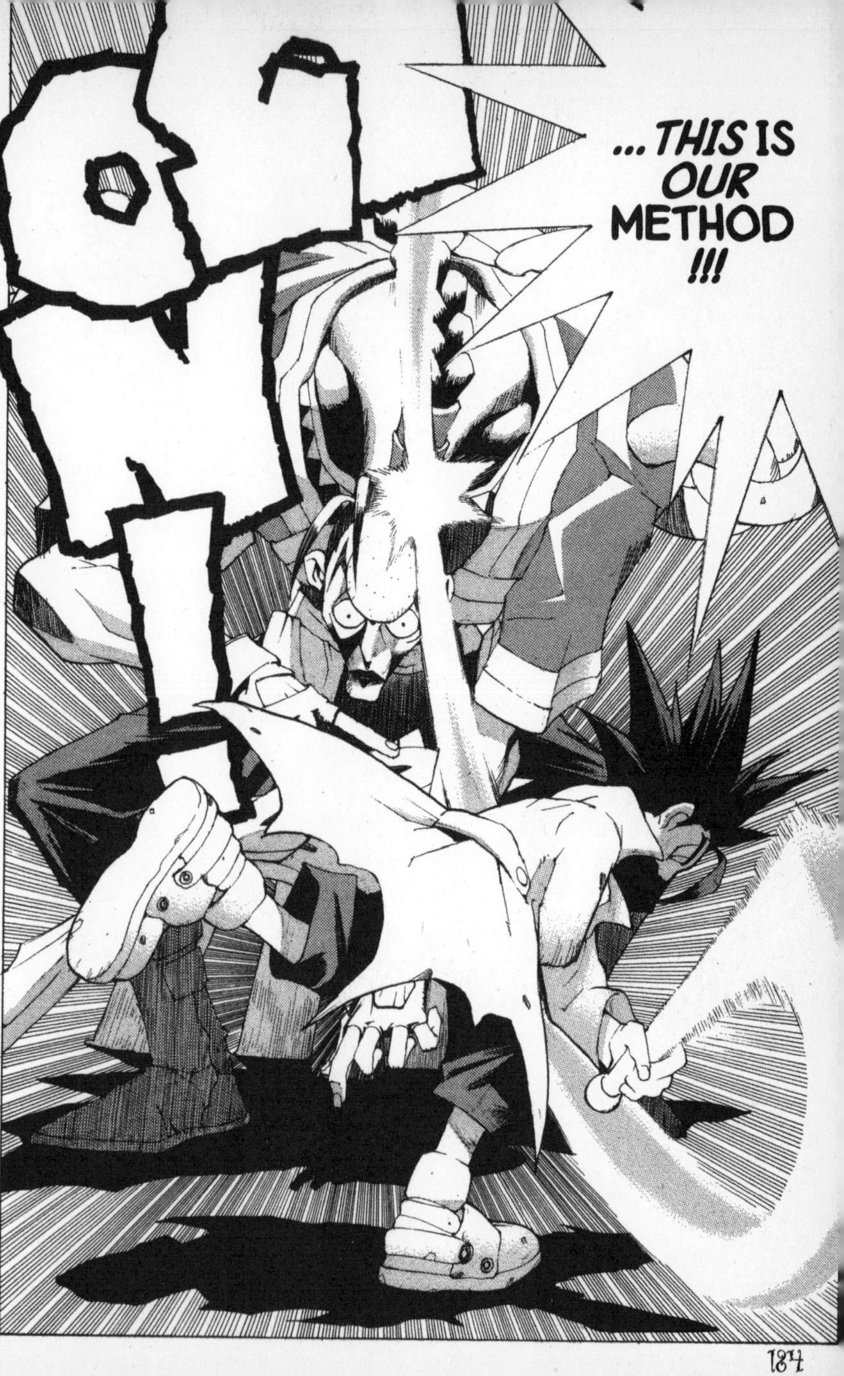
...THIS IS OUR METHOD !!!

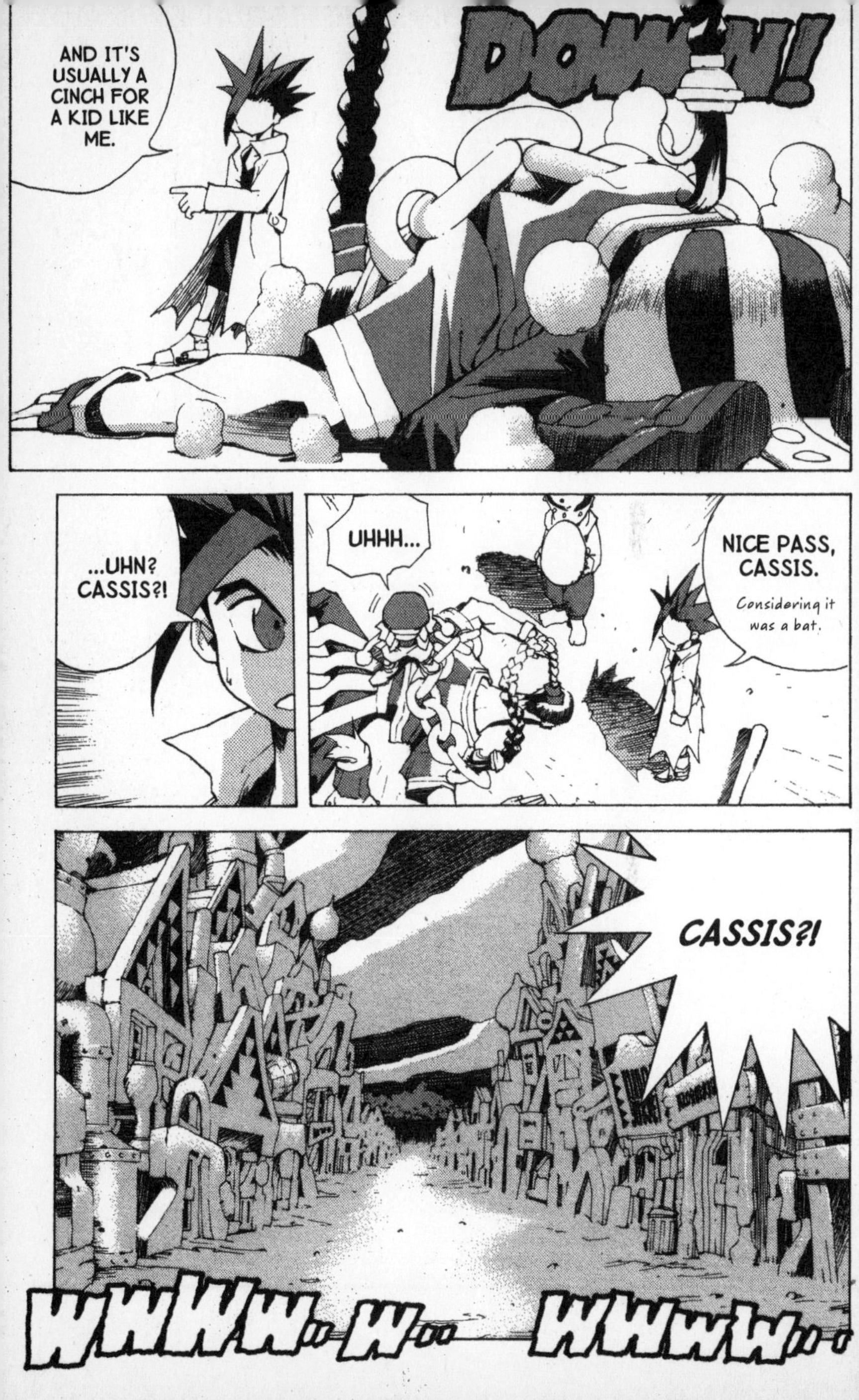
DOWN!
AND IT'S USUALLY A CINCH FOR A KID LIKE ME.
NICE PASS, CASSIS.
Considering it was a bat.
UHHH...
...UHN? CASSIS?!
CASSIS?!
WWWWW.. W.. WWWWW..

Girls more than boys,
children more than adults,
Loneliness more than crowds,
Sidestreets more than main streets...

A-R-E D-A-N-G-E-R-O-U-S!!!

(A warning message sent out into the streets of Balalaika)

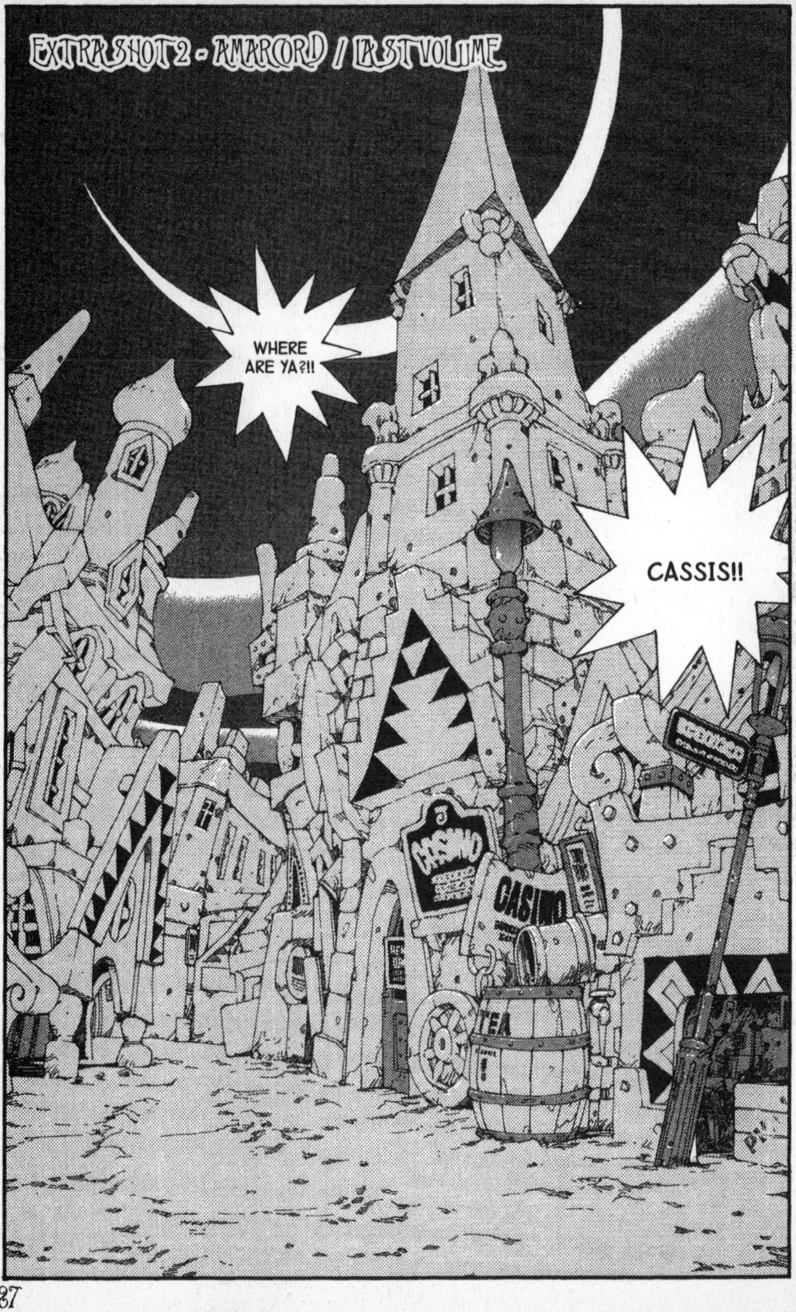
EXTRA SHOT 2 - AMARCORD / LAST VOLUME
WHERE ARE YA?!!
CASSIS!!
CASINO
TEA

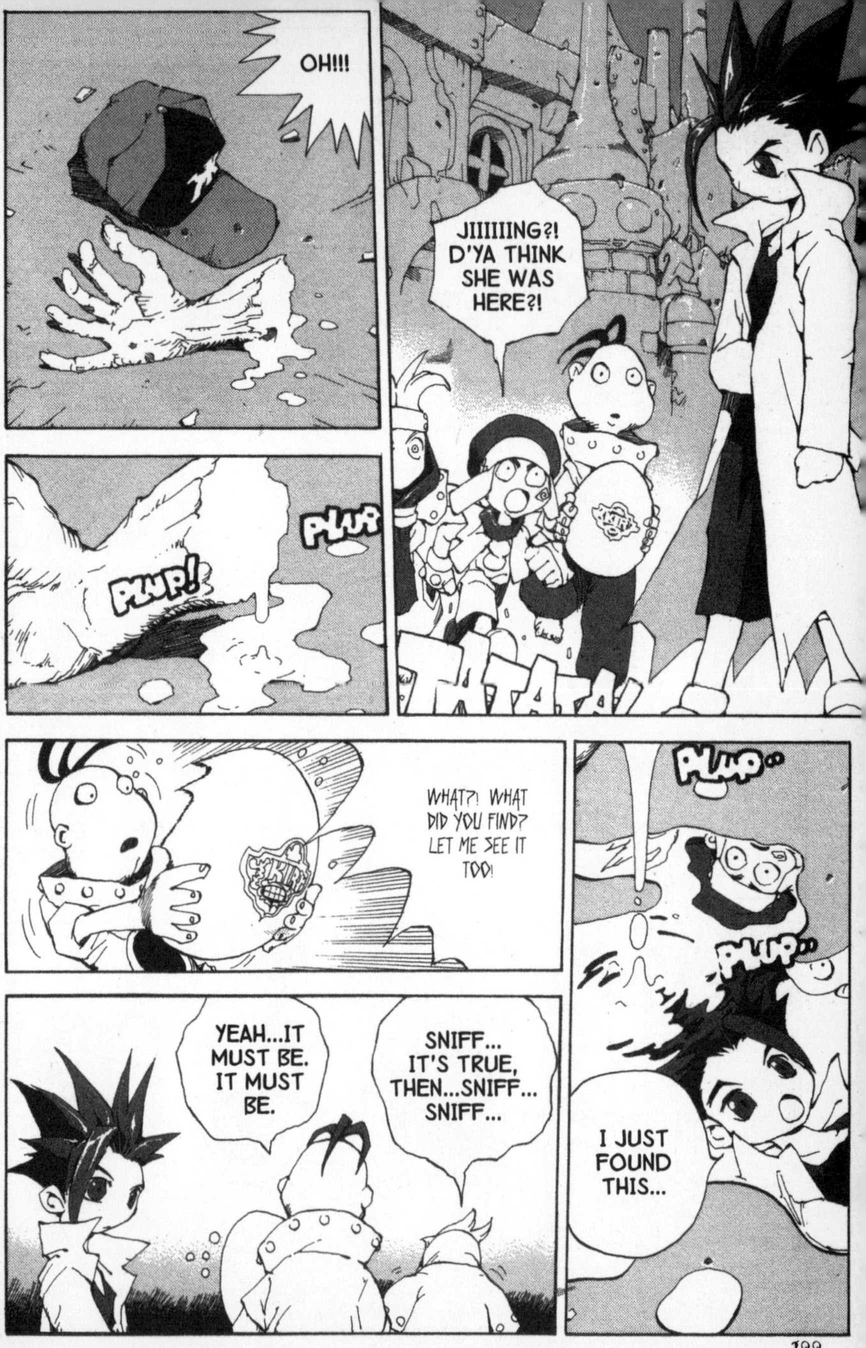
JIIIIIING?! D'YA THINK SHE WAS HERE?!
TATATA!
OH!!!
PLUP!
PLUP
PLUP..
PLUP..
I JUST FOUND THIS...
WHAT?! WHAT DID YOU FIND? LET ME SEE IT TOO!
SNIFF... IT'S TRUE, THEN...SNIFF... SNIFF...
YEAH...IT MUST BE. IT MUST BE.

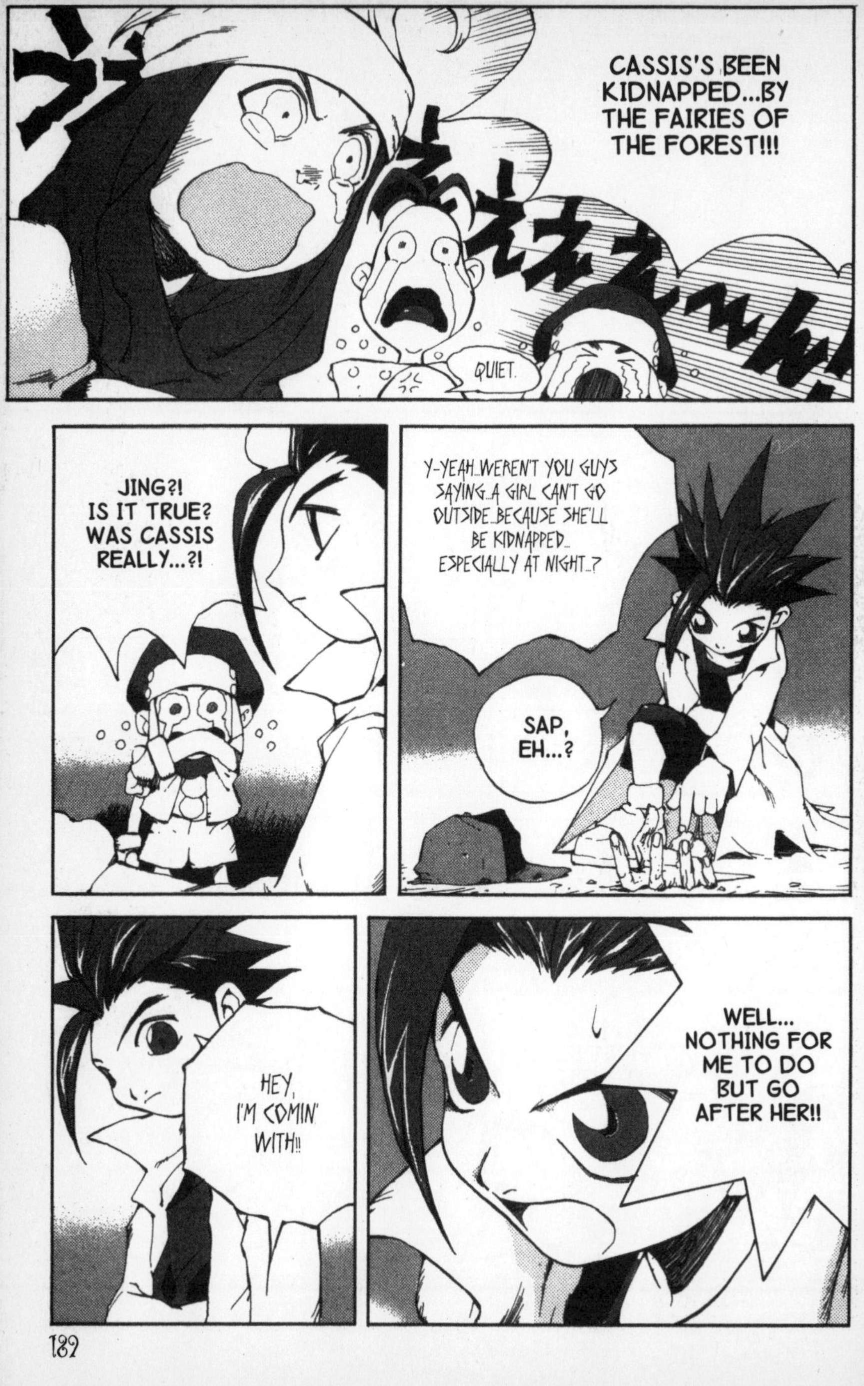
CASSIS'S BEEN KIDNAPPED...BY THE FAIRIES OF THE FOREST!!!
QUIET.
Y-YEAH...WEREN'T YOU GUYS SAYING...A GIRL CAN'T GO OUTSIDE...BECAUSE SHE'LL BE KIDNAPPED... ESPECIALLY AT NIGHT...?
SAP, EH...?
JING?! IS IT TRUE? WAS CASSIS REALLY...?!
WELL... NOTHING FOR ME TO DO BUT GO AFTER HER!!
HEY, I'M COMIN' WITH!!

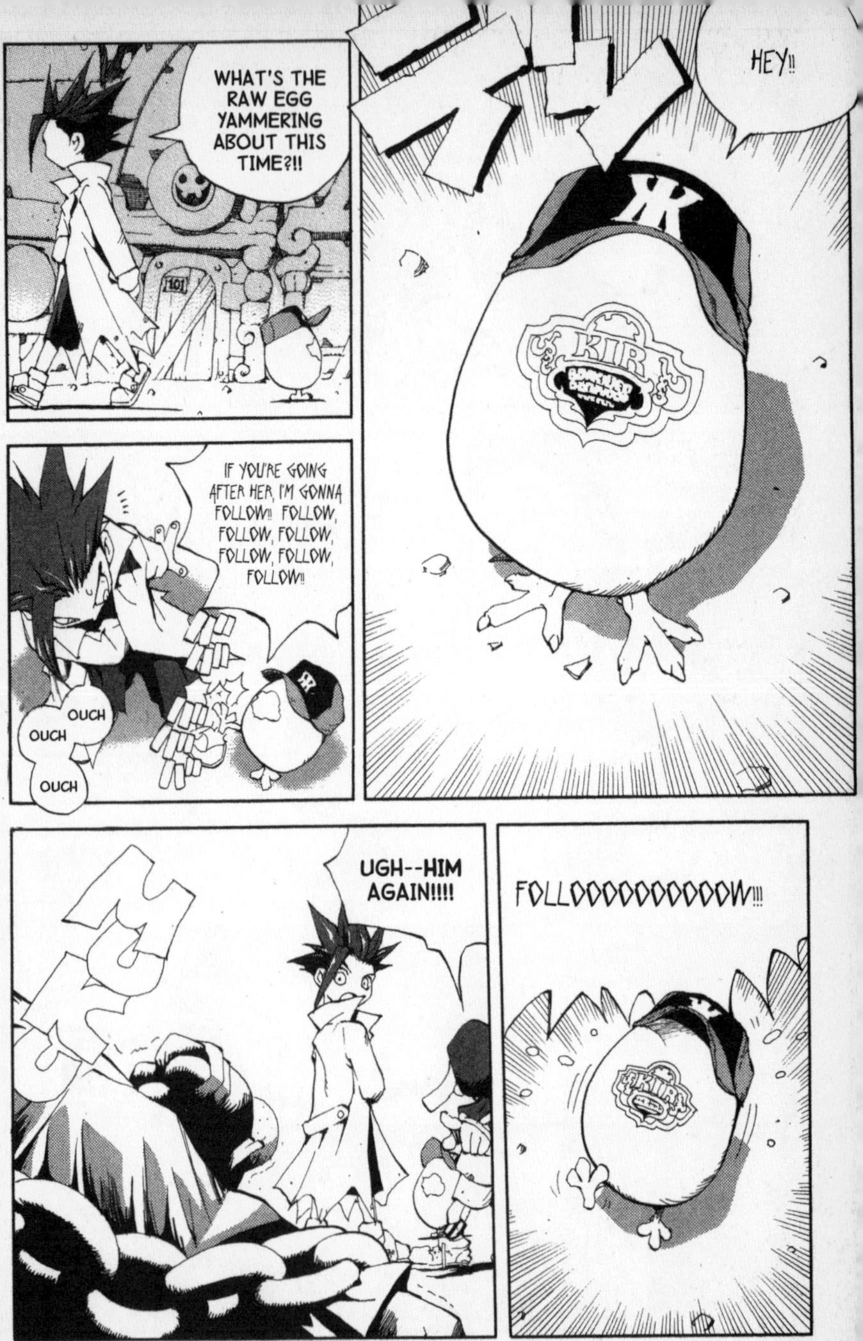
HEY!!
WHAT'S THE RAW EGG YAMMERING ABOUT THIS TIME?!!
IF YOU'RE GOING AFTER HER, I'M GONNA FOLLOW!! FOLLOW, FOLLOW, FOLLOW, FOLLOW, FOLLOW, FOLLOW!!
OUCH
OUCH
OUCH
FOLLOOOOOOOOOOW!!!
UGH--HIM AGAIN!!!!

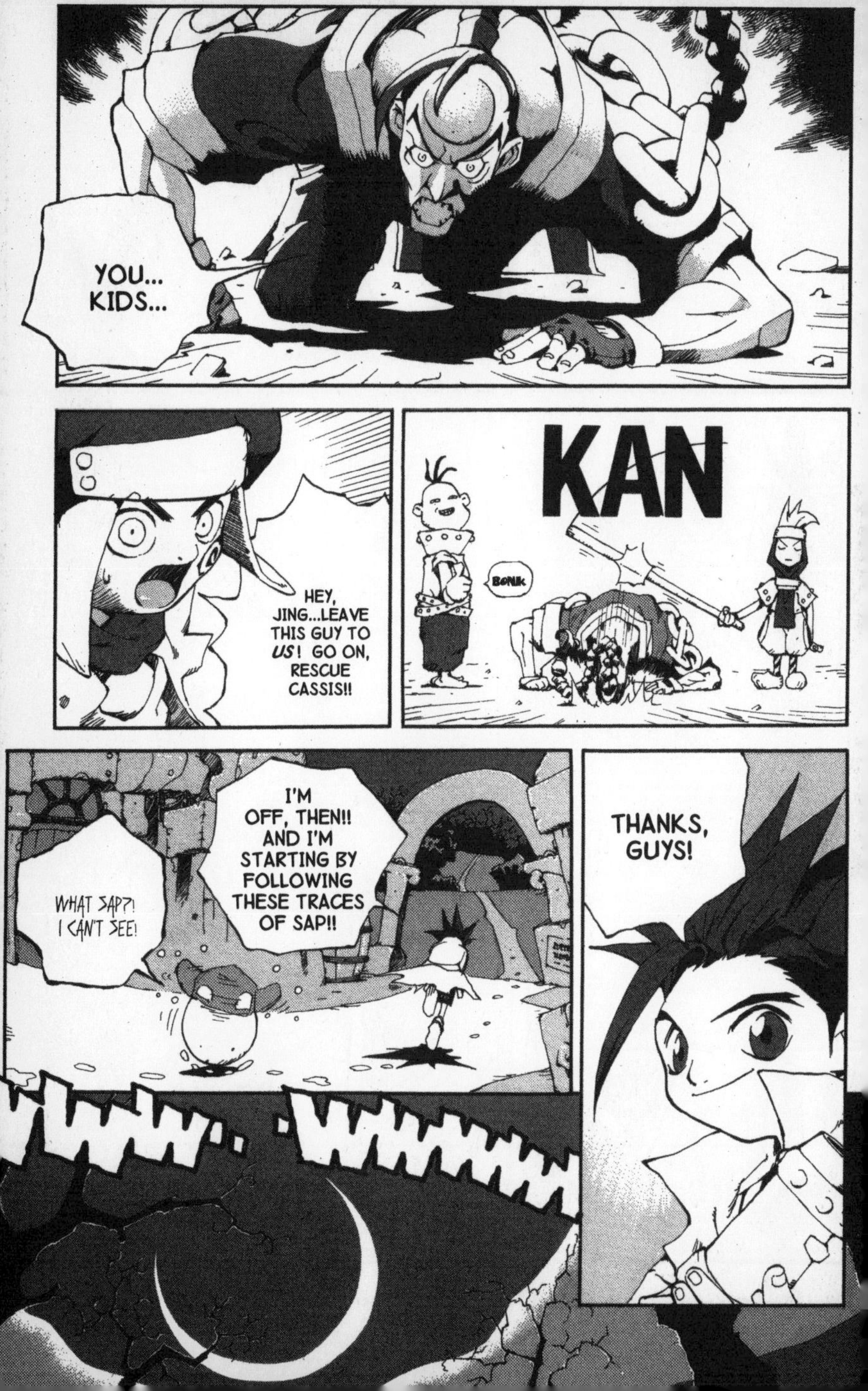
YOU... KIDS...
KAN
BONK
HEY, JING...LEAVE THIS GUY TO US! GO ON, RESCUE CASSIS!!
THANKS, GUYS!
I'M OFF, THEN!! AND I'M STARTING BY FOLLOWING THESE TRACES OF SAP!!
WHAT SAP?! I CAN'T SEE!

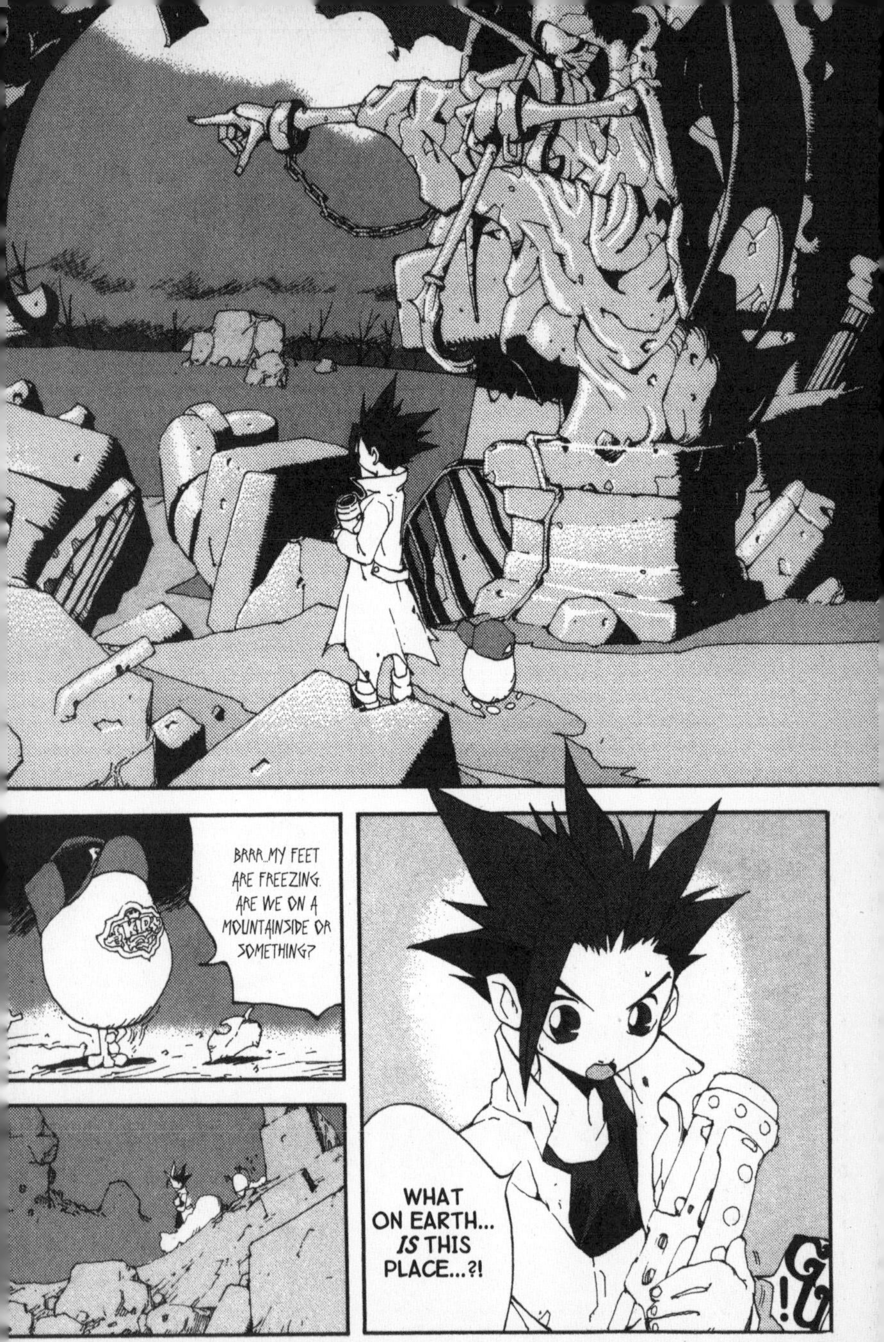
WHAT ON EARTH... *IS* THIS PLACE...?!
BRRR...MY FEET ARE FREEZING. ARE WE ON A MOUNTAINSIDE OR SOMETHING?

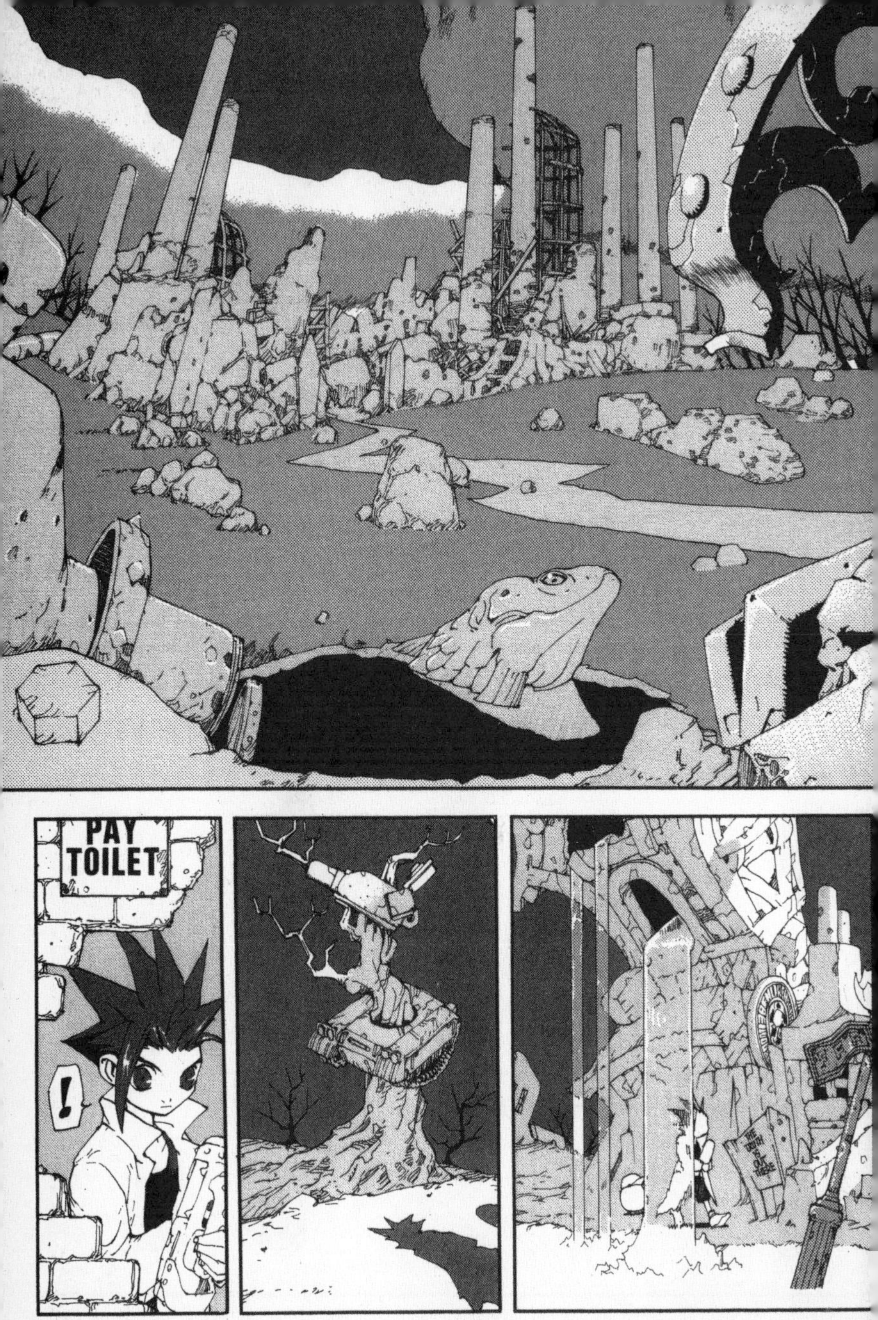
THE TRUTH IS OUT THERE
PAY TOILET
!

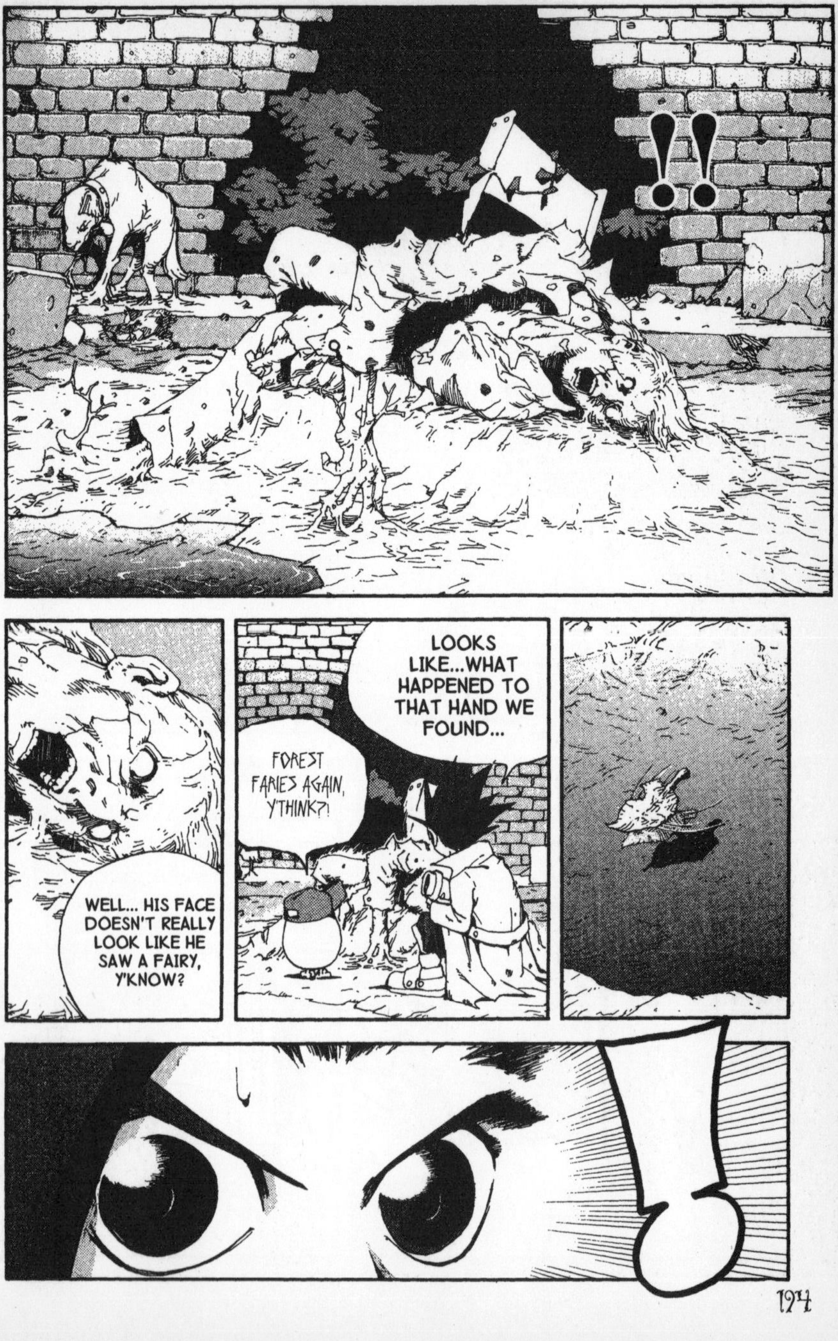
!!
LOOKS LIKE...WHAT HAPPENED TO THAT HAND WE FOUND...
FOREST FARIES AGAIN, Y'THINK?!
WELL... HIS FACE DOESN'T REALLY LOOK LIKE HE SAW A FAIRY, Y'KNOW?
!

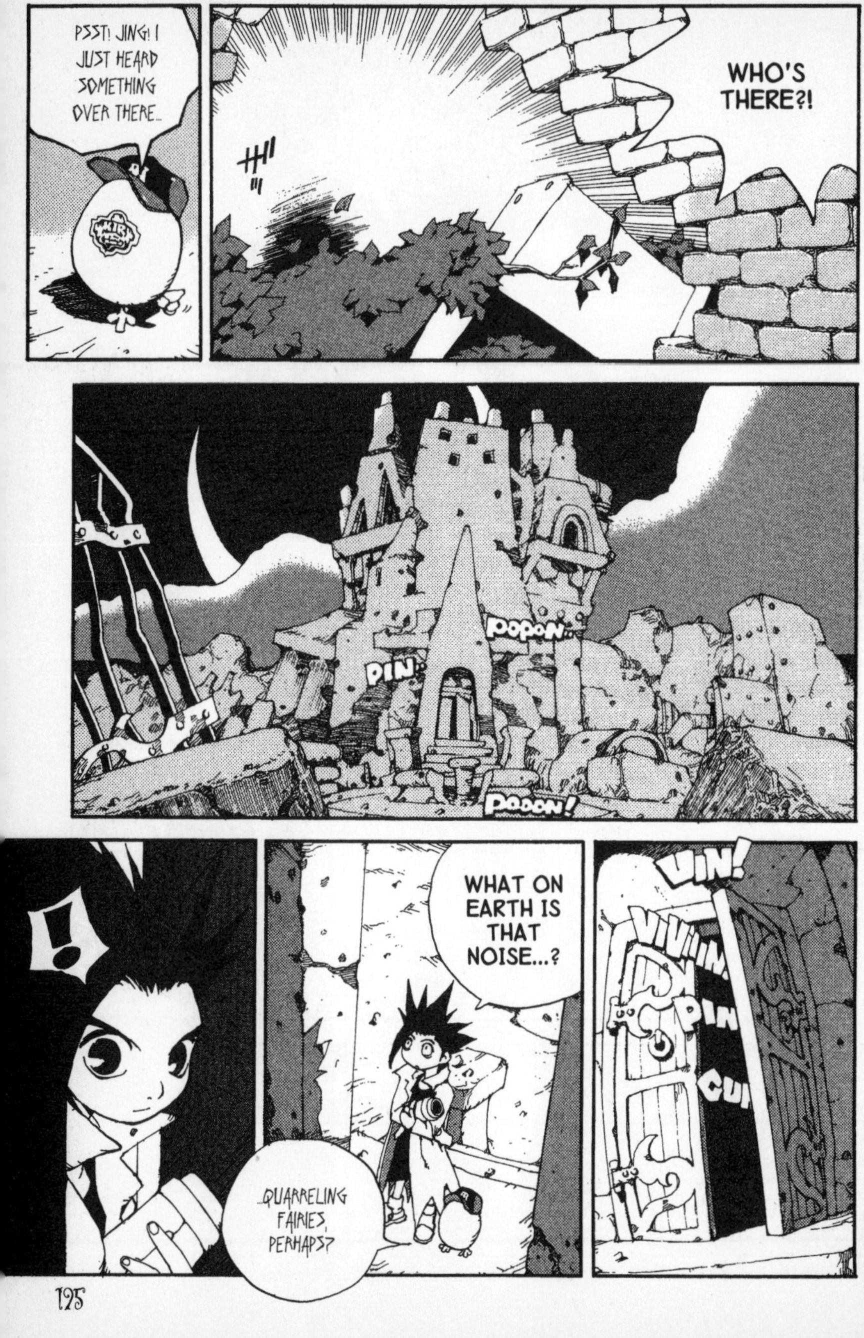
WHO'S THERE?!
PSST! JING! I JUST HEARD SOMETHING OVER THERE...
POPON..
PIN..
PODON!
VIN!
VIVIIIN..
PIN
CUI
WHAT ON EARTH IS THAT NOISE...?
...QUARRELING FAIRIES, PERHAPS?
!

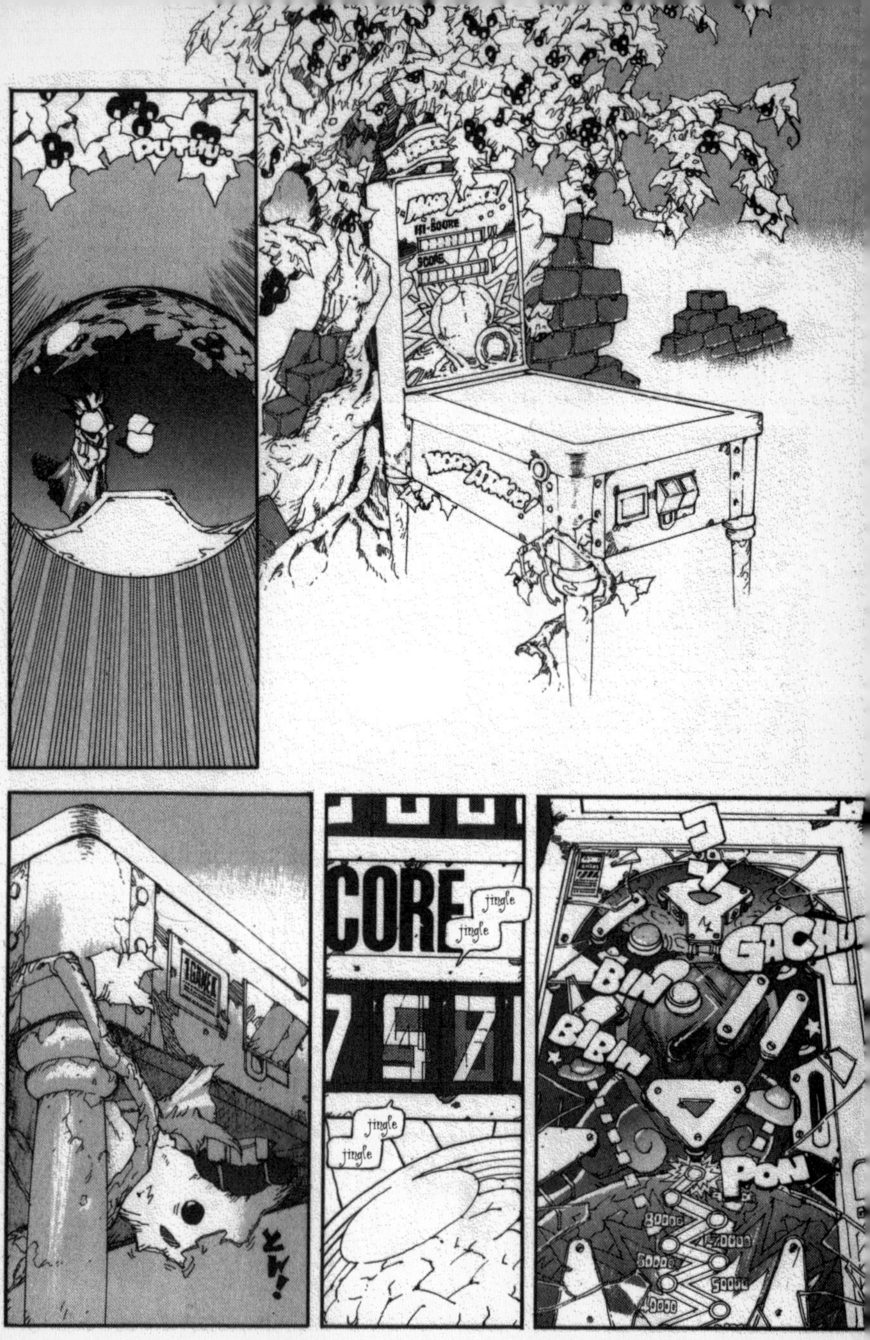
HI-SCORE
SCORE
PUTHU..
GACHU
BIN
BIBIN
PON
CORE
jingle
jingle
jingle
jingle

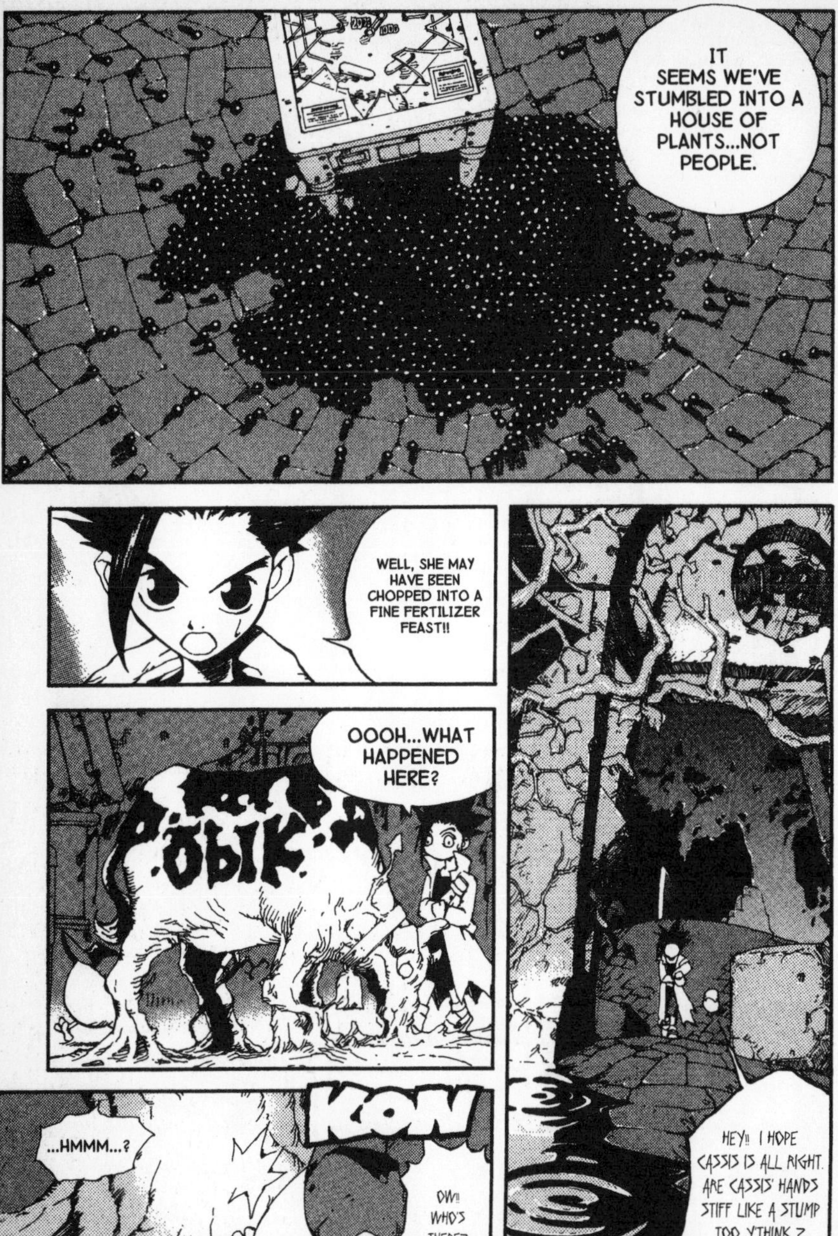
IT SEEMS WE'VE STUMBLED INTO A HOUSE OF PLANTS...NOT PEOPLE.
HEY!! I HOPE CASSIS IS ALL RIGHT. ARE CASSIS' HANDS STIFF LIKE A STUMP TOO, Y'THINK..?
WELL, SHE MAY HAVE BEEN CHOPPED INTO A FINE FERTILIZER FEAST!!
OOOH...WHAT HAPPENED HERE?
KON
OW!! WHO'S THERE?
...HMMM...?

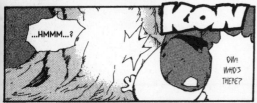

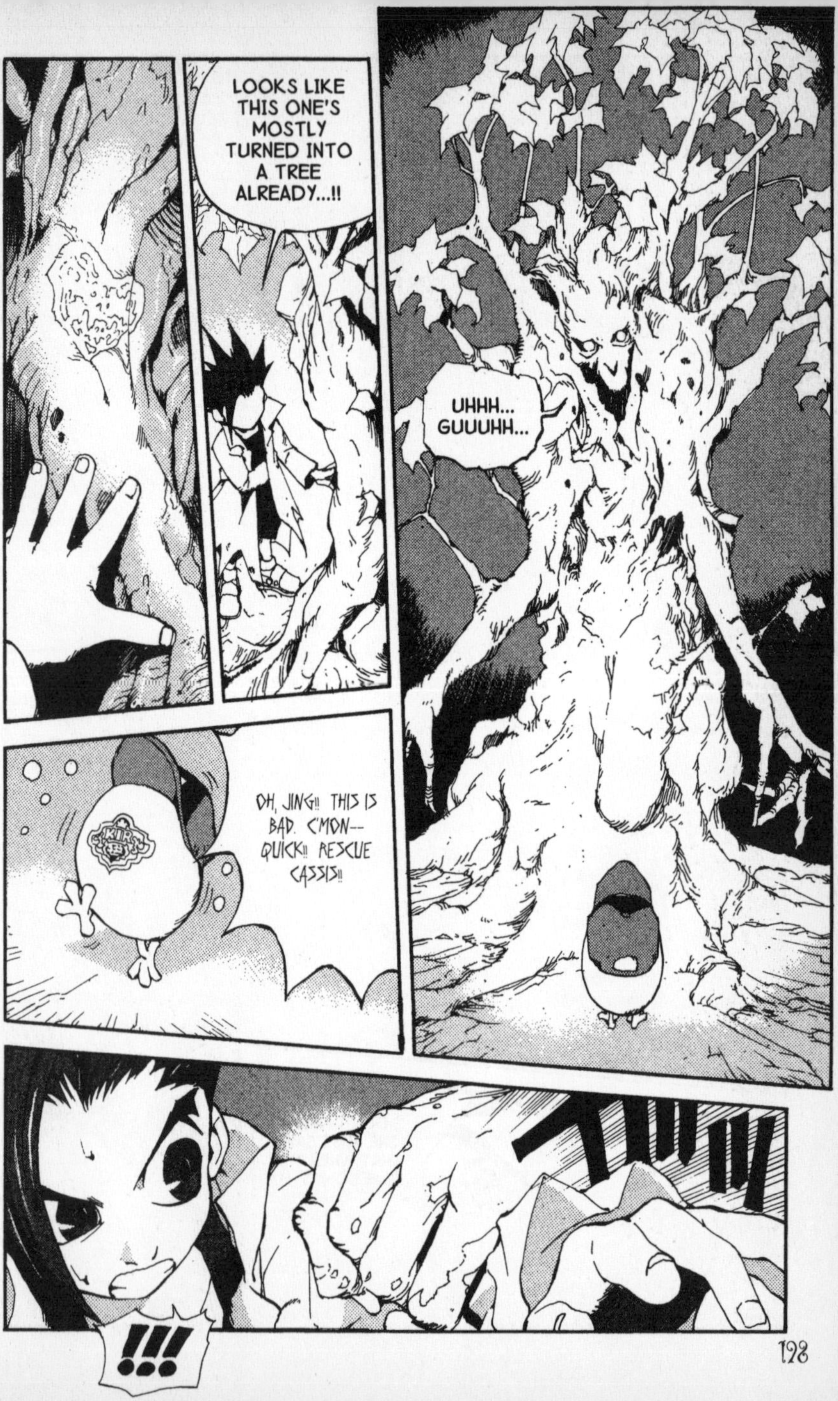
UHHH... GUUUHH...
LOOKS LIKE THIS ONE'S MOSTLY TURNED INTO A TREE ALREADY...!!
OH, JING!! THIS IS BAD. C'MON-- QUICK!! RESCUE CASSIS!!
!!!

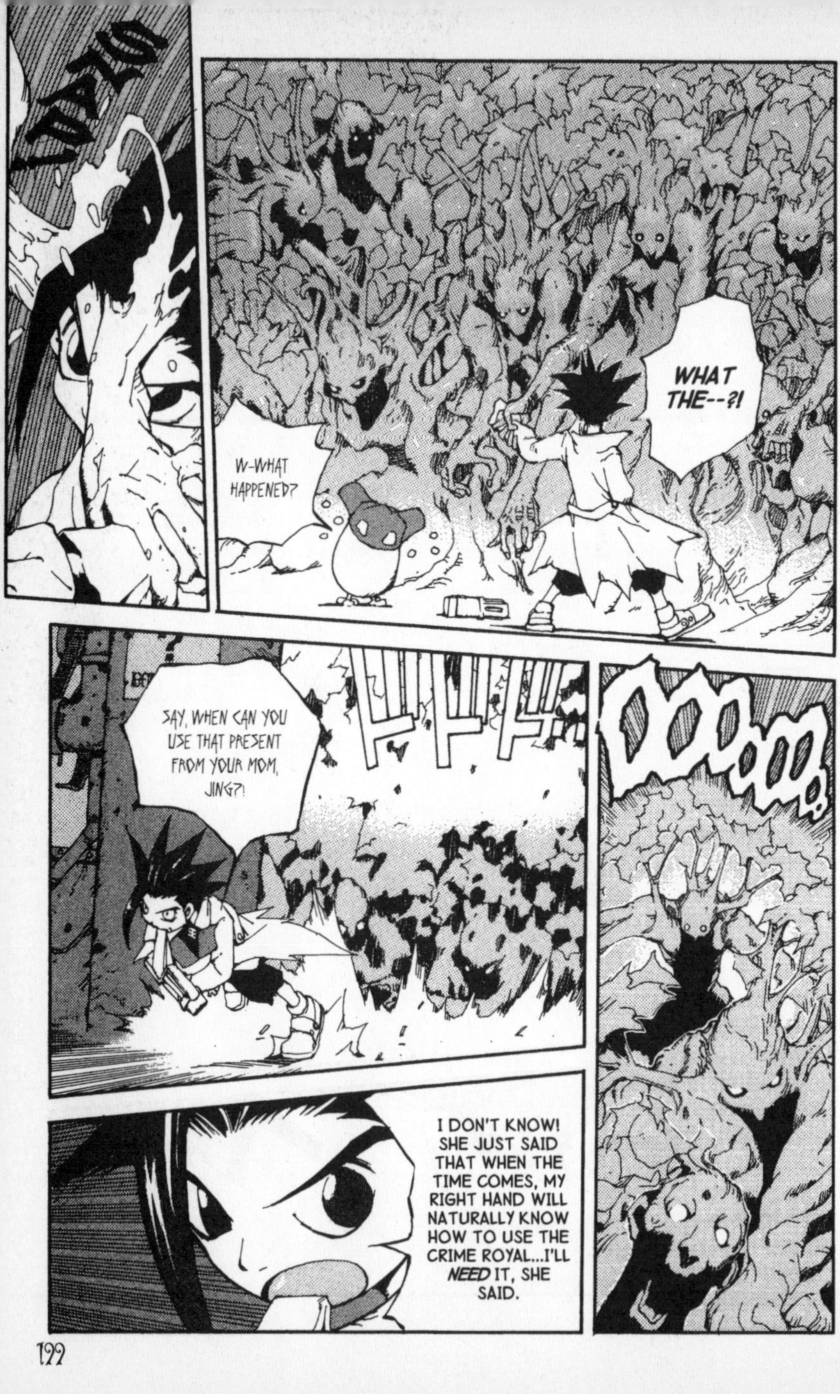
WHAT THE--?!
W-WHAT HAPPENED?
SAY, WHEN CAN YOU USE THAT PRESENT FROM YOUR MOM, JING?!
I DON'T KNOW! SHE JUST SAID THAT WHEN THE TIME COMES, MY RIGHT HAND WILL NATURALLY KNOW HOW TO USE THE CRIME ROYAL...I'LL *NEED* IT, SHE SAID.

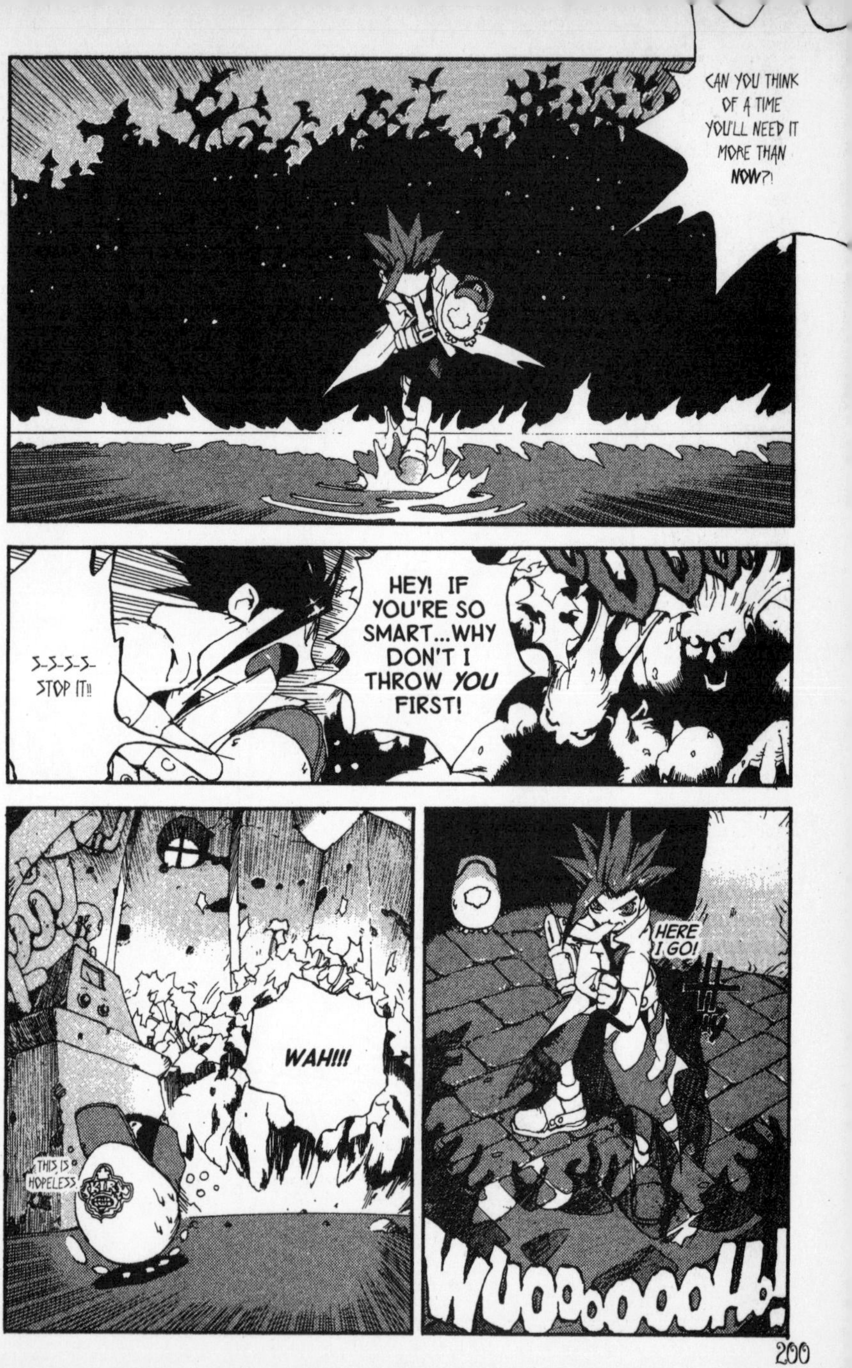
CAN YOU THINK OF A TIME YOU'LL NEED IT MORE THAN NOW?!
HEY! IF YOU'RE SO SMART...WHY DON'T I THROW YOU FIRST!
S-S-S-S-STOP IT!!
HERE I GO!
WUOOOOOOH!
WAH!!!
THIS IS HOPELESS.

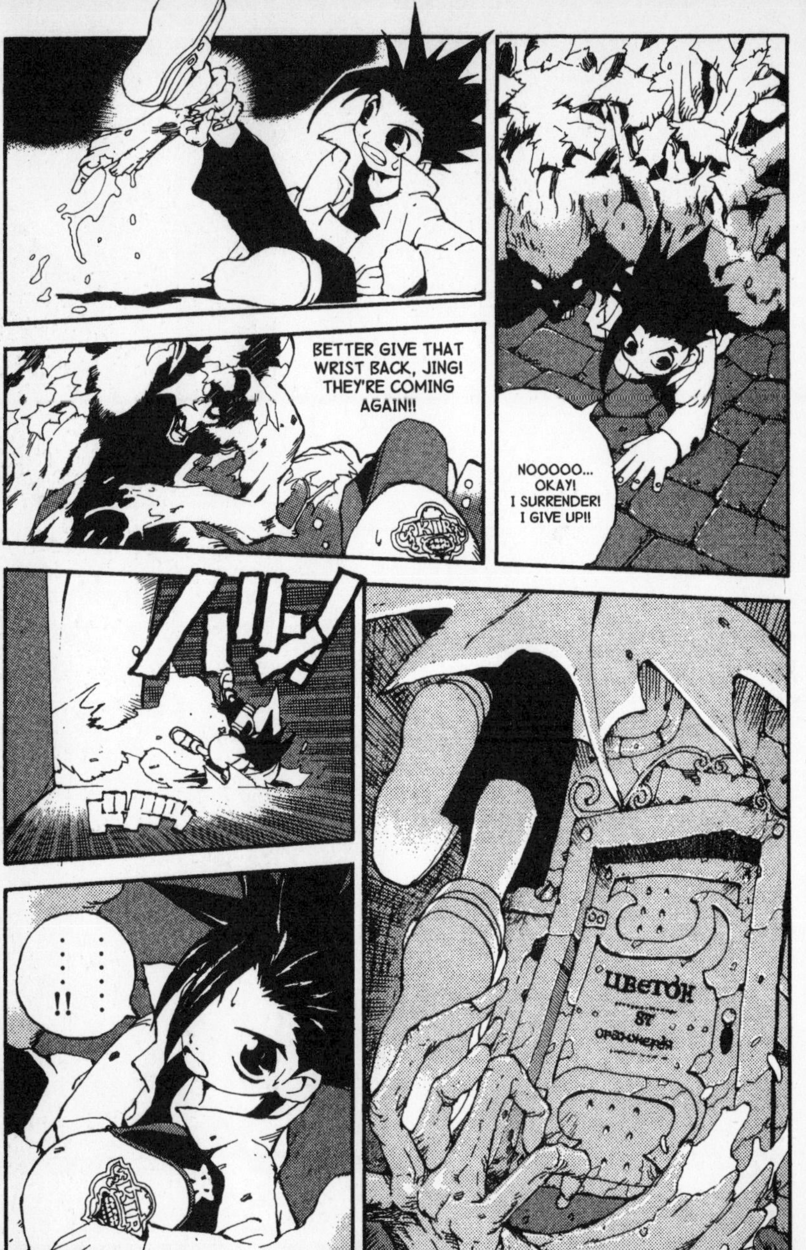
NOOOOO... OKAY! I SURRENDER! I GIVE UP!!
BETTER GIVE THAT WRIST BACK, JING! THEY'RE COMING AGAIN!!
......!!

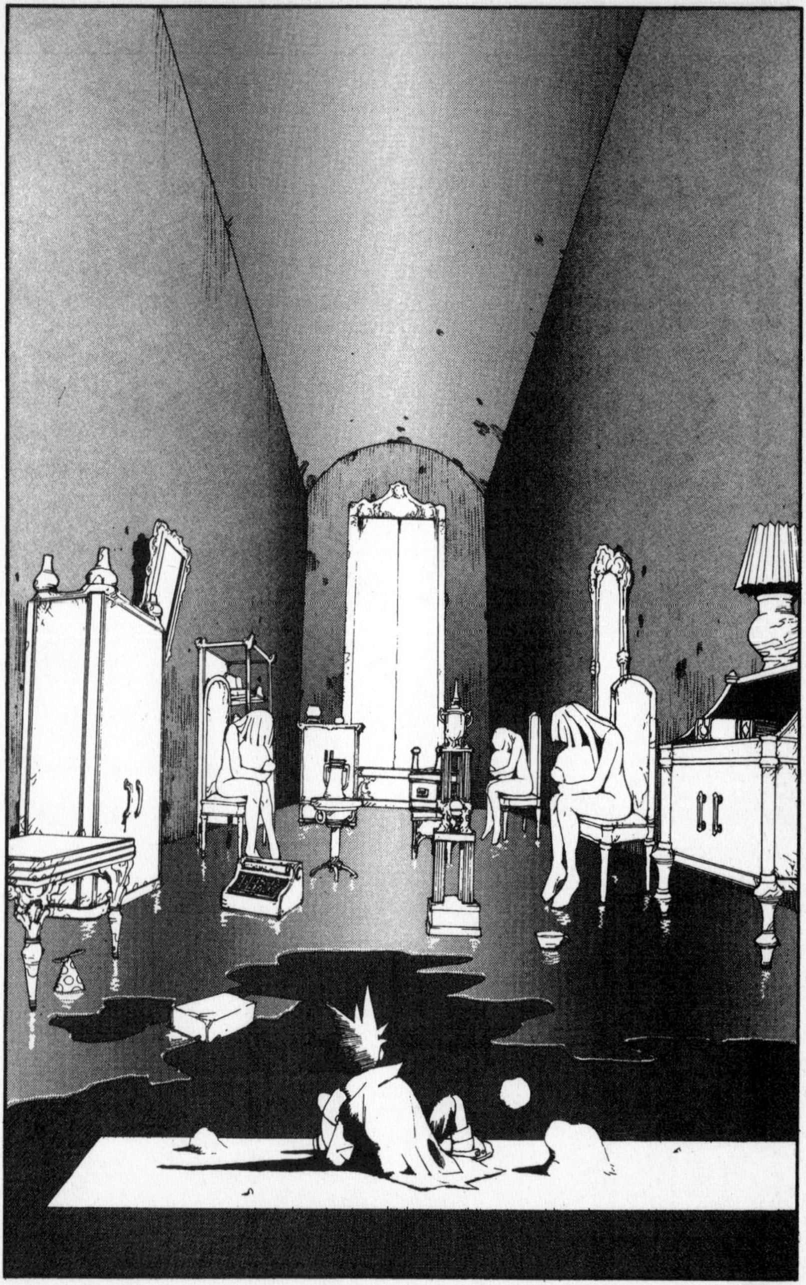

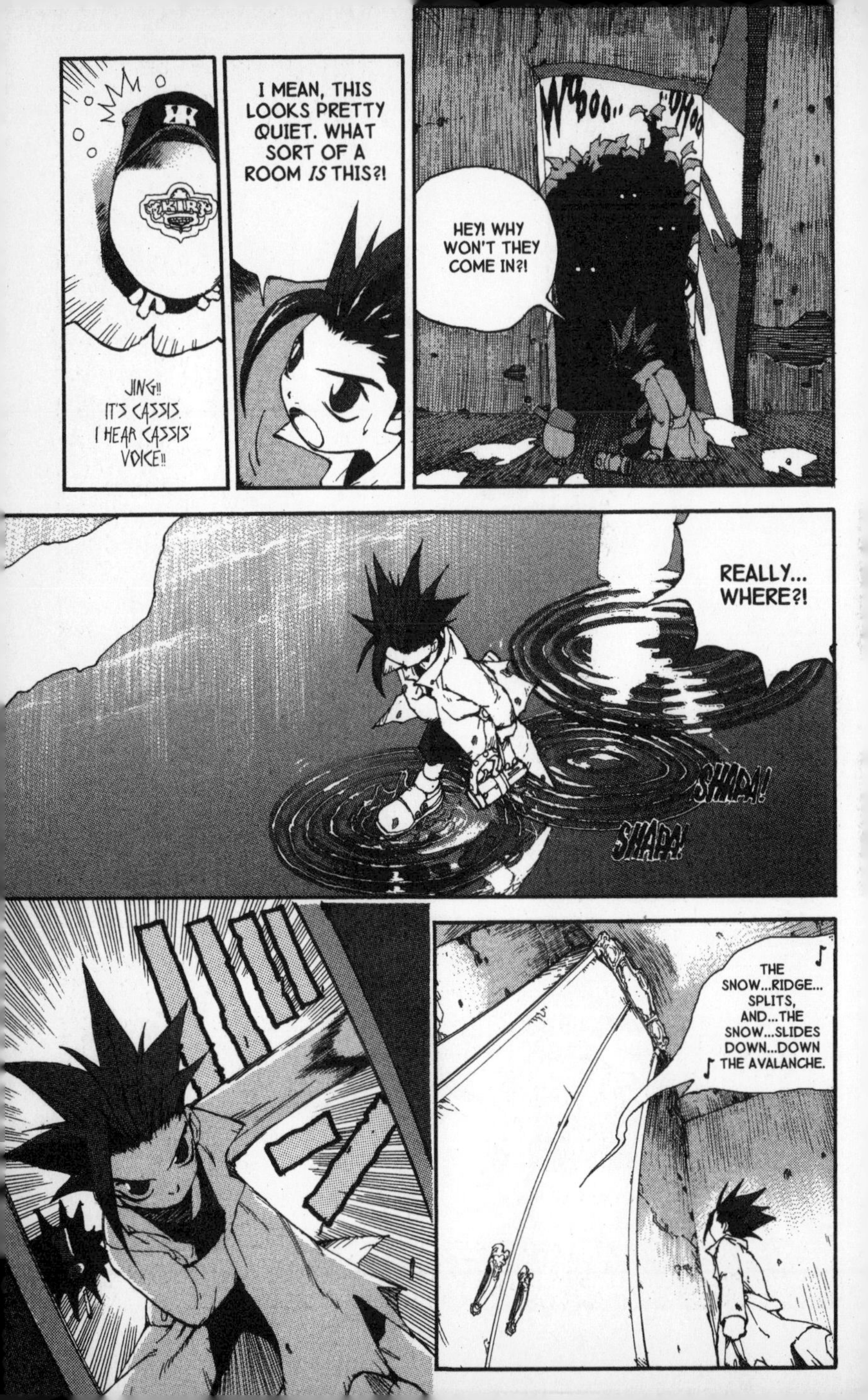
HEY! WHY WON'T THEY COME IN?!
I MEAN, THIS LOOKS PRETTY QUIET. WHAT SORT OF A ROOM IS THIS?!
JING!! IT'S CASSIS. I HEAR CASSIS' VOICE!!
REALLY... WHERE?!
SHAPA!
SHAPA!
THE SNOW...RIDGE... SPLITS, AND...THE SNOW...SLIDES DOWN...DOWN THE AVALANCHE.

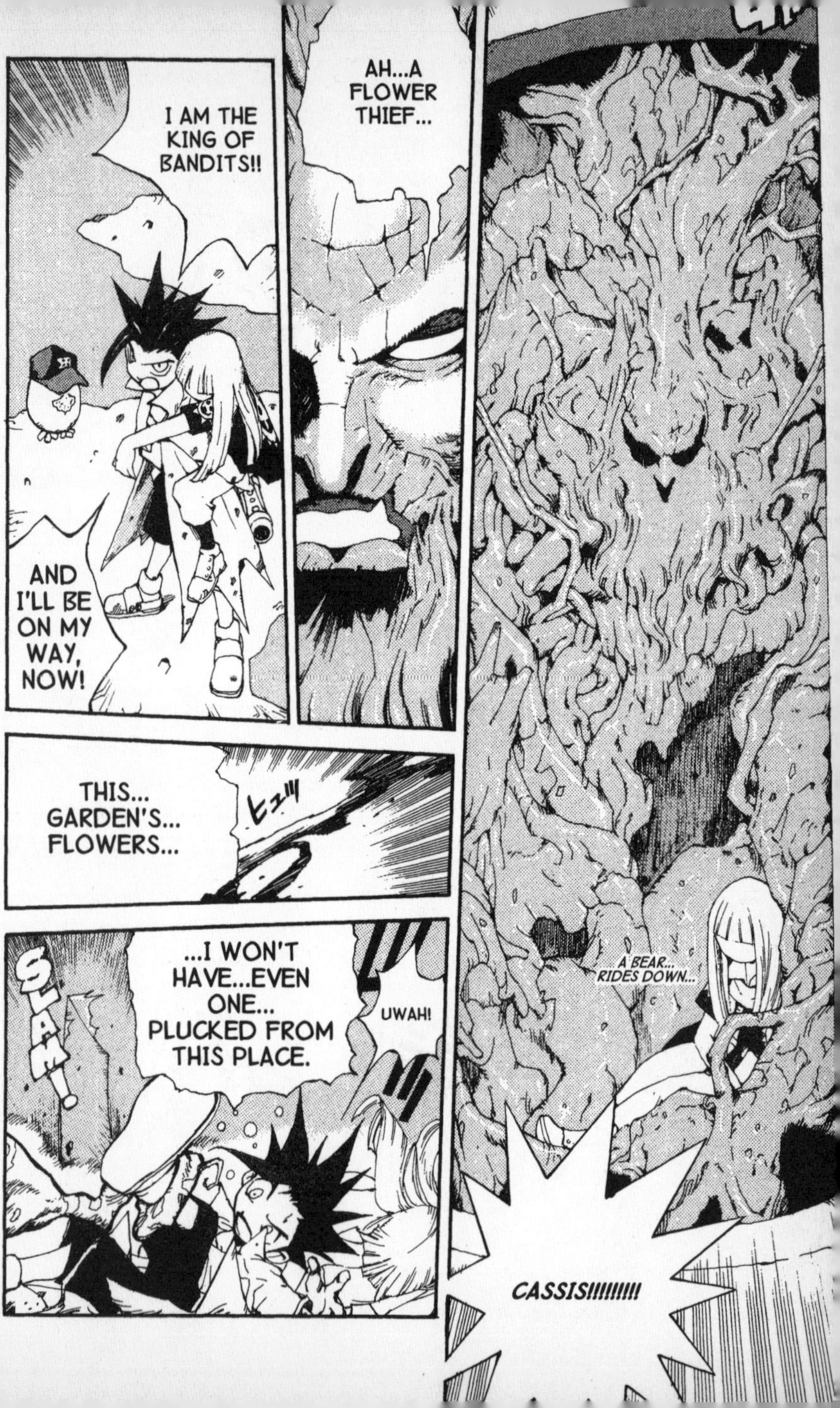
A BEAR... RIDES DOWN...
CASSIS!!!!!!!!!
AH...A FLOWER THIEF...
I AM THE KING OF BANDITS!!
AND I'LL BE ON MY WAY, NOW!
ヒュッ
THIS... GARDEN'S... FLOWERS...
UWAH!
...I WON'T HAVE...EVEN ONE... PLUCKED FROM THIS PLACE.
SLAM!

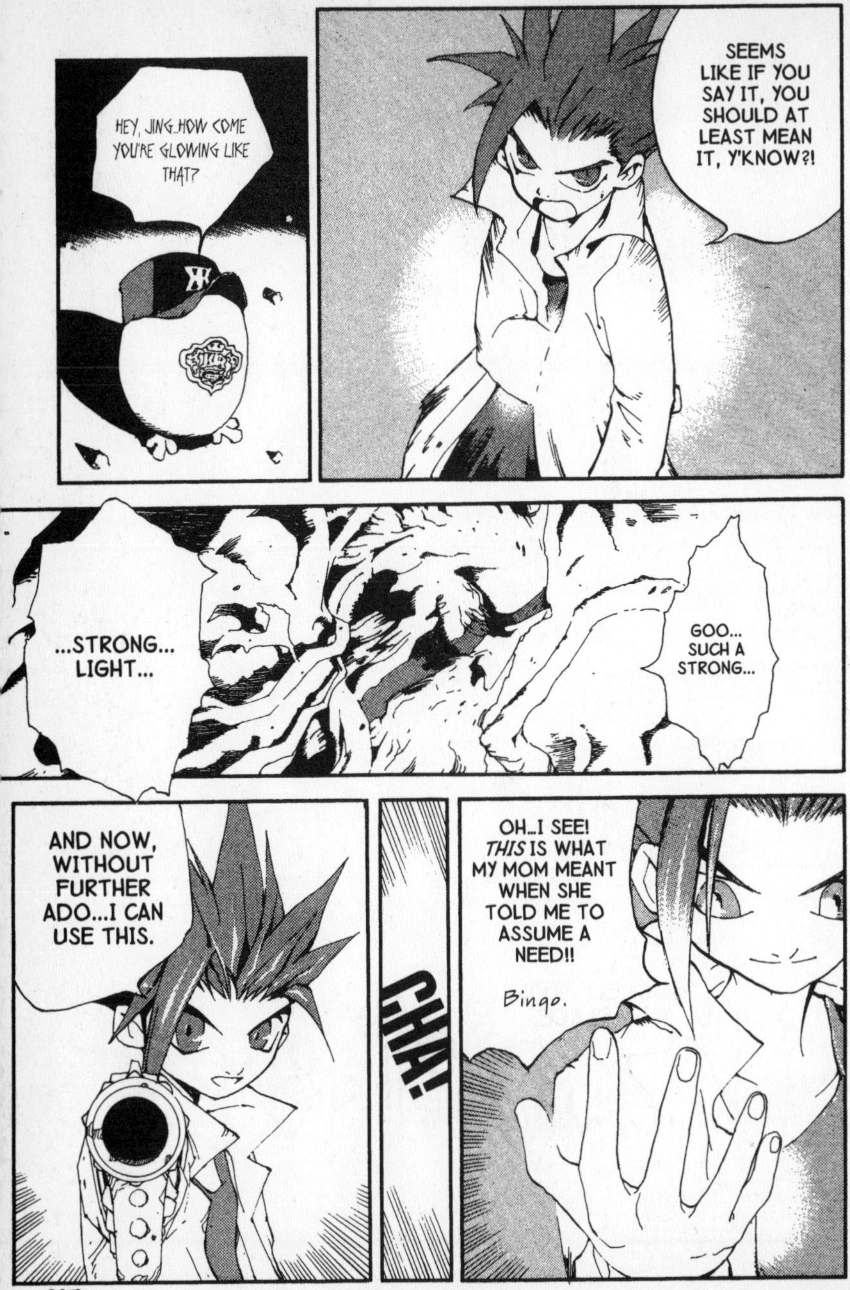
SEEMS LIKE IF YOU SAY IT, YOU SHOULD AT LEAST MEAN IT, Y'KNOW?!
HEY, JING...HOW COME YOU'RE GLOWING LIKE THAT?
GOO... SUCH A STRONG...
...STRONG... LIGHT...
OH...I SEE! *THIS* IS WHAT MY MOM MEANT WHEN SHE TOLD ME TO ASSUME A NEED!!
Bingo.
CHA!
AND NOW, WITHOUT FURTHER ADO...I CAN USE THIS.

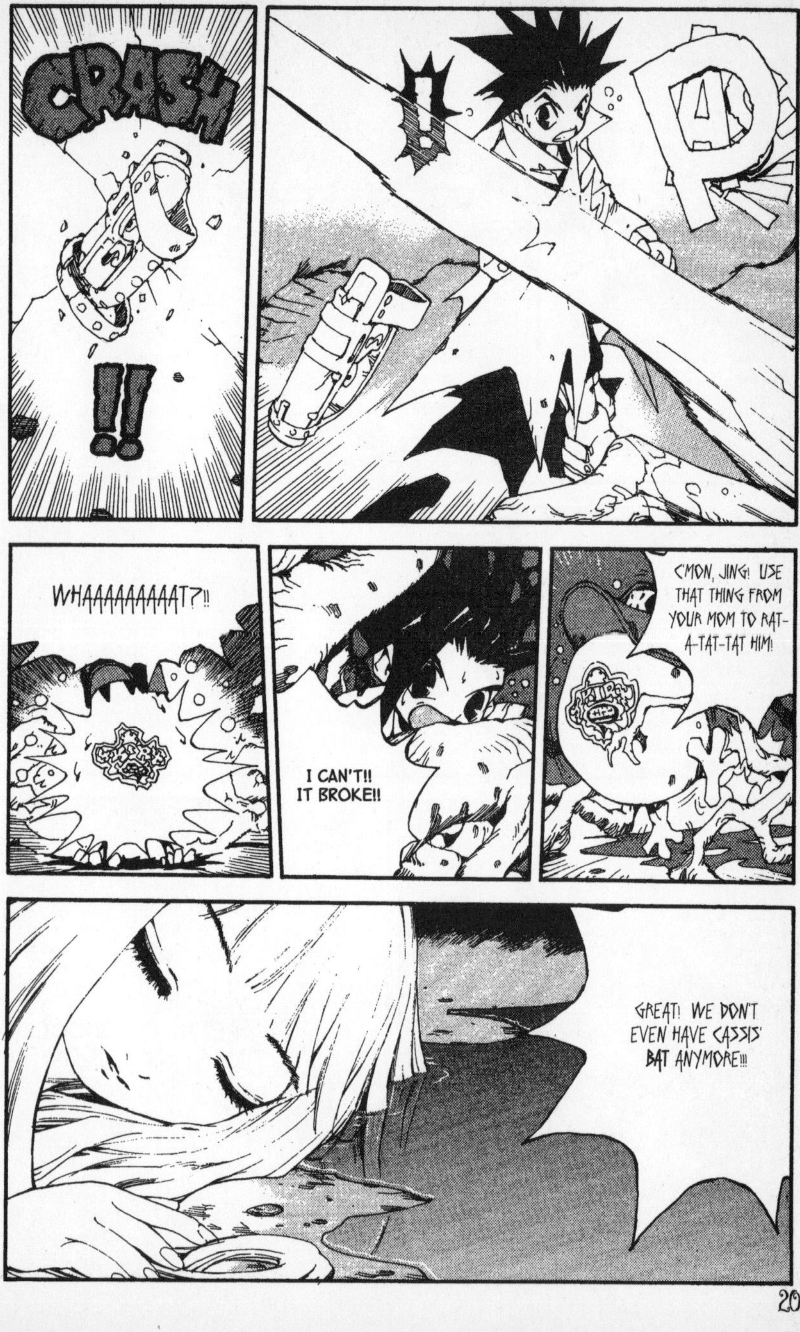
!
CRASH
!!
C'MON, JING! USE THAT THING FROM YOUR MOM TO RAT-A-TAT-TAT HIM!
I CAN'T!! IT BROKE!!
WHAAAAAAAAAT?!!
GREAT! WE DON'T EVEN HAVE CASSIS' BAT ANYMORE!!!

SHOOO-
OOOOT!!

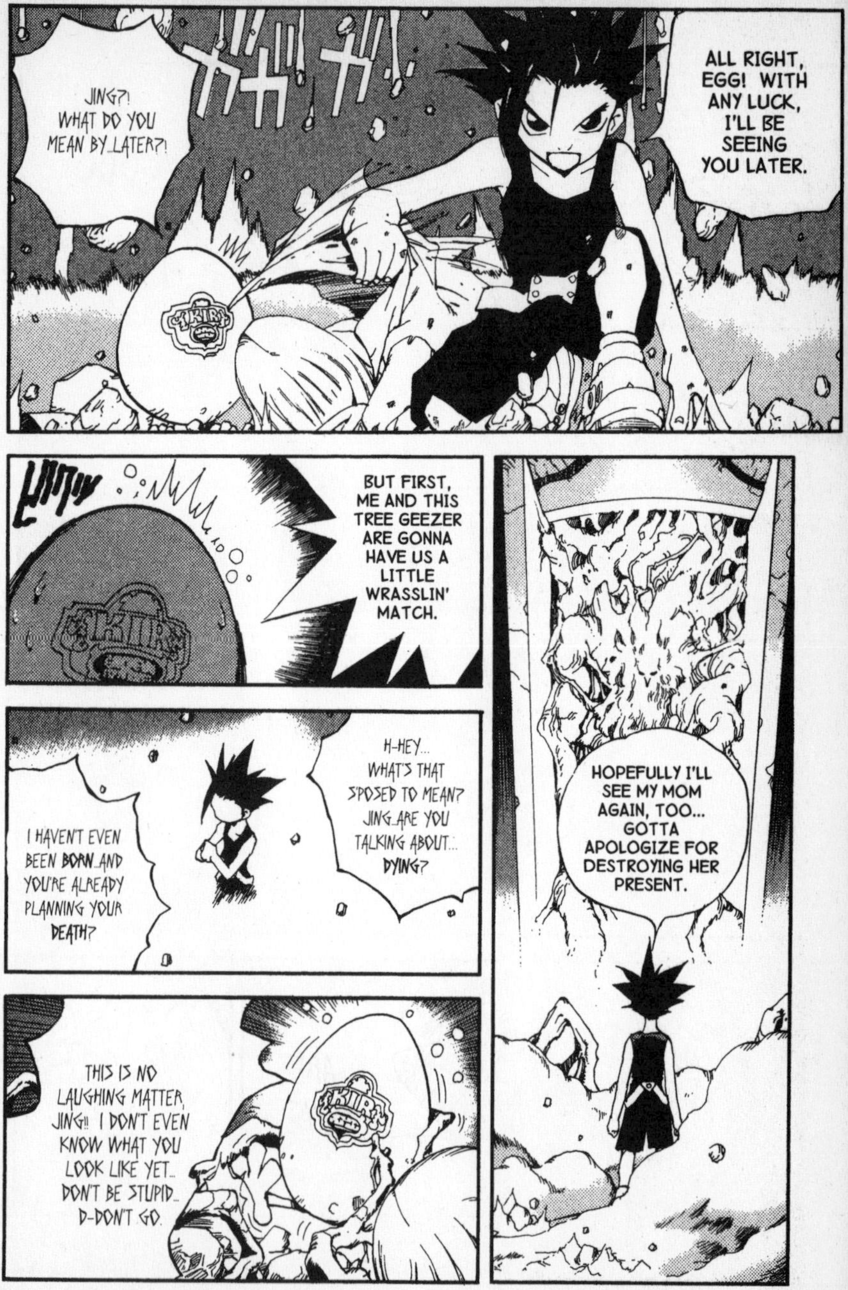
ALL RIGHT, EGG! WITH ANY LUCK, I'LL BE SEEING YOU LATER.
JING?! WHAT DO YOU MEAN BY...LATER?!
HOPEFULLY I'LL SEE MY MOM AGAIN, TOO... GOTTA APOLOGIZE FOR DESTROYING HER PRESENT.
BUT FIRST, ME AND THIS TREE GEEZER ARE GONNA HAVE US A LITTLE WRASSLIN' MATCH.
H-HEY... WHAT'S THAT S'POSED TO MEAN? JING...ARE YOU TALKING ABOUT... **DYING**?
I HAVEN'T EVEN BEEN **BORN**...AND YOU'RE ALREADY PLANNING YOUR **DEATH**?
THIS IS NO LAUGHING MATTER, JING!! I DON'T EVEN KNOW WHAT YOU LOOK LIKE YET... DON'T BE STUPID... D-DON'T GO.

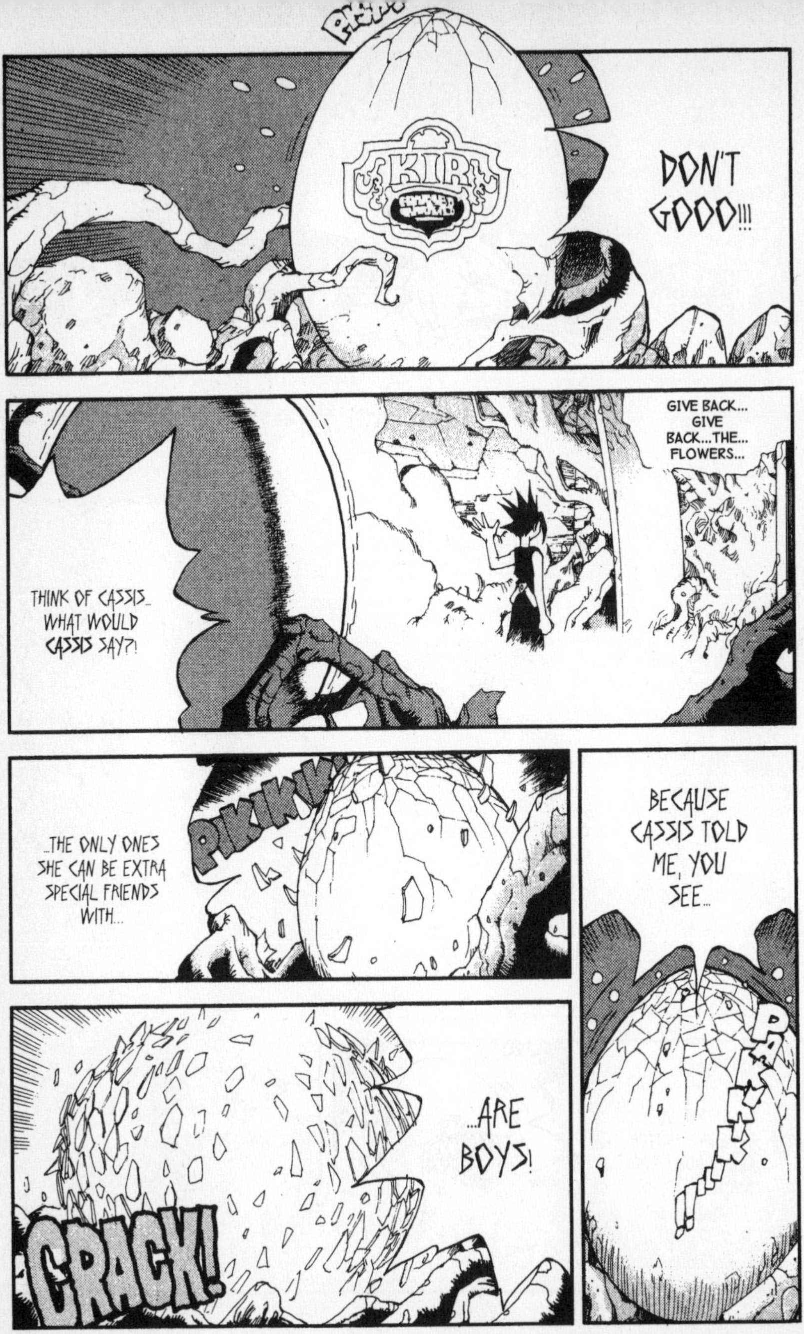
KIRI
DON'T GOOD!!!
GIVE BACK... GIVE BACK...THE... FLOWERS...
THINK OF CASSIS... WHAT WOULD CASSIS SAY?!
BECAUSE CASSIS TOLD ME, YOU SEE...
...THE ONLY ONES SHE CAN BE EXTRA SPECIAL FRIENDS WITH...
...ARE BOYS!
CRACK!

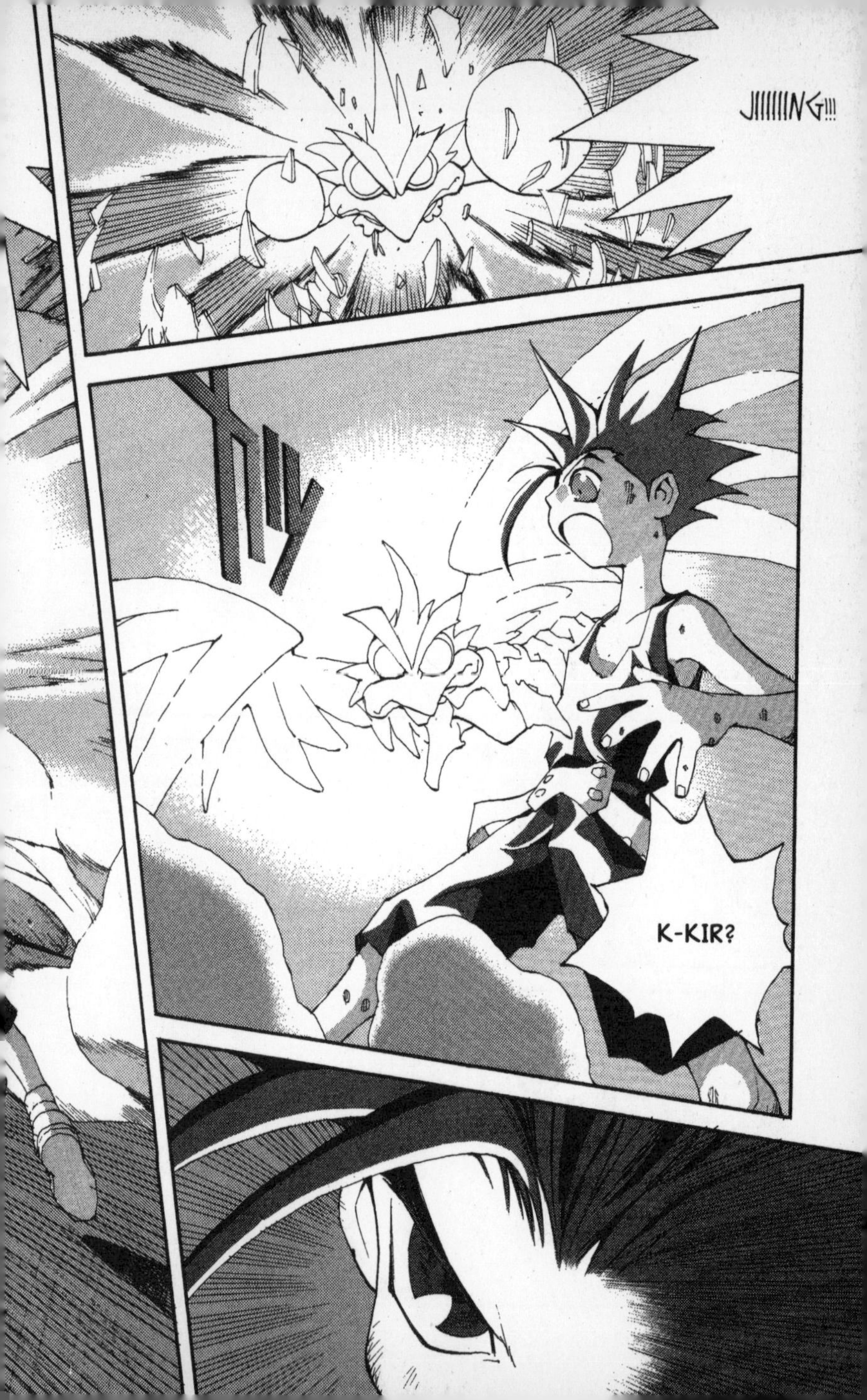
JIIIIIING!!!
YANK
K-KIR?

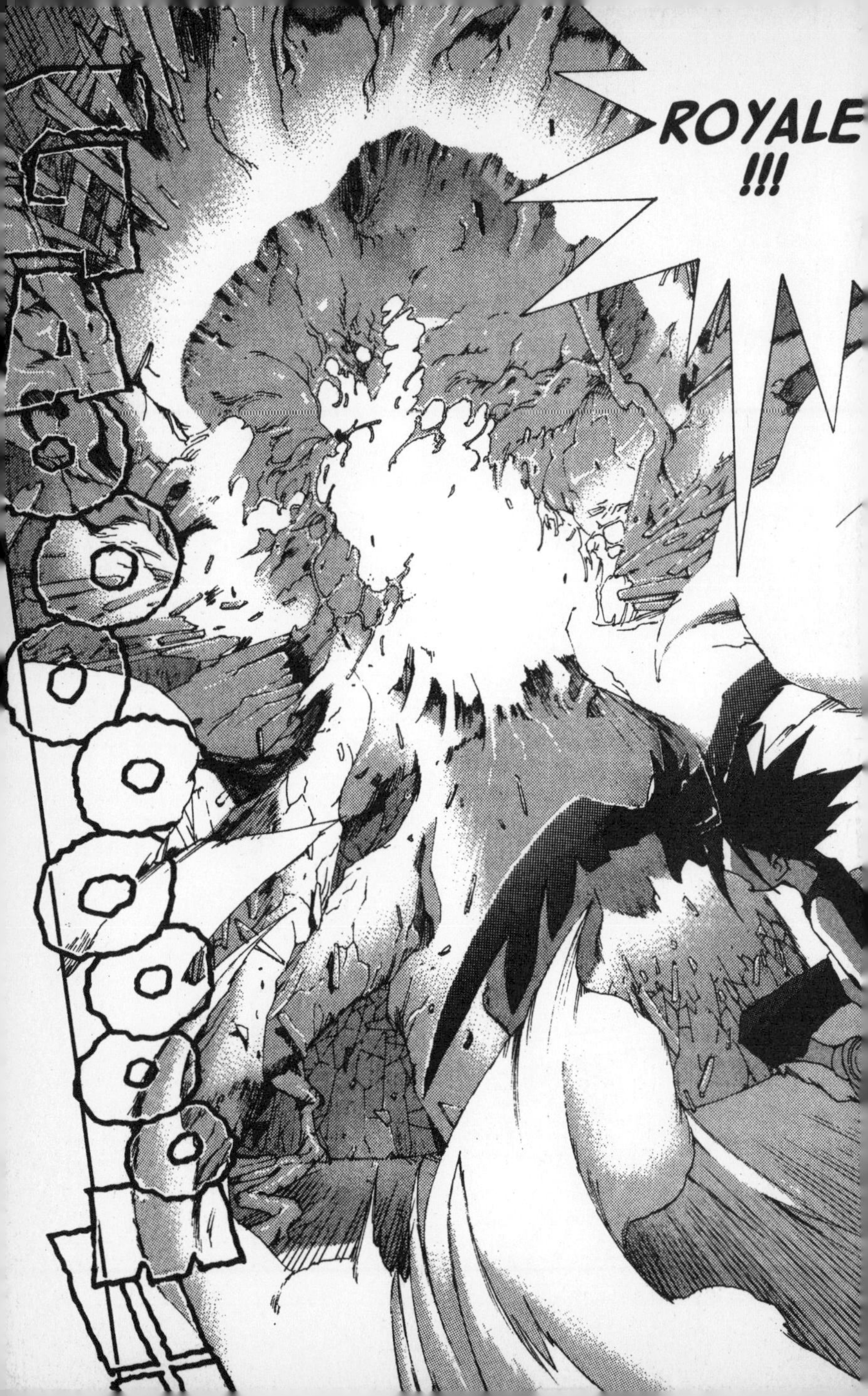
ROYALE
!!!

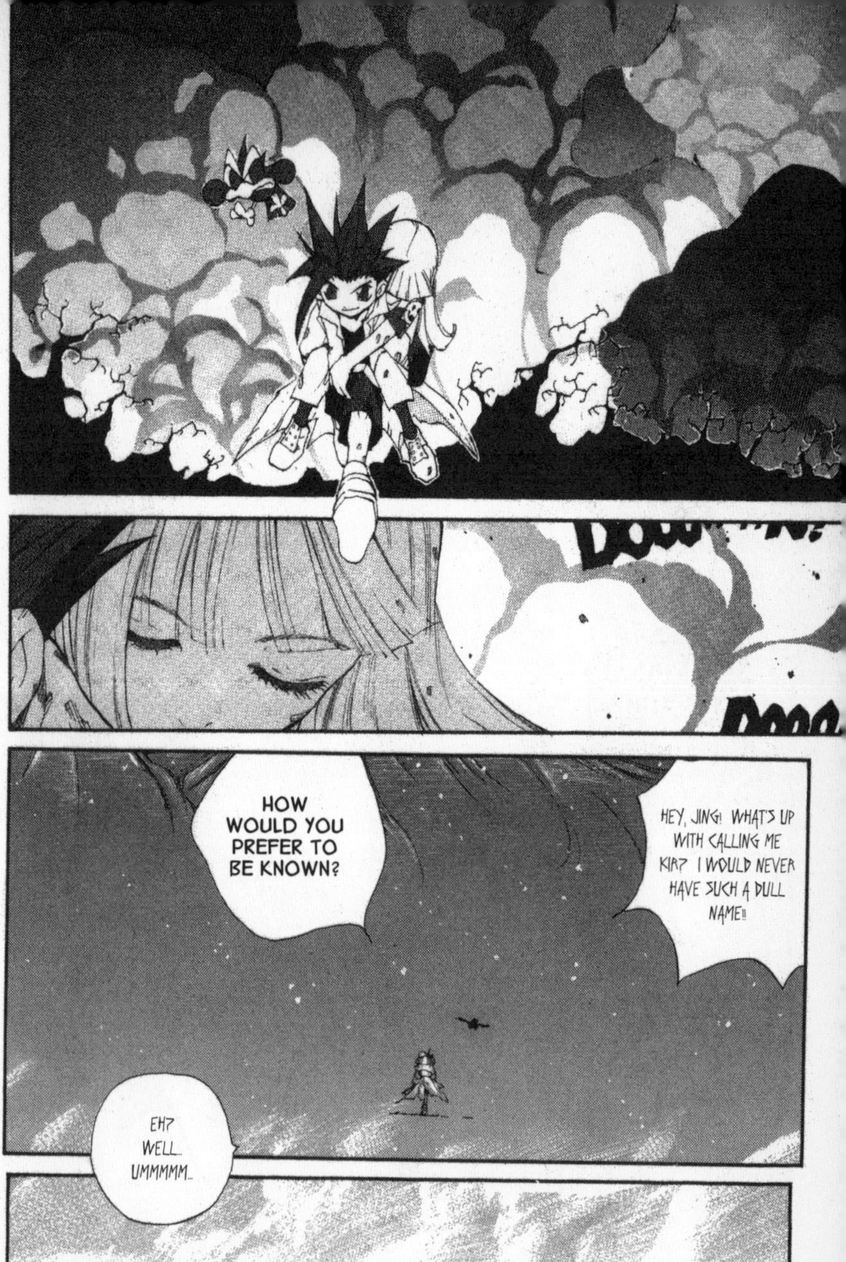
HEY, JING! WHAT'S UP WITH CALLING ME KIR? I WOULD NEVER HAVE SUCH A DULL NAME!!
HOW WOULD YOU PREFER TO BE KNOWN?
EH? WELL... UMMMMM...

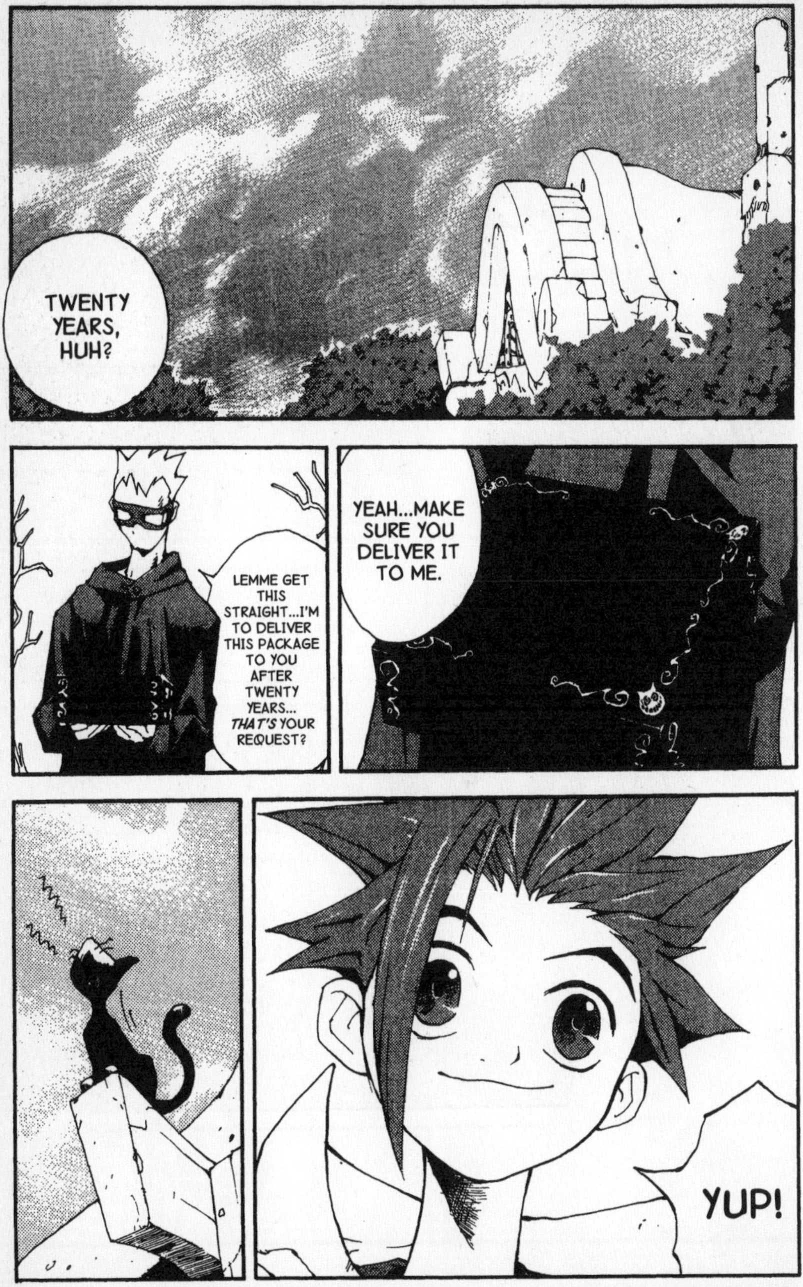
TWENTY YEARS, HUH?
YEAH...MAKE SURE YOU DELIVER IT TO ME.
LEMME GET THIS STRAIGHT...I'M TO DELIVER THIS PACKAGE TO YOU AFTER TWENTY YEARS... *THAT'S* YOUR REQUEST?
YUP!

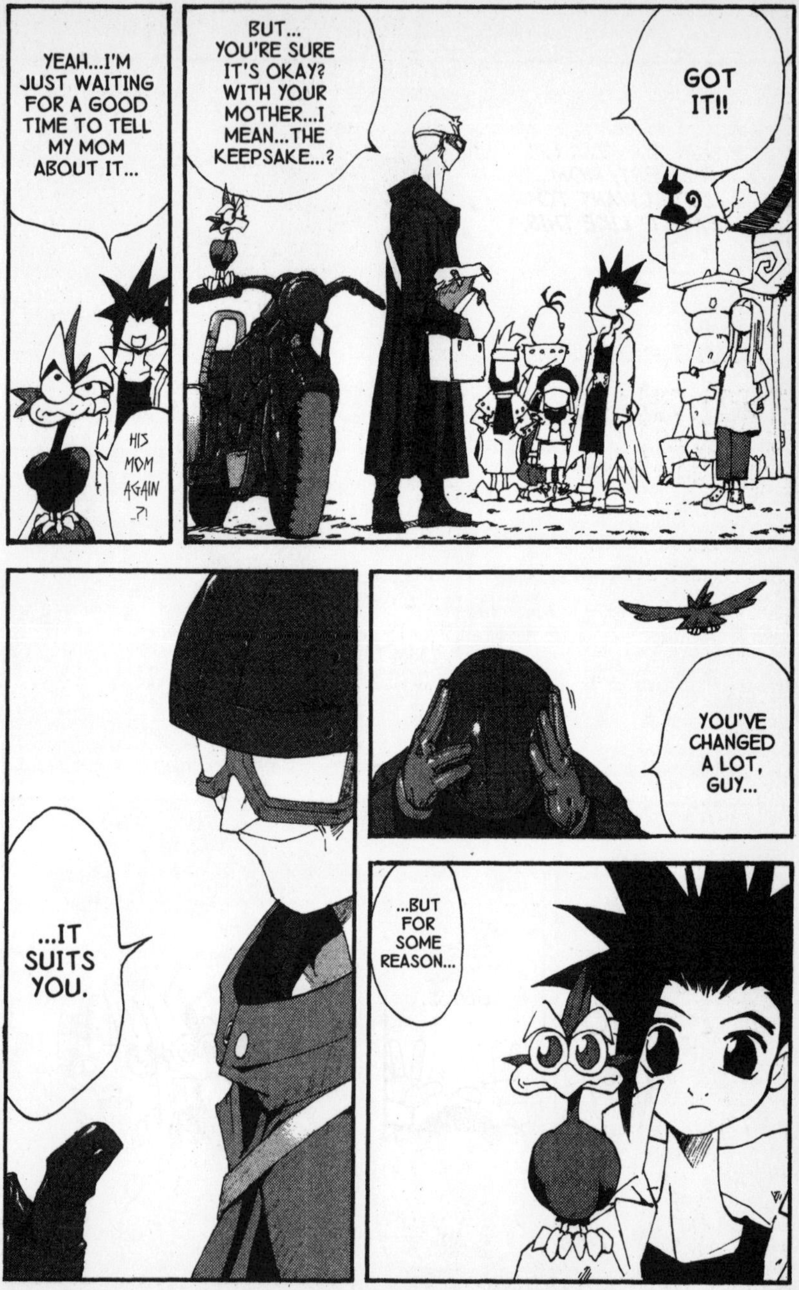
GOT IT!!
BUT... YOU'RE SURE IT'S OKAY? WITH YOUR MOTHER...I MEAN...THE KEEPSAKE...?
YEAH...I'M JUST WAITING FOR A GOOD TIME TO TELL MY MOM ABOUT IT...
HIS MOM AGAIN..?!
YOU'VE CHANGED A LOT, GUY...
...BUT FOR SOME REASON...
...IT SUITS YOU.

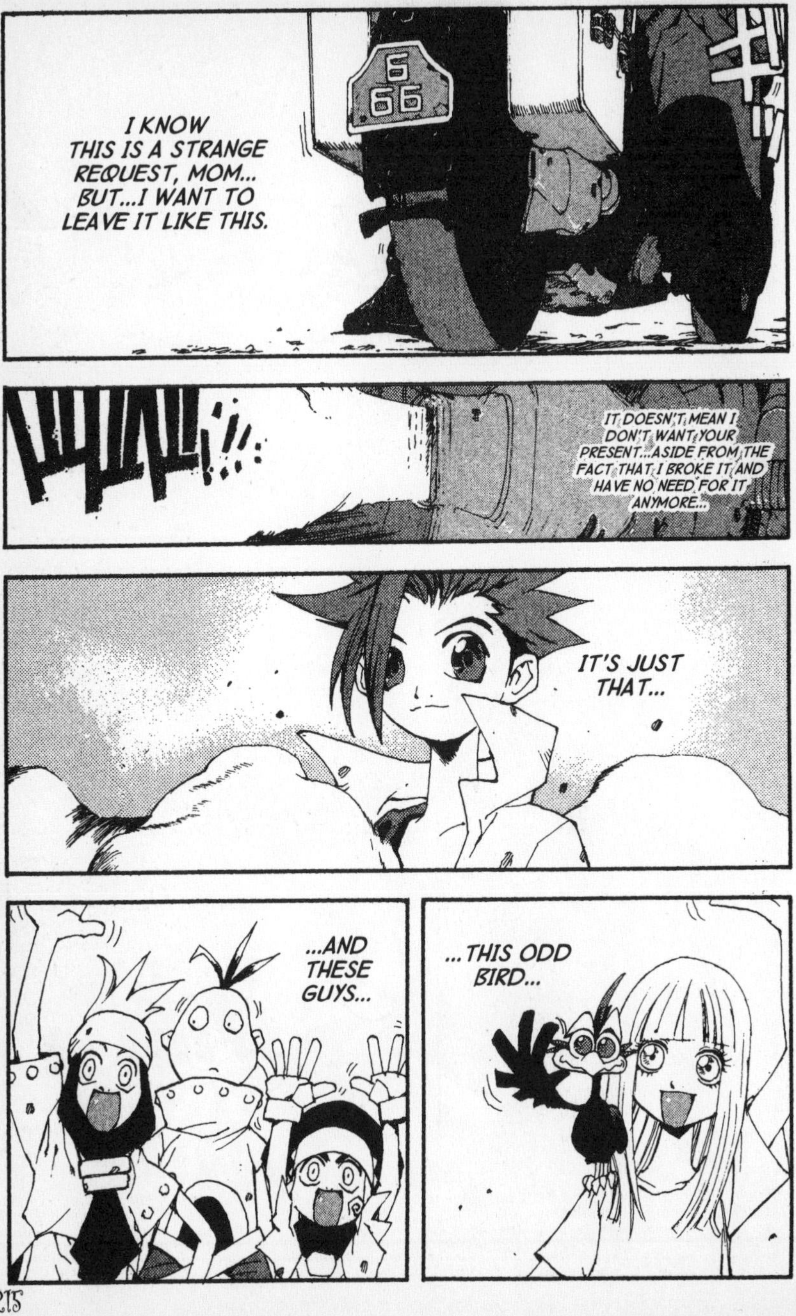
I KNOW THIS IS A STRANGE REQUEST, MOM... BUT...I WANT TO LEAVE IT LIKE THIS.
IT DOESN'T MEAN I DON'T WANT YOUR PRESENT...ASIDE FROM THE FACT THAT I BROKE IT AND HAVE NO NEED FOR IT ANYMORE...
IT'S JUST THAT...
...THIS ODD BIRD...
...AND THESE GUYS...

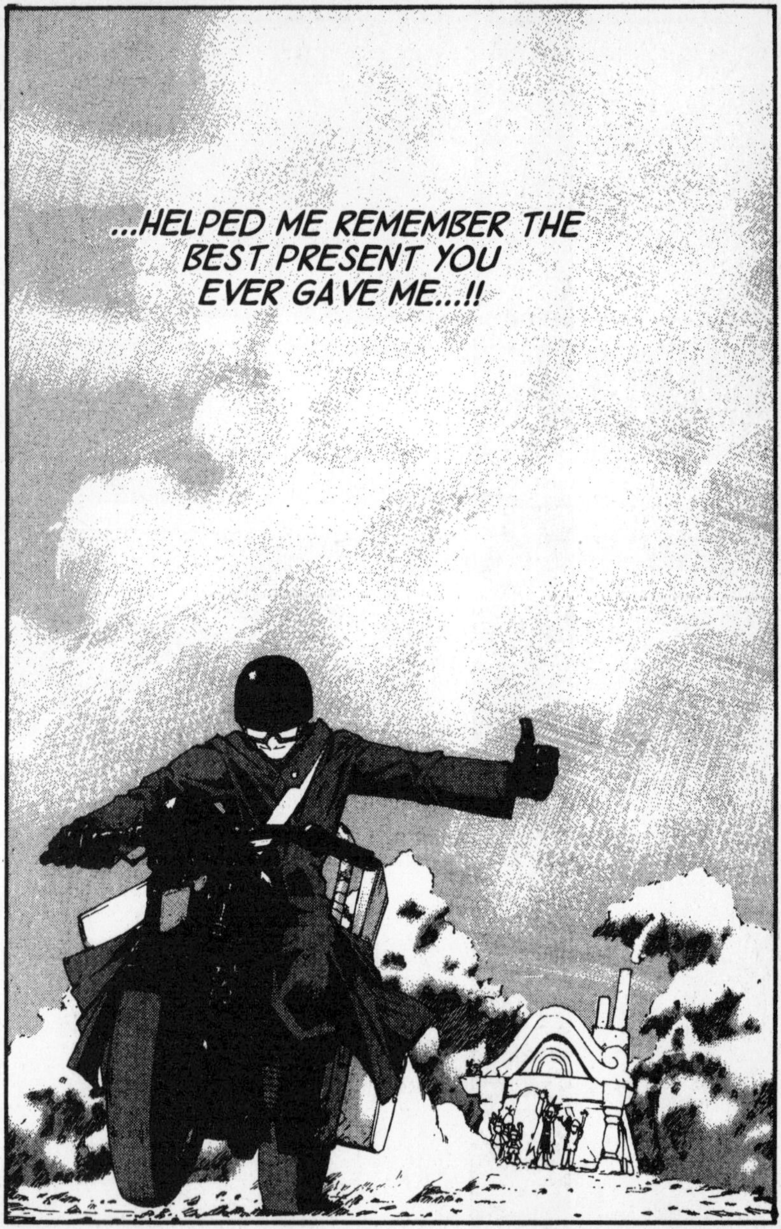
...HELPED ME REMEMBER THE BEST PRESENT YOU EVER GAVE ME...!!

CONTINUED IN VOLUME 5

JING, KING OF BANDITS INITIAL SETUP COLLECTION (4)

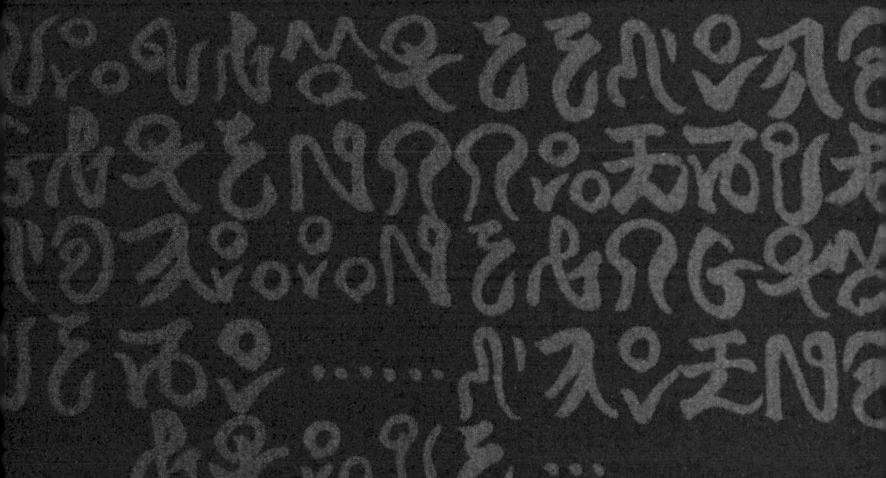

The enigmatic language uttered by the mysterious doll that Jing and the others followed in the prison of dreams. These are special characters designed just for that scene, specially manufactured and written in ink on hanshi!!

villain

He looks evil, but in a foolish way.
This is the precursor to Vodka!!
Everyone knows how he finally turns
out, but this one is pretty personal.
The current one does cry at the
reunion of the Double Mermaid. I
think that side of his personality
balances out the evil just right.

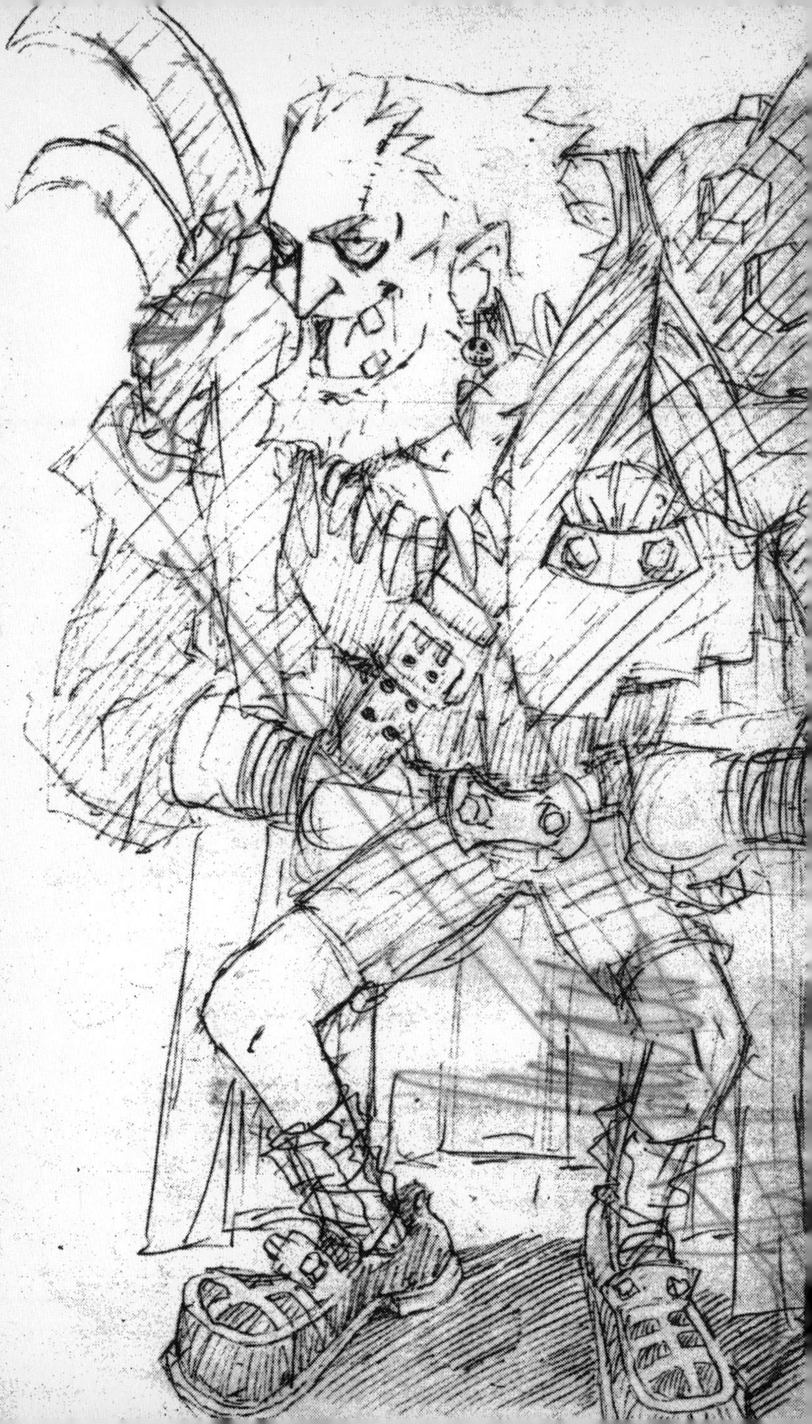

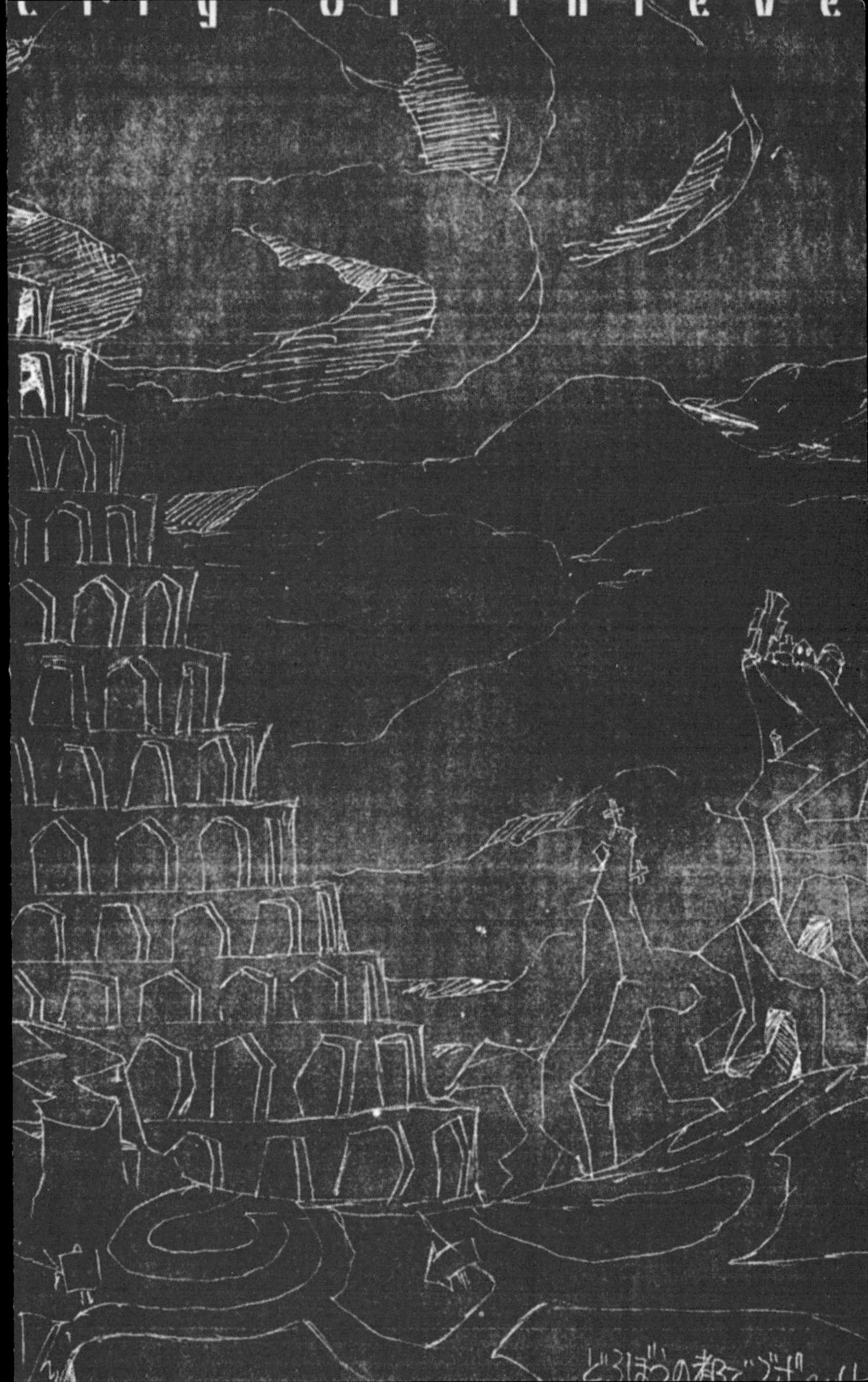
どろぼうの都で

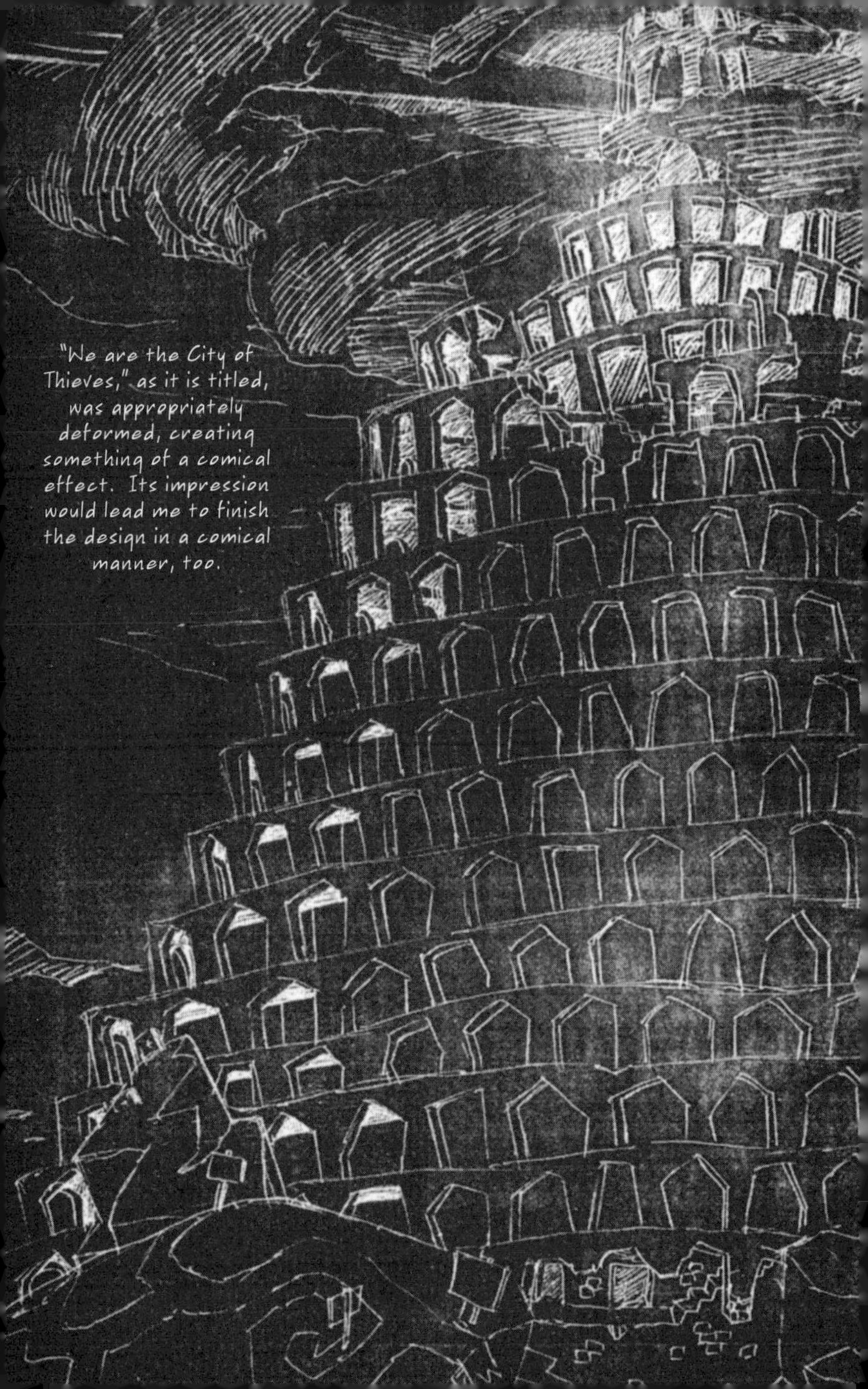

"We are the City of Thieves," as it is titled, was appropriately deformed, creating something of a comical effect. Its impression would lead me to finish the design in a comical manner, too.

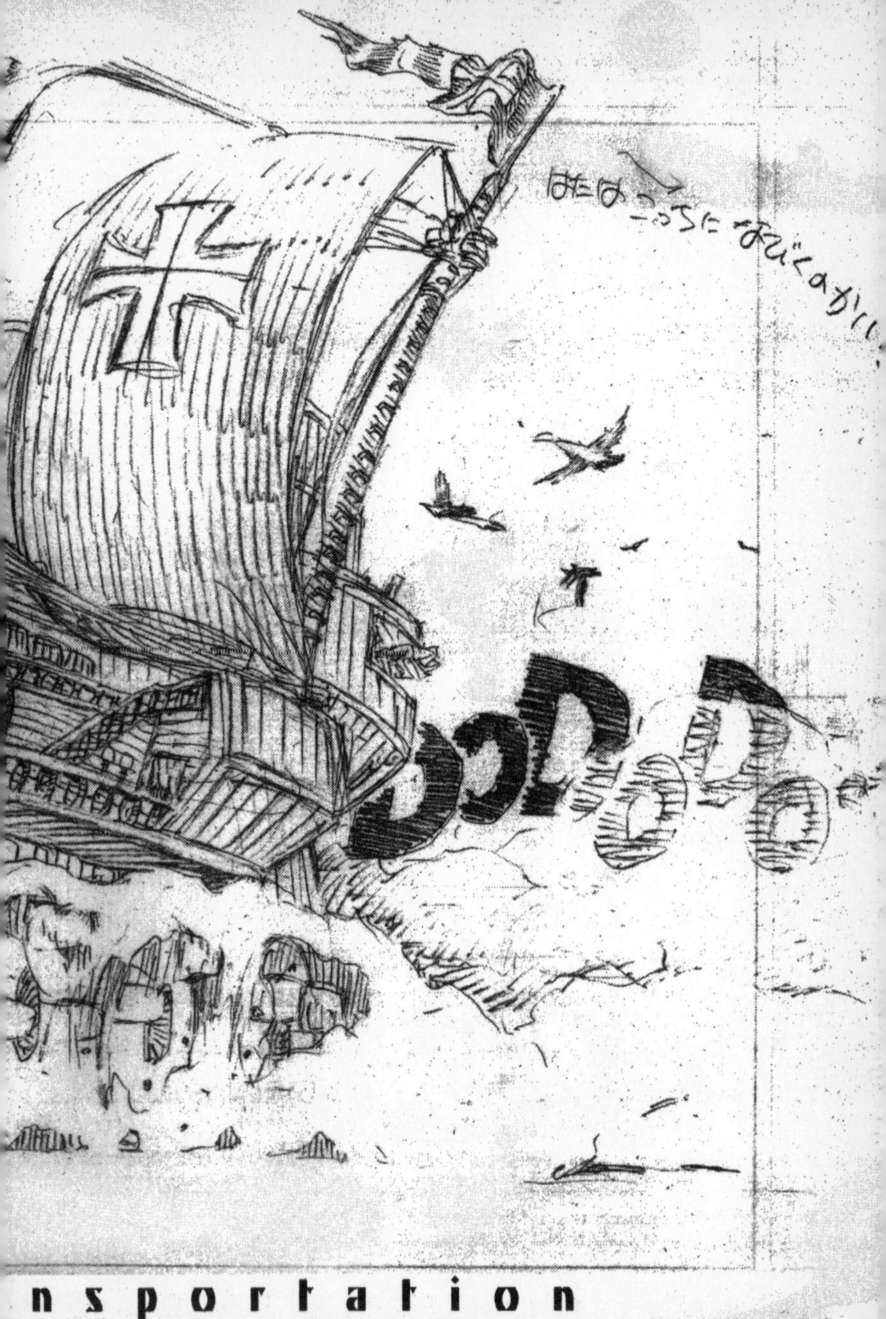
はたはこっちになびくのがいい

nsportation

Here is a design where the weightiness of a wooden ship moving slowly forward, trying to plane the earth, came through splendidly. The design itself is very realistic...one certainly wouldn't have guessed this form was a precursor to the current version.

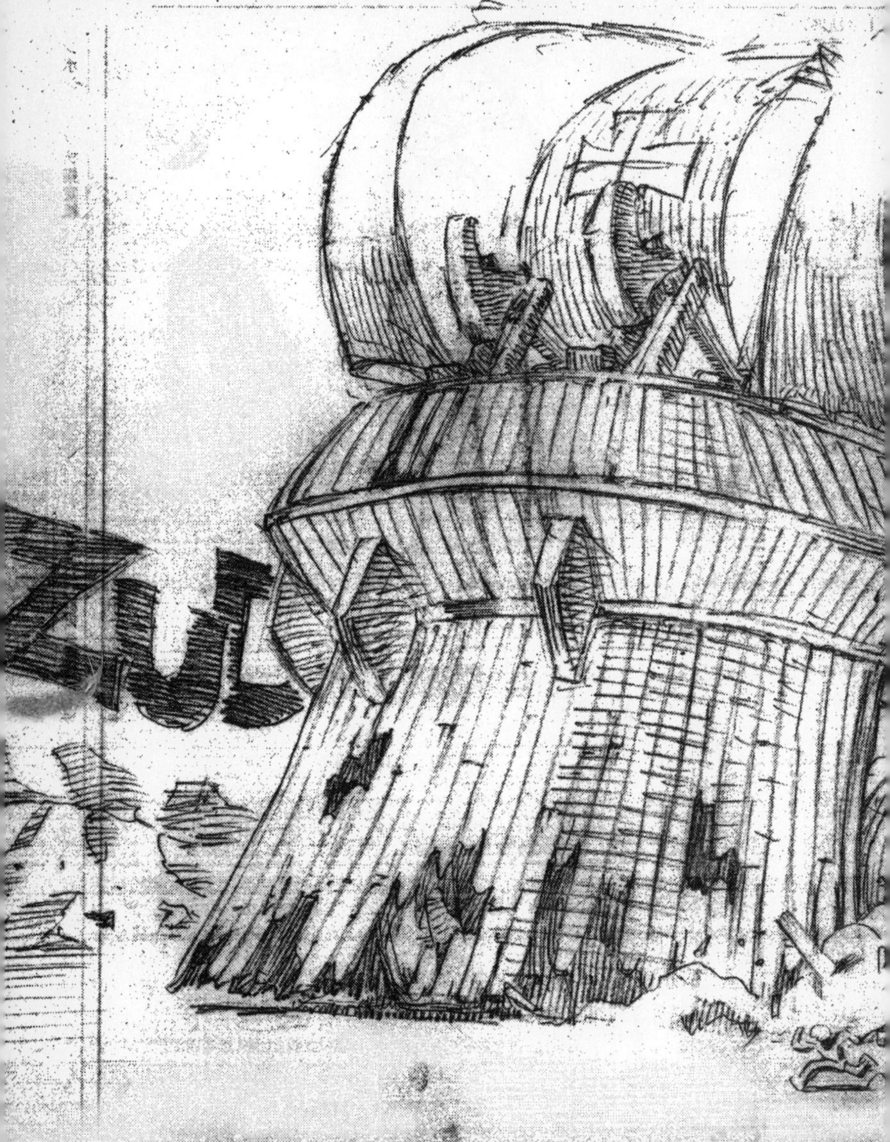
ZUL

gigantic public tr

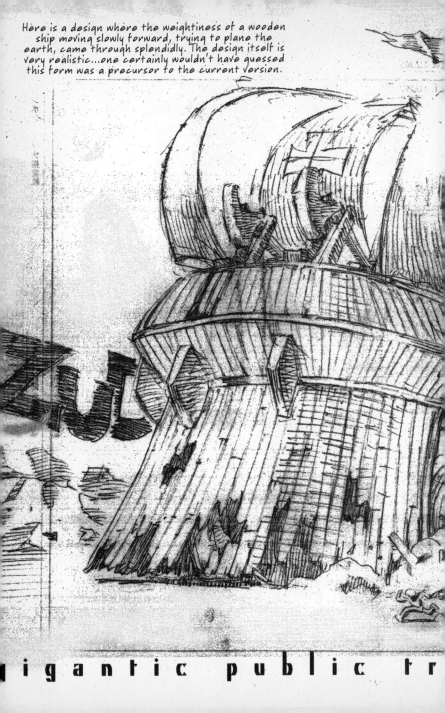

Another land-ship sailing across the infinite wasteland--again, quite a different impression from the final edition. The decision to change the ship into a land-whale was made between when this was drawn and the writing was started.

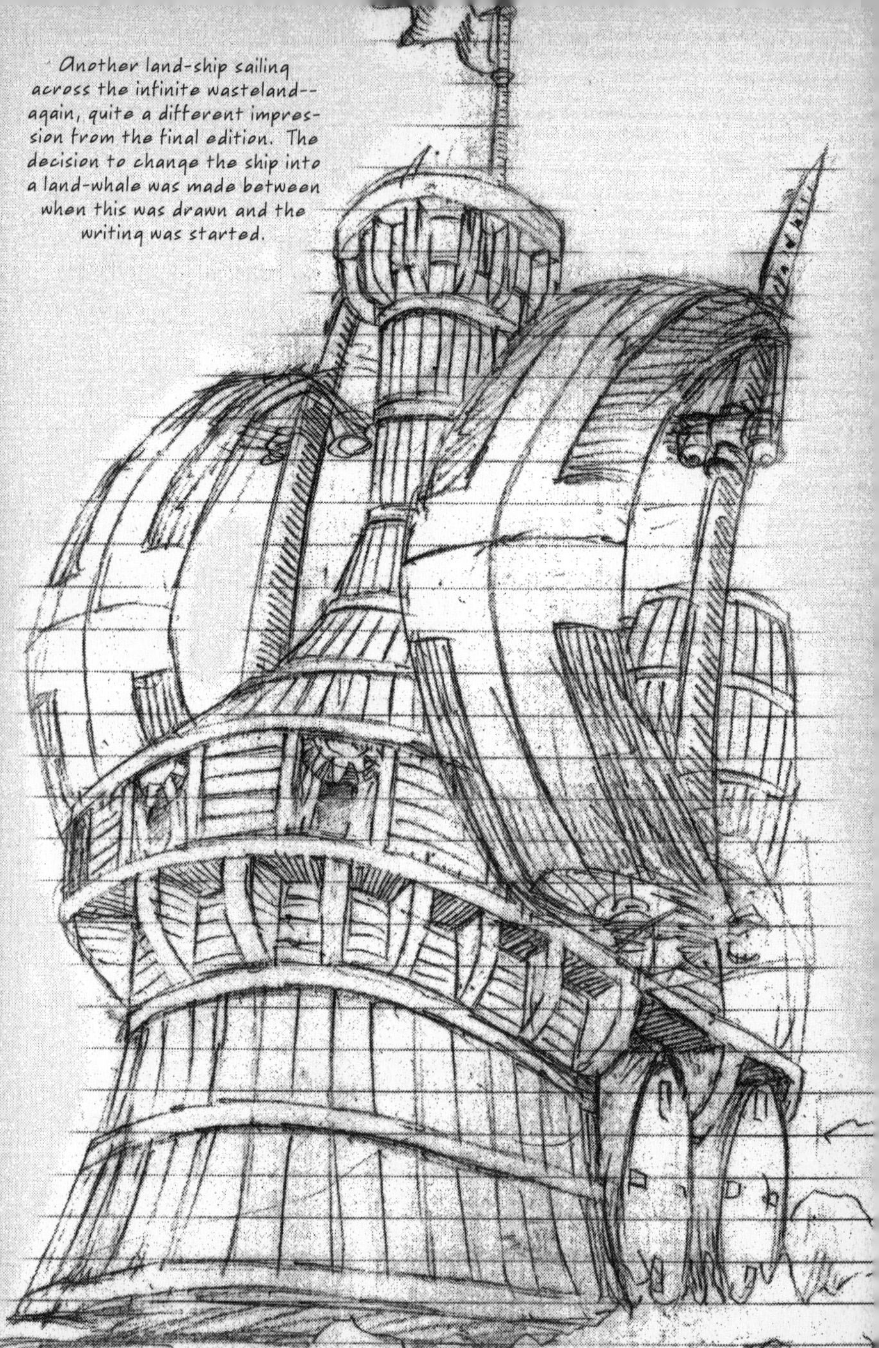

LANDSHiPb

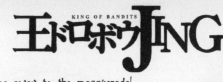

KING OF BANDITS

王ドロボウJING

Oh, take me away to the masquerade!
It seems our chap Jing and his avian ally are en route to Zaza,
a town renowned for its yearly masked ball.
Pity our heroes have no idea there will be
a lot more brawling on the ballroom floor than they'd expected.
For it is a fine line indeed between
a masquerade and a masked arena.

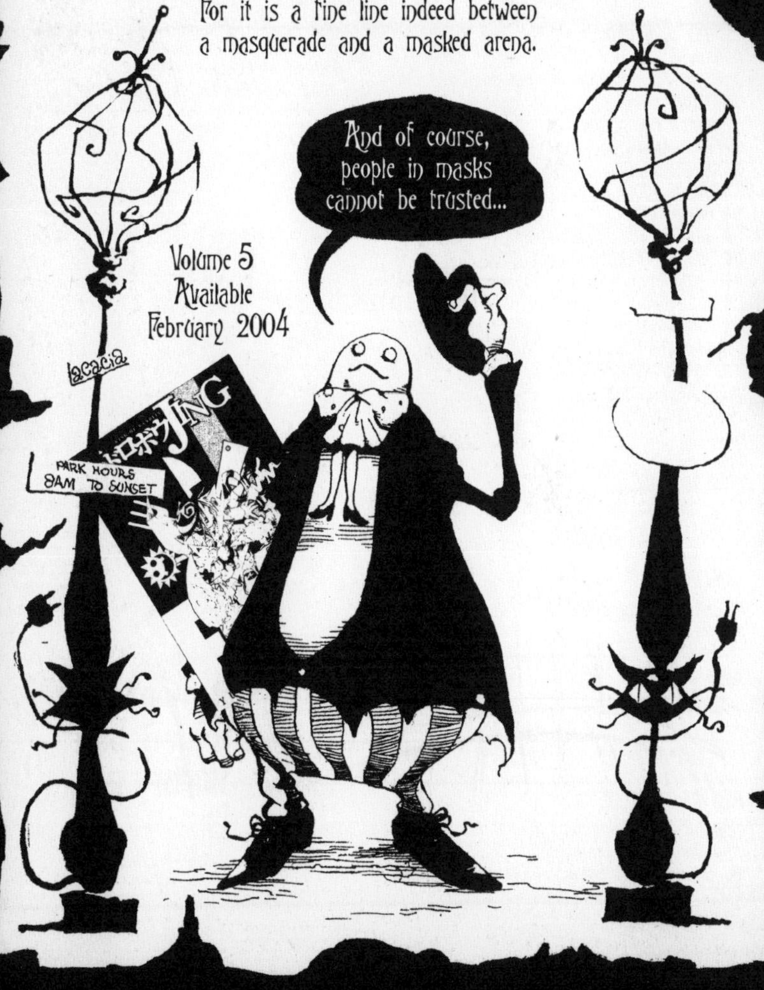
And of course, people in masks cannot be trusted...
Volume 5 Available February 2004
lacacia
PARK HOURS 8AM TO SUNSET

ALSO AVAILABLE FROM 🐾TOKYOPOP®

For more information visit www.TOKYOPOP.com

10103

ALSO AVAILABLE FROM TOKYOPOP®

MANGA

.HACK//LEGEND OF THE TWILIGHT
@LARGE
A.I. LOVE YOU February 2004
AI YORI AOSHI January 2004
ANGELIC LAYER
BABY BIRTH
BATTLE ROYALE
BATTLE VIXENS April 2004
BIRTH May 2004
BRAIN POWERED
BRIGADOON
B'TX January 2004
CARDCAPTOR SAKURA
CARDCAPTOR SAKURA: MASTER OF THE CLOW
CARDCAPTOR SAKURA: BOXED SET COLLECTION 1
CARDCAPTOR SAKURA: BOXED SET COLLECTION 2
  March 2004
CHOBITS
CHRONICLES OF THE CURSED SWORD
CLAMP SCHOOL DETECTIVES
CLOVER
COMIC PARTY June 2004
CONFIDENTIAL CONFESSIONS
CORRECTOR YUI
COWBOY BEBOP: BOXED SET THE COMPLETE
  COLLECTION
CRESCENT MOON May 2004
CREST OF THE STARS June 2004
CYBORG 009
DEMON DIARY
DIGIMON
DIGIMON SERIES 3 April 2004
DIGIMON ZERO TWO February 2004
DNANGEL April 2004
DOLL May 2004
DRAGON HUNTER
DRAGON KNIGHTS
DUKLYON: CLAMP SCHOOL DEFENDERS
DV June 2004
ERICA SAKURAZAWA
FAERIES' LANDING January 2004
FAKE
FLCL
FORBIDDEN DANCE
FRUITS BASKET February 2004
G GUNDAM
GATEKEEPERS
GETBACKERS February 2004
GHOST! March 2004
GIRL GOT GAME January 2004
GRAVITATION
GTO

GUNDAM WING
GUNDAM WING: BATTLEFIELD OF PACIFISTS
GUNDAM WING: ENDLESS WALTZ
GUNDAM WING: THE LAST OUTPOST
HAPPY MANIA
HARLEM BEAT
I.N.V.U.
INITIAL D
ISLAND
JING: KING OF BANDITS
JULINE
JUROR 13 March 2004
KARE KANO
KILL ME, KISS ME February 2004
KINDAICHI CASE FILES, THE
KING OF HELL
KODOCHA: SANA'S STAGE
LAMENT OF THE LAMB May 2004
LES BIJOUX February 2004
LIZZIE MCGUIRE
LOVE HINA
LUPIN III
LUPIN III SERIES 2
MAGIC KNIGHT RAYEARTH I
MAGIC KNIGHT RAYEARTH II February 2004
MAHOROMATIC: AUTOMATIC MAIDEN May 2004
MAN OF MANY FACES
MARMALADE BOY
MARS
METEOR METHUSELA June 2004
METROID June 2004
MINK April 2004
MIRACLE GIRLS
MIYUKI-CHAN IN WONDERLAND
MODEL May 2004
NELLY MUSIC MANGA April 2004
ONE April 2004
PARADISE KISS
PARASYTE
PEACH GIRL
PEACH GIRL CHANGE OF HEART
PEACH GIRL RELAUNCH BOX SET
PET SHOP OF HORRORS
PITA-TEN January 2004
PLANET LADDER February 2004
PLANETES
PRIEST
PRINCESS AI April 2004
PSYCHIC ACADEMY March 2004
RAGNAROK
RAGNAROK: BOXED SET COLLECTION 1
RAVE MASTER
RAVE MASTER: BOXED SET March 2004

10103

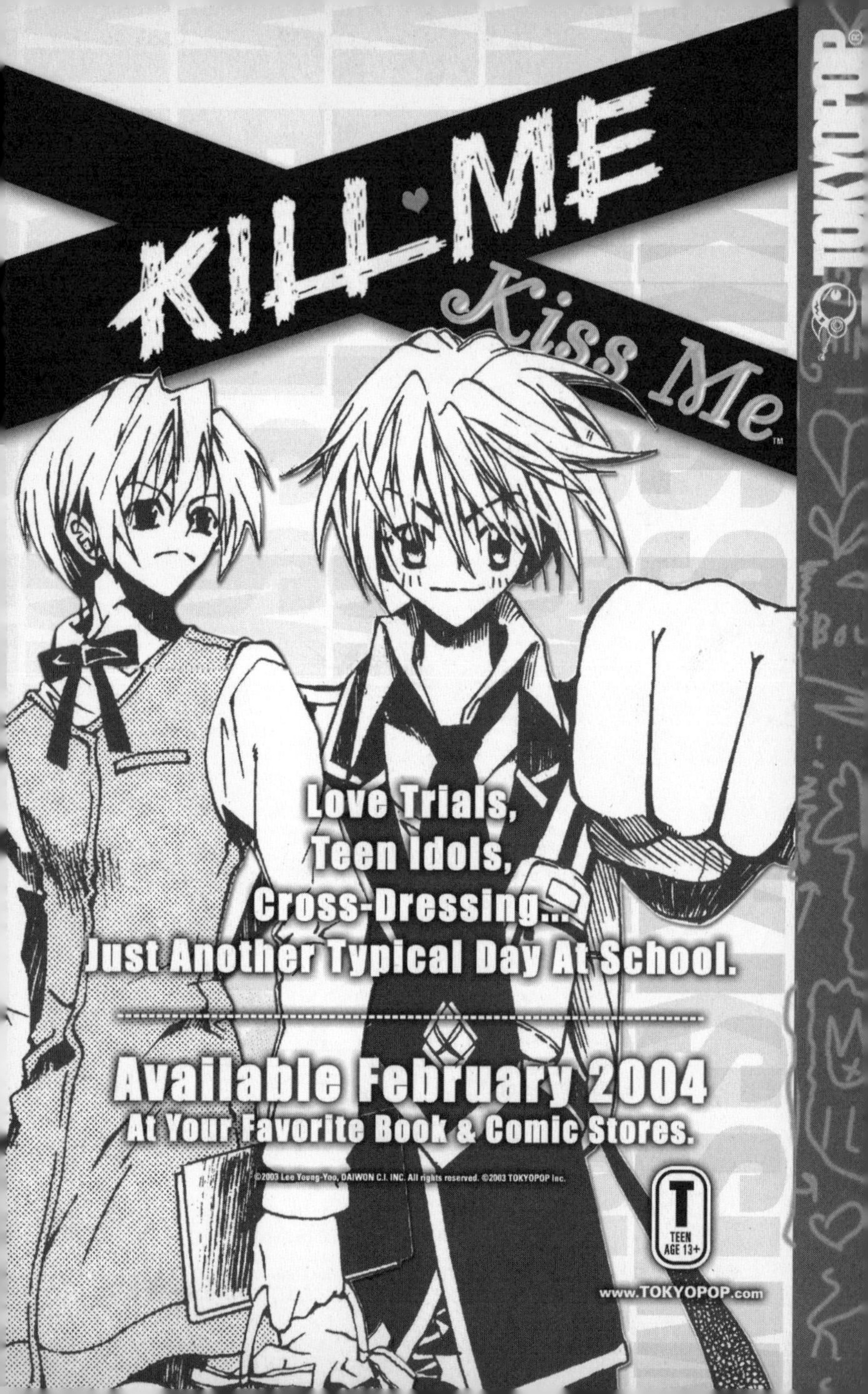
TOKYOPOP
KILL ME Kiss Me™
Love Trials,
Teen Idols,
Cross-Dressing...
Just Another Typical Day At School.
Available February 2004
At Your Favorite Book & Comic Stores.
©2003 Lee Young-Yoo, DAIWON C.I. INC. All rights reserved. ©2003 TOKYOPOP Inc.
T
TEEN
AGE 13+
www.TOKYOPOP.com

STOP!

This is the back of the book. You wouldn't want to spoil a great ending!

This book is printed "manga-style," in the authentic Japanese right-to-left format. Since none of the artwork has been flipped or altered, readers get to experience the story just as the creator intended. You've been asking for it, so TOKYOPOP® delivered: authentic, hot-off-the-press, and far more fun!

WITHDRAWN FROM COLLECTION OF
SACRAMENTO PUBLIC LIBRARY

DIRECTIONS

1
2
3
4
5
6
7
8
9
10

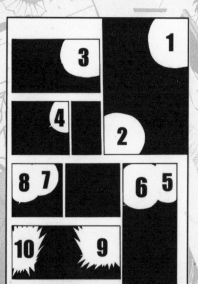

If this is your first time reading manga-style, here's a quick guide to help you understand how it works.

It's easy... just start in the top right panel and follow the numbers. Have fun, and look for more 100% authentic manga from TOKYOPOP®!

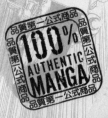